For Reference

Not to be taken from this room

Today's Foreign Policy Issues

Today's Foreign Policy Issues

Democrats and Republicans

TREVOR RUBENZER

Across the Aisle

An Imprint of ABC-CLIO, LLC
Santa Barbara, California • Denver, Colorado

Library of Congress Cataloging-in-Publication Data

Names: Rubenzer, Trevor, author.
Title: Today's foreign policy issues : Democrats and Republicans / Trevor Rubenzer.
Description: Santa Barbara, California : ABC-CLIO, 2017. | Series: Across the aisle | Includes bibliographical references and index.
Identifiers: LCCN 2016058357 (print) | LCCN 2017000075 (ebook) | ISBN 9781440843662 (hardcopy : alk. paper) | ISBN 9781440843679 (ebook)
Subjects: LCSH: United States—Foreign relations—21st century. | Democratic Party (U.S.) | Republican Party (U.S. : 1854-)
Classification: LCC JZ1480 .R83 2017 (print) | LCC JZ1480 (ebook) | DDC 327.73—dc23
LC record available at https://lccn.loc.gov/2016058357

ISBN: 978-1-4408-4366-2
EISBN: 978-1-4408-4367-9

21 20 19 18 17   1 2 3 4 5

This book is also available as an eBook.

ABC-CLIO
An Imprint of ABC-CLIO, LLC

ABC-CLIO, LLC
130 Cremona Drive, P.O. Box 1911
Santa Barbara, California 93116-1911
www.abc-clio.com

This book is printed on acid-free paper ∞

Manufactured in the United States of America

Contents

Introduction

At the dawn of the Cold War in 1947, Republican senator Arthur Vandenberg, who also served as chairman of the Senate Foreign Relations Committee, delivered a famous speech in which he argued that Americans needed to leave "partisan politics at the water's edge." In other words, whatever political tensions might be at work in the United States, America should speak with a united voice to the rest of the world. From the beginning of the Cold War until the escalation of the Vietnam War in the mid-1960s, U.S. foreign policy did enjoy a certain amount of bipartisan consensus, especially on issues related to preventing the spread of Communism and the Soviet Union. The post–Cold War period, however, has been marked by partisan rancor on some issues, though the two parties have continued to find common ground on others.

Generally speaking, Republicans have favored a more muscular approach to foreign policy since the end of the Cold War. From defending higher defense budgets, and protecting those budgets from cuts to other programs, to criticizing the president for not taking a more proactive role in responding to terrorist threats and cybersecurity vulnerabilities, Republicans have made it clear that they desire the continued assertion of hard power. Democrats, by contrast, are more willing to make at least limited defense cuts, were more prepared to end the wars in Iraq and Afghanistan, and are more likely to favor multilateral approaches to defusing conflict. The Joint Comprehensive Plan of Action (JCPOA) designed to limit Iran's nuclear ambitions, is an example of the type of multilateralism supported by Democrats.

At the same time, differences in rhetoric are not always matched by differences in policy. Republican and Democrats, for example, describe the threat of terrorist organizations like the Islamic State of Iraq and Syria (ISIS) in different terms, with Republicans favoring the idea of a global war on terror to defeat radical Islam and Democrats focusing either on individual organizations like ISIS or Al Qaeda or speaking of the struggle against terrorism in general. Republicans and Democrats also criticize each other for the relative strength and coherence of their response to the threat of terrorism. It is unclear, however, that Democratic strategies for defeating ISIS, including air strikes, Special Forces troops, coalition-building, training and equipping the Iraqi military, and training and equipping anti-ISIS forces in Iraq, Libya, and Syria, is significantly different from the Republican variant. Again on the issue of military spending, Democrats and Republicans have both proposed budgets that would maintain spending levels in excess of $550 billion per year.

Some of the greatest partisan gaps occur on "intermestic" issues. Intermestic issues are those that relate to both foreign and domestic policy in a significant way. Climate change, for example, is intermestic in that it requires both coordinated international action and domestic political action to address. Issues related to immigration, refugees, and free trade are very similar in this regard. There has historically been some partisan convergence on trade. On the issues of immigration, refugee policy, and climate change, however, the parties have taken almost polar positions.

Overall, both the Democratic and Republican Parties claim that they have the best interests of the nation and its people at heart, and they are equally adamant that they have the best policy solutions to address America's problems and challenges. This volume in ABC-CLIO's *Across the Aisle* series examines the proposals and positions of the two parties—from profound disagreements to areas of common ground—in the realm of foreign policy.

Today's Foreign Policy Issues: Democrats and Republicans sorts through the rhetorical clutter and partisan distortions that typify so many disputes between Republicans and Democrats in the 21st century in order to provide an accurate, balanced, and evenhanded overview of the parties' respective policy positions and attitudes on the most important and divisive social issues in the United States. Coverage also details instances in which the rhetorical positions staked out by Democrats and Republicans are inconsistent with their voting records and policy priorities.

Finally, in addition to explaining the differences between the two parties on today's hot-button foreign policy issues, this volume also documents significant differences of opinion *within* the parties where present. After all, neither Republicans nor Democrats march in complete lockstep on a wide range of issues, from free trade to terrorism to nuclear proliferation to challenges related to specific regions or countries. Nor do the policy positions of Republican and Democratic politicians always reflect the views of Republican and Democratic voters. For that reason, each entry examines the nature of partisan public opinion.

Throughout this volume, the text features actual quotes from Democratic and Republican Party leaders, party platforms, public opinion poll results, and other valuable, authoritative information to enhance its coverage. This information serves as the foundation for the volume's summaries of the philosophies and records of the two parties in such diverse realms as arms control, climate change, foreign aid, and drug interdiction policy.

Entry Features

Each essay in *Today's Foreign Policy Issues: Democrats and Republicans* begins with an At a Glance summary of the prevailing sentiments and policies of the two parties on the issue being discussed. This section also includes reader-friendly "bullet points" listing the most important views of each party.

Each essay then provides an Overview of historical trends, events, and attitudes displayed by both Republicans and Democrats regarding the issue in question. This section explores party attitudes toward key pieces of legislation, details their political alliances, and tracks evolutions in party thought over time.

From there each essay moves into a deeper exploration of the history and attitudes of the two parties on the foreign policy issue in question. Every essay features two special sections—one devoted to the Democratic record on the issue, the other concerned with the Republican record. As with the At a Glance and Overview sections, these sections are carefully crafted to provide both an accurate and an impartial overview of the parties' respective positions.

Every essay in this collection is further supplemented with sidebars featuring illuminating excerpts from key speeches and domestic and international laws, and coverage of particularly pivotal events. Each essay then concludes with a helpful Further Reading section to direct users to other information sources. The collection is also enhanced with a helpful Glossary of foreign policy terms, programs, and organizations mentioned in the book.

Afghanistan

At a Glance

Originally guided by the goal of defeating Al Qaeda and removing the Taliban from power in favor of a democratic, antiterrorist government, U.S. foreign policy toward Afghanistan is now guided by the quest for stability. As concerns about the Islamic State of Iraq and Syria (ISIS) grow, the situation in Afghanistan has fallen down the list of U.S. foreign policy and national security priorities. However, the resurgence of the Taliban and reemergence of Al Qaeda have caused the Obama administration to reevaluate its policies toward Afghanistan. At the same time, partisan debates about how to best proceed continue within Congress and the foreign policy elite in general.

According to many Democrats, U.S. foreign policy toward Afghanistan . . .

- Should be based on the goal of withdrawing remaining U.S. troops as soon as reasonably possible;
- Should focus on supporting the peace talks between the Afghan government and the Taliban;
- Must redouble efforts to train Afghan security and police forces to reduce dependence on American military forces; and
- Should not consider building permanent U.S. bases in Afghanistan.

According to many Republicans, U.S. foreign policy toward Afghanistan . . .

- Should recognize that earlier troop drawdowns in Afghanistan were a mistake, and delay further drawdown until Afghan forces are ready to assume all security responsibilities;
- Should be based on "on-the-ground" assessments by military advisers rather than on political calculations based on war weariness;
- Must redouble efforts to train Afghan security and police forces; and

- Should consider permanent military bases in Afghanistan in the event that their placement is deemed to be in the national interest of the United States.

Overview

The United States and Afghanistan have had a significant diplomatic relationship dating back to the early stages of the Cold War, when the two countries exchanged ambassadors. However, the roots of current U.S. foreign policy toward Afghanistan go back to the decision to support the mujahideen, a somewhat fragmented group of Islamist fighters opposed to Soviet rule, in its battle against first Soviet influence and later Soviet occupation, which began in late 1979. In the short term, the decision benefited the United States as it made the Soviet occupation of Afghanistan very costly in lives, time, and money. However, the withdrawal of the Soviets in 1988–1989 created a power vacuum in Afghanistan that was eventually filled by the Taliban, who were welcomed by many as a unifying source of order in spite of their draconian teachings and rules. Human rights abuses perpetrated by the Taliban, especially against women, were significant enough that the United Nations Security Council ultimately imposed sanctions on the country in the late 1990s. The Taliban provided safe haven to the terrorist group Al Qaeda before the terrorist attacks of September 11, 2001. Also, Osama bin Laden, mastermind of the 9/11 attacks, had been a member of the mujahideen.

After 9/11, President George W. Bush demanded that the Taliban extradite Osama bin Laden to the United States, along with several other terrorist suspects. For its part, Congress passed an Authorization for the Use of Military Force (AUMF) resolution with nearly unanimous support in the House and Senate. The AUMF was broad and permitted the use of force against either nations or organizations deemed to be involved in almost any way with the 9/11 attacks. After the Taliban refused to meet several U.S. demands, the United States and Great Britain invaded Afghanistan on October 7, 2001, under the moniker "Operation Enduring Freedom." Other North Atlantic Treaty Organization (NATO) countries became involved with the International Security Assistance Force (ISAF), mandated by the United Nations to help restore security and stability to Afghanistan. NATO became involved in the conflict after the invocation of Article 5, the mutual defense provision, of the treaty.

The Taliban were defeated within a few months by a mixture of U.S., British, and indigenous forces known as the Northern Alliance, who had been brought into a cooperative arrangement with the United States before the full invasion began. However, both Osama bin Laden and Mohammed Omar, the leader of the Taliban, evaded capture. An interim government was established headed by Hamid Karzai, who eventually became president of Afghanistan. Although the Taliban was defeated, it was not vanquished. From 2002 onward, the Taliban, along with other disaffected groups in Afghanistan, has fought an insurgency against United

President Obama Revisits His 2014 Plan to Remove All U.S. Troops from Afghanistan

In 2015, with Afghanistan still staggering under continued violence, terrorist activity, and political instability, President Obama decided to revisit his plan to withdraw all American troops from Afghanistan by the end of his presidency. Faced with the need for additional training for Afghanistan security forces as well as the need to "flush out the remnants of Al Qaeda," the president announced a revision to the troop withdrawal strategy in Afghanistan. Obama said, in part:

> Afghan forces are still not as strong as they need to be. They're developing critical capabilities—intelligence, logistics, aviation, command and control. And meanwhile, the Taliban has made gains, particularly in rural areas, and can still launch deadly attacks in cities, including Kabul. Much of this was predictable. We understood that as we transitioned, that the Taliban would try to exploit some of our movements out of particular areas, and that it would take time for Afghan security forces to strengthen. Pressure from Pakistan has resulted in more al Qaeda coming into Afghanistan, and we've seen the emergence of an ISIL presence. The bottom line is, in key areas of the country, the security situation is still very fragile, and in some places there is risk of deterioration.
>
> First, I've decided to maintain our current posture of 9,800 troops in Afghanistan through most of next year, 2016. Their mission will not change. Our troops will continue to pursue those two narrow tasks that I outlined earlier—training Afghan forces and going after al Qaeda. But maintaining our current posture through most of next year, rather than a more rapid drawdown, will allow us to sustain our efforts to train and assist Afghan forces as they grow stronger—not only during this fighting season, but into the next one.
>
> Second, I have decided that instead of going down to a normal embassy presence in Kabul by the end of 2016, we will maintain 5,500 troops at a small number of bases, including at Bagram, Jalalabad in the east, and Kandahar in the south.
>
> Again, the mission will not change. Our troops will focus on training Afghans and counterterrorism operations. But these bases will give us the presence and the reach our forces require to achieve their mission. In this sense, Afghanistan is a key piece of the network of counterterrorism partnerships that we need, from South Asia to Africa, to deal more broadly with terrorist threats quickly and prevent attacks against our homeland.

Source:

"Statement by the President on Afghanistan." The White House. Last modified October 15, 2015. https://www.whitehouse.gov/the-press-office/2015/10/15/statement-president-afghanistan.

States and NATO forces in the country. In 2006, control over security operations in Afghanistan switched to the ISAF. Suicide bombing, the use of improvised explosive devices, and other attacks continued to take a significant toll.

Under President Obama, the number of troops in Afghanistan initially increased. In 2009, Obama announced that, after a comprehensive review, the United States would deploy an additional 30,000 troops to Afghanistan in an attempt to quell the violence and stabilize the government (The White House 2009). The additional troops were to be withdrawn by 2011. Partisan debates over the drawdown in 2011 and again in 2015 were intense and will be described below. In 2010, NATO agreed that responsibility for security would be handed over to Afghanistan by 2014. The actual portfolio exchange occurred in June 2013. In May 2011, Osama bin Laden was killed by Navy SEALS at his previously hidden compound in Pakistan. It is also during this time that talks began between the United States and Afghanistan on a longer-term military and security agreement. The United States, Great Britain, and NATO formally ended combat in 2014. The violence associated with sectarianism and the insurgency continued, however, claiming more lives than any year since the initial invasion of 2001 (BBC News 2015). A disputed election in 2014 resulted in the presidency of Ashraf Ghani, a former university chancellor who has also worked for the World Bank.

In 2015, the Obama administration announced that it would delay final troop withdrawal from Afghanistan in order to assist in the maintenance of stability and security, provide further training for Afghan security forces, and provide political space for ongoing peace talks between the government and the Taliban to occur (Jaffe and Ryan 2015). As part of the revised plan, nearly 10,000 U.S. troops would remain in Afghanistan through 2016, with 5,500 to remain in the country beyond Obama's presidency. As part of his statement, Obama in essence admitted that he would not meet the goal of having all U.S. troops out of Afghanistan by the end of his presidency. There has been a significant debate within the ranks of Obama's chief military advisers as to whether the final drawdown will leave sufficient U.S. presence in Afghanistan to address security concerns (Barnes and Lubold 2015).

Democrats on U.S. Relations with Afghanistan

The 2016 Democratic Party Platform mentions Afghanistan eight times. Democrats are eager to emphasize in the platform that Afghanistan is continuing the transition to taking on responsibility for its own security. Democrats also promise to put pressure on both Pakistan and Afghanistan to deny terrorists sanctuary on either side of their shared border. The border region between Afghanistan and Pakistan is prone to terrorist activity because of its poverty, lack of government capacity, and low levels of willingness to confront militant groups in the region. Finally, Democrats point out that the United States will maintain a residual force in the region beyond the 2016 election. Although most Democrats would prefer that the United States remove its troops completely from the country, it has become clear that Afghanistan lacks the capacity to provide for its own security and combat terrorist groups without U.S. and NATO assistance.

Since the mid-2000s, many Democrats have charged that the war in Iraq distracted the United States—and the administration of Republican president George

W. Bush in particular—from the struggle to defeat Al Qaeda. Of course, the emergence of ISIS in Iraq and Syria has further complicated these plans, even as remnants of Al Qaeda have reemerged in Afghanistan.

Within the general public, the war in Afghanistan enjoyed enormous bipartisan support at its inception. In times of international crisis it is common for a "rally 'round the flag" effect to occur, whereby public approval of military action, and the president ordering such action, dramatically increases. By 2014, well over a decade into the war, the percentage of Americans who believe going to war with Afghanistan was a mistake exceeded the number who believed it was the correct decision for the first time (Newport 2014). In addition, the same survey notes a very large partisan gap that has emerged on public opinion concerning the war. In the survey, 59 percent of Democrats indicated the war was a mistake. By contrast, 36 percent of Republicans believed that the United States entered the war in error. In 2011, only 5 percent of Democrats believed that President Obama's military drawdown plan for Afghanistan would result in troops being removed too quickly (Clement 2011). Most thought that the plan was "about right."

In American foreign policy, goal setting is often the property space of the presidency, which controls the executive bureaucracy, and hence much of the diplomatic and war-making apparatus of government. When President Obama took office, his goal, and the goal of most Democrats both inside and outside of government, was to responsibly end the wars in both Afghanistan and Iraq. Continued instability and sectarian violence in Afghanistan has forced the president to continuously reevaluate that goal. In 2009, as mentioned above, the president announced a troop surge in Afghanistan that would last for two years. The money to fund the surge was ultimately provided by Congress, but not without a significant amount of resistance from congressional Democrats. President Obama also made the decision to extend the surge into 2012, at which point most of the additional troops had been withdrawn. Again in 2015, President Obama set the agenda on U.S. foreign policy toward Afghanistan by announcing that a residual force of 9,500 troops would remain in Afghanistan through 2016 and that 5,500 troops would remain after that. Overall, the president has faced significant resistance from within the Democratic Party at each decision to extend or intensify the war and praise from his Democratic colleagues each time that he has withdrawn troops.

It should be recognized that it is very difficult politically for Congress to use the power of the purse to limit a war. Once troops are deployed, lawmakers who support defunding military operations run the risk of being framed by political opponents as turning their backs on American troops. This phenomenon occurred during the 2008 election season, when Republicans accused Democrats of wanting to defund the troops in Iraq and Afghanistan. Democrats won the battle in that they gained the presidency and seats in Congress. However, faced with the prospect of defunding the troops, Congress under complete Democratic Party control continued to fund the war effort. Against this backdrop, it is perhaps not surprising that Congress decided ultimately to fund the troop surge.

At the outset of the debate, Speaker of the House Nancy Pelosi stated pointedly that Obama would have to make the case for the surge himself (Kane 2009). Pelosi was unwilling to push Democrats in her caucus to approve deepening the nation's involvement in a war than many of them strongly opposed. Obama laid out his reasoning in a December 1, 2009, speech in which he argued that the surge was a sensible and necessary action crafted in response to a detailed internal review of Afghan security and stability needs (The White House 2009). Secretary of Defense Robert Gates and Secretary of State Hillary Clinton were both dispatched to Congress to make the case directly. In the end, the bill passed easily in the Senate. In the House, the bill passed by a vote of 308–114. The bill needed a two-thirds majority to pass because it was considered under a suspension of the rules, a procedure designed to limit debate and further amendments. Democrats were split, with 148 supporting and 110 opposing the resolution (Dinan 2010). Antiwar Democrats like Wisconsin Representative Dave Obey argued that the money could be better spent on domestic concerns (Silverman 2010). Representative Silvestre Reyes, a Democrat from Texas, argued in support of the surge. He asserted that the correct decision was to support the advice of the generals on the ground, a sentiment echoed by many Republicans (Miller 2009). Democratic Party reactions to President Obama's 2015 decision to delay withdrawing the last troops from Afghanistan were far more muted. The Congressional Progressive Caucus, known for its antiwar stance, did not issue a statement in response to the decision (Bendery 2015).

There existed a significant degree of unity between former secretary of state Hillary Clinton, who secured the 2016 Democratic presidential nomination, and Senator Bernie Sanders, her closest competition for the nomination, on issues related to Afghanistan. Both Clinton and Sanders voted for the AUMF related to terrorism, which permitted the war in Afghanistan. Both candidates also have expressed support, though it was somewhat more reserved in the case of Senator Sanders, for the decision to leave a small residual force in Afghanistan, especially given the rise of ISIS in Iraq after more complete troop withdrawal there. Secretary Clinton was one of the major supporters of the 30,000 troop surge in Afghanistan and helped to lobby Congress for the funding bill that made it possible. Though he supports a small residual force in Afghanistan, Senator Sanders expressed the belief that U.S. troops have been deployed there for too long (Sanders 2016).

Republicans on U.S. Relations with Afghanistan

The 2016 Republican Party Platform mentions Afghanistan three times. The Republican messages on Pakistan and Afghanistan are very similar, with a focus on the need to defeat the Taliban in both countries. There are two departures related to Afghanistan within the platform. First, the platform mentions Afghanistan within the context of clamping down on the international narcotics trade, a logical extension given the fact that U.S. involvement in Afghanistan has done little to reduce the cultivation and export of opiates (see Narcotics and Drug Policy entry). The platform also takes a moment to criticize President Obama for troop commitments in Afghanistan. Republicans charge that the president's original decision to withdraw troops from Afghanistan was politically motivated rather than reflective of the advice of commanders on the ground. Although Republicans have given Obama a degree of credit for reversing course and agreeing to a residual force, they have argued that the decision on the size of the residual force was also politically motivated.

A review of public opinion polls concerning Afghanistan over the past several years reveals that Republicans are generally more supportive of the war than Democrats are, though support among Republicans for the war effort has decreased significantly over time. To a degree, however, Republican lawmakers and other critics who have opposed a complete withdrawal from Afghanistan are fighting an uphill battle against public opinion in both parties. A 2014 poll published after Obama announced the original time frame to end the war revealed overall support of nearly 75 percent for ending the war that year (Washington Post 2014). Although Democrats were more favorable toward the proposal than Republicans were, 60 percent of self-identified Republicans expressed support for completely ending U.S. troop involvement in Afghanistan by the end of 2016. According to the same survey, the partisan breakdown on the question of how Obama is handling Afghanistan was much more traditional. Two-thirds of Republicans did not approve of the president's performance on the issue, whereas nearly two-thirds of Democrats approved of the effort (Washington Post 2014).

Within Congress, Republicans have generally supported the president at any point where he has decided to deepen or maintain the war in Afghanistan, but they have opposed any effort in the opposite direction. For example, Republicans in both the House and Senate were supportive of the decision to send an additional 30,000 troops to Afghanistan in 2009 and 2010. Indeed, overwhelming majorities of Republicans in both chambers voted for the surge. In the House, Republicans were decisive in the ability to pass the funding provision for the additional troops under the suspension procedure described above. There was even an attempt by Republicans before Obama and his top advisers completed deliberations to compel top military officials to testify before Congress in the hopes that it would further the case for the surge at an earlier date. The effort failed, mostly because the Democratic Party controlled both chambers of Congress in 2009.

Some Republicans in Congress argued that the president should have sent at least 40,000 additional troops to Afghanistan rather than the 30,000 Obama ultimately requested. That number comes from a report leaked to journalist Bob Woodward by someone with access to a report by General Stanley McChrystal, head of the ISAF. The report suggested a minimum of 40,000 troops for regional stabilization, or a minimum of 80,000 troops for more robust national-level action (Woodward 2009). After Woodward's story was published, Republican politicians like David Vitter of Louisiana charged that President Obama was making a political, rather than a military, decision (Rushing and Youngman 2009). The criticism continued when Obama announced that the surge would end just before the 2012 election. Republicans believed, as reflected in the 2012 GOP platform, that the decision was made because of the declining popularity of the war effort, especially among Democrats. Republican presidential nominee Mitt Romney accused the president of making a primarily political decision as well. He spoke out against the 2014 deadline for the end of combat operations and the 2016 deadline for the withdrawal of all U.S. troops. Many Republicans, including Romney, chided the president for statements he made during the campaign when he later decided to maintain a residual force in Afghanistan beyond the end of his presidency.

The issue of U.S. relations with Afghanistan was not a top priority in the 2016 Republican presidential primary. None of the party's leading candidates discussed Afghanistan in the national security sections of their campaign Web sites. Ohio Governor John Kasich did argue in 2014 that the United States should maintain a continued presence in Afghanistan, but beyond that was not specific (Vogel 2014). Eventual nominee, Donald Trump, who had previously suggested that the war in Afghanistan was a mistake, later backtracked on that position, bringing his stance closer to that of most of the other candidates. He also agreed with the decision to maintain a residual force of approximately 5,000 soldiers in the country after 2016.

Further Reading

Barnes, Julian E., and Gordon Lubold. "U.S., Allied Military Review New Options for Afghan Pullback." *Wall Street Journal*. Last modified September 24, 2015. http://www.wsj.com/articles/u-s-allied-military-review-new-options-for-afghan-pullback-1443139109.

BBC News. "Afghanistan Profile—Timeline." Last modified December 24, 2015. http://www.bbc.com/news/world-south-asia-12024253.

Bendery, Jennifer. "Democrats Are Oddly Quiet on Obama's Decision to Keep Waging War." The Huffington Post. Last modified October 19, 2015. http://www.huffingtonpost.com/entry/democrats-obama-war-afghanistan_us_56251990e4b02f6a900d169c.

Clement, Scott. "Public Opinion on Afghanistan: Partisan Mix on War Ratings and Obama's Approval." *Washington Post*. Last modified June 27, 2011. https://www.washingtonpost.com/blogs/behind-the-numbers/post/public-opinion-on-afghanistan-partisan-mix-on-war-ratings-and-obamas-approval/2011/06/27/AG3h90nH_blog.html?utm_term=.b7d390d09e0a.

Dinan, Stephan. "House GOP Helps Obama Fund War." *The Washington Times*. Last modified July 27, 2010. http://m.washingtontimes.com/news/2010/jul/27/house-gop-helps-obama-fund-war/.

Jaffe, Greg, and Missy Ryan. "Obama Outlines Plan to Keep 5,500 Troops in Afghanistan." *Washington Post*. Last modified October 15, 2015. https://www.washingtonpost.com/world/national-security/obama-expected-to-announce-new-plan-to-keep-5500-troops-in-afghanistan/2015/10/14/d98f06fa-71d3-11e5-8d93-0af317ed58c9_story.html.

Kane, Paul. "Pelosi Says Rallying Votes for Troop Surge in Afghanistan Will Be Obama's Job." *Washington Post*. Last modified December 17, 2009. http://www.washingtonpost.com/wp-dyn/content/article/2009/12/16/AR2009121604161.html.

LoBianco, Tom. "Donald Trump Backtracks on Afghanistan War: Not a Mistake." CNN. Last modified October 20, 2015. http://www.cnn.com/2015/10/20/politics/donald-trump-afghanistan-war-not-a-mistake/.

Miller, Paul D. "How Do the Republican Candidates Stack Up on Afghanistan?" *Foreign Policy*. Last modified July 21, 2015. http://foreignpolicy.com/2015/07/21/how-do-the-republican-candidates-stack-up-on-afghanistan/.

Miller, S. A. "Key Democrats Align with Military on Afghan Buildup." *The Washington Times*. Last modified October 9, 2009. http://www.washingtontimes.com/news/2009/oct/09/key-democrats-align-with-military-on-buildup/?page=all.

Newport, Frank. "More Americans Now View Afghanistan War as a Mistake." Gallup.com. Last modified February 19, 2014. http://www.gallup.com/poll/167471/americans-view-afghanistan-war-mistake.aspx.

Richardson, Bradford. "Cruz: Change of Course on Afghanistan Reveals Obama's 'Failure.'" *The Hill*. Last modified October 18, 2015. http://thehill.com/policy/defense/257267-cruz-change-of-course-on-afghanistan-reveals-obamas-failure.

Rushing, J. T., and Sam Youngman. "GOP Warns Obama on Troop Surge." *The Hill*. Last modified October 21, 2009. http://thehill.com/homenews/administration/64025-gop-warns-obama-on-troop-surge.

Sanders, Bernie. 2016. "On the Issues: War and Peace." Bernie 2016. Last modified 2016. https://berniesanders.com/issues/war-and-peace/.

Silverman, Graham. "Money for Afghan Troop Surge Divides Democrats." *The Fiscal Times*. Last modified May 25, 2010. http://www.thefiscaltimes.com/Articles/2010/05/25/Money-for-Afghan-Troop-Surge-Divides-Democrats.

Vogel, Kenneth P. "Kasich Bonds with Adelson in Vegas." *Politico*. Last modified March 29, 2014. http://www.politico.com/story/2014/03/john-kasich-sheldon-adelson-105168#ixzz3BebAo0h2.

Washington Post. 2014. "June 2014 *Washington Post*–ABC News poll." Last modified June 8, 2014. https://www.washingtonpost.com/politics/polling/june-2014-washington-postabc-news-poll/2014/06/02/5a8b391c-ea77-11e3-b10e-5090cf3b5958_page.html?tid=a_inl.

The White House. 2009. "Remarks by the President in Address to the Nation on the Way Forward in Afghanistan and Pakistan." Whitehouse.gov. Last modified December 1, 2009. https://www.whitehouse.gov/the-press-office/remarks-president-address-nation-way-forward-afghanistan-and-pakistan.

Woodward, Bob. "McChrystal: More Forces or 'Mission Failure.'" *Washington Post*. Last modified September 21, 2009. http://www.washingtonpost.com/wp-dyn/content/article/2009/09/20/AR2009092002920.html.

Arms Control and Disarmament

At a Glance

In the general sense of the term, arms control occurs any time a country or group of countries decides to restrict the development, creation, proliferation, or use of a certain weapon or class of weapons. In practice, however, U.S. arms control policy since the end of World War II has focused on weapons of mass destruction (WMD), especially nuclear weapons. Weapons of mass destruction are defined by their ability to cause widespread damage and their inability to distinguish between types of targets. Generally speaking, nuclear weapons, chemical weapons, and biological weapons/agents are the three main types of weapons of mass destruction. Within the realm of U.S. foreign policy, significant partisan gaps exist in the area of arms control. Although these gaps have not prevented the United States from entering a wide variety of arms control agreements under both Republican and Democratic presidential administrations, they have had an impact on the scope of these agreements as well as their timing.

According to many Democrats, U.S. arms control policy . . .

- Should be based on a willingness to reduce, and in some cases eliminate, stocks of weapons of mass destruction;
- Can enhance the security of the United States by increasing transparency and confidence building within the international community;
- Should include a goal of "global zero" for nuclear weapons, even if the achievement of that goal is not practical at the present time;
- Should focus on limiting the proliferation of WMD to other countries; and
- Should include a reduction in U.S. nuclear stockpiles.

According to many Republicans, U.S. arms control policy . . .

- Should reflect the fact that U.S. nuclear weapons provide a credible deterrent against international threats;
- Should focus on limiting the proliferation of WMD to other countries;

- Should not include measures such as the Comprehensive Test Ban Treaty, which the GOP believes limits the ability of the U.S. to ensure the safety and effectiveness of its nuclear stockpile; and
- Should consider a reduction in nuclear stockpiles only if other concessions, such as the abandonment of U.S. ballistic missile defenses, are not part of the negotiations.

Overview

The pursuit of arms control and disarmament as a part of U.S. foreign policy dates back as far as 1817 when the United States and Great Britain agreed to demilitarize the Great Lakes as part of the Rush–Bagot Pact and Convention ("Rush–Bagot Pact," U.S. Department of State 2016). In the late 19th and early 20th century, the United States became a party to parts of the Hague Conventions on war and armed conflict. Notably, the United States did not become a party to the portion of the Hague Conventions prohibiting the use in war of "asphyxiating gases" (the term used in that era for chemical weapons).

In order for a treaty to become binding on the United States, the treaty or convention must be both signed (by the president or the president's designate) and ratified. Ratification requires a two-thirds vote in the Senate on a resolution of ratification. The United States did agree to a ban on the use of asphyxiating gases as part of its ratification of the 1925 Geneva Protocol. After World War I, the United States became involved in arms control efforts related to conventional armaments. Conventional arms are weapons that are widely used in armed conflict and are not weapons of mass destruction, as defined above. The Five Power Treaty between the United States, the United Kingdom, France, Italy, and Japan, which limited naval ships by tonnage, is an example of such an effort (Office of the Historian, "The Washington Naval Conference," 2016). Ultimately, efforts to circumvent the treaty and increases in armaments before World War II derailed what had originally been successful negotiations. From that point onward, with the partial exception of the Conventional Forces in Europe Treaty of 1990, most U.S. arms control and disarmament efforts focused on weapons of mass destruction. World War II, as well as the emerging Cold War, made conventional arms control, and, for a time, arms control in the realm of weapons of mass destruction, exceedingly difficult. When the United Nations Charter was adopted in June 1945, it reflected some of this thinking. Both Article 11 and Article 47 of the Charter, written with heavy U.S. influence, differentiate between the regulation of armaments, which today is referred to as arms control, and disarmament, which relates to the elimination of armaments (Charter of the United Nations 1945). The General Assembly of the United Nations quickly clarified that the goal with regard to weapons of mass destruction would be disarmament, while the goal related to conventional weapons would be arms control (Duarte 2011).

The Nuclear Nonproliferation Treaty (NPT)

The NPT, which entered into force in 1970, serves as the cornerstone of international nuclear arms control efforts. In contrast to the voluminous treaties of recent times, the 11 articles of the NPT take up only two pages of text. The treaty's main provisions are as follows:

Article I

Each nuclear-weapon State Party to the Treaty undertakes not to transfer to any recipient whatsoever nuclear weapons or other nuclear explosive devices or control over such weapons or explosive devices directly, or indirectly; and not in any way to assist, encourage, or induce any non-nuclear-weapon State to manufacture or otherwise acquire nuclear weapons or other nuclear explosive devices, or control over such weapons or explosive devices.

Article II

Each non-nuclear-weapon State Party to the Treaty undertakes not to receive the transfer from any transferor whatsoever of nuclear weapons or other nuclear explosive devices or of control over such weapons or explosive devices directly, or indirectly; not to manufacture or otherwise acquire nuclear weapons or other nuclear explosive devices; and not to seek or receive any assistance in the manufacture of nuclear weapons or other nuclear explosive devices.

Article III

1. Each non-nuclear-weapon State Party to the Treaty undertakes to accept safeguards, as set forth in an agreement to be negotiated and concluded with the International Atomic Energy Agency in accordance with the Statute of the International Atomic Energy Agency and the Agency's safeguards system, for the exclusive purpose of verification of the fulfilment of its obligations assumed under this Treaty with a view to preventing diversion of nuclear energy from peaceful uses to nuclear weapons or other nuclear explosive devices . . .

Article VI

Each of the Parties to the Treaty undertakes to pursue negotiations in good faith on effective measures relating to cessation of the nuclear arms race at an early date and to nuclear disarmament, and on a treaty on general and complete disarmament under strict and effective international control.

To the United States, the provisions of Articles I, II, and III are critical to preventing the spread of nuclear weapons. To the non-nuclear-weapons states, the lack of progress on Article VI, which would hypothetically require the elimination of all nuclear weapons, remains an area of concern. The NPT remains the only current treaty related to weapons of mass destruction that contains separate provisions for states that possess a certain class of weapon and those that do not.

Source:

"NPT Treaty." United Nations. Accessed March 21, 2016. http://www.un.org/en/conf/npt/2005/npttreaty.html.

During and immediately after the Cold War, the United States became a state party to several multilateral disarmament treaties. In 1970, the Nuclear Nonproliferation Treaty (NPT) entered into force. The treaty divides states into nuclear weapons states (NWS) and nonnuclear weapons states (NNWS). NNWS signatories agreed not to develop or otherwise acquire nuclear weapons. NWS signatories, such as the United States, promised not to assist NNWS to develop weapons, although they pledged to transfer peaceful nuclear technology to the NNWS. NNWS are required to enter into monitoring agreements with the International Atomic Energy Agency (IAEA) in order to safeguard against the use of peaceful technology in the development of nuclear weapons.

The United States also became a party to the Biological Weapons Convention (BWC), which entered into force in 1975. The BWC was the first treaty to ban the production of an entire class of weapons. However, the BWC does not contain enforcement provisions like those of the NPT, which limits its effectiveness to those states genuinely committed to not producing biological weapons. For its part, the United States maintains a biodefense program but does not actively produce or use biological weapons.

Finally, the United States is a party to the Chemical Weapons Convention (CWC), which entered into force in 1997. The treaty is the first to mandate the elimination of all weapons within a category and includes intrusive verification methods, including challenge inspections of national and business facilities.

The United States has also entered into a variety of bilateral agreements related to arms control and disarmament. Many of these treaties relate to nuclear weapons and were concluded with the Soviet Union and, after its collapse, with Russia. For example, the Strategic Arms Limitation Talks (SALT) led to the creation of the Antiballistic Missile (ABM) Treaty. The ABM Treaty limited the number of missile interceptors to two (later one), enabling the United States and the Soviet Union to maintain their nuclear deterrent and consider a reduction in the number of deployed warheads (see Ballistic Missile Defense entry). A second round of SALT talks broke down after the Soviet Union invaded Afghanistan. In 1991, the United States and USSR concluded the Strategic Arms Reduction Treaty (START). START limited the number of warheads that could be possessed by either nation to 6,000 and the number of delivery vehicles to 1,600 (Treaty Between the United States of America and the Union of Soviet Socialist Republics 2011). Although attempts to develop a START II Treaty failed for a variety of reasons, the New START Treaty entered into force in 2011. New START caps the number of nuclear warheads at 1,550 and the number of nuclear delivery vehicles at 700. The number of launchers is capped at 800 per country.

Democrats on Arms Control and Disarmament Policy

Generally speaking, Democrats are more likely to favor arms control and disarmament than are Republicans. For example, the 2012 Democratic Party platform lauds the entry into force of the New START Treaty between the United States and Russia (Democratic National Committee 2012). The platform also calls for U.S. ratification of the Comprehensive Test Ban Treaty (CTBT), which would ban the testing of nuclear weapons. Democrats see banning nuclear testing as a necessary step toward the ultimate elimination of nuclear weapons, arguing that there are other means to ensure the safety and operational effectiveness of the existing nuclear stockpile until general and complete nuclear disarmament is achieved. The Democratic Party platform is also committed to nonproliferation (preventing the spread of nuclear weapons from countries that have them to countries that do not) through strengthening the NPT and IAEA inspection regimes.

Public opinion among Democrats is also broadly supportive of disarmament. For example, a 2013 survey found that 73 percent of Democrats would favor the U.S. signing a treaty providing for the elimination of all nuclear weapons, including those held by the United States (Moore 2013). On this issue, there was a 44-point gap between Democrats and Republicans on willingness to engage in full nuclear disarmament. Democrats are also slightly more likely than Republicans to place a high priority on limiting the proliferation of nuclear weapons to other countries, though majorities of both parties believe that limiting the spread of nuclear weapons is a key foreign policy goal (Chicago Council on Global Affairs 2015). Majorities of both parties would also vote, if the opportunity were provided, for the reduction of U.S. and Russian nuclear stockpiles (Jones 2013). Unfortunately, the paucity of data on the partisan dimension of public opinion on issues related to disarmament makes it impossible to move beyond the surface of the issue.

President Barack Obama has taken positions on arms control and nuclear disarmament that are broadly in line with the Democratic Party consensus on the issue. For example, upon signing the New START Treaty, Obama stated that Russia and the United States were moving toward "responsible global leadership" (Phillips 2010). Obama also delivered a speech in 2009 in which he called on the international community to strive toward the goal of eliminating nuclear weapons. The Obama administration has also supported Senate ratification of the CTBT, which would ban all forms of nuclear testing using a complex system of seismic and radiation detection devices. However, Obama has not resubmitted the CTBT to the Senate for ratification. Generally, a president will not submit a treaty to the Senate for ratification unless the president is either sure of ratification or the goal is to have opponents on record as being against a popular treaty. In this case, the CTBT would not pass with the required two-thirds vote on ratification in the Senate due to the number of Republicans who oppose the treaty. In addition, while the CTBT is popular, it is not an issue to which the news media has devoted much attention. In 1999, when the CTBT was last submitted for ratification by Democratic president Bill Clinton, 60 percent of the public was unaware of the result of the Senate vote against ratification (Moore 1999).

Democrats in Congress have, for the most part, backed disarmament efforts when they have come before the House or Senate for a vote. One of the best

---

President Obama on the New START Treaty

In April 2010, President Obama and President Medvedev of Russia signed the New START Treaty. During the signing ceremony, Obama made several key assertions related to the New START Treaty, as well as nuclear disarmament in general.

> Together, we've stopped that drift, and proven the benefits of cooperation. Today is an important milestone for nuclear security and non-proliferation, and for U.S.–Russia relations. It fulfills our common objective to negotiate a new Strategic Arms Reduction Treaty. It includes significant reductions in the nuclear weapons that we will deploy. It cuts our delivery vehicles by roughly half. It includes a comprehensive verification regime, which allows us to further build trust. It enables both sides the flexibility to protect our security, as well as America's unwavering commitment to the security of our European allies . . .
>
> While the New START treaty is an important first step forward, it is just one step on a longer journey. As I said last year in Prague, this treaty will set the stage for further cuts. And going forward, we hope to pursue discussions with Russia on reducing both our strategic and tactical weapons, including non-deployed weapons . . .
>
> And the spread of nuclear weapons to more states is also an unacceptable risk to global security—raising the specter of arms races from the Middle East to East Asia. Earlier this week, the United States formally changed our policy to make it clear that those [non]-nuclear weapons states that are in compliance with the Nuclear Non-Proliferation Treaty and their non-proliferation obligations will not be threatened by America's nuclear arsenal.

Source:

"Remarks by President Obama and President Medvedev of Russia at New START Treaty Signing Ceremony and Press Conference." Whitehouse.gov. Last modified April 8, 2010. https://www.whitehouse.gov/the-press-office/remarks-president-obama-and-president-medvedev-russia-new-start-treaty-signing-cere.

---

places to examine Democratic support for disarmament is in treaty ratification votes before the Senate. For example, in the vote on ratification of the New START Treaty, all 56 Senate Democrats voted in favor of the treaty (*New York Times* 2010). When the CTBT came before the Senate for ratification, 44 of 45 Democrats in the chamber voted in favor of acceding to the treaty. Senator Robert Byrd, the only Democratic senator not to vote in favor of the CTBT, voted "present" as a form of protest for the unwillingness of Senate Republicans to delay a vote on the treaty (Arms Control Association 1999).

It is common for the Senate to allow indefinite postponement of a vote on ratification in cases where the president has signed a treaty and submitted it to the Senate for consideration, but the votes for ratification are lacking. The goal is to avoid a vote that might embarrass the United States internationally. In this case, a group of Republican senators, arguing that the CTBT would not allow the United

States to maintain its nuclear deterrent and that provisions of the treaty would be too easy to evade, decided to force a vote in order to end the ratification battle outright. Similarly, all 45 Democrats in the Senate in 1997 voted in favor of ratifying the Chemical Weapons Convention (*New York Times* 1997). In this case, the Senate was willing to delay the vote until after the 1996 presidential election in order to increase the odds of an affirmative vote.

Arms control and disarmament, at least in terms of agreements that require disarmament by the United States, are not a significant issue in the 2016 Democratic Presidential Primary. Neither former secretary of state Hillary Clinton nor Senator Bernie Sanders has highlighted arms control and disarmament as a key issue. Both candidates favor current efforts to deny Iran a nuclear weapon. It is also the case that as secretary of state, Clinton was involved in the negotiations that led to the New START Treaty and advocated for early ratification in the Senate. For his part, Senator Sanders voted in favor of ratification. Sanders has also called for reductions in the nuclear weapons budget and for the eventual elimination of all nuclear weapons (Sanders 2009).

Republicans on Arms Control and Disarmament Policy

On balance, Republicans are more skeptical of arms control efforts than are Democrats. The 2012 Republican Party platform is a case in point. Although the GOP platform does not express direct opposition to the New START Treaty, it is critical of the Obama administration for not taking adequate steps to modernize U.S. nuclear weapons infrastructure (Republican National Committee 2012). The platform posits that modernization was part of the compromise that allowed ratification of the treaty in the first place. Republicans tie the unwillingness of the Obama administration to upgrade the nuclear arsenal to his willingness to cancel the deployment of ballistic missile defense systems to the Czech Republic and Poland. The essential argument they make is that Democrats are too eager to appease Russia in order to advance a disarmament agenda that is contrary to U.S. national interests. It is also worth noting that the 2000 Republican platform staked out a position against ratification of the CTBT, charging that its measures were unverifiable and that it would strip the United States of its ability to ensure the reliability and effectiveness of its nuclear stockpile (American Presidency Project 2000).

On issues related to chemical and biological weapons, the Republican position appears more mixed. For example, the 1988 Republican platform called for the modernization of existing U.S. chemical weapons in order to maintain their deterrent value. However, the platform also called for the creation of an instrument leading to the elimination of all chemical and biological weapons (American Presidency Project 1988). The 1992 Republican platform, adopted one year before the CWC was opened for signature, only mentioned chemical and biological weapons in the context of threats from "rogue states" such as Iraq (American Presidency Project 1992). Taken in the context of the Iraqi invasion of Kuwait and subsequent expulsion by U.S.-led coalition forces, the emphasis on Iraq was understandable. This is especially the case in light of the discovery of chemical, biological, and nuclear weapons programs in Iraq in the early 1990s. Whether the dominance of the first U.S.-led Gulf War accounts for the omission of a call for a verifiable treaty providing for the elimination of chemical and biological weapons is unclear.

Republicans within the general public also tend to be less supportive than their Democratic Party counterparts of arms control and disarmament efforts. When questioned in 2013 about support for an international convention eliminating nuclear weapons, 29 percent of Republicans in one poll favored the proposal while 37 percent expressed direct opposition (Moore 2013). According to the same study, only 18 percent of Republicans favored unilateral U.S. reduction of its nuclear inventory. By contrast, 55 percent of self-identified Democrats favored unilateral reductions in nuclear weapons. Majorities of both Democrats and Republicans agreed that the threat of Iranian nuclear weapons was at least somewhat serious (Moore 2013). Overall, these findings, coupled with those presented above, suggest that Republican and Democrat perceptions of the threat from weapons in other countries are more similar than their views on the proper course of action with respect to limiting U.S. stockpiles.

Republicans in Congress have also expressed displeasure at U.S. disarmament efforts. However, Republican opposition has been less unified overall than Democratic Party support. For example, a majority of Senate Republicans voted against Senate ratification of the New START Treaty. However, 13 Republicans crossed party lines and voted with the Democrats (*New York Times* 2010). Many of the Republican defections occurred after passage of an amendment offered by Senator John McCain to pressure the Obama administration on ballistic missile defense (Nuclear Threat Initiative 2010). A similar phenomenon occurred with regard to ratification of the CWC. In this case, Republicans were even more divided, with 29 voting in favor of ratification and 26 voting against it (*New York Times* 1997). The larger number of "aye" votes by Republicans is explained, in part, by the fact the Senate leadership favored the CWC while opposing the New START Treaty. By contrast, Senate Republicans were much more unified in their opposition to ratification of the CTBT. In this case, only four Republicans, all known as moderates, crossed party lines to vote with the Democrats, who favored ratification (Dewar 1999). Republican leadership was united in opposition to the treaty, which was a factor in the level of party unity displayed on the vote.

Much like the party at large, the 2016 Republican presidential candidates expressed skepticism about arms control and disarmament—although as with Democrats, the issue was not prominent in the debates, candidate Web sites, or candidate speeches. In the speech announcing his candidacy, Donald Trump called for the modernization of the U.S. nuclear arsenal, arguing "even our nuclear arsenal doesn't work" (*Time* Staff 2015). Trump also appeared to take nuclear disarmament off the table in an interview with *GQ* Magazine in 2015 (Heath 2015). Senator Ted Cruz expressed a desire to strengthen and modernize the nuclear triad, which consists of long-range bombers, submarine-launched missiles, and intercontinental ballistic missiles. Although this is not incompatible with arms control and disarmament (a smaller nuclear force can be more modern) Cruz did not mention arms control or disarmament when discussing the modernity of the nuclear triad. Ohio Governor John Kasich also supported modernization without mentioning the prospect of arms control or disarmament.

Overall, Republicans, especially in presidential campaigns, tend to strike a more hawkish position on issues related to preparedness. The SALT process demonstrated that Republicans are willing to negotiate arms control and disarmament agreements. Overall, however, Republicans are less likely to favor arms control than are Democrats.

Further Reading

American Presidency Project. "Republican Party Platforms: Republican Party Platform of 1988." Last modified August 16, 1988. http://www.presidency.ucsb.edu/ws/?pid=25846.

American Presidency Project. "Republican Party Platforms: Republican Party Platform of 1992." Last modified August 17, 1992. http://www.presidency.ucsb.edu/ws/?pid=25847.

American Presidency Project. "Republican Party Platforms: Republican Party Platform of 2000." Last modified July 31, 2000. http://www.presidency.ucsb.edu/ws/?pid=25849.

Arms Control Association. "Senate Rejects Comprehensive Test Ban Treaty; Clinton Vows to Continue Moratorium." Last modified September 1, 1999. https://www.armscontrol.org/act/1999_09-10/ctbso99.

Charter of the United Nations. 1945. United Nations Treaty Collection. Accessed March 20, 2016. https://treaties.un.org/doc/publication/ctc/uncharter.pdf.

Chicago Council on Global Affairs. "America Divided: Political Partisanship and US Foreign Policy." Last modified 2015. http://www.thechicagocouncil.org/sites/default/files/CCGA_PublicSurvey2015.pdf.

Democratic National Committee. "The 2012 Democratic Platform." Last modified 2012. https://www.democrats.org/party-platform.

Dewar, Helen. "Senate Rejects Test Ban Treaty." *Washington Post*. Last modified October 4, 1999. http://www.washingtonpost.com/wp-srv/politics/daily/oct99/senate14.htm.

Duarte, Sergio. "Disarmament and Non-Proliferation: A Historical Review." United Nations. Last modified March 28, 2011. http://www.un.org/disarmament/HomePage/HR/docs/2011/2011-03-28_OAS_statement.pdf.

Heath, Chris. "This Donald Trump Interview Is the Best. You're Gonna Love It." GQ. Last modified November 23, 2015. http://www.gq.com/story/best-donald-trump-interview-gq-men-of-the-year.

Jones, Jeffrey M. "In U.S., 56% Favor U.S.-Russian Nuclear Arms Reductions." Gallup.com. Last modified March 11, 2013. http://www.gallup.com/poll/161198/favor-russian-nuclear-arms-reductions.aspx.

Moore, David W. "Public Supports Comprehensive Test Ban Treaty in Principle." Gallup.com. Last modified November 5, 1999. http://www.gallup.com/poll/3487/public-supports-comprehensive-test-ban-treaty-principle.aspx.

Moore, Peter. "Americans Back Nuclear Disarmament." YouGov: What the World Thinks. Last modified November 13, 2013. https://today.yougov.com/news/2013/11/15/americans-back-nuclear-disarmament/.

"New START." U.S. Department of State. Last modified 2015. http://www.state.gov/t/avc/newstart/index.htm.

New York Times. "How the Senators Voted on Treaty." Last modified April 25, 1997. http://www.nytimes.com/1997/04/25/world/how-the-senators-voted-on-treaty.html.

New York Times. "Senate Vote 298—Final Passage for Arms Treaty." Last modified December 22, 2010. http://politics.nytimes.com/congress/votes/111/senate/2/298.

Nuclear Threat Initiative. "U.S. Senate Ratifies New START in 71–26 Vote, Despite Top GOP Opposition." Last modified December 22, 2010. http://www.nti.org/gsn/article/us-senate-ratifies-new-start-in-71-26-vote-despite-top-gop-opposition/.

Office of the Historian. "Rush-Bagot Pact, 1817 and Convention of 1818—1801–1829—Milestones." U.S. Department of State. Last modified 2016. https://history.state.gov/milestones/1801-1829/rush-bagot.

Office of the Historian. "The Washington Naval Conference, 1921–1922—1921–1936—Milestones." U.S. Department of State. Last modified 2016. https://history.state.gov/milestones/1921-1936/naval-conference.

Phillips, Macon. "The New START Treaty and Protocol." Whitehouse.gov. Last modified April 8, 2010. https://www.whitehouse.gov/blog/2010/04/08/new-start-treaty-and-protocol.

Republican National Committee. "2012 Republican Platform." Last modified 2012. https://prod-static-ngop-pbl.s3.amazonaws.com/docs/2012GOPPlatform.pdf.

Sanders, Bernie. "Statement: Sanders Calls for Limiting Nuclear Proliferation." Senator Bernie Sanders. Last modified October 8, 2009. http://www.sanders.senate.gov/newsroom/press-releases/statement-sanders-calls-for-limiting-nuclear-proliferation.

Time Staff. "Donald Trump's Presidential Announcement Speech." TIME.com. Last modified June 16, 2015. http://time.com/3923128/donald-trump-announcement-speech/.

"Treaty between the United States of America and the Union of Soviet Socialist Republics on Strategic Offensive Reductions (START I)." Nuclear Threat Initiative I. Last modified 2011. http://www.nti.org/learn/treaties-and-regimes/treaties-between-united-states-america-and-union-soviet-socialist-republics-strategic-offensive-reductions-start-i-start-ii/.

Ballistic Missile Defense (BMD)

At a Glance

Ever since the development of intercontinental ballistic missiles armed with nuclear warheads, the United States has been interested in developing the technology to destroy such missiles in flight. However, the ability to construct a robust missile defense has significant foreign policy implications, including assertions that development of a U.S.-based shield might actually make a ballistic missile attack more likely. In addition, the terrorist attacks of September 11, 2001, against the United States increased fears that either rogue states or terrorist organizations might acquire ballistic missiles capable of striking portions of the United States. As a result, missile defense has become a key foreign policy issue with clear, though sometimes narrow, delineation between Democratic and Republican Party positions.

According to many Democrats, U.S. missile defense . . .

- Makes ballistic missile attacks against the United States more likely;
- Should be limited to intercept missiles from key targets such as Iran and North Korea;
- Makes it more difficult to negotiate nuclear disarmament agreements with countries like Russia; and
- Can be useful, in certain cases, against short- and medium-range missiles.

According to many Republicans, U.S. missile defense . . .

- Is vital to protect the United States from attacks by rogue states or terrorist organizations that acquire ballistic missiles;
- Is technologically possible if developed as a multilayered defense system;
- Projects the strength necessary to maintain peace in an uncertain world;
- Poses no threat to countries with significant numbers of missiles, like Russia and China, and so should not make disarmament talks more difficult; and
- Can be useful against short-, medium-, and long-range and intercontinental ballistic missiles.

Overview

Serious efforts on the part of the United States and the Soviet Union to develop ballistic defense systems date to the 1950s, during the beginning stages of the Cold War. At that time, both the United States and the Soviet Union developed and later deployed intercontinental ballistic missiles (ICBMs). A ballistic missile is powered early in its flight by liquid or solid fuel and then falls toward its target under the pull of gravity. By contrast, a cruise missile is powered during the entire course of its flight. During the early Cold War, U.S. missile defense was predicated on using one missile to intercept another. In 1962, the United States achieved the first successful midair intercept of an unarmed test missile (Missile Defense Agency 2015).

Initially, the United States believed that it might one day be able to use a missile defense system to protect the entire United States from a Soviet or Chinese nuclear missile attack. For a variety of reasons, though, including cost and available technology, it became clear that this strategy was not feasible. As a result, the United States focused its missile defense on protecting its own ICBMs. The goal was to protect enough land-based missiles to provide for a credible counterstrike capability in the event of a Soviet first strike (Council on Foreign Relations 2002). The Soviets developed similar technology during roughly the same time period. To political realists, the ability to protect ICBMs from a first strike would make preemptive nuclear war less likely as a result of the heavy cost that could be imposed on the aggressor. Gradually, the idea that the cost of nuclear war would be too high for either the United States or the Soviet Union to attempt it (given the destructive power of the counterstrike) became known as the doctrine of mutually assured destruction (MAD).

As time passed, however, believers in MAD, who came to dominate the foreign policy establishment in both the United States and the Soviet Union, expressed growing concern that if one side were able to develop a missile defense shield that could protect its major population centers and its own ICBMs from nuclear attack, it might come to believe that it could win a nuclear war. They worried that such a development would make the odds of a first strike more likely. In addition, if either the Soviet Union or the United States detected the building of such a system, it would be tempted to begin a nuclear war before the shield was completed. Hence, a robust missile defense might actually increase the probability of nuclear war by decreasing the probability of MAD.

As a result of this realization, the United States and the Soviet Union concluded the Anti-Ballistic Missile (ABM) Treaty in 1972. The treaty limited the number of ABM cites to two per county (later amended to one). The ABM Treaty remained in effect during the remainder of the Cold War and beyond, with Russia assuming responsibilities under the treaty after the collapse of the Soviet Union. Over time, the development of missiles with multiple reentry vehicles (MRVs) rendered the application of traditional missile defense obsolete. As a result, the United States shuttered its ABM system in 1976.

In 1983, the idea of missile defense was reborn with the Reagan administration's launch of the Strategic Defense Initiative (SDI). SDI, which quickly became known unofficially as "Star Wars," depended on the development of sophisticated missile interception technologies ranging from electromagnetic rail guns to X-ray lasers. SDI was eventually scrapped in favor of new, more limited programs. However, the program has been credited by Republicans with helping to win the Cold War. They argue that Star Wars forced the Soviet Union to increase its own defense spending so much that the Soviet economic and political system finally crumbled under the strain.

By the end of the Cold War, the United States had come to the conclusion that the most significant missile threat came from limited numbers of missiles launched by nonstate actors (Missile Defense Agency 2015). The United States also began to focus on short- and medium-range missile defense systems, such as the Patriot System used during the first Gulf War against Iraq. The United States was able to remain in the ABM Treaty at the time because these short range defenses were not designed to protect against ICBMs. By the early 2000s, however, the George W. Bush administration had become convinced that it needed greater protection against the threat of limited ICBMs launched by "rogue states." A defense against this type of attack would require a multilayer system deployed at more than two locations. With this in mind, the Republican administration of President George W. Bush gave notice to Russia that it was withdrawing from the ABM Treaty. The United States formally withdrew from the Treaty in July of 2002, after completing the mandatory six-month notification period under the ABM Treaty. In January 2002, the Missile Defense Agency (MDA) was created to manage the new program.

Democrats on Missile Defense Policy

The Obama administration has broken sharply with the Bush administration, and with Republicans in general, on issues related to missile defense. Although Democrats do not favor abandoning the shield altogether, they expressed concerns that Bush administration plans to deploy missile defense systems in Poland and the Czech Republic would be seen as a direct threat by Russia. As a result of issues relating to Russia, as well as cost and feasibility concerns, the Obama administration decided in 2009 to delay deployment of ballistic missile defense (BMD) systems in Eastern Europe. Obama argued that sea-based missile defense, coupled with later plans for ground-based defenses in Europe, would be a superior option (The White House 2009). Obama denied that the planned deployment had ever been intended as a threat to Russia, but rather had always been designed to intercept missiles targeting Europe or the United States from Iran. Polish and Czech officials, as well as heads of state and government throughout Europe, saw the move as critical to decreasing Russian fears that the missile shield was designed to target Russian missiles. In 2013, the United States canceled the deployment as part of nuclear disarmament negotiations with Russia. The United States has deployed sea-based systems to Europe as well as a land-based system in Romania.

The 2012 Democratic Party platform mentions missile defense twice, both within the context of the NATO alliance. The first mention relates to the phased adaptive approach unveiled by the Obama administration in 2009 to replace the Bush administration policy of more aggressive deployment (Democratic National Committee 2012). The second mention relates to BMD with Turkey, a NATO ally, as well as Eastern Europe. The United States did deploy Patriot batteries to Turkey in 2013. However, it withdrew the missiles in 2015 as part of revised threat assessments (Neuman 2015). The deployment of BMD in Europe remains fluid as the United States evaluates threats in other regions, such as Southeast Asia, and contemplates sea-based BMD deployment.

There is little public opinion research concerning a possible partisan gap as it relates to missile defense. The data that does exist, gathered in the early 2000s as the United States prepared to withdraw from the ABM Treaty, suggests that most of the general public supports the idea of BMD. Overall, 51 percent of Americans surveyed in 2001—before the attacks of 9/11—supported the deployment of a BMD system (Pew Research Center 2001). However, there was a clear partisan gap on the issue. Whereas nearly 63 percent of Republicans supported BMD, only 47 percent of Democrats supported the shield.

Traditionally, though, BMD has not generally been a high salience issue for the American public. A 2001 survey by Gallup suggested that only 11 percent of Americans claimed to have been following the issue of BMD very closely (Moore 2001). After 9/11, the Bush administration highlighted the role of BMD in stopping a terrorist group or rogue state from targeting the United States. Given those developments, it is possible that the issue is of greater importance to voters.

Congressional Democrats have been broadly supportive of President Obama's scaled-down BMD policy. Democrats in Congress had originally been skeptical of President Bush's missile defense policy. On September 7, 2001, every Democratic member of the House Armed Services Committee voted to cut BMD funds in the hope of preventing abrogation of the ABM Treaty (Shanker 2001). However, the events of 9/11 led them to mute their criticism until a more opportune time (Levin 2001). By October 2011, Democrats ceased their attempt to remove BMD funds from the budget. Even so, Senator Carl Levin (D-MI) was critical of a Bush-era defense budget that prioritized BMD over other forms of military research and development. In 2003, Representative Nancy Pelosi (D-CA) argued that missile defense "has no justification in terms of threat, technology, budget . . . and is harmful to our disarmament agreements with other countries and multilateral agreements" (Council on Foreign Relations 2003). In 2006, a majority of House Democrats voted for an amendment that would have substantially cut funding for the missile defense program (House Report 109-468 2006). The amendment failed due to unanimous Republican opposition and opposition from 65 Democrats who broke ranks and voted no.

Democrats in Congress continued to favor scaling back BMD during the Obama administration. Congressional Democrats, for example, supported Obama's decision to not place missile defense systems in Poland or the Czech Republic. Democrats also applauded the decision to delay development of the multiple kill vehicle (MKV) designed to destroy multiple missiles with a single launch. Democrats have argued that the technology behind such a system, as well as more basic components of BMD, has failed so often in tests that the programs are of extremely limited utility (Oliveri 2013). However, Democrats in Congress did support the president's decision to enhance BMD cooperation, including the deployment of detection and interception capability in Japan, with the potential for future cooperation with South Korea and Australia. Recent North Korean nuclear and ballistic missile testing may well speed up this cooperation. In fact, the United States and South Korea will soon begin talks concerning the deployment of a high-altitude missile defense system (Shalal and Brunnstrom 2016).

Both of the former Democratic Party candidates for president, Senator Bernie Sanders and former senator and secretary of state Hillary Clinton, have expressed positions on missile defense issues. In some ways, Clinton is willing to take missile defense further than the Obama administration. Clinton was a key part, while serving as secretary of state, in the negotiations that would have placed BMD in Poland and the Czech Republic. As a senator, Clinton also voted to deploy BMD against the threat of Iranian missiles (Willis 2015). Where Clinton may be more conservative than President Obama on issues related to missile defense, Senator Sanders is more liberal. For example, Sanders voted against the missile defense deployment favored by Clinton (Willis 2015). As far back as 1991, Senator Sanders argued that missile defense programs were unnecessary in the post–Cold War world (Crowley 2016).

Overall then, Democrats are more likely to be skeptical of missile defense than are Republicans. Although Democrats do not appear to favor abandoning the idea of BMD, they are willing to scale back programs in terms of funding and deployment, especially if doing so will make cooperation on other disarmament issues with countries like Russia more likely. Democrats do favor the limited deployment of BMD systems in regions potentially threatened by states such as North Korea and Iran. However, they are also more likely to view the use of such systems as a potential barrier to meaningful arms control talks with Russia and, potentially, China.

Republicans on Missile Defense Policy

The 2012 Republican Party platform mentioned missile defense four times. The thrust of the platform is that the Obama administration has imperiled the country and its allies by not taking missile defense seriously. The platform cites the decision to cancel the deployment of BMD installations to Poland and the Czech Republic, as well as reducing the number of U.S. interceptors, as examples of complacency

(Republican National Committee 2012). The platform suggests that the Obama administration is taking these actions in order to appease Russia, which objects to placing BMD in Eastern Europe out of fear that such a move would decrease the credibility of its nuclear arsenal as a deterrent against Western strikes. Overall, the platform suggests that the Obama administration's insufficient commitment to missile defense is indicative of its willingness to let military preparedness fall to the wayside through budget cuts, appeasement, and lack of commitment to U.S. allies.

In terms of public opinion, Republican support for missile defense is more robust than that of Democrats, though, as mentioned above, there is a degree of bipartisan support discernable within opinion polls on this issue. Although public opinion data is not plentiful, it does suggest that Republicans are more likely than Democrats to view the Iranian and North Korean nuclear programs as significant threats to the United States (Chicago Council on Global Affairs 2015). Given the close relationship between concerns about nuclear programs and concerns about delivery systems, which make nuclear weapons a more significant threat to the United States, it can be inferred that heightened concerns about Iran and North Korea's nuclear programs may well translate into increased support for BMD.

Current and former elected Republicans have also been highly critical of Democratic Party policies related to missile defense. Former vice president Dick Cheney, for example, criticized the Obama administration for being unwilling to deploy missile defense systems to Poland and the Czech Republic, especially in light of Russia's actions in Ukraine (Curry 2014). Former minority leader and Speaker of the House John Boehner has argued that Democratic Party attempts to cut missile defense place the United States on weaker footing in the war on terror, the effort to ensure security against rogue states, as well as the effort to ensure that Israel maintains a qualitative military advantage in the Middle East (Speaker.gov 2007). Republicans in Congress have also argued, at times against both Democrats and Department of Defense, that the United States needs to supplement its BMD on the West Coast and in Alaska. Republicans have asserted that North Korean and Iranian ICBM programs (the latter successfully placed a satellite in orbit in 2015) require a more robust missile defense (Judson and Herb 2015).

Missile defense as part of U.S. foreign policy has become part of the Republican presidential nomination process, though it has not assumed the level of importance of other defense issues. Senator Ted Cruz, who has always been outspoken on issues related to missile defense, has been the most vociferous proponent of allocating increased resources to BMD. In 2014, Cruz argued that the United States should restore those installations in Eastern Europe canceled by the Obama administration in 2009 and 2013 (McCormack 2014). As part of his presidential campaign, Cruz made a similar argument, as well as pushing for the installation of BMD sites in the eastern United States (Cruz 2016). He has accused the Obama administration of "dithering" on missile defense issues.

President Obama Rejects Deploying BMD to Poland and the Czech Republic

In September 2009, President Obama announced that, as a result of a review of missile defense policy, the United States would replace plans for BMD installations in the Czech Republic with a "phased adaptive approach." As part of the argument, Obama stated:

> This new approach will provide capabilities sooner, build on proven systems, and offer greater defenses against the threat of missile attack than the 2007 European missile defense program . . .
>
> To put it simply, our new missile defense architecture in Europe will provide stronger, smarter, and swifter defenses of American forces and America's allies. It is more comprehensive than the previous program; it deploys capabilities that are proven and cost-effective; and it sustains and builds upon our commitment to protect the U.S. homeland against long-range ballistic missile threats; and it ensures and enhances the protection of all our NATO allies . . .
>
> We will continue to work cooperatively with our close friends and allies, the Czech Republic and Poland, who had agreed to host elements of the previous program. I've spoken to the Prime Ministers of both the Czech Republic and Poland about this decision and reaffirmed our deep and close ties. Together we are committed to a broad range of cooperative efforts to strengthen our collective defense, and we are bound by the solemn commitment of NATO's Article V that an attack on one is an attack on all.

Source:

"Remarks by the President on Strengthening Missile Defense in Europe." Whitehouse.gov. Last modified September 17, 2009. https://www.whitehouse.gov/the-press-office/remarks-president-strengthening-missile-defense-europe.

Senator Marco Rubio and Governor John Kasich also favored the expansion of U.S. missile defense capabilities. As a member of the House of Representatives, Kasich voted in favor of the development of SDI. During one of the February 2016 Republican debates, Kasich also argued the United States should place interceptors in South Korea in response to the North Korean threat (*New York Times* 2016). Senator Marco Rubio's campaign Web site argued in favor of speeding up the deployment of BMD in Europe. Rubio was also the only candidate to specifically mention the desirability of a missile defense system that can defend against cruise missiles (Rubio 2016).

Of all the candidates seeking the Republican presidential nomination in 2016, Donald Trump has the most mixed record on BMD. On one hand, he has criticized the Obama administration for its willingness to delay or cancel the deployment of BMD in Eastern Europe, and he has also stated that missile defense systems may be necessary to counter Chinese military development (Trump 2011). On the other hand, Trump had previously argued that missile defense systems were not "the right defense for our times" (Trump 2000, 150). It is possible that Trump's position changed in the wake of the terrorist attacks of 9/11 and in response to advancements in Chinese missile systems.

Further Reading

Chicago Council on Global Affairs. "America Divided: Political Partisanship and US Foreign Policy." Last modified 2015. http://www.thechicagocouncil.org/sites/default/files/CCGA_PublicSurvey2015.pdf.

The Cold War Museum. "The Strategic Defense Initiative (SDI): Star Wars." Accessed March 9, 2016. www.coldwar.org/articles/80s/SDI-StarWars.asp.

Council on Foreign Relations. "Chronology of National Missile Defense Programs." Last modified June 1, 2002. http://www.cfr.org/missile-defense/chronology-national-missile-defense-programs/p10443.

Council on Foreign Relations. "The David A. Morse Lecture with Nancy Pelosi." Last modified March 7, 2003. http://www.cfr.org/united-states/david-morse-lecture-nancy-pelosi/p5669.

Crowley, Michael. "Bernie Sanders' Military Record: Past Support for Drastic Cuts Could Hurt Him." *Politico*. Last modified February 18, 2016. http://www.politico.com/story/2016/02/bernie-sanders-defense-budget-pentagon-219386.

Cruz, Ted. "American Resolve: Rebuilding America's Military." Cruz for President. Last modified 2016. https://www.tedcruz.org/american-resolve/.

Curry, Tom. "Republicans Heighten Criticism of Obama's Ukraine Response." NBC News. Last modified March 9, 2014. http://www.nbcnews.com/storyline/ukraine-crisis/republicans-heighten-criticism-obamas-ukraine-response-n48386.

Democratic National Committee. "The 2012 Democratic Platform." Last modified 2012. https://www.democrats.org/party-platform.

Judson, Jen, and Jeremy Herb. "GOP, Pentagon Tussle over East Coast Shield." Politico. Last modified April 27, 2015. http://www.politico.com/story/2015/04/missile-shield-east-coast-shield-republicans-pentagon-117323.

Levin, Carl. "A Debate Deferred: Missile Defense after the September 11 Attacks." *Arms Control Today* 31 (November 2001): 3–5. http://legacy.armscontrol.org/act/2001_11/levinnov01.

Library of Congress. "H. Rept. 109-468—Providing for further Consideration of H. CON. RES. 376, the Concurrent Resolution on the Budget for Fiscal Year 2007." Last modified May 17, 2006. https://www.congress.gov/congressional-report/109th-congress/house-report/468.

McCormack, John. "Cruz Continues Push to Reverse Obama's 'Disastrous Missile Defense Policies.'" *Weekly Standard*. Last modified March 19, 2014. http://www.weeklystandard.com/cruz-continues-push-to-reverse-obamas-disastrous-missile-defense-policies/article/785550.

Missile Defense Agency. "MDA—History Resources." U.S. Department of Defense. Last modified 2015. http://www.mda.mil/news/history_resources.html.

Moore, David W. "Public Supports Concept of Missile Defense." Gallup.com. Last modified May 7, 2001. http://www.gallup.com/poll/1555/public-supports-concept-missile-defense.aspx.

Neuman, Scott. "U.S. Says It Will Remove Patriot Missile Defense from Turkey in October: The Two-Way: NPR." NPR.org. Last modified August 16, 2015. http://www.npr.org/sections/thetwo-way/2015/08/16/432486072/u-s-says-it-will-remove-patriot-missile-defense-from-turkey-in-october.

New York Times. "Transcript of the Republican Presidential Debate." Last modified February 6, 2016. http://www.nytimes.com/2016/02/07/us/politics/transcript-of-the-republican-presidential-debate-in-new-hampshire.html?_r=0.

Oliveri, Frank. "Chambers Split on East Coast Missile Defense Site: Roll Call Policy." Roll Call. Last modified July 30, 2013. http://www.rollcall.com/news/chambers_split_on_east_coast_missile_defense_site-226754-1.html.

Pew Research Center. "Other Important Findings and Analyses: Partisan Gap on Missile Defense." Pew Research Center for the People and the Press. Last modified June 11, 2001. http://www.people-press.org/2001/06/11/other-important-findings-and-analyses-10/.

Republican National Committee. "2012 Republican Party Platform." Last modified 2012. https://prod-static-ngop-pbl.s3.amazonaws.com/docs/2012GOPPlatform.pdf.

Rubio, Marco. "Restoring and Modernizing American Strength." Marco Rubio for President. Last modified 2016. https://marcorubio.com/sidebar-featured/marco-rubio-military-defense-spending-policy/.

Shalal, Andrea, and David Brunnstrom. "North Korea Rocket Launch May Spur U.S. Missile Defense Buildup in Asia." Reuters. Last modified February 9, 2016. http://www.reuters.com/article/us-northkorea-satellite-missiledefense-idUSKCN0VH034.

Shanker, Thom. "Senate Committee Cuts Money from Missile Defense Plan." *New York Times*, September 8, 2001.

Speaker.gov. "Boehner: Missile Defense Cuts Weaken American Security." Last modified May 16, 2007. http://www.speaker.gov/press-release/boehner-missile-defense-cuts-weaken-american-security.

Trump, Donald. *The America We Deserve*. Los Angeles: Renaissance Books, 2000.

Trump, Donald. *Time to Get Tough: Making America #1 Again*. Washington, D.C.: Regnery Pub., 2011.

White House. "Remarks by the President on Strengthening Missile Defense in Europe." Whitehouse.gov. Last modified September 17, 2009. https://www.whitehouse.gov/the-press-office/remarks-president-strengthening-missile-defense-europe.

Willis, Derek. "The Senate Votes That Divided Hillary Clinton and Bernie Sanders." *New York Times*—Breaking News, World News & Multimedia. Last modified May 27, 2015. http://www.nytimes.com/2015/05/28/upshot/the-senate-votes-that-divided-hillary-clinton-and-bernie-sanders.html?_r=0.

Brexit and the European Union

At a Glance

The European Union (EU) is a common European market that includes significant political integration. Common markets have either no or very few tariffs between members and have a common external tariff on goods and (often) services from states outside of the common market. Common markets are often characterized by free flow of labor and capital across national boundaries. On June 23, 2016, the United Kingdom of Great Britain and Northern Ireland held a referendum to vote on whether to remain in the European Union. By a margin of 52 percent to 48 percent, British citizens voted to leave the EU. The decision became known as "Brexit," a clever combination of the words "Britain" and "exit." In this case, the term "Britain," which excludes Northern Ireland, is being used by Brexit supporters and opponents as shorthand for the entire United Kingdom, which contains England, Scotland, and Wales (the Great Britain component) plus Northern Ireland, which collectively make up the U.K. Brexit, which won't take complete effect until the end of 2018 at the earliest, has sent partisan ripples through Europe and the United States. Although there are few signs that Brexit will cause the United States, under either Democratic or Republican Party rule, to reevaluate its relationship with Great Britain or the European Union, there are significant differences in the way each party views the merits of Brexit as well as the lessons that might be learned from the process. These differences, in turn, may become manifest in other areas of foreign policy, such as immigration and free trade.

According to many Democrats . . .

- Brexit was a bad idea brought on by fears about immigration and exaggerated claims about external regulation and job losses;
- Brexit will not affect the "special relationship" between the United States and Great Britain;
- Brexit will not affect the U.S. relationship with the European Union; and
- Brexit represents a "wake-up" call that Americans are concerned that the free flow of labor and capital can result in job losses and other economic dislocations.

According to many Republicans . . .

- Brexit represents a rejection of the type of globalism preferred by Democrats;
- Brexit will not affect the "special relationship" between the United States and Great Britain; and
- Brexit reflected public desire for increased security, economic sovereignty, and a more restrictive immigration policy.

Overview

What is today the European Union began in 1951 as the European Coal and Steel Community (ECSC), which was created by the Treaty of Paris. Besides seeking economic benefits from a common market in coal and steel, the six founders of the ECSC sought to foster the type of economic interdependence, especially between France and Germany, that would make war less likely on the continent. Great Britain remained outside of the ECSC in order to preserve as much of its economic sovereignty as possible. Great Britain did join the European Economic Community (EEC), a successor organization to the ECSC in 1973. Over time, the EEC developed the European Political Cooperation (EPC). The goal of the EPC was to create increased political integration within the EEC and to develop a common foreign policy for the organization.

The modern EU began in 1987 with the signing of the Single European Act (SEA). The SEA created social programs to address income variation in the EEC and gave more legitimacy to joint foreign policy decision making. Perhaps most important, the SEA set the timetable for the establishment of a full common market, which would in practice remove all economic barriers between members and establish a common external tariff on goods from outside the EEC. In 1993, the Maastricht Treaty, which established the European Union, took effect. At this point, the economic component of the EU (the EEC) was renamed the European Community (EC). The EC became one of the three pillars of the new EU. The second pillar was the Common Foreign and Security Policy (CFSP), a strengthened version of the EPC. The third pillar was the establishment of judicial and police cooperation, which was designed to increase coordination between national judicial authorities, customs agencies, and national police forces. The Maastricht Treaty and the creation of the EU also laid the groundwork for the creation of a European Monetary Union (EMU), which began in 1999. Of the 28 countries that are part of the EU, 19 are also part of the EMU. Two of the nine EU countries that are not part of the EMU—Great Britain and Denmark—opted out of EMU and the common monetary policy it mandates. Both countries objected to the fact that under the EMU, countries cannot adjust their own monetary policy (by lowering interest rates to increase access to currency, for instance) in response to economic shocks from inside and outside of the EMU. The other seven EU members that are not in the EMU have yet to meet EMU qualifications in terms of budget deficits, inflation rates, and other qualification terms.

The modern EU contains several key institutions that accomplish the work of the organization. The European Commission serves as the executive branch of the EU and consists of one commissioner appointed from each member state. The commission is responsible for implementing most EU policies. The European Council decides the overall direction of EU policy. It consists of the heads of government of each member of the EU. A related, but not an identical institution is the Council of the European Union. The Council adopts EU-wide laws together with the European Parliament. The Council consists of one ministerial level individual from each member state. A minister is a member of a country's government that has responsibility for policy within a certain area. Although they are not identical and have more power (in part because they are elected officials), ministers are somewhat similar to cabinet secretaries in the United States. The European Parliament also plays a role in enacting most EU laws. The difference between the Parliament and the Council of the European Union is that its members are directly elected by EU voters as a whole. This means that members of the European Parliament (MEPs) do not represent a specific country. Disputes over EU laws are settled with the Court of Justice of the European Union (CJEU), which contains one justice from each member state. For countries that are part of the Euro-zone (meaning they are part of the EMU) the European Central Bank lends to banks in member states, manages reserve currencies, and sets interest rates, thereby controlling monetary policy.

In 2016, the people of Britain voted to leave the European Union, a dramatic decision that garnered considerable political attention in the United States. Over time, increasing numbers of British citizens had become agitated by policies that they saw as being imposed by "Brussels" (shorthand for the seat of power for most EU institutions). In addition, the economic downturn that began in 2008 and affected countries worldwide soured many British citizens to the open immigration policies among EU members. Polish citizens, for example, have increasingly come to Great Britain in search of economic opportunity and are willing to work for lower wages. The European migrant crisis, involving refugees and asylum seekers from Syria and elsewhere, further shook British confidence in the EU. Although Great Britain is toward the low end of EU states for asylum applications, the number has increased over time. Euro-skeptic political parties such as the U.K. Independence Party (UKIP) have expressed a desire to leave the EU in part to gain national control over immigration policy.

As the debate over remaining in the EU intensified, Prime Minister David Cameron, a member of the Conservative Party, committed to holding a national referendum on EU membership if the Conservatives remained in power after the 2015 national elections. By doing so, Cameron was able to temporarily unify the Euro-skeptic wing of his party with the other factions. The Conservative Party remained in power, and Cameron kept his promise to put the issue to a referendum. Almost immediately, a "remain" and a "leave" camp formed to campaign from the U.K. to either stay in the EU or for "Brexit." Cameron and most other elected officials in the United Kingdom, with the exception of UKIP members and "hard" Euro-skeptics in the Conservative Party, favored and openly campaigned for the remain option. As the migration crisis worsened in Europe, however, the Brexit campaign strengthened, though migration was not the only issue at play. By the day of the referendum, most outside political observers expected a narrow victory for "remain." This was not the case. Citizens of the United Kingdom voted to leave the European Union by a 52–48 margin. After the vote, David Cameron announced his resignation, arguing that a pro-Brexit prime minister should negotiate the terms of a British exit from the EU.

Republicans on the EU and Brexit

The 2016 Republican Party platform made only a single, indirect, reference to Brexit. The platform states that Republicans "respect their decision concerning their nation's relationship with the European Union and pledge that, however, much other international relationships may change, those who were first to our side in our hour of loss will always rank first in our policies and our esteem" (Republican National Committee 2016). The decision to neither endorse nor condemn the decision is reflective of at least two main factors. First, Republicans have almost always tended to view the overall relationship with Great Britain as more important than the relationship with European institutions. This is partially reflected in the "first to our side" language that refers to the British response to the terrorist attacks of September 11, 2001, even under a Labor Government (the Labor Party in the U.K. more closely resembles the Democratic Party than the Republican Party). Second, as demonstrated below, Republicans are not of one mind concerning Brexit. It is the case that there were more Republicans favoring Brexit than there were Democrats. However, there were also Republicans who believed that it would be best for the U.K. to remain part of the EU. In the end, the Republican position is a balance that reflects the desire to respect the wishes of a close, sovereign ally. The platform contains 3 other mentions of the word "European" and 11 mentions of the word "Europe." Apart from one mention designed to tie Democrats to large, and heavily regulated European financial institutions, the other mentions do not relate to the European Union, but to either bilateral relationships or to the North Atlantic Treaty Organization (NATO).

U.S. public opinion on the issue of Brexit is sparse. However, a *USA Today*–sponsored public opinion poll in 2016 found that Republican voters were more likely to see Brexit as a global trend than Democrats. Three in four Republicans believe that Brexit is part of a larger trend of political dissatisfaction that applies to countries like the United States as well (Page and Crescente 2016). Unsurprisingly, a plurality of Republicans believed that the trend embodied by Brexit would help Donald Trump, their 2016 presidential nominee, win the White House in November 2016. It is also worth noting that a majority of Democrats and independents view Brexit as part of a trend, rather than an isolated political incident. A Harris Poll taken just after the British referendum on EU membership found that Americans, overall, were divided on Brexit. Supporters of Brexit, opponents of Brexit, and those with no preference were split into nearly equal thirds (Harris Poll 2016). However, a majority of Republicans (56 percent) supported Great Britain's decision to leave the European Union. A Huffington Post poll, conducted in conjunction with online pollster YouGov, found more decisive results. In the poll, Republicans who favored Brexit outnumbered those who thought that Great Britain should remain in the EU by over 2–1 (Edwards-Levy 2016).

On the broader issue of the European Union, there are some areas of partisan consensus in the general public. For example, sizable majorities of both Republicans (84 percent) and Democrats (82 percent) want the European Union to exert strong leadership in global affairs (Chicago Council on Global Affairs 2015. The same survey also indicated that majorities of both Republicans (77 percent) and Democrats (62 percent) believe that the EU can deal responsibly with world problems. The wider gap, in this case, can probably be attributed to general Republican skepticism about the efficacy of international organizations. Although Republicans are much more confident in the EU than they are in more global organizations like the United Nations, it is still the case that Republicans tend to be more pessimistic than Democrats about the ability of multilateralism to solve important international problems. It should also be noted that it is common in opinion polling to find that large percentages of both Republicans and Democrats are unfamiliar with the structures and functions of the European Union. This was also the case in Great Britain, where estimates concerning the percentage of U.K. law that comes directly from the EU varied wildly in part because of the difficulty in determining what parts of a given law are determined nationally and which parts are designed to comply with EU regulations.

Overall, Republican political elites favored Brexit, with some variation on the level of vigor. Trump, for example, praised the British for "taking their country back" (McCaskill 2016), and he argued that the vote in Great Britain would have a ripple effect in the United States where antiglobalism sentiment would help push him to the presidency. Former Alaska governor Sarah Palin, who supported Trump and spoke on his behalf at some campaign stops, praised the decision as an avoidance of "apocalyptic one-world government" (Guarino 2016). Defense of national sovereignty against the threat of globalism, while normally reserved for organizations like the United Nations, is likely to resonate among more conservative Republicans, as well as Democrats who believe that the United States has ceded too much of its sovereignty to intergovernmental organizations. Alabama Senator Jeff Sessions, who endorsed Trump in the race for president, argued that it is "now America's turn" to reject globalism by voting for Donald Trump (Sessions 2016).

Other Republicans struck a more measured tone. Speaker of the House Paul Ryan stated "I respect the decision made by the people of the United Kingdom. The U.K. is an indispensable ally of the United States, and that special relationship is unaffected by this vote" (Ryan 2016). It is likely that part of the reason for Ryan's measured response is that he serves as Speaker of the House, and hence speaks, at least to a degree, for Republicans in general. It is also the case that Ryan recognizes that a majority of elected officials in the U.K. opposed Brexit, and that working diplomatically in the future with these same officials could become more complicated, especially under a potential Republican president, if Republicans were seen as too enthusiastic about a policy that many members of the Conservative Party opposed. Republican Senator Kelly Ayotte of New Hampshire reacted to Brexit in a manner almost identical to Ryan, stating that she respected the decision, but that no result would have changed the relationship between the United States and the United Kingdom.

Democrats on the EU and Brexit

As a general rule, Democrats have been less likely to favor Brexit, and more likely to favor the EU in general, than their Republican counterparts. The Democratic Party platform does not mention Brexit either directly or indirectly. Instead, the platform reaffirms the U.S. commitment to its "special relationship" with Great Britain as well as a commitment to the European Union. One could perhaps infer that this implies support for both entities regardless of status. However, it is clear that the Democrats are not willing to go as far as Republicans in terms of a reaction to the fact that the referendum did take place and that "leave" carried the day. This is perhaps not surprising given the fact that some Democrats, including President Obama, campaigned openly for Great Britain to remain in the EU. Party platforms are known for trying, when possible, to avoid discussions of issues that might adversely reflect on the party.

Overall, Democratic voters are more favorably disposed toward the European Union, and British membership in the organization, than are Republicans. For example, in the Huffington Post/YouGov poll mentioned above, only 17 percent of self-identified Democrats supported Brexit, creating a 42-point anti-Brexit gap with Republicans (Edwards-Levy 2016). Unlike many issues, where political independents tend to lean heavily toward Democrats or Republicans, independents occupy a midway point between Democrats and Republicans, with 32 percent approving of Brexit according to the Huffington Post/YouGov poll. According to the 2016 Harris Poll, 55 percent of Democrats opposed Brexit, compared to 13 percent of Republicans (Harris Poll 2016). Including independents, Americans were more likely to think that Brexit will have a more negative than positive impact on the United States. On the issue of the impact of Brexit on U.S. politics, a majority of Democrats agree with Republicans that the Brexit vote was a sign of anger that goes beyond the United Kingdom (Page and Crescente 2016). As one might expect, Democrats were more likely to believe that Brexit would hurt Donald Trump more than Hillary Clinton in the same way that Republicans believed the opposite. However, in the case of Democrats, the plurality category was "no impact," suggesting that Democrats are somewhat less bullish of the positive impact that Brexit will have on their preferred candidate.

Among Democratic political elites, President Obama was by far the strongest voice against Brexit. During a joint press conference with Prime Minister David Cameron in April 2016, Obama argued that "the United States wants a strong United Kingdom as a partner, and the United Kingdom is at its best when it's helping to lead a strong Europe . . . It leverages U.K. power to be part of the European Union" (Nelson and Gross 2016). Obama also made the argument that trade deals with the U.K. alone would be of lower priority than those of the EU, implying that the economic power of Great Britain is naturally magnified by being part of the much larger European common market. Obama also made the point that if Brexit took place, any new trade agreement between the two countries would be difficult to achieve, due to the partisan conflicts that arise when free trade deals are presented to Congress. Many politicians, especially pro-Brexit officials in Great Britain, were displeased by the president's remarks, arguing that a foreign official should not intervene in a sovereign, domestic decision (even if that decision has international implications).

Other Democrats were more muted in their response to Brexit. Vice President Joe Biden, for example, stated that the Brexit vote would not change the special relationship between the United Kingdom and the United States. Former senator and Democratic presidential nominee Hillary Clinton expressed concern that Brexit would lead to short-term "economic uncertainty" but that she respected the decision of the British people (Flores 2016). Senator Bernie Sanders, who pressed Clinton for the Democratic nomination, argued that Brexit should serve as a warning to Democrats in the United States that there is a strong reaction against globalism (or in this case regional multilateralism) on both the left and the right of the political spectrum. Overall, Democrats in Congress were less likely to speak out on Brexit than Republicans. Part of this can be attributed to the fact that, especially after the referendum, the Brexit storyline contains more potential Republican talking points than Democratic talking points. Some Democrats did attempt to make a political point in the aftermath of the referendum when some supporters of Brexit appeared to have second thoughts. Overall, though, Republicans had more to say about the various implications of the vote. In addition, while Congress often speaks out on U.S. foreign policy issues, it tends not to take strong positions on domestic affairs in other countries. In this respect, Republicans in Congress also spoke less on Brexit issues before the referendum than they did after.

In the final analysis, the Brexit process itself is unlikely to have a direct impact on U.S. foreign policy toward the U.K. or the European Union. However, the partisan gap between Democrats and Republicans on the issue has implications for both foreign and domestic U.S. policies. With regard to domestic policy, the Brexit divide is indicative of a broader partisan divide on domestic issues related to globalization. This divide manifests itself, for example, on immigration, with Republicans and Democrats on opposite sides of the immigration reform debate.

On foreign policy issues, Republican assertions of sovereignty related to organizations like the United Nations and Organization of American states have become stronger at the same time as support for Brexit. Democrats, by contrast, continue to embrace multilateral organizations and increased integration. In this sense, the Brexit vote was seen by Republicans as an affirmation of their worldview and a rebuke to the Democratic position.

Further Reading

Chicago Council on Global Affairs. "America Divided: Political Partisanship and US Foreign Policy." Last modified 2015. https://www.thechicagocouncil.org/sites/default/files/CCGA_PublicSurvey2015.pdf.

Edwards-Levy, Ariel. "Republicans Are Totally in Favor of Brexit." Huffington Post. Last modified June 27, 2016. http://www.huffingtonpost.com/entry/republicans-favor-brexit_us_577198e0e4b0dbb1bbbbaf25.

Flores, Reena. "U.S. Politicians React to Brexit Vote—CBS News." CBS News—Breaking News, U.S., World, Business, Entertainment & Video. Last modified June 24, 2016. http://www.cbsnews.com/news/donald-trump-us-politicians-react-to-brexit-vote/.

Guarino, Ben. "Sarah Palin Celebrates Brexit, Says U.K. Avoided 'Apocalyptic One World Government.'" *Washington Post*. Last modified June 27, 2016. https://www.washingtonpost.com/news/morning-mix/wp/2016/06/27/sarah-palin-celebrates-brexit-says-uk-avoided-apocalyptic-one-world-government/.

Harris Poll. "America Split over Brexit Vote." Last modified July 1, 216. http://www.theharrispoll.com/politics/Americans_Divided_Over_Brexit.html.

Huffington Post. "Republicans Are Totally in Favor of Brexit." Last modified June 27, 2016. http://www.huffingtonpost.com/entry/republicans-favor-brexit_us_577198e0e4b0dbb1bbbbaf25.

McCaskill, Nolan D. "Republicans Echo Trump's Brexit Applause." Politico. Last modified June 24, 2016. http://www.politico.com/story/2016/06/brexit-republicans-react-224767.

Nelson, Colleen M., and Jenny Gross. "Obama Urges U.K. to Remain in EU." *Wall Street Journal*. Last modified April 2016. http://www.wsj.com/articles/during-london-visit-obama-urges-u-k-voters-to-stay-in-eu-1461318148.

Page, Susan, and Fernanda Crescente. "USA TODAY Poll: Americans See Brexit Anger as Widespread." *USA Today*. Last modified June 30, 2016. http://www.usatoday.com/story/news/politics/elections/2016/06/30/poll-americans-brexit-anger-widespread/86546786/.

Republican National Committee. "Republican Party Platform 2016." Last modified 2016. https://prod-static-ngop-pbl.s3.amazonaws.com/media/documents/DRAFT_12_FINAL[1]-ben_1468872234.pdf.

Ryan, Paul. "Statement on Brexit." Speaker.gov. Last modified June 24, 2016. http://www.speaker.gov/press-release/statement-brexit.

Sessions, Jeff. "Sessions Statement following Brexit Vote: Now It's America's Turn." Senator Jeff Sessions. Last modified June 24, 2016. http://www.sessions.senate.gov/public/index.cfm/news-releases?ID=C55023D7-0A87-4485-9A80-65D6AA0121E6.

China

At a Glance

U.S. foreign policy toward China is complex. On the one hand, the two world powers diverge on several key international issues, including trade, human rights, and military policy. On the other hand, the United States and China are economically interdependent, which gives each state a stake in the well-being of the other. Partisan gaps in the debate over U.S.–China relations have become more significant over time.

According to many Republicans, U.S. foreign policy toward China . . .

- Should focus on countering China's growing military power and power projection;
- Must deter China from cyberattacks on the United States;
- Should respond to Chinese currency manipulation with countervailing duties;
- Must deter China from further violations of U.S. intellectual property;
- Should assist Taiwan in maintaining the status quo as it relates to the "one China" policy; and
- Should focus on isolating China for its poor human rights record.

According to many Democrats, U.S. foreign policy toward China . . .

- Must address the adverse impact China has on the global environment;
- Should focus on ensuring that China follow current international trade rules;
- Should encourage cooperation with China on security issues such as North Korea and the Iranian nuclear program;
- Should assist Taiwan in maintaining the status quo as it relates to the "one China" policy; and
- Should prioritize speaking out against China's poor human rights record.

———————

Overview

The historical relationship between the United States and China has normally been characterized by mixtures of cooperation and conflict dating back to the first unsuccessful attempt of the United States to make diplomatic contact with China in 1784. In the early 19th century, American merchants began to participate in the opium trade, hoping to successfully follow their British counterparts. During the first Opium War from 1839 through 1842, the United States experienced a boom in its opium sales to China, and the British triumph and signing of the Treaty of Nanking set the stage for further U.S. access. The U.S. gained favorable treatment with regard to exports and imports to and from China in the 1844 Treaty of Wangxia (Office of the Historian n.d.).

In the late 19th and early 20th centuries, immigration from China into the United States became an issue between the two countries. Chinese laborers and fortune-seekers arrived in the United States to participate in the California gold rush and help build railroads in the West. Eventually, protests grew in the United States based on fears about losing modest paying labor jobs to the Chinese immigrants. This led to a series of attempts to limit Chinese immigration, including the famous Chinese Exclusion Act of 1882. Ultimately, this led to a boycott of U.S. goods in China. The impact of the boycott, however, was limited by the previous defeat of China in the first Sino-Japanese war as well as reparations due from the Qing Dynasty to the United States after the failure of the Boxer Rebellion. In 1911, the Qing Dynasty fell and, a year later, the Republic of China was born. China, however, was not reunified until 1925.

In 1921, the Chinese Communist Party formed. The United States did not formally react to this event. However, the United States did formally recognize the Nationalist government in 1928. The Nationalists beat back the Communist insurgency and appeared to be on the way to eliminating the movement until the outbreak of the second Sino-Japanese war, as well as World War II. Both of these events weakened the Nationalist government in significant ways. The United States provided assistance to shore up the government, extending credit to the Nationalists in their efforts to defeat the Japanese, but maintained neutrality in the war until the December 7, 1941, Japanese attack on Pearl Harbor. China and the United States formed an official alliance during the war, and the United States rescinded many of the unequal elements of its previous treaties with the Qing. After the war, the United States offered to mediate—but not directly intervene in— the renewed Chinese Civil War. Weakened by World War II, and having lost a significant amount of its nationalist credibility to the Chinese Communist Party, the Nationalists lost the war and fled across the Taiwan Straits to the island of Taiwan, where they continued to maintain that the Communists were ruling illegitimately.

The United States did not formally recognize the Chinese Communist government until 1979, eight years after the People's Republic of China (PRC) joined the United Nations, taking the permanent UN Security Council seat held by the Republic of China (ROC), which had been controlled by the defeated Nationalist forces on Taiwan. In the period between PRC victory and UN membership, the United States and China clashed in both the Korean War and the Vietnam War, as well as over Chinese development of nuclear weapons capabilities during the 1960s. In Korea, American and Chinese troops met on the battlefield after U.S. military personnel neared the Chinese border in 1950. Although the Chinese suffered far more numerous losses, they were able to force a retreat of UN forces, led by the United States. China's success in defending its borders from the United States became an important part of Chinese revolutionary identity. Participation by China in the Vietnam War on the side of the North Vietnamese was more indirect. China supplied military and civilian training, as well as some financial assistance, to North Vietnam, the Communist regime that in 1975 conquered South Vietnam despite major military, economic, and political assistance from the United States.

Despite tensions over Vietnam, however, U.S.–China relations generally improved during the 1970s and 1980s. "Ping pong diplomacy," a reference to a diplomatic exchange of visits by the U.S. and Chinese ping-pong teams to each other's country, and Nixon's historic visit to China in 1972 brought about eventual full diplomatic recognition. The death of Chinese Revolutionary figure and Communist Party leader Mao Zedong in 1976 opened the door to economic liberalization in China, which resulted in increased opportunities for trade, though this occurred gradually at first. Sino-U.S. relations, however, deteriorated in 1989 after the Chinese government cracked down on popular protests calling for democratic reforms in Tiananmen Square, which is located in central Beijing, the Chinese capital city. China ultimately imposed martial law and forcibly cleared the square, resulting in thousands of arrests and hundreds of deaths. In response, the United States suspended diplomatic relations, though back channel communications continued. The administration of President George H. W. Bush also imposed economic and military sanctions on China in the wake of the Tiananmen Square violence, and these sanctions received bipartisan support.

The 1990s and 2000s saw the decoupling of U.S. foreign policy toward China from concerns about human rights. The Clinton administration determined that tying Chinese government respect for human rights standards to the granting of most-favored nation (MFN) status for trade purposes was no longer achieving the desired result. In 2000, the president signed a bill granting China permanent normal trade relations status (PNTR), and one year later China joined the World Trade Organization.

PNTR had replaced MFN in U.S. legislation relating to trade. The terms MFN and PNTR are, in practice, synonymous. In the Senate, the PNTR legislation passed with bipartisan majorities by a vote of 83–15. In the House, a majority of Democrats voted against the legislation while a majority of Republican favored granting PNTR. In part due to lobbying by President Clinton, a greater number of Democrats broke rank and favored the legislation, which was opposed by House leadership, than the number of Republicans who broke with their leadership to oppose the legislation. The final vote was 237–197 in favor.

Republicans on U.S. Relations with China

The 2012 Republican Party platform mentioned China 16 times. Most of these mentions related to the accusation that China uses unfair trade practices, such as artificial currency devaluation and intellectual property violations to gain an advantage in the global marketplace. China now has the world's second-largest economy and is the single largest U.S. creditor, which is part of the reason for the concern. The GOP platform suggested several measures to punish China for these alleged transgressions, including the imposition of countervailing duties to balance Chinese currency manipulation and an end to U.S. government procurement of Chinese products in the event that China refused to honor its previous agreements. The platform also mentioned the need to maintain the U.S. current nuclear arsenal as a deterrent against both Russia and China. In recent years, China's military budget has increased significantly, to the point that it exceeded $100 billion annually. Although this amount is less than one-fifth of the U.S. military budget, it reflects a pattern of increased Chinese military assertiveness, especially in Southeast Asia. Finally, the 2012 GOP platform bemoaned China's record on issues such as authoritarian governance, suppression of religious expression, arbitrary detention, and abortion.

Within the realm of public opinion, Republicans and Democrats are unified on several points. For example, both Republicans and Democrats have expressed concern about the large amount of U.S. debt held by China (Wike 2015). China holds around 1.2 trillion dollars in U.S. debt instruments, which is about 7 percent of total debt as of 2016. The overall fear is that either this amount of debt holding could translate into excessive Chinese influence over American politics and policy making, or that a Chinese decision to no longer invest in U.S. debt could lead to an economic crisis. A plurality of Americans have thus seen China as a serious problem—but not necessarily as an adversary (Pew Research Center 2011). In a 2015 Chicago Council on Global Affairs survey, Republicans and Democrats each ranked Chinese military power as the 11th greatest threat to U.S. interests (Chicago Council on Global Affairs 2015).

There are also several areas of divergence between Republicans and Democrats when one examines public opinion. Nearly two-thirds of self-identified Republicans, for example, view cyberattacks directed at the United States from China as a significant threat (Wike 2015). Slightly less than half of all Democrats hold the same view. According to the National Security Agency, China has launched more than 600 cyberattacks on the U.S. government, or on U.S.-based companies between 2010 and 2015 (Windrem 2015). Most of these attacks are designed to gain access to corporate or government secrets. Generally, Republicans are more likely to believe that these attacks warrant a punitive response, rather than solely a strengthening of U.S. countermeasures. Republicans are also more likely than Democrats to be concerned about the U.S. trade deficit with China. The trade deficit, which measures the difference between the value of exports and the value of imports stood at $266 billion (U.S.) in 2015.

Republicans Denounce U.S.–China Climate Deal

Although Democrats supported the U.S.–China joint statement on climate change, most Republican members of the Senate were heavily critical of what they perceived as the one-sided nature of the agreement. Senate majority leader Mitch McConnell argued, for example:

> I was particularly distressed by the deal that . . . requires the Chinese to do nothing at all for 16 years while these carbon emission regulations are creating havoc in my state and other states around the country.

Senator James Inhofe, a Republican member of the Senate Environment and Public Works Committee and well-known climate change denialist, also panned the agreement:

> In the President's climate change deal, the United States will be required to more steeply reduce our carbon emissions while China won't have to reduce anything. It's hollow and not believable for China to claim it will shift 20 percent of its energy to non-fossil fuels by 2030, and a promise to peak its carbon emissions only allows the world's largest economy to buy time. China builds a coal-fired power plant every 10 days and is the largest importer of coal in the world. This deal is a nonbinding charade.

Although Republicans in Congress cannot block the joint statement, which is nonbinding, it can and has resisted the president's Clean Power Plan, which is designed, in part, to implement portions of the U.S. side of the agreement. Republicans tend to believe that efforts to reduce greenhouse gas emissions are too costly in terms of American jobs and are based on unsettled science.

Sources:

Inhofe, James M. "U.S.–China Climate Deal a Nonbinding Charade." November 12, 2014. http://www.inhofe.senate.gov/newsroom/press-releases/inhofe-us-china-climate-deal-a-non-binding-charade.

McAuliff, Michael, and Kate Sheppard. "Republicans Slam China Climate Deal as They Welcome Their Senate Majority." The Huffington Post, November 12, 2014. http://www.huffingtonpost.com/2014/11/12/obama-china-congress_n_6145904.html.

Congressional Republicans have been critical of the Obama administration policies toward China on a variety of issues. In late 2014, for example, the United States reached an agreement with China related to climate change and clean energy production. Under the agreement, U.S. targets related to greenhouse gas emissions were more stringent than those made by China, but less than those previously made by major greenhouse gas producers in Western Europe. Prominent Republican lawmakers such as Senate Majority Leader Mitch McConnell and Speaker of the House John Boehner argued that the agreement would needlessly hurt the U.S. economy in general and the manufacturing sector in particular. Several states with

Republican governors also sued the Obama administration to stop implementation of the Clean Power Plan, which was part of the joint announcement with China. In February 2016 the U.S. Supreme Court enjoined the Clean Power Plan from taking effect while the litigation continues.

Congressional Republicans, much like Republicans in the general public, also have been critical of the Obama administration on issues related to cyberattacks originating in China. For example, Representative Will Hurd, a Republican from Texas who sits on the House Homeland Security Committee has pilloried the lack of a clear "red line" by the Obama administration indicating what the U.S. response would be to a Chinese cyberattack (Takala 2016). In 2015 Chinese hackers attacked the Office of Personnel Management (OPM) database, potentially compromising the personal information of millions of government workers. In this case, the Chinese government has indicated that the hack was not sanctioned by the government, a claim viewed with some skepticism in government circles. Obama announced that the United States would retaliate, but has not specified the means by which this would occur. Congressional Republicans, such as Senator Lindsey Graham of South Carolina, have called for the imposition of economic sanctions. For its part, the Obama administration fears that retaliation could lead to a trade war, which may well hurt the United States more than the original infraction. For its part, the Chinese government denies being the source of the attack.

Republican presidential hopefuls have also called for a stronger stance on China. Businessman Donald Trump, for example, has called for the imposition of countervailing duties on China for its currency manipulation. Trump would also like the United States to pressure the PRC with regard to its relationship with North Korea. Trump has asserted that, under U.S. pressure, China is capable of reigning in North Korea, which is otherwise isolated diplomatically and economically from most of the world. Finally, Trump called for the United States to be tougher with China on the issue of intellectual property. He asserted that economic sanctions and a stronger negotiating stance could convince China to improve compliance with existing intellectual property law. It is worth noting that Trump was not alone, among Republican or Democratic presidential contenders, when it came to focusing on trade with respect to U.S. foreign policy toward China. All of the major presidential candidates in 2016 focused more on trade issues than environmental, security, or human rights issues. In part, this reflected the focus on jobs and economic security that often come to the fore during presidential elections. Nonetheless, during their campaigns for the Republican presidential nomination, both Ohio governor John Kasich and Texas senator Ted Cruz brought up other issues related to China. Cruz, for example, introduced a bill into the Senate that would have renamed the street in front of the Chinese Embassy in Washington D.C. Liu Xiaobo Plaza after the prodemocracy advocate imprisoned by China for his political activities. Cruz asserted that renaming the street would call attention to China's human rights record, and he used Senate rules to block Obama's ambassador nominees to multiple countries until the bill was considered. The bill ultimately passed the Senate in a unanimous voice vote but has not progressed, in part because of opposition from Obama, who believed the bill to be a counterproductive political stunt. Ohio governor John Kasich, meanwhile, advanced the idea that the United States should do more to counter Chinese attempts to assert its military power in Asia. While on the campaign trail, Kasich suggested sending "a little carrier" group to the area to let China know that it does not own the South China Sea (Torry 2015).

Democrats on U.S. Relations with China

The 2012 Democratic Party platform mentioned China 14 times. Like its Republican counterpart, the Democratic platform is concerned primarily with trade issues, including Chinese violations of World Trade Organization rules (Democratic National Committee 2012). Both platforms also mention China's poor human rights record. However, the Democratic platform keys on some subjects not emphasized by the Republicans, including cooperation on military and environmental issues. On military issues, the Democratic position favors cooperation in areas where Chinese and U.S. interests match, such as the problem of piracy in the South China Sea. Democrats have also applauded cooperation between the two nations in placing sanctions on North Korea in response to its nuclear and missile tests, as well as their combined efforts to bring Iran to the negotiating table to curb its nuclear ambitions. The Democratic Party platform also envisioned cooperation on environmental issues, which was partially realized with a historic 2014 climate agreement.

Within the general public, both Democrats and Republicans have unfavorable views of China; however, the partisan gap is wide. Forty-two percent of Democrats view China favorably, while only 27 percent of Republicans view China favorably (Wike 2015). A 2011 poll also found that twice as many Democrats as Republicans feel that the relationship between the United States and China is improving (Pew Research Center 2011). It is important to recognize, however, that a majority of both Democrats and Republicans believes that the relationship has either stayed the same or is getting worse. Interestingly, neither Democrats nor Republicans view growing Chinese economic power as a top10 threat to the United States (Chicago Council on Global Affairs 2015). At present, the U.S. economy is larger, in absolute terms, than the Chinese economy. The Chinese economy is growing at a much faster rate, however. In any case, the rate of Chinese economic growth, as well its increased projection of military power, has not yet caused the public to believe that China is a significant threat to U.S. national interests. However, protecting the jobs of American workers is the top foreign policy goal of both Democrats and Republicans, which might explain the comparatively hawkish stances taken by both parties on issues of trade with China.

The Obama administration has sought to find common ground with China on a variety of issues, including climate change. Although the 2014 agreement between the two nations on this issue did not bind either party to specific targets,

President Obama Hails U.S.–China Climate Deal

When President Obama and President Xi of China made a joint statement containing a variety of goals related to lowering greenhouse gas emissions, many observers hailed the occasion as an important development in efforts to combat climate change. At the joint press conference, President Obama said, in part:

> Second, as the world's two largest economies, energy consumers and emitters of greenhouse gases, we have a special responsibility to lead the global effort against climate change. That's why today I am proud that we can announce a historic agreement. I commend President Xi, his team, and the Chinese government for the commitment they are making to slow, peak, and then reverse the course of China's carbon emissions . . .
>
> This is a major milestone in the U.S.–China relationship, and it shows what's possible when we work together on an urgent global challenge. In addition, by making this announcement today, together, we hope to encourage all major economies to be ambitious—all countries, developing and developed—to work across some of the old divides so we can conclude a strong global climate agreement next year.

The talks between the United States and China were related to several issues beyond climate change, including trade and security issues. However, the climate deal received the most attention and scrutiny, in part because of its proximity to the Paris climate talks, which produced a historic 195-nation agreement on greenhouse targets, and also because of the release of President Obama's controversial Clean Power Plan.

Source:

"Remarks by President Obama and President Xi of the People's Republic of China in Joint Press Conference." Whitehouse.gov. Last modified September 25, 2015. https://www.whitehouse.gov/the-press-office/2015/09/25/remarks-president-obama-and-president-xi-peoples-republic-china-joint.

it did set specific targets in a way that underscored a recognition by both governments that robust action on the issue was necessary. Given the previous lack of cooperation between the two countries on this issue, the Obama administration hailed the joint statement as a breakthrough on an issue of key importance to both states. China and the United States together account for over 40 percent of global carbon emissions, so progress by both states is required if the goal of keeping global warming at or below two degrees centigrade globally is to be met. India and Russia, the next two largest carbon emitters, make up about 10 percent of the global total. The Obama administration needed to cooperate with China in order to conclude the Joint Comprehensive Plan of Action (JCPOA), which is designed to reign in Iranian nuclear ambitions. As a permanent member of the United Nations Security Council, China could have vetoed any multilateral sanctions against Iran, which may well have scuttled any attempt to force Iran to the negotiating table.

In other areas, the Obama administration has taken a more unyielding stance with China. In general, however, the Obama administration has eschewed direct confrontation. For example, the United States has deployed an additional naval carrier and other warships to the South China Sea in 2016 to counter Chinese influence and threats over the status of several disputed islands in the region. In March 2016, China responded by deploying antiship missiles on the islands, which it claims are not targeted at the United States. For the first time in decades, the United States also has stationed troops at Subic Bay in the Philippines. The Philippine Supreme Court agreed to the U.S. request to station troops amid concerns about Chinese territorial claims in the area. China has condemned the U.S. show of force in the region, but, to this point, there has been no direct conflict between the two countries.

On the issue of Taiwan, the Obama administration has been careful to emphasize adherence to the Taiwan Relations Act, by which the United States recognized the PRC and broke formal relations with Taiwan. Taiwan and the United States maintain a de facto diplomatic relationship. In late 2015, however, Obama authorized the sale of 1.83 billion in arms sales to Taiwan, which angered China (Brunnstrom and Zengerle 2015).

In Congress, Democrats have been mixed in their support of the president's agenda as it relates to China. For example, many Democrats praised the climate agreement between the United States and China. Minority Leader Nancy Pelosi, for example, referred to the agreement as "a commitment to confronting climate change with the seriousness it requires" (Pelosi 2014). Democrats in Congress have also supported the decision by the Obama administration to bring an increased number of Chinese trade violation cases before the Dispute Settlement Mechanism of the World Trade Organization. However, on other issues, Democrats have been more critical of the president. On the issue of Chinese cyberattacks against U.S. government and business sites, for example, Democrats have urged the president to make a more forceful response. Democratic representative Jim Langevin, ranking member of the House Armed Services Committee, argued in 2015 that the president should consider economic sanctions, criminal indictments, and/or publicly naming the offending parties, even though President Obama has argued that this would likely significantly increase tensions with the Chinese government (Marks 2015).

In 2016, both of the major candidates for the Democratic Party presidential nomination vowed to take an aggressive stance toward China. Former secretary of state Hillary Clinton argued that China needed to be held more accountable for the promotion of cybersecurity and rules-based international trade (Hillary for America 2016). Clinton also argued in favor of Obama's decision to display U.S. military might in the South China Sea. As First Lady, Clinton delivered her famous "women's right are human rights" speech during the UN Fourth World Conference on Women in Beijing in 1995. The speech drew significant criticism from China, but praise in the United States. Although she supported the decision to decouple

Chinese–U.S. trade relations from human rights issues, she has been a vocal critic of human rights abuses in China.

Vermont senator Bernie Sanders has primarily viewed U.S.–Chinese relations through the lenses of trade and human rights. On trade, Sanders was one of the few members of Congress to vote against granting PNTR status to China. He has consistently argued that, on balance, trade agreements between the United States and countries with a large supply of unskilled labor and/or low levels of respect for workers' rights—such as China—results in lost American jobs and a race to the bottom on wages. Sanders, like his Republican counterparts, has accused China of manipulating its currency in order to lower the price of its exports, a move that can cost manufacturing jobs in the United States. Sanders cosponsored a bill in 2001 that would have directly criticized China for its poor human rights record. The bill did not make it out of committee but was heavily supported by Democrats.

Further Reading

"America Divided: Political Partisanship and U.S. Foreign Policy." Chicago Council on Global Affairs. Last modified 2015. http://www.thechicagocouncil.org/sites/default /files/CCGA_PublicSurvey2015.pdf.

Brunnstrom, David, and Patricia Zengerle. "Obama Administration Authorizes $1.83-billion Arms Sale to Taiwan." Reuters. Last modified December 17, 2015. http://www.reuters .com/article/us-usa-taiwan-arms-idUSKBN0TZ2C520151217.

Democratic National Committee. "The 2012 Democratic Platform." Democrats.org. Last modified 2012. https://www.democrats.org/party-platform.

GovTrack.us. "H.R. 4444 (106th): China Trade Bill." Accessed April 4, 2016. https://www .govtrack.us/congress/votes/106-2000/h228.

Hillary for America. "National Security | Issues | Hillary for America." Hillary for America Starts Right Here | Hillary for America. Last modified 2016. https://www.hillaryclinton .com/issues/national-security/.

Marks, Joseph. "GOP to Obama: Crack Down on Chinese Hackers." Politico. Last modified June 10, 2015. http://www.politico.com/story/2015/06/republicans-obama-chinese -hackers-crack-down-118802.

Office of the Historian. "U.S.–China Chronology." Accessed April 3, 2016. https://history .state.gov/countries/issues/china-us-relations.

Pelosi, Nancy. "Pelosi Statement on U.S.–China Climate Agreement." Congresswoman Nancy Pelosi. Last modified November 11, 2014. https://pelosi.house.gov/news/press -releases/pelosi-statement-on-us-china-climate-agreement.

Pew Research Center. "Strengthen Ties with China, But Get Tough on Trade." Pew Research Center for the People and the Press. Last modified January 12, 2011. http://www .people-press.org/2011/01/12/strengthen-ties-with-china-but-get-tough-on-trade/.

Republican National Committee. "2012 Republican Platform." Last modified 2012. https:// prod-static-ngop-pbl.s3.amazonaws.com/docs/2012GOPPlatform.pdf.

Takala, Rudy. "Republicans Push Obama to Get Tough on Chinese Hacking." Congressman Will Hurd. Last modified January 25, 2016. https://hurd.house.gov/media-center/in -the-news/republicans-push-obama-get-tough-chinese-hacking.

Torry, Jack. "John Kasich Talks Foreign Policy, Urges Tougher Stance against China." *The Columbus Dispatch*. Last modified July 8, 2015. http://www.dispatch.com/content/stories/local/2015/07/08/john-kasich-talks-foreign-policy-in-south-carolina.html#.

Wike, Richard. "Americans' Concerns About China: Economics, Cyberattacks, Human Rights Top the List." Pew Research Center's Global Attitudes Project. Last modified September 9, 2015. http://www.pewglobal.org/2015/09/09/americans-concerns-about-china-economics-cyberattacks-human-rights-top-the-list/.

Windrem, Robert. "Exclusive: Secret NSA Map Shows China Cyber Attacks on U.S. Targets." NBC News. Last modified July 30, 2015. http://www.nbcnews.com/news/us-news/exclusive-secret-nsa-map-shows-china-cyber-attacks-us-targets-n401211.

Climate Change

At a Glance

Although, at times, both political parties have elevated concerns over global climate change to a point closer to a core goal of U.S. foreign policy, virtually all support for aggressive international action against climate change resides within the Democratic Party. Most Democrats see climate change as a major threat to future generations of people in America and around the world, and they insist that as the world's leading generator of greenhouse gases (GHGs), the United States has a moral imperative to take a leadership role in responding to the threat. One example of such action is the 2014 U.S.–China Joint Announcement on Climate Change. A second example is the support of the Obama administration for the final document of the UN Conference on Climate Change in Paris.

Virtually all political opposition to laws and regulations to combat climate change comes from the Republican Party and its business and industry constituencies. In addition to expressing deep skepticism about the severity and even the reality of anthropogenic (human-caused) climate change, Republicans are critical of international agreements that, they argue, disproportionately harm the United States. Republicans are especially critical of agreements that provide more modest GHG-emission reduction goals for developing countries like China and India. They argue that such arrangements put the United States at an unacceptable economic disadvantage.

According to many Democrats, assertive U.S. actions to address climate change . . .

- Are critical in order to avoid economic, social, and political catastrophe;
- Should include specific targets for the reduction of greenhouse gases;
- Reflect a clear scientific consensus on the issue;
- Are required because climate change disproportionately affects the poor; and
- Are necessary to enlist the cooperation of other countries, including major contributors to climate change in the developing world.

According to many Republicans, assertive U.S. actions to address climate change . . .

- Would create damaging economic trade-offs without clear short- or medium-term benefits;
- Should not include specific targets except in cases where all countries, especially China, are participating on equal footing;
- Are based on an overstated scientific consensus on the role of anthropogenic (human-caused) climate change; and
- Are not a key security issue.

Overview

The political history of climate change as a part of U.S. foreign policy began during the Cold War. In the 1950s and early 1960s, climate science was part of a broader program of atmospheric research with a variety of geostrategic applications in mind (Howe 2014, 17). At the time, the impact of greenhouse gases such as carbon dioxide and methane on the atmosphere was a matter of speculation. However, previous scientists had already determined that the Earth was warming and that seawater could not absorb the new large quantities of carbon dioxide entering the atmosphere as a result of global industrialization and population growth. In 1965, a special scientific panel advised President Lyndon Johnson that the greenhouse effect, as it had become known, was a real concern. Though Johnson reported these findings to Congress, concerns about greenhouse gas emissions took a backseat to concerns about other pollutants in America's air, land, and water that were having a more visible impact on the environment.

The late 1980s and early 1990s witnessed renewed momentum on climate change policy in the United States. The United States first became involved in the Intergovernmental Panel on Climate Change (IPCC) during the Reagan administration. The IPCC was formed by the United Nations Environmental Program and the World Meteorological Association to provide scientific evidence and advice on the current state of the world's climate. The IPCC concluded that humans had contributed, through the emission of greenhouse gases, to an increase in global temperatures over the preceding century. President George H. W. Bush supported the United Nations Framework Convention on Climate Change (UNFCCC), which committed state signatories to develop and implement national strategies to decrease greenhouse gas emissions. Although some Senate Democrats expressed a concern over the fact that the convention did not set binding targets, the Senate ratified the UNFCCC without difficulty. President George H. W. Bush did promise to submit any additional protocols to the UNFCCC, especially those that would require mandatory emission reductions, to the Senate for further advice and consent (Barbour 2010).

The difference between binding and nonbinding targets became clear in the debate over the Kyoto Protocol to the UNFCCC. The 1997 Kyoto Protocol committed state parties to emission reduction targets based on their level of emissions and their development status. Developing countries, including China were not subject to mandatory targets. States unable to meet their targets would be afforded flexibility through emissions trading based on what was commonly called a cap and trade system. In advance of negotiations on the Kyoto Protocol, the U.S. Senate voted 95–0 to recommend that the Clinton administration not sign the protocol if developing countries were not required to commit to binding targets (Kahn 2003). In spite of the fact that the protocol did not contain binding targets, the United States signed the treaty. However, the treaty never became binding on the United States because it was never submitted to the Senate for ratification. The Clinton administration knew that the ratification effort would fail.

In 2001, newly inaugurated Republican president George W. Bush removed the United States from the Kyoto negotiation process. He argued that "Kyoto is, in many ways, unrealistic. Many countries cannot meet their Kyoto targets. The targets themselves were arbitrary and not based upon science. For America, complying with those mandates would have a negative economic impact, with layoffs of workers and price increases for consumers. And when you evaluate all these flaws, most responsible people will understand that it is not sound public policy" (Bush 2001). The decision by the United States not to ratify the Kyoto Protocol delayed the entrance into force of the instrument. The signatories to Kyoto placed a threshold on entry into force that prevented the treaty from becoming binding until 55 countries accounting for at least 55 percent of emissions ratified the treaty. As a significant source of greenhouse emissions, the U.S. failure to ratify delayed the entrance into force of the protocol until 2005.

Although Democrats were not generally supportive of Kyoto's omission of targets for developing countries, they were nonetheless critical of the abandonment of the process. Most Democrats—and important parts of the party coalition, like environmental and labor groups—held that even if Kyoto was unworkable, the United States still needed to engage with the world on the issue and find a path forward to combat climate change.

From that point forward, partisan divisions over the nature and severity of climate change rapidly widened. After Kyoto, Republicans became less likely to attribute climate change to human activity. Democrats, by contrast, became increasingly likely to believe that climate change is occurring and that human beings play a role in altering the climate due to greenhouse gas emissions (Dunlap 2008). Republicans also began to believe in higher numbers that the media was overstating the impact of global warming.

The last major drive for a bipartisan effort to address the climate change issue came in 2003, when Republican senator John McCain and Democratic (later independent) senator Joe Lieberman championed the Climate Stewardship Act. The act would have capped carbon dioxide emissions at year 2000 levels. In addition the

The Clean Air Act and Climate Change

The Clean Air Act, which was passed with overwhelming bipartisan support by Congress and signed by Republican president Richard Nixon in 1970, does not contain the words "global warming" or "climate change." The 1970 legislation and subsequent amendments do, however, permit the EPA to regulate any hazardous air pollutant. In the landmark Supreme Court case *Massachusetts v. EPA* (2007), the high court held that the EPA must regulate greenhouse gas emissions in the event that the agency found them to be hazardous. This ruling was a rebuke to the George W. Bush administration, which had refused to regulate greenhouse gas emissions on the grounds that such regulation did not fall under the agency's mandate.

The Clean Air Act, coupled with the *Massachusetts v. EPA* decision, cleared the way for the Barack Obama administration to establish a variety of regulations related to reduction of greenhouse gases. Automobiles, for example, may now be regulated, not just for fuel economy and sulfur emissions, but for carbon emissions as well. As a result of the intentional vagueness of the act (the idea was to make the act flexible enough to deal with current and future pollution issues) federal rules related to greenhouse gas emissions can, and have, been extended to existing and new power plants. However, it is important to recognize that the EPA is part of the executive bureaucracy. As a result, the president plays a key role on the areas of emphasis for the agency. Republican presidents are currently more likely to emphasize more traditional sources of pollution, such as sulfur dioxide, over greenhouse gases. In addition, a group of GOP-controlled states, public utilities, and portions of the energy industry have sued the EPA, arguing that the Clean Power Plan does not fall under the mandate of the EPA.

Sources:

Massachusetts v. Environmental Protection Agency. Oyez: IIT Chicago-Kent College of Law. Accessed January 23, 2016. https://www.oyez.org/cases/2006/05-1120.

"Summary of the Clean Air Act." U.S. Environmental Protection Agency. Accessed January 23, 2016. http://www.epa.gov/laws-regulations/summary-clean-air-act.

act would have established a cap and trade mechanism for use between elements of the industrial, electricity generation, transportation, and commercial sectors. The Climate Stewardship Act ultimately failed by a vote 43 in favor to 55 opposed, with two senators not voting. Although there was some bipartisanship evident in the voting, 75 percent of Democratic senators voted yes while 88 percent of Republican senators voted no. Similar versions of the bill were introduced in 2005 and 2007, but those bills failed as well.

In 2007, the U.S. Supreme Court ruled in *Massachusetts v. EPA* that the Environmental Protection Agency (EPA) must regulate greenhouse gas emissions in the event that the EPA declared them harmful. The EPA has declared that carbon dioxide and other greenhouse gases are indeed harmful. In 2015, President Obama, unable to pass climate change legislation through Congress, used the *Massachusetts v. EPA* ruling to justify the unveiling of the Clean Power Plan for existing power plants. New power plants were already covered by 2013 EPA regulations. Auto emissions are covered under a separate set of regulations as well. With respect to power plants, the largest source of carbon emissions, the goal is to lower emissions to 32 percent below 2005 levels by the year 2030 (EPA.gov 2015).

Coupled with the 2014 U.S.–China Joint Announcement on Climate Change, the Clean Power Plan ties into the overall support within the Obama administration, and among Democrats in general for compliance with the terms of the Paris Agreement. The latter accord, reached at the 21st session of the Conference of the Parties to the UNFCCC in 2015, commits states to taking unspecified measures to keep the global temperature increase at or below 1.5 degrees Celsius (European Commission 2015). The Paris Agreement was set to enter into force when ratified by 55 countries accounting for an estimated 55 percent of global greenhouse emissions. In October of 2016, the threshold was crossed with the accession of several states. Thus, the agreement enters into force in November 2016. More liberal Democrats have attempted to push the Obama administration even further, toward the establishment of a cross-sectoral emissions trading system created under the auspices of the EPA in enforcement of the Clean Air Act.

Democrats on Climate Change

During the 1990s, Democratic vice president Al Gore became perhaps America's best-known critic of government inaction on climate change. He was one of the Clinton administration's most outspoken proponents of the Kyoto Protocol, which would have created binding targets for greenhouse gas emissions for the United States as it did for other developed countries. Gore argued that "U.S. leadership was instrumental in achieving a strong and realistic agreement in Kyoto—one that couples ambitious environmental targets with flexible market mechanisms to meet those goals at the lowest possible cost. At the close of the Kyoto conference, President Clinton and I made clear his intention to sign this historic accord. In the eleven months since Kyoto, the evidence of global warming has grown only stronger, and so has our resolve" (Gore 1998).

As discussed above, the Kyoto Protocol was never ratified by the U.S. Senate. In the years since the Kyoto negotiations took place, however, Democratic support for aggressive action on climate change has become much stronger. Democrats say that this shift is directly attributable to a steady accumulation of scientific evidence that anthropogenic climate change is already occurring and could have cataclysmic consequences if effective mitigation policies and strategies are not implemented in the United States and around the world.

In 2012 the official Democratic Party platform on climate accepts the scientific consensus on global warming. The platform also supported market mechanisms, such as cap and trade schemes, to provide flexibility in carbon emissions both domestically and as part of broader international agreements (Democratic National

Committee 2012). Democrats have also chosen to list climate change as a danger to U.S. national security, describing the threat posed by climate change as "real, urgent, and severe" (Democratic National Committee 2012). The 2016 Democratic Party platform takes Republican nominee Donald Trump to task for referring to climate change as a hoax during a speech in South Carolina in 2015. The 2016 platform also refers to climate change as "real."

Democrats recognize the climate change has both international and domestic ramifications. On the international side, the aforementioned security concerns are combined with the assertion that climate change is something that must be addressed in a global, foreign policy context. In the domestic realm, the party platform argues that clean energy initiatives provide the best avenue for the United States to reduce its own emissions.

Public opinion polls indicate that large majorities of people who identify as Democrats believe that climate change is real. A 2013 Pew poll, for example, found that roughly two-thirds of all Democrats believe that human activity is the main cause of climate change (Pew Research Center 2013). A clear majority of Democrats also believe that evidence of global warming is emerging across the planet in the form of record high temperatures, increasingly common and severe weather events, and loss of ice in glaciers and arctic regions. In addition, very few Democrats believe that the media is exaggerating the nature of climate change. Finally, Democrats, once again by a strong majority, favor the idea of the United States becoming party to an international treaty with binding limits on greenhouse gas emissions (Russonello 2015).

Democrats in Congress have also exhibited a comparatively high degree of unity on issues and legislation related to climate change since President Barack Obama—himself a strong advocate for clean energy and other efforts to address climate change—took office. For example, in 2015, shortly after Obama announced the Clean Power Plan, Senate Democrats proposed a plan that would have required even more significant cuts. Although the legislation had no hope of passing the Republican-controlled Senate, it was a sign that the Democrats believe that climate change has become a winning issue for them (Davenport 2015). The bill was specifically timed to match efforts at the UN in advance of the UNFCCC talks in Paris, demonstrating the significant foreign policy dimensions of the issue.

Unity within the Democratic Party on the issue of climate change, however, is not absolute. This is, in part, because climate change is both a domestic and a foreign policy issue. Specifically, domestic regulations designed to combat climate change, whether or not they occur within the context of a broader international effort, can have an impact on local industries, especially in areas that depend more on fossil fuels for power generation or as a component of the economy. For example, 44 House Democrats voted against the American Clean Energy and Security Act of 2009 (Office of the Clerk of the U.S. House of Representatives 2009). The bill would have created a cap and trade mechanism similar to the system that exists in Europe.

Many of these Democrats either represented conservative districts or resided in states like West Virginia with significant economic dependence on fossil fuel industries.

A second example of imperfect Democratic Party unity within Congress occurred in 2015 during House debate on the contentious Keystone Pipeline. Democrats have argued, and the Department of State agreed in 2014, that the pipeline would increase carbon emissions, especially from Canadian tar sands (U.S. Department of State 2014). First, while most Democrats voted against the bill to authorize the pipeline to proceed, 31 Democrats broke ranks and voted for the bill. Most of these Democratic supporters of the pipeline represented traditionally "red" states with large numbers of conservative voters. Democrats in this situation are often referred to as "blue dog" Democrats. Blue dog Democrats are more likely to be moderate or even conservative in their ideological and voting tendencies, a fact that underscores the mismatch that sometimes occurs between party identification and ideology.

Divisions within the Democratic Party also emerged with respect to climate change on the Senate version of the bill. Democrats were able to mount a successful filibuster attempt, succeeding by a single vote (in the Senate, 40 senators can block many pieces of legislation from coming to a vote). However, 14 Democrat senators broke ranks and voted with the Republicans, following the same basic pattern as the vote in the House of Representatives. Second, Senator Bernie Sanders, who, though an independent, normally caucuses with the Democrats, and Senator Joe Manchin, a blue dog Democrat from West Virginia, sponsored rival amendments on the nature of climate change. Both amendments declared that humans have a significant impact on climate change (part of the effort to get Republicans on record on the issue). However, the Manchin amendment specifically envisioned a role for fossil fuels in the future economy, while the Sanders amendment called for a complete transition away from fossil fuels (Foran 2015). As a moderate, Manchin's amendment was an attempt to walk the fine line that exists in coal- and oil-rich states between environmental and economic concerns. Eventually, the Democrats agreed to table both amendments, and were only able to get vague wording relating to climate change, as opposed to anthropogenic climate change, being real.

The framing of climate change as a threat to U.S. security and international political and economic stability was also frequently heard in the 2016 Democratic presidential primary. For example, Senator Bernie Sanders described climate change as the single greatest threat to U.S. national security. He also tied the issue of climate change directly to the growth of terrorism in cases like the emergence of the Islamic State of Iraq and the Levant (ISIL) (Sanders 2016). Hillary Clinton, meanwhile, described climate change as "an urgent challenge that threatens us all" (Hillary for America 2016, and she has proposed a wide range of programs and policies to increase investment in clean energy and reduce American reliance on GHG-generating fossil fuels.

Republicans on Climate Change

The 2012 Republican Party platform mentioned climate change only once, compared to Democrats, who mention the issue 18 times. Moreover, the sole mention of climate change in the GOP platform comes within a context in which the party criticized Democrats for exaggerating climate change's impact on national security (Republican National Committee 2012). Republicans argued in the platform the Democrats have placed more of an emphasis of climate change as a security issue than on terrorism as a security issue. On more general issues related to the environment, the Republican platform focused on an "all of the above" approach to energy security, including taking advantage of low-cost fossil fuels such as coal. The essential argument is that any transition toward renewable energy should be based on market principals such as supply and demand, rather than government intervention in a way that favors particular portions of the energy sector. Consistent with this approach, the Republican platform focuses on the domestic side of the climate change equation, arguing that strict federal regulation, as opposed to cooperative agreements with energy producers, has harmed the energy industry and resulted in a net loss of jobs in the energy sector. The 2016 party platform offers continuity with the 2012 variant; arguing the IPCC is a political mechanism, rather than a purely scientific body.

The climate change language in the 2012 Republican Party platform suggests a shift to the right on climate change when compared to the previous (2008) platform. Although neither platform elevates climate change to the level of a security issue, the 2008 platform mentions climate change a total of 13 times. The 2008 platform acknowledges that humans may have an impact on the climate through carbon emissions, though it also argues that the science on this issue is unsettled (American Presidency Project 2008). The 2012 platform does not mention anthropogenic climate change at all. The 2008 platform mentions market mechanisms in the context of reducing greenhouse gases. The 2012 platform mentions the primacy of the market in the context of all decisions related to energy. This may be as a result of 2008 Republican presidential candidate John McCain's argument that cap and trade agreements have a positive role to play in the reduction of greenhouse gases (a belief not shared by 2012 Republican presidential candidate Mitt Romney). The 2008 Republican platform mentions international cooperation in the area of climate change. Specifically, Republicans argued that other states emitting large amounts of greenhouse gases, such as China and India, must not be given a competitive advantage over the United States. The 2012 platform does not mention international agreements or international cooperation to address climate change.

In terms of public opinion, Republicans are more likely than Democrats to be skeptical about global warming, though this skepticism is softening. In 2008, for example, 73 percent of self-identified Democrats believed that global warming is primarily caused by humans. By contrast, 42 percent of Republicans held the same belief (Dunlap 2008). In 2016, 47 percent of Republicans believed that climate change is anthropogenic (Lehmann 2016). Republicans, overall, were also much more likely to believe that global warming is exaggerated by the news media than are their Democratic-leaning counterparts. However, the rise in the number of Republicans who believe that climate change is caused by humans may lower some of the existing barriers to bipartisan cooperation on this issue.

Public opinion among self-identified Republicans appears to be more divided on issues related to climate change than opinion among Democrats. The rise of the Tea Party movement among conservatives, including Republicans, is partially responsible for the division. For example, 70 percent of Republicans who do not identify with the Tea Party movement believe that the Earth is warming (though not primarily due to human activity), while only 30 percent of those who identify with the Tea Party movement have a similar belief. There is no identifiable subset of Democrats who have the same division from Democrats at large. The rise of the Tea Party movement to political prominence during the 2010 midterm elections may be another part of the reason for the changes between the 2008 and 2012 Republican Party platforms.

By contrast, Republicans appear to be more unified in Congress than their Democratic Party counterparts on issues related to climate change. As mentioned above, the American Clean Energy and Security Act of 2009 would have created a cap and trade system in the United States. Seventeen percent of House Democrats broke ranks and voted against the act at a time when the Democrats still controlled the House of Representatives. By contrast, only 4.5 percent of House Republicans broke ranks and voted for the bill (GovTrack.us 2009). Although the bill passed the House, it was unable to overcome a GOP filibuster in the Senate. In addition to increased party unity within the Republican Party as a factor, it also should be noted that the onset of the Great Recession made it more difficult to pass environmental legislation due to fears about the impact on unemployment of increased federal regulation. Republican minority leader and future Speaker of the House John Boehner argued that "This is the biggest job-killing bill that has ever been on the floor of the House of Representatives. Right here. This bill" (CNN 2009).

Republicans in Congress, as well as candidates for the Republican Party presidential nomination, have also been unified in their condemnation of President Obama's Clean Power Plan. Former Florida governor Jeb Bush, for example, argued that the Clean Power Plan should be repealed, while businessman Donald Trump dismissed the idea of human-caused climate change as a "hoax." Texas senator Ted Cruz asserted that the Clean Power Plan is an illegal abuse of federal power and introduced legislation to block the move (League of Conservation Voters 2015). In 2016, 27 states, mostly headed by Republican governors, sued the Obama administration arguing that the Clean Power Plan relies on authority not granted to the Environmental Protection Agency under the Clean Air Act. A federal district court stayed the Clean Power Plan (prevented it from going into effect) during the lawsuit. The U.S. Supreme Court has refused to lift the stay.

Given the dramatically different perspectives of leaders of the two parties, the fate of the Clean Power Plan is likely to depend largely on whether a Democrat or Republican occupies the White House in 2016. Because of the nature of the plan, anyone elected president could abandon or expand the plan, barring a successful legal challenge, without congressional approval. The Clean Power Plan is hypothetically not subject to congressional approval because it is an interpretation of enforcement of an already existing law, the Clean Air Act.

Further Reading

American Presidency Project. "Republican Party Platforms: 2008 Republican Party Platform." Last modified September 1, 2008. http://www.presidency.ucsb.edu/ws/?pid=78545.

Barbour, Emily C. "International Agreements on Climate Change: Selected Legal Questions." Congressional Research Service. Last modified April 12, 2010. http://fpc.state.gov/documents/organization/142749.pdf.

Bush, George W. "President Bush Discusses Global Climate Change." White House. Last modified June 11, 2001. http://georgewbush-whitehouse.archives.gov/news/releases/2001/06/20010611-2.html.

CNN.com. "House Passes Energy Overhaul Bill 219-212—CNN.com." CNN—Breaking News, Latest News and Videos. Last modified June 26, 2009. http://www.cnn.com/2009/POLITICS/06/26/house.energy/index.html?eref=rss_us.

Davenport, Coral. "Senate Democrats Offer Climate Change Bill Aimed Not at Success Now, but in 2016—*New York Times*." *New York Times*—Breaking News, World News & Multimedia. Last modified September 22, 2015. http://www.nytimes.com/2015/09/23/us/politics/senate-democrats-to-unveil-aggressive-climate-change-bill.html.

Democratic National Committee. "The 2012 Democratic Party Platform." Last modified 2012. https://www.democrats.org/party-platform.

Dunlap, Riley. "Climate-Change Views: Republican–Democratic Gaps Expand in Recent Years." Gallup.com. Last modified May 29, 2008. http://www.gallup.com/poll/107569/climatechange-views-republicandemocratic-gaps-expand.aspx.

European Commission. "Paris Agreement—European Commission." Last modified 2015. http://ec.europa.eu/clima/policies/international/negotiations/future/index_en.htm.

Foran, Clare. "Democrats Divided on Climate Change: Ideological Split on Full Display Over Two Days of Senate Failures." *National Journal*. Last modified January 22, 2015. http://www.nationaljournal.com/energy/2015/01/22/democrats-divided-climate-change.

"GOP Deeply Divided Over Climate Change." Pew Research Center for the People and the Press. Last modified November 1, 2013. http://www.people-press.org/2013/11/01/gop-deeply-divided-over-climate-change/.

Gore, Al. "Gore Statement on U.S. Signing of Kyoto Protocol." Common Dreams. Last modified November 12, 1998. http://www.commondreams.org/pressreleases/Nov%2098/111298c.htm.

GovTrack.us. "H.R. 2454 (111th): American Clean Energy and Security Act of 2009." Last modified June 26, 2009. https://www.govtrack.us/congress/votes/111-2009/h477.

Hillary for America. "Taking on the Global Threat of Climate Change | Issues | Hillary for America." Accessed January 23, 2016. https://www.hillaryclinton.com/issues/climate/.

Howe, Joshua P. *Behind the Curve: Science and the Politics of Global Warming*. Seattle: University of Washington Press, 2014. http://search.ebscohost.com/login.aspx?direct=true&scope=site&db=nlebk&db=nlabk&AN=709398.

Kahn, Greg. "The Fate of the Kyoto Protocol under the Bush Administration." *Berkeley Journal of International Law* 21, no. 3 (2003): 548–571. http://scholarship.law.berkeley.edu/cgi/viewcontent.cgi?article=1248&context=bjil.

League of Conservation Voters. "In Their Own Words 2016 Presidential Candidates on the Clean Power Plan." Last modified January 15, 2015. http://www.lcv.org/assets/docs/presidential-candidates-on-cpp.pdf.

Lehmann, Evan. "Many More Republicans Now Believe in Climate Change." Scientific American. Last modified April 27, 2016. https://www.scientificamerican.com/article/many-more-republicans-now-believe-in-climate-change/.

Lewis, Phillip. "Donald Trump On Climate Change: 'I Believe It Goes Up and It Goes Down.'" The Huffington Post. Last modified September 22, 2015. http://www.huffingtonpost.com/entry/trump-global-warming_us_5601d04fe4b08820d91aa753.

New York Times. "House Vote 519—Directs Administration to Proceed on Keystone Pipeline." Last modified November 14, 2014. http://politics.nytimes.com/congress/votes/113/house/2/519.

Office of the Clerk. "FINAL VOTE RESULTS FOR ROLL CALL 477 (American Clean Energy and Security Act)." U.S. House of Representatives. Last modified June 26, 2009. http://clerk.house.gov/evs/2009/roll477.xml.

Republican National Committee. "Republican Platform 2012." Last modified 2012. https://prod-static-ngop-pbl.s3.amazonaws.com/docs/2012GOPPlatform.pdf.

Russonello, Giovanni. "Two-Thirds of Americans Want U.S. to Join Climate Change Pact." *New York Times.* Last modified November 30, 2015. http://www.nytimes.com/2015/12/01/world/americas/us-climate-change-republicans-democrats.html?_r=0.

Sanders, Bernie. "Full Plan: Combating Climate Change to Save the Planet." Accessed January 21, 2016. https://berniesanders.com/issues/climate-change/.

U.S. Department of State. "Final Supplemental Environmental Impact Statement: Keystone XL Project." Last modified April 214. https://keystonepipeline-xl.state.gov/documents/organization/221190.pdf

U.S. Environmental Protection Agency. "FACT SHEET: Clean Power Plan by the Numbers | Clean Power Plan | US EPA." Last modified 2015. http://www.epa.gov/cleanpowerplan/fact-sheet-clean-power-plan-numbers.

White House. "U.S.–China Joint Announcement on Climate Change." Whitehouse.gov. Last modified November 12, 2014. https://www.whitehouse.gov/the-press-office/2014/11/11/us-china-joint-announcement-climate-change.

Cuba

At a Glance

For most of the period since Cuban independence, the issue of U.S. foreign policy toward Cuba was one where politics stopped "at the water's edge." That is to say that, in spite of small areas of disagreement, the Republican and Democratic parties were largely unified over the direction of policy toward the small island nation. Leaders of both parties agreed that the Communist nation should be treated as an international pariah, and they balked at any suggestion that America engage in any trade or diplomacy with Cuba.

In recent years, however, a partisan gap has opened between Democrats and Republicans on the diplomatic relationship between the United States and Cuba as well as the economic embargo against Cuba that has been in place since the Eisenhower administration. Given Florida's importance in Electoral College politics, coupled with high levels of political activity among Cuban Americans in Florida, the emerging partisan gap has significant implications.

Most support for normalization of the U.S. relationship with Cuba came from within the Democratic Party. In December 2014, in fact, the Obama administration announced that it would begin the process of establishing diplomatic relations with Cuba. In July 2015, the United States and Cuba reopened their embassies, ending decades of diplomatic isolation. Advocates of normalization argue that the previous approach to U.S. relations with Cuba, exemplified by the Cuban embargo and the virtual absence of a diplomatic relationship, had failed to produce the results sought by the architects of the policy from both parties.

Much of the opposition to normalization came from within the Republican Party. The essential argument of the GOP is that normalization of relations between the two countries rewards the regime in Cuba for continuing to abuse human rights and preventing the emergence of democracy. From this perspective, the continued isolation of Cuba, both economically and diplomatically, is necessary to secure the fundamental rights of the Cuban people.

It is important to recognize that a full reconciliation between the United States and Cuba would require bipartisan support. Although the president, under Article II of the Constitution, maintains the power to send and receive ambassadors, the machinery of the Cuban embargo is largely governed by Congress, which is currently controlled by the Republican Party. The Obama administration has the power to ease certain travel and humanitarian restrictions. Most of the trade and other economic restrictions, however, are governed by laws such as the Cuban Democracy Act of 1992 and the Cuban Liberty and Democratic Solidarity Act of 1996 (also known as the Helms-Burton Act).

According to many Democrats, normalization of relations with Cuba would . . .

- Make it easier for Cubans to promote democracy from within by increasing their access to the Internet and other sources of information not subject to governmental censorship;
- Improve the day-to-day lives of Cubans living without access to basic goods or being forced to pay exorbitant prices for those goods; and
- Provide the United States with increased leverage to push for improvements in Cuba's human rights record.

According to many Republicans, normalization of relations with Cuba would . . .

- Provide legitimacy to the dictatorial Cuban regime;
- Increase the staying power of the regime by ending certain financial restrictions; and
- Project U.S. weakness by demonstrating a willingness to negotiate with tyrannical regimes.

Overview

The U.S. relationship with Cuba has evolved significantly over time. The Spanish-American War resulted in U.S. occupation of Cuba from 1898 until Cuban independence in 1902. The period from 1902 until the Cuban Revolution began in 1953 was characterized by periods of direct and indirect U.S. control over the island nation. The Platt Amendment of 1901 and the treaty that resulted from the amendment granted the United States the right to intervene in Cuba under a variety of circumstances, ensuring U.S. hegemony over Cuban affairs. Ultimately, the provisions of the Platt Amendment also led to the U.S. lease of Guantanamo Bay in Cuba as a naval base.

U.S. interests in Cuba were based on several factors, including the geostrategic importance of Cuba in controlling access to the Panama Canal and the economic importance of sugar and other valuable crops that thrive in Cuba's tropical climate (Staten 2003, 45–46).

United States foreign policy toward Cuba during the prerevolutionary era privileged political stability over polity type. Against this backdrop, corruption among political elites became increasingly common. Average Cubans, who had hoped for genuine independence from Spain, became increasingly disenchanted with America's role in supporting dictators who governed primarily in the interests of economic elites in Cuba and the United States. One such dictator was Fulgencio Batista. Having previously been elected president of Cuba, Batista returned to power as part of a military coup in 1952. Initially, the United States supported the Batista regime, which became notorious for high levels of corruption, indifference to rising poverty and economic inequality, and human rights abuses.

As internal dissatisfaction with Batista grew, so did the prospects for rebellion. On July 26, 1953, rebel leader Fidel Castro led an attack on a military barracks near Santiago de Cuba. Although the attack was unsuccessful and Castro was captured and imprisoned, the attack became known as the beginning of the Cuban Revolution. Over time, the United States began to withdraw its support from what the government saw as an ineffective and chaotic Batista regime. The Cuban government, in spite of initial success, was unable to defeat the rebellion. In 1959, Batista fled Cuba in defeat, leading to the ascension of Fidel Castro.

As Castro consolidated his power, he undertook several initiatives that quickly soured relations with the United States. Land reform policies initiated under Che Guevara led to the confiscation of over 500,000 acres of land formerly owned by U.S. corporations (Kellner 1989, 58). Ownership of land under sugar cultivation was restricted to Cuban citizens or the Cuban government. Castro also nationalized the oil industry in Cuba and placed significant restrictions on all foreign corporate ownership. Finally, the Soviet Union and Cuba established close economic ties, including agreements on sugar importation (the United States cut sugar importation in response to Castro's agricultural reforms), the extension of credit, and scientific exchange (Walters 1966, 74).

The United States responded to Castro's rise to power and embrace of Communist ideology in a variety of ways. In 1960 the Eisenhower administration, with the support of Congress, imposed an economic embargo on Cuba, exempting only humanitarian and medical supplies. Sanctions were further strengthened under the Kennedy administration in 1962. The United States also attempted various forms of military intervention in order to destabilize or overthrow the Castro regime. The most famous of these interventions was the failed Bay of Pigs invasion in 1961. The Bay of Pigs invasion enabled Castro to further consolidate his rule by providing a pretext for the imprisonment and/or execution of thousands of political opponents (Staten 2003, 97). In 1962, the Cuban missile crisis, during which the United States blockaded Cuba in order to prevent the Soviet Union from deploying missiles equipped with nuclear warheads in Cuba, brought the United States to the brink of war with the Soviet Union. War was averted when the United States agreed not to invade Cuba again and the Soviets agreed to dismantle all offensive weapons systems in Cuba and not to attempt to deploy nuclear weapons to the nation.

Title III of the Cuban Liberty and Democratic Solidarity Act

The Cuban Liberty and Democratic Solidarity Act (LIBERTAD) of 1996, also known as the Helms-Burton Act, codified into law some of the strongest sanctions ever imposed by the U.S. government against a foreign nation. Perhaps the most controversial provision of Helms-Burton is Title III, which allows U.S. citizens to file suit in U.S. civil courts against any individual or company, regardless of nationality, trafficking in confiscated U.S. property (Library of Congress 1995–1996). Given the scope of land and property confiscation by the Castro regime in the wake of the Cuban Revolution, Helms-Burton opened the door to a large number of lawsuits by U.S. citizens against virtually anyone conducting trade with Cuba. These provisions were controversial with America's trading partners, and the European Union even filed a grievance with the World Trade Organization.

So controversial was Title III of the Helms-Burton Act that President Bill Clinton negotiated waiver language into the bill before it became a law. The language allowed the president to suspend the application of Title III for renewable six-month periods. There was no limit placed on the number of renewals. In order to avoid international trade conflicts with countries in the European Union, as well as Canada and Mexico, Clinton waived Title III every six months during the remainder of his two terms in office. In a move that surprised some observers, Republican president George W. Bush continued this practice, as did Democratic president Barack Obama. Most political observers note that the waiver of Title III across party lines represents an attempt by the executive branch to maintain a portion of its power over the Cuban embargo. In any event, the informal understanding that Title III would always be waived allowed the European Union to drop its grievance before the World Trade Organization.

The Cuban exile community in the United States also played a major role in shaping the U.S. relationship with Cuba. The Cuban Revolution, as well as subsequent Cuban and U.S. policies, led hundreds of thousands of Cubans to seek refuge in the United States. In 1981, a group of Cuban exiles, in cooperation with the Reagan administration officials, founded the Cuban American National Foundation (CANF). Over time, the CANF became a significant voice in favor of maintaining and strengthening the Cuban embargo. At its apex, the CANF was powerful enough to help maintain support for the Cuban embargo across traditional partisan divisions (Haney and Vanderbush 1999, 341). The importance of South Florida as an electoral battleground within the larger battleground state of Florida, coupled with the political significance of the Cuban exile community, played a key role in embargo politics for several decades.

Administration of the Cuban embargo changed in a significant way in 1992 with passage of the Cuban Democracy Act and in 1996 with the passage of the Cuban Liberty and Democratic Solidarity Act (also known as the Helms-Burton Act). Not only did these laws strengthen the Cuban embargo in a variety of ways, the acts served to codify the embargo into statutory law. In practice, this meant that ending the Cuban embargo would now require the agreement of Congress and the president. Before the Cuban Democracy Act and Helms-Burton, individual presidents were free to alter the embargo by executive order. Codification of the Cuban embargo had significant implications for any politician or interest group that wished to weaken or abandon the Cuban embargo as part of the process of diplomatic and economic normalization.

Over time, especially after the end of the Cold War, support for normalization of U.S. relations with Cuba began to increase. Even among Cuban Americans in Florida, the group that has traditionally favored the embargo with the most political fervor, support for the embargo began to wane (FIU Cuban Research Institute 2014, 9). In part due to changing public perceptions of the Cuban embargo and in part due to recognition that the embargo has not achieved the desired result of democratization of the island, President Obama announced several changes to the relationship in a speech on December 17, 2014. The content of these changes, which were supported by many Democratic lawmakers, serves as the new starting point for a discussion of partisan differences on the direction of U.S. foreign policy toward Cuba. It is important to recognize, however, that the announced change in policy does not alter the status of the Cuban embargo. As mentioned above, most elements of the embargo are controlled by Congress under the provisions of the Helms-Burton Act.

Democrats on U.S. Relations with Cuba

The historic shift in the Democratic Party's position on U.S. relations with Cuba is summarized in the 2014 White House brief announcing the new course toward Cuba being charted by the Obama administration (White House 2014). As the brief indicated, the administration intended to implement changes to provide for:

- Reestablishment of diplomatic relations with Cuba;
- Increasing the amount of remittances that may be sent from the United States to Cuba;
- Expansion of travel between the United States and Cuba;
- Easing import and export restrictions;
- Increasing telecommunications access for Cubans;
- Promoting dialogue related to human rights and fundamental freedoms; and
- Removing Cuba from the list of state sponsors of terrorism.

With regard to economic issues, the Obama administration is limited by congressional control over most of the details of the economic embargo, including prohibitions on the import of Cuban goods. Overall, Democrats have supported President Obama's position that normalization of the U.S. diplomatic relationship with Cuba, as well as a comprehensive reevaluation of the Cuban embargo, is more likely to achieve the goal of democratization than the previous approach of diplomatic and economic isolation that had been in place for more than a half century.

President Obama Announces a Landmark Change in American Relations with Cuba

In December 2014 the Obama administration ushered in a new and friendlier era in U.S.–Cuba relations. Following are excerpts from President Obama's speech announcing his administration's new stance toward the island nation:

In the most significant changes in our policy in more than fifty years, we will end an outdated approach that, for decades, has failed to advance our interests, and instead we will begin to normalize relations between our two countries. Through these changes, we intend to create more opportunities for the American and Cuban people, and begin a new chapter among the nations of the Americas.

First, I've instructed Secretary Kerry to immediately begin discussions with Cuba to reestablish diplomatic relations that have been severed since January of 1961. Going forward, the United States will reestablish an embassy in Havana, and high-ranking officials will visit Cuba.

Second, I've instructed Secretary Kerry to review Cuba's designation as a State Sponsor of Terrorism . . . At a time when we are focused on threats from al Qaeda to ISIL, a nation that meets our conditions and renounces the use of terrorism should not face this sanction.

Third, we are taking steps to increase travel, commerce, and the flow of information to and from Cuba. This is fundamentally about freedom and openness, and also expresses my belief in the power of people-to-people engagement . . . Today, America chooses to cut loose the shackles of the past so as to reach for a better future—for the Cuban people, for the American people, for our entire hemisphere, and for the world.

Source:

Obama, Barack. "Statement by the President on Cuba Policy Changes." December 17, 2014. https://www.whitehouse.gov/the-press-office/2014/12/17/statement-president-cuba -policy-changes.

The move toward normalization represents a departure for Democrats, who had historically supported both the economic and diplomatic portions of the embargo. The 2012 Democratic Party platform does not mention diplomatic normalization, though it does establish positions in favor of some relaxation of rules related to travel and remittances. As an additional example, before becoming secretary of state, Hillary Clinton expressed support for the embargo while running for the Senate in 2000 as a means to pressure the Castro regime toward democratic reforms. As Obama's secretary of state and during the 2016 presidential campaign, however, Clinton expressed support for diplomatic normalization and a comprehensive reexamination of the economic embargo (Edwards 2014).

The movement toward normalization for Democrats corresponds with shifts in public opinion on the Cuban embargo, both nationwide and in South Florida. A 2014 poll indicated that 71 percent of Cubans in South Florida believed that the embargo has either not worked at all, or has not worked very well (FIU Cuban Research Institute 2014, 8). Of those surveyed, 52 percent believed that the embargo should be discontinued (FIU Cuban Research Institute 2014, 9). This marks a significant downturn in Cuban American support for the embargo since the 1991 end of the Cold War when support was over 80 percent. Within the population at large, support for the resumption of diplomatic relations as well as support for ending the embargo has also grown over time (Gallup 2016). Given the salience of the issue to Cuban Americans, public opinion among this portion of the population has always had more resonance with politicians than the opinion of the public at large, which typically has higher issue priorities.

For its part, even CANF has appeared to soften its stance on Cuba in a way that provides some political cover for Democrats attempting to appeal to the Cuban vote in Florida. The CANF requested a seat at the table as part of the process of reevaluating the U.S.–Cuba relationship. The organization also emphasized that democracy must remain the goal of U.S. foreign policy toward Cuba. However, the official CANF response did not denounce any specific portion of the "new course" nor did it call on Congress to take action to prevent the Obama administration from implementing the change in policy (*South Florida Caribbean News* 2014).

The Democratic Party has not enjoyed unanimity on the issue of normalizing ties between the United States and Cuba, however. For example, Democratic National Committee chairperson Debbie Wasserman Shultz suggested in July 2015 that Cuba must earn the benefits of normalization by improving its human rights record in a more significant way (Gass 2015). Shultz's position is closer in many ways to the traditional Democratic Party stance on the U.S. relationship with Cuba. Part of Shultz's difference of opinion with the Obama administration may stem from the fact that she is part of the Florida congressional delegation, which has traditionally been more conservative on issues related to Cuba.

By far, the harshest critique of the president's policy departure from within the Democratic Party came from New Jersey senator Robert Menendez, whose parents were Cuban immigrants. Menendez argued that "this is the only government in the Western Hemisphere which the Obama administration has chosen to establish relations with that is not elected by its citizens. The message is democracy and human rights take a back seat to a legacy initiative" (Menendez 2015). Menendez's positions on the Cuban embargo have been more hawkish on issues related to Cuba than other Democrats, especially in recent years.

Other Democrats, as a whole, have been more supportive of the move toward liberalization. Democratic senator Bernie Sanders of Vermont expressed strong support for the move, arguing that the policy of isolation had been counterproductive and ineffective and that the embargo cost the United States a great deal of potential revenue from trade (Sanders 2014). Other Democrats have also expressed support for lifting the embargo and normalizing relations with Cuba. The fact that President Obama became the first candidate to carry Cuban Americans in Florida since the Cuban Revolution may well have altered the political calculations of Democrats running for office, especially in Florida.

As younger Cuban Americans continue to moderate their positions on issues relating to Cuba the political space for Democrats to moderate their positions on Cuba continues to grow. In a state critical to the path to the presidency for both parties, one would expect foreign policy outcomes to more closely mirror public opinion than they do in cases where the electoral calculus is less clear. In this context, it is likely that the 2016 Democratic Party platform will align closely with the Obama administration's policy shift on Cuba.

Republicans on U.S. Relations with Cuba

The Republican Party position on Cuba lies much closer to the party platform unveiled as part of the 2012 presidential campaign. The Republican Party platform charged that Cuba's government was autocratic and corrupt and a sponsor of terrorism. It also rejected the transition of power in Cuba from Fidel Castro to his brother Raul as immaterial and declared free and fair elections in Cuba were a prerequisite to any discussion of removing the economic embargo (Republican National Committee 2012).

Traditionally, Republican Party candidates for office have fared better among Cuban Americans (traditionally a fairly conservative political constituency) than their Democratic Party counterparts. This is especially the case among older Cuban Americans. As noted above, however, the gap has narrowed in recent years. What remains unclear is what impact the more aggressive move toward normalization undertaken by Democrats will have.

Several key members of the Republican Party stated their opposition to Obama's normalization of relations with Cuba, his efforts to ease the embargo, and his decision to remove Cuba from the list of state sponsors of terror. Florida Representative Mario Diaz-Balart commemorated the one-year anniversary of President Obama's decision to begin normalization of relations with Cuba by stating:

> And what have the U.S., and the Cuban people, gained from President Obama's policy? Just take a look at the facts. Political arrests totaled 1,447 in November, the highest monthly tally this year, and there have been 7,686 political arrests this year to date. More than half of the Obama–Castro so-called "list of 53" political prisoners have been re-arrested in the past year. Desperate Cuban refugees are fleeing the regime in ever greater numbers. Meanwhile, the Castro regime is sending members of its military to prop up fellow dictator Assad in Syria and smuggling military weapons to rogue international actors. (Diaz-Balart 2015)

Florida senator Marco Rubio, a Cuban American senator representing Florida who made a failed bid for the Republican Party nomination for president in 2016, vowed to roll back President Obama's Cuba policy changes in the event that he was elected president. These opinions have been echoed by each Cuban American member of Congress, as well as by most of the 2016 Republican presidential hopefuls.

Continued Republican Party support for the embargo, and opposition to normalization has various policy consequences. First, it prevents full normalization of relations between the United States and Cuba. Although the president has the constitutional authority to establish diplomatic relations, the Senate must provide its advice and consent for any ambassador-level appointment. Republican control of the Senate makes this prospect very unlikely. As a result, President Obama is unlikely to nominate an ambassador to Cuba. The lack of an ambassador does not preclude a high-level diplomatic relationship. The president is free to appoint someone at the level of *chargé d'affaires*. In diplomacy, this is the head of a diplomatic mission to another country or to an international organization. Senator Lindsay Graham of South Carolina has promised to block funding for a U.S. embassy in Havana and has enjoyed support on this score from most Republican Party politicians. As long as the Republicans control Congress, the normalization of diplomatic relations between the U.S. and Cuba is unlikely to be accompanied by economic normalization. Republicans in key positions within the House and Senate support the continuation of the embargo in its current form.

As is the case within the Democratic Party, however, there is some division on issues related to Cuba within the Republican Party. Much of this internal tension is due to the emergence of an antiembargo/pronormalization majority among Republican voters (Pew Research Center 2015). Republican lawmakers from heavily agricultural states such as Kansas have also been more receptive to trade and normalization. The essential argument from these Republicans is that, with the exception of sugar, the United States would likely enjoy positive terms of trade with Cuba on agricultural goods (LaFranchi 2015). Arizona senator Jeff Flake, the only Republican to visit Cuba as part of the U.S. delegation led by Obama administration secretary of state John Kerry, has argued that increasing trade and travel ties with Cuba is more likely to promote than prevent freedom. Flake has consistently supported the expansion of travel and humanitarian efforts in Cuba. Utah representative Jason Chaffetz has argued that the travel ban is "ridiculous" and that dropping the ban would further the cause of freedom in Cuba (French 2014).

A second area of disagreement within the Republican Party relates to the "wet-foot, dry-foot" policy created by the Cuban Adjustment Act of 1966 as amended. The act created a preference system for Cuban refugees fleeing Cuba for the United States. It also allowed any Cuban who successfully reaches U.S. soil to be considered for citizenship after a period of one year. Some Republicans have argued that the Cuban Adjustment Act creates special privileges for Cuban refugees that are no longer warranted (Ross 2015). Most Republicans, as part of their contention that the United States should not normalize relations with Cuba, have argued for keeping the existing policy. If normalization continues to move forward, especially if travel restrictions between the two countries weaken significantly, calls for revisiting the policy within the Republican Party are likely to increase.

Further Reading

"Cuban American National Foundation (CANF) Responds to Today's Announcement Regarding U.S.–Cuba Policy." *South Florida Caribbean News*. December 17, 2014. https://sflcn.com/cuban-american-national-foundation-canf-responds-to-todays-announcement-regarding-u-s-cuba-policy/.

Democratic National Committee. "Our Platform." Democratic Party. n.d. https://www.democrats.org/party-platform.

Diaz-Balart, Mario. "One Year Later: The Results of Obama's Concessions to the Castros." Congressman Mario Diaz-Balart. Last modified December 17, 2015. https://mariodiazbalart.house.gov/media-center/press-releases/one-year-later-the-results-of-obama-s-concessions-to-the-castros.

Edwards, Haley S. "Why Democrats Changed Their Minds on Cuba." TIME.com. Last modified December 17, 2014. http://time.com/3637887/cuba-normalize-democrats/.

Florida International University (FIU) Cuban Research Institute. Accessed January 7, 2016. https://cri.fiu.edu/research/cuba-poll/2014-fiu-cuba-poll.pdf.

French, Lauren. "Obama's Republican Ally on Cuba." *Politico*. Last modified December 20, 2014. http://www.politico.com/story/2014/12/jeff-flake-obama-cuba-113717.

Gallup.com. "Cuba | Gallup Historical Trends." Accessed January 7, 2016. http://www.gallup.com/poll/1630/cuba.aspx.

Gass, Nick. "Debbie Wasserman Schultz Breaks with Obama on Cuba." *Politico*. Last modified July 19, 2015. http://www.politico.com/story/2015/07/debbie-wasserman-schultz-cuba-stance-119903.

Haney, Patrick J., and Walt Vanderbush. 1999. "The Role of Ethnic Interest Groups in U.S. Foreign Policy: The Case of the Cuban American National Foundation." *International Studies Quarterly* 43 (2). [International Studies Association, Wiley]: 341–361. http://www.jstor.org/stable/2600759.

Hohmann, James, and Kyle Cheney. "The Democrats' Risky Cuba Bet." Politico. Accessed December 30, 2015. http://www.politico.com/story/2014/12/cuba-democrats-florida-politics-113659.

Kellner, Douglas. *Ernesto "Che" Guevara*. New York: Chelsea House Publishers, 1989.

LaFranchi, Howard. "US–Cuba Relations: Why Republicans Are Divided on New Rules (+video)—CSMonitor.com." *Christian Science Monitor*. Last modified January 15, 2015. http://www.csmonitor.com/USA/Foreign-Policy/2015/0115/US-Cuba-relations-why-Republicans-are-divided-on-new-rules-video.

Leatherby, Lauren. "Republicans Stand Against Cuba Change Despite Public Opinion Shift: It's All Politics: NPR." NPR.org. Accessed December 30, 2015. http://www.npr.org/sections/itsallpolitics/2015/07/27/424736858/republicans-stand-against-cuba-change-despite-public-opinion-shift.

Library of Congress. "Bill Text H.R. 927—104th Congress (1995–1996)—THOMAS (Library of Congress)." Congress.gov | Library of Congress. Accessed January 7, 2016. http://thomas.loc.gov/cgi-bin/query/z?c104:H.R.927.ENR.

Menendez, Robert. "Sen. Menendez on U.S.–Cuba Embassy Announcement." Bob Menendez for New Jersey. Last modified July 1, 2015. www.menendez.senate.gov/news-and-events/press/sen-menendez-on-uscuba-embassy-announcement.

Office of the Historian. "The United States, Cuba, and the Platt Amendment, 1901—1899–1913—Milestones." Accessed January 6, 2016. https://history.state.gov/milestones/1899-1913/platt.

Pew Research Center. "Growing Public Support for U.S. Ties with Cuba—And an End to the Trade Embargo." Pew Research Center for the People and the Press. Last modified July 21, 2015. http://www.people-press.org/2015/07/21/growing-public-support-for-u-s-ties-with-cuba-and-an-end-to-the-trade-embargo/.

Republican National Committee. "Republican Party Platform 2012." Accessed January 7, 2016. https://prod-static-ngop-pbl.s3.amazonaws.com/docs/2012GOPPlatform.pdf.

Ross, Janell. "Why the 'Wet-Foot, Dry-Foot' Debate Could Soon Be Coming to a Head—*Washington Post.*" *Washington Post.* Last modified October 10, 2015. https://www.washingtonpost.com/news/the-fix/wp/2015/10/16/why-the-wet-foot-dry-foot-debate-could-soon-be-coming-to-a-head/.

Sanders, Bernie. "Americans Favor Ties with Cuba—Senator Bernie Sanders of Vermont." Sen. Bernie Sanders. Accessed February 11, 2014. http://www.sanders.senate.gov/newsroom/recent-business/americans-favor-ties-with-cuba.

Staten, Clifford L. *The History of Cuba.* Westport, CT: Greenwood Press, 2003.

Walters, Robert S. "Soviet Economic Aid to Cuba: 1959–1964." *International Affairs* 42, no. 1 (1966): 74–86. http://doi.org/10.2307/2612437.

White House. "Charting a New Course on Cuba." Accessed December 30, 2015. https://www.whitehouse.gov/issues/foreign-policy/cuba.

Cyberterrorism and Security

At a Glance

Since the advent of the Internet, terrorist groups, companies bent on espionage, foreign governments, and hacker activists of every ideological stripe have used the technology to ferret out the secrets of their foes or damage their telecommunications operations. Democrats and Republicans agree that cybersecurity is a significant issue. However, the nature of the policy initiatives necessary to combat such unlawful and/or threatening activities have often been the subject of significant partisan debate. The focus of this entry is on cyberterrorism undertaken by nongovernment actors or foreign governments against U.S. government interests. Actions taken by "hacktivists" and companies engaging in corporate espionage are beyond the scope of this volume.

According to many Republicans . . .

- The United States must develop increased offensive cyberwarfare capabilities
- Increased cooperation between the private and public sector is needed to improve cybersecurity;
- Current government regulations make it more difficult for private entities and the government to innovate in the realm of cybersecurity; and
- The United States should directly retaliate against countries like China and North Korea when cyberattacks are traced back to those countries.

According to many Democrats . . .

- Cybersecurity does not require a specific public deterrence protocol; though, responding to cyberattacks with countercyberattacks is always an option;
- Cybersecurity policy should focus on defensive capabilities to harden U.S. systems against attack;
- Any new policy or law related to cybersecurity should balance the need for security with legitimate concerns about protecting individual privacy; and

- Enhanced cybersecurity will require both public–private partnerships as well as increased international cooperation in order to be successful.

Overview

From the initial conceptualization of computer networking over a phone line to the development of the World Wide Web in 1989, the idea of computers and other electronic devices communicating and sharing information over vast distances has captivated much of the world. Although it is difficult to pin down, the first Internet-based cyberattack, though it probably was not malicious in intent, was carried out by Robert Tapan Morris, who developed a computer "worm" in an attempt to determine the size of the Internet in 1988. The worm morphed into a virus, began replicating itself, and damaged 6,000 computers, doing millions of dollars in damage. Shortly later, the General Accounting Office (GAO) suggested that the White House science adviser should develop strategies to counter future viruses. In 1992, Congress amended the Computer Fraud and Abuse Act to cover the transmission of computer viruses.

Leading up to the year 2000, the government commissioned a variety of reports and working groups to consider America's readiness to respond to potential Y2K issues—a fear that computer system programming would have difficulty reading years accurately when the 1900s ended and the year 2000 arrived. Although the Y2K computing threat turned out to have been overblown, it led indirectly to the first commitments to the development of a national cybersecurity strategy. Though it was not known by the general public until well after the fact, the year 2000 was also the year that officials discovered the Moonlight Maze attack on U.S. government computer systems, including NASA and the Pentagon (Public Broadcasting Service 2003). The attack exposed several classified documents and was ultimately traced to a computer system in Russia. However, the Russian government denies all responsibility for the attack.

In 2002, President George W. Bush signed the Cybersecurity Research and Development Act into law. The bill passed with large bipartisan majorities in both the House and the Senate. In the House of Representatives, all "nay" votes came from Republicans (H.R. 3394 2002) who expressed concern that the act would lead either to excessive business regulation or government intrusion on personal privacy. That same year, the Department of Homeland Security (DHS) was established, and it quickly became a hub for cybersecurity operations.

Cyberattacks on government networks have increased virtually every year since then, however. Many of these attacks, which have sought to either slow or disable U.S. computer networks or access classified or sensitive information, have been traced to China and North Korea. Many times, however, the origin of the attack is never known. Such an unknown foreign attack occurred in 2006 and obtained designs for NASA shuttle launch vehicles (NATO Review 2013). A similar attack occurred on the Pentagon in 2007. Attacks on U.S. companies, including Google, occurred as well during this time. The general aim of business attacks is to gain access to intellectual property.

In response to these and other attacks, the United States launched the U.S. Cyber Command (USCYBERCOM) in 2010. USCYBERCOM is an operational part of the U.S. Army and is designed to protect Department of Defense systems. Most government agencies and departments are protected by the National Security Deployment Division, located in the Department of Homeland Security. It maintains the National Cybersecurity Protection System.

Though incidents are often difficult to verify, the United States has also engaged at times in offensive cyberwarfare operations against alleged national security threats. The most famous of these cases was the deployment of the Stuxnet virus, developed by U.S. and Israeli experts to target Iran's nuclear facilities. The program was developed during the George W. Bush administration, sometime around 2006, to attack Iranian centrifuges, and ordered fully operational by President Barack Obama in early to mid-2009 (Nakashima and Warrick 2012). The attack, which occurred over time and was designed to evade detection, was highly successful, destroying over 1,000 Iranian centrifuges, which are used to enrich uranium. China has also accused the United States of cyberattacks against its interests. Unlike conventional warfare, cyberwarfare is difficult to track because it is normally carried out in secret. Even in cases where the identity of the attackers is known, such as the case of the Chinese attack on the Office of Personnel Management in 2015, the state carrying out the attack denies that it occurred and the United States does not publicly reveal its response.

Cyberwarfare, and the efforts to combat it, has also led to concerns among many civil liberties advocates that the United States is too willing to erode constitutional rights in the service of cybersecurity. Bulk e-mail data collection, as well as specific intercepts, came to light as a result of the Edward Snowden revelations. Snowden, who worked for the CIA and as a subcontractor for the National Security Agency, released documents obtained illegally during his employment that demonstrated U.S. involvement in extensive phone and Internet surveillance of U.S. citizens. Many of these efforts were designed to keep the United States secure from more conventional forms of terrorism. Privacy advocates claim, however, that the government surveillance program, known as PRISM, is not subject to enough legal or public oversight to protect individuals from unreasonable government intrusion (Savage 2015). Similar concerns have been expressed over the National Cybersecurity Protection Advancement Act of 2015, which passed Congress as an amendment to the consolidated appropriations bill.

Republicans on Cybersecurity Policy

The 2012 Republican Party platform mentioned issues related to cybersecurity and cyberterrorism 20 times and spent approximately twice as much copy space on cybersecurity issues as the Democratic Party platform. The Republican platform began by tying cybersecurity issues to national defense issues, and criticizing the Obama administration for being willing to cut the military budget as part of the sequestration process (Republican National Committee 2012). The platform also referred to the possibility of a "cyber Pearl Harbor" and the need for more public–private cooperation on cybersecurity issues. The platform also charged that government information concerning cyberthreats was not adequately shared with the business community in a timely manner, exposing businesses to domain name system (DNS) attacks and cyberespionage. The platform also asserts that the Obama administration was preoccupied with cyberdefense in a way that precluded the United States from taking cyberwarfare to its enemies, either preemptively or in response to cyberattacks from overseas. The 2016 version of the platform adds that the electrical grid in the United States remains vulnerable to cyberattacks. And adds a specific call for retaliation against states, such as Russia and China, that engage in cyberattacks against the United States.

Within the realm of public opinion, Republicans and Democrats appear to be fairly unified on the threat of cyberterrorism. A 2016 survey revealed that 77 percent of self-identified Republicans believe that cyberterrorism is a critical threat to the United States (McCarthy 2016). In a 2015 survey, Republicans ranked cyberterrorism as the fifth-most serious threat to U.S. security, behind various other types of terrorist acts and the Iranian nuclear program (Chicago Council on Global Affairs 2015). Although it can be unwise to compare responses from across polls, it is worth noting that a similar poll commissioned by the *Washington Post* in 2012 found a somewhat lower percentage of Republican and Democrats were concerned about cyberattacks on the U.S. government (*Washington Post* 2012). Even in this survey, however, a majority of individuals from both parties expressed at least some level of concern with the issue. Given the fact that cyberattacks have grown in number over time, coupled with increased media reporting about the attacks on both public and private entities, it would not be surprising to find that concerns about cybersecurity have also grown over time.

Republicans in Congress appear to have a nuanced opinion on issues related to cybersecurity. On one hand, Republicans in Congress and elsewhere have been critical of Democrats, especially President Obama, for not taking a strong enough stance on cyberterrorism and cybersecurity. On the other hand, Republicans want to make sure that cybersecurity measures do not alienate their probusiness constituency. The fact that much of our cybernetwork in the United States was created or enhanced by the private sector means that attempts to improve security against foreign threats will sometimes include regulation of domestic firms. One example of the Republican position was manifest in the debate on the Cybersecurity Act of 2012, introduced by Senator Joe Lieberman, a Democrat who became an independent after losing the Democratic Senate primary in 2006 and cosponsored by Republican senator Susan Collins. The bill would have required the DHS to conduct a comprehensive review of existing cybersecurity procedures. It would

The National Chamber of Commerce "Key Vote" Letter on the Cybersecurity Act of 2012

Just like in domestic politics, interest groups sometimes seek to influence U.S. foreign policy. One common technique is to "score" important congressional votes on legislation of interest to its members. In 2012, the National Chamber of Commerce wrote a "key vote" letter to members of Congress concerning a cybersecurity bill that the chamber opposed:

> The flawed process by which S. 3414 was developed has led to a flawed bill. The Chamber appreciates the willingness of senators to engage with the business community on this important issue, and we hope that these efforts will continue. Still, as the Chamber asserted at a meeting last Friday hosted by Sens. Lieberman, Feinstein and Coons, there are no "quick-fix" amendments that can achieve what should be a central goal of S. 3414: legislation that enhances U.S. cybersecurity by helping the business community thwart cyber threats.
>
> The Chamber believes S. 3414 could actually impede U.S. cybersecurity by shifting businesses' resources away from implementing robust and effective security measures and toward meeting government mandates.
>
> Cybersecurity relies on the business community and the federal government working collaboratively. The regulatory approach provided in S. 3414 would likely create an adversarial relationship, which should be unacceptable to lawmakers. The Chamber urges Congress to not complicate or duplicate existing industry-driven security standards with government mandates and bureaucracies, even if they are couched in language that would mischaracterize these standards as "voluntary . . .
>
> The Chamber strongly opposes S. 3414, the Cybersecurity Act of 2012 and may consider votes on, or in relation to S. 3414 in our annual *How They Voted* scorecard.

In this case, the chamber achieved its desired outcome. The Cybersecurity Act of 2012 died via a Republican-led filibuster in the Senate. It is impossible to know, of course, what role, if any, the key vote letter played in the decision. Three years later, the Cybersecurity Act of 2015 was signed into law without the standards, voluntary or otherwise, to which the chamber objected.

Source:
"Key Vote Letter on S. 3414, the 'Cybersecurity Act of 2012.'" U.S. Chamber of Commerce. Last modified July 30, 2012. https://www.uschamber.com/letter/key-vote-letter-s-3414-cyber security-act-2012%E2%80%9D.

have also required the Office of Personnel Management to establish a cybersecurity awareness curriculum for all federal employees. Information sharing databases would also have been established to facilitate cooperation between public and private entities. Finally, the bill would have created optional standards for information security that would apply to both government and businesses in cases where critical systems, whether they are public or private, are involved (Congress.gov 2012).

It was the optional standards provision that led Republican senators to fili-buster the bill. Republican senator John McCain of Arizona argued that even the optional standards would be too burdensome on private businesses and would divert attention; effectively diverting attention from innovations that might better enhance cybersecurity. The U.S. Chamber of Commerce, a probusiness lobbying and advocacy group with over three million business organizations as members argued that the bill would create and "adversarial relationship" between businesses that might oversee critical infrastructure and government agencies (U.S. Chamber of Commerce 2012). The chamber felt strongly enough about the bill to issue what they call a key vote letter. Interest groups that provide campaign funds or critical endorsements often inform elected officials that they are scoring, rating, or keying a piece of legislation. That means that the senator's vote on the bill will, in part, determine the rating of that senator by the interest group, which in turn helps determine endorsements and future campaign contributions.

To overcome the Republican-led filibuster, the Democrats needed 60 votes to invoke cloture or end debate on the bill. Supporters were only able to muster 52 votes, and the bill died in the Senate. To end the filibuster, 45 Democrats joined 5 Republicans and 2 independents voting. To maintain the filibuster, 6 Democrats joined 40 Republicans (Senate Vote 187 2012).

In late 2015, however, the Republican-controlled Congress passed and President Obama signed into law the Cybersecurity Act of 2015 by amendment as part of the appropriations process. The act gives companies the right to monitor information systems, broadly construed in order to defend their networks from attack and for general cybersecurity purposes. It also provides for information sharing between businesses and the government in a way previously opposed by the Obama admin-istration (see below) and still opposed by privacy advocates (Kerr 2015). The act also provides protection from civil liability for companies that monitor activity in a way that complies with the act. The U.S. Chamber of Commerce supported the act, as did an overwhelming number of Republicans and most Democrats. In the House, where the full version of the act was voted on, rather than as an amendment, the bill passed 355–63. Only 19 Republicans opposed the legislation, mostly based on concerns about privacy and civil liberties. In the Senate, only five Republicans voted against the act when it was originally presented in the nonamendment form.

Although cyberterrorism and cybersecurity were not a marquee issue in the 2016 Republican primary process, eventual nominee Donald Trump claimed in an interview that "we're so obsolete in cyber" (*New York Times* 2016). Trump also expressed concern that the United States is falling behind rivals such as Russia and China in the area of cyberwarfare.

Democrats on Cybersecurity Policy

The 2012 Democratic Party platform mentioned cybersecurity issues 13 times and had a small section of the platform dedicated to the issue. Like Republicans, the

The Cybersecurity Act of 2015

On December 18, 2015, President Obama signed a compromise appropriations bill to fund the government through most of 2016. One component of the budget legislation was the Cybersecurity Act of 2015, which proponents believed would have a better chance of passing as part of the budget deal between the Republican-controlled Congress and the president. The act contains the following key provisions:

- Liability protections for private entities that share threat information with the federal government through the Department of Homeland Security (DHS);
- Provisions that allow the government to only use shared information for security purposes;
- A requirement that the DHS develop measures to protect information that is being shared;
- The requirement that government agencies address staffing shortages in skilled positions related to cybersecurity;
- A requirement that the State Department must negotiate with foreign governments to develop international cyberspace behavior agreements that protect government data and intellectual property;
- Development of more comprehensive inoperability plans for states in the event that emergency communications systems are targeted by cyberattacks; and
- Development of contingency plans for public health in the event of a cyberattack on critical infrastructure.

Passage of the Cybersecurity Act of 2015 angered many privacy advocates, who accused both Republicans and the Obama administration of hiding the bill in a larger piece of "must-pass" legislation.

Source:
"Summary: S.754—114th Congress (2015–2016)." Congress.gov. Last modified October 27, 2015. https://www.congress.gov/bill/114th-congress/senate-bill/754.

Democratic Party advances the claim the cyberattacks, both domestic and foreign, are a critical threat to national security. The platform also hails the establishment of USCYBERCOM (Democratic National Committee 2012). Democrats also defended the Cybersecurity Act of 2012, which died in the Senate due to a GOP filibuster, as a piece of compromise legislation that would have strengthened U.S. information security while addressing key privacy and civil liberties concerns. Finally, the platform addressed the willingness of the president to use executive orders to enhance cybersecurity. During his second term, President Obama, working first with a divided Congress, then with a unified Republican Congress, has shown a greater propensity to use executive orders in an attempt to shape foreign policy on issues such as immigration and climate change. Cybersecurity is no exception, as noted below. The 2016 version of the platform largely echoes the 2012 platform, adding language applauding President Obama for taking additional steps (outlined below) to enhance cybersecurity.

As already noted, Democrats and Republicans within the general public largely see eye to eye on the general issue of cybersecurity. Any differences are matters of degree. For example, one 2015 poll found that Democrats rate cyberattacks on U.S. computer networks as the number one threat to national interests over the next 10 years while Republicans claim that it is the fifth greatest threat to security (Chicago Council on Global Affairs 2015). In the same survey, Democrats were less likely than Republicans to support offensive cyberwarfare against countries like Iran in the face of its nuclear threat. The same 2016 survey that found 77 percent of Republicans concerned about cyberterrorism as a critical threat found that 72 percent of Democrats share that view. One additional issue where Republicans and Democrats, at least in the general public, share an opinion is on the issue of security versus privacy. Majorities of both Democrats and Republicans believe that the government and the private sector are collecting too much information about them (Doherty 2013).

At the executive level, President Obama supported both the cybersecurity legislation that failed to overcome a Republican filibuster in the Senate in 2012 and the Cybersecurity Act of 2015, which ultimately passed Congress with bipartisan support. The main difference between the two pieces of legislation is that the former contained voluntary standards for businesses in terms of cybersecurity while the 2015 legislation did not. Both pieces of legislation provided for public–private information sharing, something that the president was only willing to agree to if the legislation also addressed privacy concerns related to private businesses sharing sensitive personal information about customers with government agencies. Obama argued that the legislation addressed privacy concerns by redacting unnecessary personal information and requiring companies to protect personal information that must be shared if they wish to receive liability protection (White House 2015).

The president also issued several executive orders related to cybersecurity in 2013–2015. Executive order 13636, for example, directs the National Institute for Standards and Technology to work on developing model cybersecurity practices in cooperation with the private sector (White House 2013). The development of model standards and practices was the main element that made the 2012 cybersecurity bill unacceptable to a number of Senate Republicans. In 2015, the president signed an executive order imposing sanctions on individuals determined by the secretary of the Treasury to have been involved in cyberattacks on critical infrastructure or for the purpose of industrial espionage. In 2016, President Obama announced the Cybersecurity National Action Plan (CNAP). The president has proposed that $3.1 billion be set aside for government information technology modernization as part of the CNAP (White House 2016). The plan also includes a public outreach component, designed to convince Americans to keep their home and work computers more secure.

Democrats in Congress have the opposite tightrope to walk as their Republican colleagues. On one hand, Democrats tend to favor the standard-setting, even if it is mandatory, that Republicans and the U.S. Chamber of Commerce opposed. On the other hand, Democrats are much less likely than Republicans to support information-sharing and business liability protections, two provisions that Republicans support. In spite of this, a majority of congressional Democrats favored both the 2012 and 2015 cybersecurity legislation, though Democrats preferred the 2012 version because of the voluntary cybersecurity standards provision explained above. Democrats also believed that the 2012 legislation more thoroughly addressed privacy concerns by limiting the circumstances under which data could be shared between private and public entities. In the end, however, a majority of Democrats also supported the Cybersecurity Act of 2015. Over twice as many Democrats as Republicans opposed the legislation, mainly due to privacy concerns and the promise of immunity, under certain circumstances, to private companies monitoring their networks and sharing information with the federal government. Privacy advocates argued that the bill would significantly increase surveillance of individuals in their online activities.

Both of the major Democratic Party candidates for president in 2016 had discernibly distinct positions on cybersecurity. Senator Bernie Sanders voted against the Cybersecurity Information Sharing Act (CISA) and the 2015 Cybersecurity Act because of concerns that the act did not do enough to protect privacy. However, Sanders supported the 2012 Cybersecurity Act on the grounds that it did more to protect individual privacy while promoting security. Sanders did not maintain a position on cybersecurity on his campaign Web site, under the category labeled "war and peace."

Former secretary of state Hillary Clinton, who eventually secured the party's 2016 presidential nomination, stated during a February 2016 town hall that cybersecurity would be a significant challenge for the next president. Clinton argued that countries like Russia and China, as well as "rogue hackers" and cyberterrorists, would be significant threats in coming years.

Further Reading

Chicago Council on Global Affairs. "America Divided: Political Partisanship and US Foreign Policy." Last modified 2015. http://www.thechicagocouncil.org/sites/default/files/CCGA_PublicSurvey2015.pdf.

Congress.gov. "Text—S.2105—112th Congress (2011–2012): Cybersecurity Act of 2012." Last modified February 14, 2012. https://www.congress.gov/bill/112th-congress/senate-bill/2105/text.

Democratic National Committee. "2012 Democratic Platform." Last modified 2012. https://www.democrats.org/party-platform.

Doherty, Carroll. "Balancing Act: National Security and Civil Liberties in Post-9/11 Era." Pew Research Center. Last modified June 7, 2013. http://www.pewresearch.org/fact-tank/2013/06/07/balancing-act-national-security-and-civil-liberties-in-post-911-era/.

GovTrack.us. "H.R. 1731: National Cybersecurity Protection Advancement Act of 2015." Last modified April 23, 2015. https://www.govtrack.us/congress/votes/114-2015/h173.

"H.R. 3394: Cyber Security Research and Development Act." Last modified February 7, 2002. https://www.govtrack.us/congress/votes/107-2002/h13.

Kasich, John. "National Security Plan." Kasich for America. Last modified March 21, 2016. https://www.johnkasich.com/nationalsecurity/.

Kerr, Orin. "How Does the Cybersecurity Act of 2015 Change the Internet Surveillance Laws?" *Washington Post*. Last modified December 24, 2015. https://www.washington post.com/news/volokh-conspiracy/wp/2015/12/24/how-does-the-cybersecurity -act-of-2015-change-the-internet-surveillance-laws/.

McCarthy, Justin. "Americans Cite Cyberterrorism Among Top Three Threats to U.S." Gallup. Last modified February 10, 2016. http://www.gallup.com/poll/189161/americans -cite-cyberterrorism-among-top-three-threats.aspx.

Nakashima, Ellen, and Joby Warrick. "Stuxnet Was Work of U.S. and Israeli Experts, Officials Say." *Washington Post*. Last modified June 2, 2012. https://www.washingtonpost .com/world/national-security/stuxnet-was-work-of-us-and-israeli-experts-officials -say/2012/06/01/gJQAlnEy6U_story.html.

NATO Review. "The History of Cyber Attacks—A Timeline." Last modified 2013. http:// www.nato.int/docu/review/2013/cyber/timeline/EN/index.htm.

New York Times. "Senate Vote 187—S.3414: On the Cloture Motion S. 3414." Last modified August 2, 2012. http://politics.nytimes.com/congress/votes/112/senate/2/187.

New York Times. "Transcript: Donald Trump Expounds on His Foreign Policy Views." Last modified March 26, 2016. http://www.nytimes.com/2016/03/27/us/politics/donald -trump-transcript.html.

Public Broadcasting Service. "The Warnings? | Cyber War! | *FRONTLINE*." PBS. Last modified April 24, 2003. http://www.pbs.org/wgbh/pages/frontline/shows/cyberwar/warnings/.

Republican National Committee. "2012 Republican Platform." Last modified 2012. https:// cdn.gop.com/docs/2012GOPPlatform.pdf.

Savage, Charlie. "File Says N.S.A. Found Way to Replace Email Program." *New York Times*. Last modified November 19, 2015. http://www.nytimes.com/2015/11/20/us/politics /records-show-email-analysis-continued-after-nsa-program-ended.html?_r=0.

"U.S. Chamber Policy Accomplishments for 2012." U.S. Chamber of Commerce. Last modified 2012. https://www.uschamber.com/sites/default/files/legacy/about/2012Policy Accomplishments--January2013.pdf.

Washington Post. "Public Concern over Cyber-attack." Last modified June 6, 2012. https:// www.washingtonpost.com/page/2010-2019/WashingtonPost/2012/06/07/National -Politics/Polling/release_90.xml?uuid=sD1ccrA8EeGw96SQqoz3hw.

White House. "Foreign Policy Cyber Security Executive Order 13636." Last modified February 12, 2013. https://www.whitehouse.gov/issues/foreign-policy/cybersecurity/eo -13636.

White House. "SECURING CYBERSPACE—President Obama Announces New Cybersecurity Legislative Proposal and Other Cybersecurity Efforts." Whitehouse.gov. Last modified January 13, 2015. https://www.whitehouse.gov/the-press-office/2015/01/13 /securing-cyberspace-president-obama-announces-new-cybersecurity-legislat.

White House. "FACT SHEET: Cybersecurity National Action Plan." Whitehouse.gov. Last modified February 9, 2016. https://www.whitehouse.gov/the-press-office/2016/02/09 /fact-sheet-cybersecurity-national-action-plan.

Williams, Katie B. "Clinton: Cybersecurity Will Be Challenge for Next President." *The Hill*. Last modified February 3, 2016. http://thehill.com/policy/cybersecurity/268121 -clinton-cybersecurity-one-of-the-most-important-challenges-for-next.

Debt Relief for Developing Countries

At a Glance

The United States has the largest absolute amount of debt of any country in the world, standing at approximately $19.5 trillion in August 2016. However, the size of the U.S. economy, the status of the dollar as a reserve currency, the low-interest rates on U.S.-issued debt instruments, and other factors make it possible for the United States to service its debt (pay the minimum payment) without significant difficulty. For a variety of reasons, including primary commodity dependence, macroeconomic mismanagement and corruption, periods of predatory lending, poor terms of trade, and external economic shocks, developing countries are often in a less favorable debt service position. Many of the poorest countries in the world have had significant portions of their debt written off by bilateral and multilateral lenders. However, many developing countries, especially in Latin America and Asia, were too wealthy by developing-country standards to receive relief, leaving them with unsustainable debt levels. Generally, Republicans and Democrats have agreed on the need for debt forgiveness for the poorest countries (often called least developed countries or LDCs). However, partisan gaps exist on debt forgiveness and restructuring policy to developing countries that are not LDCs. Partisanship has also entered the debate over the interaction between debt relief and foreign aid.

According to many Republicans . . .

- Debt relief should be accompanied by lower amounts of foreign aid, especially concessional loans;
- Debt relief should be minimal for all but the LDCs;
- The debt crisis was caused mainly by corruption and macroeconomic mismanagement in developing countries; and
- Debt relief in non-LDCs should be tied to democratic and macroeconomic reforms.

According to many Democrats . . .

- Debt relief programs should be expanded to have an impact on more countries;
- Developed countries should help developing countries maintain low debt levels by providing more aid in the form of grants instead of loans;
- The debt crisis, especially in resource-rich developing countries was caused as much by predatory lending as by macroeconomic mismanagement or corruption; and
- Debt relief should be tied to the willingness of developing countries to channel the money saved on debt service toward poverty reduction.

Overview

There are three main types of external debt that may be incurred by a developing country. For research-rich developing countries, especially oil-rich states like Nigeria, commercial debt is a possibility. Commercial loans, provided at market rates, are based on collateral, in the form of facilities or receipts from the sale of resources, such as oil. During the oil boom of the later 1960s through the 1970s, commercial banks lent to developing countries based on the promise of continued high prices. Global recession caused a significant price adjustment, with wide fluctuation in oil prices becoming the norm. Developing countries accrued significant commercial debt during this time frame. Because commercial loans generally involve stricter repayment terms, countries suffering from commercial indebtedness have had difficulty having loans forgiven. Nevertheless, the "London Club" of commercial creditors, which meets on an ad hoc basis, has been willing at times to extend repayment terms for developing countries in order to avoid default. Unlike other creditors, commercial institutions are unlikely to write off significant portions of developing-country debt.

Developing countries can also find themselves with balance of payment difficulties due to bilateral debt. Many developed countries, including the United States, provide a portion of their foreign aid in the form of concessional loans. A concessional loan is any loan that has below market interest rates, extended repayment terms, or both. Developing countries, especially those pursuing import substitution industrialization policies in the 1970s, incurred significant bilateral debt. Import substitution industrialization is a strategy that attempts to stimulate domestic production by using tariffs (taxes on imports) to make imports more expensive and domestic products more competitive. Developing countries that pursue this strategy must finance their industrial infrastructure rather than build more incrementally. The Paris Club, a group of 19 countries holding significant amounts of developing-country debt, meets several times a year to consider debt rescheduling and, more recently, debt write-offs.

The third source of debt for developing countries is multilateral debt. Developing countries who take out loans from international lending institutions such as the International Monetary Fund (IMF), the International Bank for Reconstruction and Development (better known as the World Bank), and several regional development banks are taking on multilateral debt. The LDCs, who normally do not have access to bilateral loans or to conventional multilateral loans, can access development funding from the International Development Association (IDA), a branch of the World Bank. As developing countries began to default on multilateral debt, multilateral agencies began to offer debt rescheduling and partial write-offs in exchange for financial austerity programs collectively known as "structural adjustment." Structural adjustment often proved insufficient for developing countries for a variety of reasons, including increased political instability caused by decreased funding for social programs.

In the mid-1990s, the World Bank and the IMF introduced the Highly Indebted Poor Countries (HIPC) Initiative, which began to write-off debt for countries with high debt-to-export ratios. HIPC also required countries to focus a portion of the proceeds from debt relief into national poverty reduction strategies. HIPC also required structural adjustment, but of the type that would maintain elements of the social safety net in developing countries. When HIPC proved helpful, the Group of 8 Developed Countries, which includes the United States, created the Multilateral Debt Relief Initiative (MDRI). Although there are limits to MDRI debt relief, including the fact that not all of the regional development banks are participating, total MDRI relief exceeded $45 billion (U.S.) as of 2009, the peak implementation year of the program. The United States contributes to MDRI both by writing off bilateral loans in concert with multilateral MDRI relief and by using a portion of the foreign aid budget to provide additional resources to the IMF and World Bank to write off loans.

The United States also provides debt relief to some countries for more strategic reasons. For example, the United States has provided over $7 billion dollars in debt relief to Egypt in recognition of its willingness to make peace with Israel and its role in the Persian Gulf War (Tarnoff and Lawson 2016). After ousting President Saddam Hussein from Iraq, the United States provided billions in debt relief and encouraged other countries to do the same. The MDRI was born, in part, out of negotiations over Iraqi debt relief. During times of humanitarian crisis, the United States may forgive additional debt as it has in the Philippines and in Haiti. This additional debt relief is considered as part of the foreign aid budget, which requires budgetary approval from Congress. Multilateral write-offs only require congressional approval in the event that the United States provides additional financial resources to the multilateral lending institutions to help absorb the cost of the write-off.

It should also be noted that it can be difficult to isolate partisan currents within the debt relief debate for several reasons. First, multilateral debt relief, while it often involves U.S. leadership, is provided by international financial institutions like the World Bank and the IMF. If the president decides to support relief through these mechanisms he can do so without congressional approval, except in cases where the United States is reimbursing some of the cost. As a result, multilateral debt relief is not always subject to significant partisan debate. Second, even if U.S. money, and hence congressional authorization, is involved, most debt relief comes from the foreign aid budget. Hence, the debate over debt relief can be lost in the broader debate concerning foreign aid. Third, debt relief to specific countries, especially in times of crisis is often bipartisan, even if the overall debate over debt relief is not. In this environment, we must look to key votes, and nonvotes, to determine the partisan dimensions of the issue.

Democrats on Debt Relief for Developing Countries

The last Democratic Party platform to specifically mention debt relief for developing countries was the 2008 platform, which mentions debt relief in the context of economic and political reform. The 2004 platform also mentions the idea of sensible debt relief. Debt relief was a salient enough issue to make it into the platform closer to the turn of the millennium because of the popularity of the Jubilee 2000 effort to eliminate developing-country debt as well as the Millennium Development Goals (MDGs), which were developed by the United Nations and supported by the United States. The Democratic Party supported the MDGs, including goal 8D, which sets indicators for sustainable debt service for developing countries. Interestingly, the Democratic Party of Washington State favored the inclusion of a platform plank that specifically mentioned using foreign aid to write off developing-country debt. However, this plank did not make it into the final platform.

The lack of emphasis on debt relief within the Democratic Party platform is broadly reflected in public opinion. However, we can glean some useful information on differences in public opinion on debt relief by examining public opinion related to foreign aid (which is where the United States budgets its debt-relief funds). In this regard, 33 percent of Democrats asserted in a 2013 poll that aid to the world's needy should be increased, whereas 25 percent believe it should be decreased (Pew Research Center 2013). However, a 2015 poll found that only 17 percent of Democrats believe that economic aid to developing countries is a "very effective" way of advancing U.S. foreign policy goals (Chicago Council on Global Affairs 2015). Generally, Democrats are also likely to believe that foreign aid should be provided in grant form rather than loan form. This would prevent developing countries from incurring more debt even in the face of increased aid.

Democrats in Congress have often expressed support for debt relief for developing countries over the years. For several consecutive years, the Jubilee Act for Responsible Lending and Expanded Debt Cancellation came before Congress. The act would have required debt forgiveness beyond MDRI terms, and would have required the president to support increased debt relief from multilateral lending institutions. The bill would also have required that most future economic and humanitarian aid, as opposed to military aid, to developing countries be made as grants rather than loans.

Majorities of Democrats in the House and Senate have supported the legislation on each occasion. In 2008, when the House held its only recorded floor vote on the measure, 216 of 222 Democrats voted in favor of the legislation (GovTrack. us 2008). Six Democrats, all in districts vulnerable to Republican takeover, voted no. For a variety of reasons, including concerns that the bill could not overcome a Republican filibuster, the act was never voted on by the full Senate. A majority of Democrats supported the bill in committee, however.

The 2010 midterm elections resulted in significant victories for Republicans, including the rise of the Tea Party movement. From that point on, large-scale debt relief bills became unlikely to pass Congress. Maxine Waters, who sponsored the Jubilee Act, did successfully support passage of debt relief for Haiti after an earthquake killed over 200,000 Haitians in 2010. It is worth noting, however, that large amounts of U.S. disaster relief to countries such as the Philippines—developing countries too wealthy to be declared LDCs—have been provided as loans rather than grants.

President Barack Obama and Democratic presidential nominee Hillary Clinton have also expressed support for increased debt relief for developing countries. For example, President Obama's State Department funding request for FY 2016 included $111 million for debt relief for countries only eligible for IDA loans (U.S. Department of State 2016). Obama has also supported the Enterprise Institute for the Americas (better known by its Spanish-language acronym of EAI), which provides debt relief to countries in Latin America and the Caribbean. The amount of funds requested for debt relief has decreased over time, in part because the United States has already forgiven significant portions of HIPC debt. Debt relief to other developing non-HIPCs has been less forthcoming. In 2008, Obama announced during his first presidential campaign that he supported 100 percent debt cancellation for the HIPCs, a pledge that has been largely kept. Congress does not always fund 100 percent of the debt relief request, however, which explains why there continue to be IDA debt relief requests in 2016–2017 (the IDA line item of the State Department budget contains most of the money requested for debt relief. Senator Clinton, who participated in the rollout of President Bill Clinton's debt relief initiative in Africa while serving as First Lady, also supports debt forgiveness for HIPCs.

Republicans on Debt Relief for Developing Countries

Overall, Republicans are less supportive of debt relief for developing countries, especially if that relief takes the form of outright debt forgiveness. However, there are deeper intraparty divisions within the Republican Party on this issue than there are within the Democratic Party. Specifically, for some evangelical Republicans, the idea of debt forgiveness fits well with certain tenets of the Christian faith. In this context, it makes sense that the year 2000 Republican Party platform is the only Republican Party platform of the past 20 years to specifically mention debt relief for developing countries. The year 2000 was viewed by many Christians as a "Great Jubilee." In biblical terms, a traditional jubilee celebrated every 50 years in the biblical Old Testament, was an occasion for debt forgiveness. The Grad Jubilee, according to many Christians, including the Pope, should be an occasion for debt forgiveness for developing countries.

As mentioned above, direct debt forgiveness to developing countries normally falls under the foreign aid budget within the Department of State. With this in mind, we can at least approximate public attitudes toward debt relief by examining partisan attitudes toward foreign aid. Self-identified Republicans within the general public are not strong proponents of foreign aid. In a 2013 Pew Research Center survey 70 percent of Republicans argued that foreign aid should be decreased while only 7 percent believed that it should be increased (Pew Research Center 2013). The 45-point partisan gap in public opinion on this issue is one of the largest recorded on a foreign policy issue. Republicans and Democrats are more similar in their skepticism of foreign aid as a tool to advance the U.S. foreign policy agenda. Only 7 percent of Republicans believe that economic aid is a "very effective" way to meet U.S. foreign policy goals (Chicago Council on Global Affairs 2015). Recall, however, that only 17 percent of Democrats believe that economic aid is "very effective." The partisan gap is thus much smaller on the issue of aid effectiveness (to the United States) than it is on whether aid should be increased or decreased.

Republicans in Congress are more divided on debt relief than are Democrats. In the vote on the 2008 Jubilee Act, for example, 126 Republicans voted against the measure while 69 Republicans favored the legislation. Republican leadership, including then House minority leader John Boehner, opposed the legislation. Instead, Boehner favored a counterproposal that would have provided debt relief to some countries but blocked debt relief to any developing country conducting business with Iran (Boehner 2008). The Republican alternative failed because of opposition from Democrats who tend to oppose secondary sanctions (sanctions or punishments against a country for dealing with another country) and Republicans who desired to pass the original Jubilee Act. Alabama Republican Spencer Bachus, a member of the Congressional Prayer Caucus, for example, became a cosponsor of the Jubilee Act. Bachus argued that "doing the right thing (passing the Jubilee Act) is not only morally imperative, it serves our national interests" (Jubilee Blog 2008).

At the executive level, Republican president George W. Bush was a strong proponent of debt relief for developing countries, especially HIPCs in Africa. Bush and former British prime minister Tony Blair pushed a plan to the Group of Eight (G8), an organization of the world's largest economies, to forgive over $40 billion in HIPC debt. The proposal, which was approved, resulted in a 100 percent write-off of all HIPC debt owed at the time to the IMF, the World Bank, and the African Development Bank. HIPC countries, as well as other developing countries, still owe debt to the IMF, some non–Paris Club bilateral lenders, and other regional development banks. The G8 deal did not require congressional approval because it was not a treaty or congressional-executive agreement. However, the plan, which became known as the MDRI, did require enough congressional support to fund the IDA line of the foreign aid budget. Congress, including Republicans in Congress, have generally been supportive in this regard.

The GOP's 2016 presidential nominee, Donald Trump, had not declared a public position on debt relief for developing countries as of the fall of 2016. Trump has expressed a general distaste for foreign aid, however, arguing that the United States should not be "sending foreign aid to countries that hate us" (Trump 2015). Trump's macrolevel argument is that sending foreign aid, which includes debt relief, to developing countries, trades off with more important priorities in the United States. In expressing this sentiment, Trump has tapped into a line of thinking shared by many Americans: that foreign aid spending is not appropriate in an era when (1) so many other domestic spending priorities exist, and (2) the United States itself is currently carrying a national debt.

Further Reading

Boehner, John. "Boehner Praises House Passage of GOP Proposal to Block Taxpayer-Funded Debt Relief for Allies of Iran." Speaker.gov. Last modified April 15, 2008. http://www.speaker.gov/press-release/boehner-praises-house-passage-gop-proposal-block-taxpayer-funded-debt-relief-allies.

Chicago Council on Global Affairs. "America Divided: Political Partisanship and US Foreign Policy." Last modified 2015. https://www.thechicagocouncil.org/sites/default/files/CCGA_PublicSurvey2015.pdf.

GovTrack.us. "H.R. 2634 (110th): Jubilee Act for Responsible Lending and Expanded Debt Cancellation of 2008." Last modified April 16, 2008. https://www.govtrack.us/congress/votes/110-2008/h199.

Jubilee Blog. "Jubilee Act Markup Opening Statement of Ranking Member Spencer Bachus." Last modified April 4, 2008. http://jubileeusa.typepad.com/blog_the_debt/2008/04/opening-stateme.html.

Pew Research Center. "Wide Partisan Gap Exists Over U.S. Aid to World's Needy." Last modified March 13, 2013. http://www.pewresearch.org/daily-number/wide-partisan-gap-exists-over-u-s-aid-to-worlds-needy/.

Tarnoff, Curt, and Marian L. Lawson. "Foreign Aid: An Introduction to U.S. Programs and Policy." Congressional Research Service. Last modified June 17, 2016. https://www.fas.org/sgp/crs/row/R40213.pdf.

Trump, Donald J. "Donald J Trump Presidential Announcement." Donald J. Trump for President. Last modified June 16, 2015. https://www.donaldjtrump.com/media/donald-j-trump-presidential-announcement.

U.S. Department of State. "Congressional Budget Justification Foreign Assistance Summary Tables Fiscal Year 2016." Last modified 2016. http://www.state.gov/documents/organization/238223.pdf.

Defense Spending

At a Glance

The U.S. military has always been a significant instrument of U.S. foreign policy. The United States, with an inclusive military budget of approximately $596 billion in 2015, accounts for about 36 percent of all military spending in the world (SIPRI 2016). Military spending in 2016 should be very similar based on budget projections. China, the next largest spender in percentage terms, accounts for about 13 percent of all military spending. The United States spends about 3.3 percent of its gross domestic product on defense, making this the largest discretionary item in the U.S. budget. In spite of these large numbers, defense spending has actually decreased since the end of combat operations in Iraq and Afghanistan, when annual military spending, in constant dollar terms (adjusted for inflation) neared $800 billion. Frequent partisan debates over military spending are driven partially by this decrease, partially by debates concerning the state of U.S. military equipment, and partially by threats faced by the United States.

According to many Republicans . . .

- U.S. military expenditures are too low given the wide-ranging and severe threats faced by the United States;
- Falling military budgets are degrading weapons systems in a variety of areas;
- Decreasing military budgets sends a message of weakness to America's enemies; and
- Robust defense spending is good for the U.S. economy.

According to many Democrats . . .

- U.S. military expenditures are about right and reflect a compromise between Democrats (who want lower spending) and Republicans (who want higher spending);
- The military budget contains a great deal of waste; including funding levels beyond those requested by the Department of Defense for some weapons systems;

- The United States spends a sufficient amount on defense to project qualitative and quantitative military strength; and
- Money not spent on defense can be used for social programs and other discretionary spending that are also beneficial to the American public.

Overview

U.S. defense expenditures have varied significantly over time. Before the end of World War II in 1945, the best predictor of spending levels was whether America was at war. As a result, there are spikes in military spending, relative to their time, around events like the War of 1812, the Mexican-American War, The U.S. Civil War, the Spanish-American War, World War I, and World War II. The United States emerged from World War II as a global hegemon (a predominant military and economic power) with all of the accompanying costs of setting and maintaining the global order. In addition, World War II transitioned quickly into the Cold War between the United States and the Soviet Union, which led to the maintenance of high spending levels through 1991 (the end of the Cold War). As a result, though defense spending went down after a peak in World War II (in constant dollar terms), it has remained higher than at any other point in history. Since the early 1950s, the military budget in constant dollars has tended to fluctuate between $400 billion and $780 billion annually (*Washington Post* 2013).

Because of its sheer size, the U.S. military budget can be quite complicated. What follows are some of the major components of military spending from year to year:

- Operations and Maintenance: Normally, this is the largest component of the defense budget. Money from this appropriations title is used to fight wars (including supplies and equipment), transport troops, maintain bases, and maintain existing equipment.
- Military Personnel: This functional component includes the costs of salary and a variety of benefits for members of the Armed Forces. It is generally the second-largest component of the defense budget. Normally, this is the least controversial area, from a partisan standpoint, of the defense budget.
- Procurement: Old equipment needs to be replaced with new equipment over time, whether or not the new equipment is a completely new weapons system of simply replacements for worn out weapons and equipment. The procurement budget can vary significantly depending on whether the Department of Defense is purchasing completely new systems. The procurement budget is also subject to significant partisan debate, as demonstrated below.
- Research and Development: Normally making up about 10 percent of the defense budget, research and development is the smallest of the main

components. However, given the overall size of the budget, this functional area often results in over $60 billion in annual spending. The Department of Defense conducts and sponsors research in a variety of areas, from new weapons and equipment to mental health issues related to warfare.

An additional area of the budget that can vary significantly from year to year is the Overseas Contingency Operation (OCO) budget. Each of the functional areas listed above has an OCO component. OCO is designed as a sort of supplemental fund (critics often refer to it as a "slush fund") designed to provide money for unanticipated costs related to the fight against terrorist groups in places like Syria and Libya (Epstein and Williams 2016). During the George W. Bush administration, OCO was called Global War on Terror (GWoT) in funding requests. OCO/GWoT funding requests were at their highest during the peak fighting years of the wars in Iraq and Afghanistan (fiscal years 2004–2011). When one party or candidate accuses another of "putting a war on the credit card," as Barack Obama argued during the 2008 presidential campaign, that reference is normally to the OCO portion of the budget. Total OCO/GWoT funds for Iraq and Afghanistan equaled well over $1 trillion total from 2004–2011.

In 2015, after two years of sequestration cuts to the defense, the Bipartisan Budget Control Act restored military spending to near presequestration levels. Under sequestration, the defense budget for the year 2015, for example, would have been automatically set at $498 billion. Instead, including OCO funding, the total defense budget stands at $533 billion (Pellerin 2015). This amounts to approximately 98 percent of the amount that the DoD requested from Congress. The act has set up a key debate between proponents, who argue that the budget deal is a compromise that leaves the military in an excellent position to protect U.S. interests, and opponents, who either believe that military spending is too high or too low. As one might imagine, the divide falls, at least partially, along partisan lines.

Republicans on Defense Spending

Generally, Republicans and Democrats have been supportive of the large defense budgets that have existed since World War II. It is also the case, however, that Republicans tend to be more bullish overall on defense spending than are Democrats. In a budgetary environment where just a few percentage points of difference in preferred spending points can amount to tens of billions of dollars, the differences between parties are worth exploring.

The 2016 Republican Party platform mentions defense spending 11 times. The mentions can be divided into three rough categories. First, Republicans argue that sequestration has reduced the military budget, in real terms, by 25 percent, and that this is an unacceptable level of funding given the threats, such as global terrorism, faced by the United States. Second, the platform expresses dissatisfaction with President Obama's veto of the 2016 National Defense Authorization Act.

Republicans argue that the act was the first step in restoring the military to presequestration levels. Finally, Republicans argue Democrats are too willing to sacrifice necessary military spending to domestic spending priorities. For example, most Democrats were unwilling to restore military funding to presequestration levels unless other domestic priorities, such as social safety net spending, received similar treatment.

There is also a demonstrable partisan gap in public opinion as it relates to defense spending as an instrument of U.S. foreign policy. Since 2011, for example, the number of Republicans and Democrats who say that the United States is spending "too little" on defense has increased. However, Republicans are the only category where a majority of individuals (56 percent, according to one 2015 poll) believe that the government spends too little on defense (McCarthy 2015). In 2013, a plurality of Americans polled in a Pew Research study believed that military spending ought to be kept about the same (Drake 2014). What is interesting about this finding is that it occurred during the first year of sequestration, when the defense budget was the lowest it had been since the beginning of the wars in Iraq and Afghanistan. Given that these are different survey instruments in different years, it is possible that the divergent findings are simply a product of the nature of sampling from a population. It is also possible that they broadly reflect the trend, noted by Gallup, that the percentage of people who believe that the U.S. spends too little on the military is growing over time. Another distinct possibility is that most Americans are not aware of the amount of money spent on the military, which influences their perceptions of "appropriate levels of spending." It has been well documented, for example, that Americans significantly overestimate the amount of money spent on foreign aid (the U.S. spends less than 1 percent of its budget on foreign aid while the average American places the figure at around 25 percent) according to a 2015 poll by the Kaiser Family Foundation (DiJulio, Firth, and Brodie 2015). With regard to defense spending, there is no annual survey available. However, the most recent available data (from 2011) indicates that Americans underestimate the amount of money allocated to defense spending to the point that it creates inconsistencies in survey responses (Rasmussen Reports 2011).

In October and November of 2015, Congress debated two measures related to defense spending. The first, the National Defense Authorization Act of for Fiscal Year (FY) 2016, passed both houses of Congress but was vetoed by President Obama. The second bill, the Bipartisan Budget Act of 2015, provided an additional $80 billion in defense spending for FY 2016 and 2017. The first resolution passed along party line votes in the House and the Senate, both of which were controlled by the GOP. In the House, 233 Republicans supported the bill while only 10 of those voting opposed it (GovTrack.us 2015). The few Republicans who voted against the measure primarily argued that the spending caps imposed by the 2011 Budget Control Act should apply to all areas of spending, even the military (Wingerter 2015). In the Senate, 49 Republicans voted in favor of the legislation, while two opposed it (three Senators did not vote). The two "no" votes, Senators

Rand Paul (R-Ky.) and Ted Cruz (R-Tex.) were both high-profile senators arguing, like their dissenting House colleagues, that the legislation was a direct attempt to remove congressionally imposed spending caps.

The vote on the 2015 Bipartisan Budget Act of 2015 was, in some ways a mirror image of the Defense Authorization Act. The Bipartisan Budget Act was passed in violation of the famous, but informal, Hastert Rule (named after former Republican of the House Dennis Hastert), which requires a majority of Republican lawmakers in the House to support a piece of legislation for it to be brought to the floor. Because the bill lifted spending caps, imposed by the original 2011 Budget Control Act, on a variety of spending areas, only 79 Republicans favored the act while 167 Republicans opposed the legislation (GovTrack.us 2015). The most notable of the "yea" votes was then Speaker of the House John Boehner, who voted for the act as part of his promise to "clean the barn" of contentious pieces of legislation before leaving office. The bill passed the House because all 187 Democrats voted in favor of the legislation (see below). In the Senate, only 18 of 53 Republicans supported the legislation. However, it passed because 44 Democrats voted in favor of the legislation. Originally, the number of senators opposing the legislation would have been enough to sustain a filibuster, which requires at least 41 senators. However, using a procedural maneuver, the bill was passed as part of another piece of legislation related to the Trade Act of 2015, circumventing what had been a successful filibuster attempt.

The debate over defense spending also featured prominently in the 2016 presidential election. Republican nominee Donald Trump argued that increased defense spending is required to make the military "so big, so powerful, so strong, that nobody—absolutely nobody—is going to mess with us" (Trump 2016). It is worth noting that, in 2013, Trump stated in an interview with Fox News's Greta Van Susteren that he supported the sequester cuts, which were, in his words "a very small percentage of the cuts that should be made" (On The Record with Greta Van Susteren 2013). However, Trump's statements were in regard to the sequester as a whole, and he was not asked if he would create an exemption for defense spending. On the campaign trail in 2016, Trump argued that defense cuts have left the armed forces to perform maintenance on complex weapons systems such as fighter craft using what amounts to junkyard equipment. In this context, Trump has asserted that the defense procurement budget needs to be increased to fully address challenges such as cybersecurity and defeating ISIS.

Democrats on Defense Spending

The 2016 Democratic Party platform refers to defense spending four times. Thematically, the platform is concerned with two primary issues. First, Democrats blame Republicans for the sequestration process that brought about across the board cuts in areas such as defense, rather than "smart" defense budgeting. Overall, Democrats believe that Republicans have used the debt ceiling, a device that

Republicans argue is vital to rein in spending, as a blackmailing tool to force cuts in social programs. During the 2013 budget showdown, Democrats believed that they needed to avoid compromise unless targeted cuts were made in both defense and nondefense items. They blame the lack of compromise on Republicans entrenching around the social spending cuts, requiring Democrats to dig in to make sure that the military budget bore its fair share of the belt-tightening. Second, the platform argues that the Pentagon and high-dollar defense contractors should be audited in order to produce targeted cuts that reduce waste while not reducing the ability of the armed forces to carry out its mission. There appears to be some room for bipartisan compromise in this area, as the Republican Party platform also calls for an audit of the Pentagon, though it does not refer to defense contractors.

Among members of the general public that self-identify as Democrats, support for military spending is lower than among Republicans or independents. For example, while the number of Democrats saying that the current amount of defense spending is "too little" has grown, these respondents still make up only 17 percent of all Democrats according to one 2015 poll (McCarthy 2015). It is worth noting that the single largest year-over-year increases in Democrats who believe that defense spending is too low occurred after sequestration. For their part, according to the same poll, independents are situated midway between Republicans and Democrats. Thirty-three percent of independents believe that defense spending is too low, versus 56 percent of Republicans. Once again, the inferences that can be made from this data are somewhat limited by the fact that the public tends to underestimate the military budget, especially when compared to public perceptions of what other countries spend on defense. In the Rasmussen survey mentioned above, only 25 percent of the public believed that the United States should spend three times as much as any other nation, a situation that occurs regularly (conditioned in part by the difficulty in estimating Chinese defense spending).

Democrats in Congress generally opposed the National Defense Authorization Act of 2016 and supported the Bipartisan Budget Act of 2015 (which applies to FY 2016–2017). In the House, only 43 of 184 Democrats who voted supported the Defense Authorization Act (GovTrack.us 2015). Democrats opposed the legislation for several reasons. First, while many Democrats supported the idea of freeing defense spending from the caps imposed during the sequester, they believed the same exemptions should have applied to other nondefense programs. Second, the act circumvented the cap on defense spending by providing more money for the OCO sections of the defense budget. Democrats, including Minority Leader Nancy Pelosi, argued that OCO funding does not provide a predictable basis for military funding and also makes it more difficult to target funding toward benefits for members of the armed forces. Third, President Obama had threatened to veto the legislation and Democrats wanted to remain loyal to the president. Finally, the act included a provision that would have allowed federal defense contractors, under the concept of religious liberty, to base certain employment decisions on the sexual orientation of a potential or actual employee. President Obama signed an executive order prohibiting this practice in 2014, and the 2015 act would have overridden the protections mandated in the executive order for LGBTQ individuals. Those House Democrats who did vote for the legislation tended to be from districts with large numbers of members of the armed forces, military bases, or from more moderate districts.

In the Senate, 21 Democrats supported the act and 22 opposed it, demonstrating that Senate Democrats were somewhat more divided than House Democrats. One reason for this is the nature of the legislation. Generally, the defense authorization bill is considered to be "must-pass" bipartisan legislation. In the Senate, where bipartisanship can be a bit more common than in the House, it is not surprising that more Democrats supported the act. Second, Senate Republicans were more willing to vote for the legislation, knowing that the votes existed in the House to sustain a presidential veto. As a result, many Democrats railed against the use of OCO funds in the legislation but ultimately voted for the bill. Senator Debbie Stabenow of Michigan, for example, voted for the legislation but stated before her vote that there were not enough votes to override a presidential veto (Johnson 2015). Finally, it is common for senators from both parties to be more hawkish on defense policy, including defense spending. Constitutionally, the Senate has more responsibility in the realm of foreign affairs, which contributes to the hawkishness. In addition, senators are much more likely than representatives to run for president, a position that normally requires candidates who are viewed as "strong" on defense. Voting against defense appropriations bills can be an unwise policy in this regard. With regard to the Bipartisan Budget Act of 2015, Democrats were completely united in the House, with all 187 voting Democrats approving the measure (recall that the measure passed with a minority of Republican votes). The same is true in the Senate, where all 44 Democratic senators, as well as the two independent senators who caucus and regularly vote with the Democrats, voted "aye."

President Obama ultimately vetoed the Defense Authorization Act and signed the Bipartisan Budget Act, a position with which Democratic presidential nominee Hillary Clinton agreed. Obama took issue with the OCO funding mechanism, arguing that it did not provide predictable funding for the military in the years to come. The president also made it clear that he would prefer spending caps on the military to be lifted in conjunction with other spending limits, a position ultimately adopted in the Bipartisan Budget Act. For her part, former secretary of state Clinton asserted that the Bipartisan Budget Act "is a promising first step in providing government agencies with much needed fiscal stability. But we must go further by ending the sequester for both defense and non-defense spending in a balanced way" (Hillary for America 2016). Clinton has also argued that the military healthcare system and the acquisition (procurement) system invite wasteful spending that can be curtailed without sacrificing benefits.

Further Reading

Clinton, Hillary. "Military and Defense." Hillary for America. Last modified 2016. https://www.hillaryclinton.com/issues/military-and-defense/.

DiJulio, Bianca, Jamie Firth, and Mollyann Brodie. "Data Note: Americans' Views on the U.S. Role in Global Health." Kaiser Family Foundation. Last modified February 23, 2015. http://kff.org/global-health-policy/poll-finding/data-note-americans-views-on-the-u-s-role-in-global-health/.

Drake, Bruce. "Plurality of Americans Support Current Level of Defense Spending." Pew Research Center. Last modified February 24, 2014. http://www.pewresearch.org/fact-tank/2014/02/24/plurality-of-americans-support-current-level-of-defense-spending/.

Epstein, Susan E., and Lynn M. Williams. "Overseas Contingency Operations Funding: Background and Status." Congressional Research Service. Last modified June 13, 2016. https://www.fas.org/sgp/crs/natsec/R44519.pdf.

GovTrack.us. "H.R. 1735: National Defense Authorization Act for Fiscal Year 2016." Last modified October 1, 2015. https://www.govtrack.us/congress/votes/114-2015/h532.

Johnson, Fawn. "Democrats Retreat in the Battle over Defense Budget 'Gimmick.'" Defense One. Last modified June 17, 2015. http://www.defenseone.com/politics/2015/06/democrats-retreat-battle-over-defense-budget-gimmick/115591/.

McCarthy, Justin. "Americans Split on Defense Spending." Gallup. Last modified February 20, 2015. http://www.gallup.com/poll/181628/americans-split-defense-spending.aspx.

On The Record with Greta Van Susteren. "Trump on the Looming Sequester: 'It's Being Over-exaggerated.'" New York: Fox News, February 22, 2013.

Pellerin, Cheryl. "DoD Comptroller: Budget Deal Offers Relief, Uncertainty." U.S. Department of Defense. Last modified 2015. http://www.defense.gov/News/Article/Article/632078/dod-comptroller-budget-deal-offers-relief-uncertainty.

Perlo-Freeman, Sam, Aude Fleurant, Pieter Wezeman, and Siemon Wezeman. "Trends in World Military Expenditure, 2015." SIPRI. Last modified April 5, 2016. https://www.sipri.org/sites/default/files/EMBARGO%20FS1604%20Milex%202015.pdf

Rasmussen Reports. "Voters Underestimate How Much U.S. Spends on Defense." Last modified February 1, 2011. http://www.rasmussenreports.com/public_content/politics/general_politics/january_2011/voters_underestimate_how_much_u_s_spends_on_defense.

Trump, Donald. "Military—Donald J. Trump for President." YouTube. January 24, 2016. https://www.youtube.com/watch?v=6iZKBv8xqyk.

Washington Post. Plumer, Brad. "America's Staggering Defense Budget, in Charts." Last modified January 7, 2013. https://www.washingtonpost.com/news/wonk/wp/2013/01/07/everything-chuck-hagel-needs-to-know-about-the-defense-budget-in-charts/.

Wingerter, Justin. "Rep. Tim Huelskamp Lone Member of Kansas Delegation to Oppose Defense Authorization Bill." Last modified October 2, 2015. http://m.cjonline.com/news/2015-10-02/rep-tim-huelskamp-lone-member-kansas-delegation-oppose-defense-authorization-bill#.

Egypt

At a Glance

The relationship between the United States and Egypt has always been a critical part of U.S. foreign policy in the Middle East. Since Egypt and Israel signed the Camp David Accords peace agreement in 1978—a landmark event that owed much to the active involvement of Democratic president Jimmy Carter in negotiations—Egypt has also been one of the largest recipients of U.S. foreign aid. In 2011, the sudden ouster of President Hosni Mubarak (regarded as a longtime ally of the United States) and the rise of an Islamist-led government in Egypt as part of the Arab Spring caused renewed tensions between the two countries. The 2013 coup in Egypt that resulted in a return to military rule opened renewed debate about U.S. policy toward the most populous country in the Middle East.

According to many Republicans, U.S. foreign policy toward Egypt . . .

- Should be contingent on having a regime in power that is friendly to the United States;
- Should be based on a recognition that positive stability in Egypt is key to stability in the wider Middle East; and
- Should reflect an overarching goal of protecting Israel from attack from neighboring states.

According to many Democrats, U.S. foreign policy toward Egypt . . .

- Should encourage a return to democratic governance;
- Should work to improve human rights in Egypt;
- Should continue to include financial aid, even in the wake of the 2013 military coup; and
- Should be based on a recognition that positive stability in Egypt is key to stability in the wider Middle East.

Overview

The United States first established diplomatic relations with Egypt in 1922, when Egypt gained limited independence from Great Britain. In 1952, the Egyptian military launched a coup against the monarchy, leading to the advent of republican government under Gamal Abdel al-Nasser. The U.S. government believed that although he was not fond of Western-style democracy, Nasser would not embrace ties with the Soviet Union. During Nasser's reign (he served as prime minister from 1954 to 1956 and president from 1956 until his death in 1970), Egypt confounded U.S. foreign policy elites, often playing the United States and Soviet Union against each other. Sensing an opening after the United States refused to provide military aid to Nasser's government, the Soviet Union did so in the mid-1950s. In 1957, the United States sided with Egypt in the Suez crisis, a moved welcomed by Egypt. However, Egypt had previously recognized the People's Republic of China (PRC), a move that angered the United States. In response to Egypt's recognition of the PRC, the United States withdrew its offer to provide financing for the Aswan High Dam, which Egypt viewed as vital to the development of its electrical infrastructure (Glass 2012). The Soviet Union ultimately agreed to assist in financing the project, a move that brought Egypt and the Soviet Union closer together.

In 1967, Egypt broke off diplomatic relations with the United States, charging that the United States had assisted Israel during its 1967 preemptive war with several Arab states. In 1970, Nasser died, leading to the presidency of Anwar Sadat. Egypt–Soviet relations had soured to the point where Sadat expelled Soviet advisers from the country. Egypt's attack on Israeli positions in the Sinai Peninsula in 1973 did not prevent the reestablishment of diplomatic relations with the United States, even in the wake of the Arab oil embargo announced after the United States provided military equipment to Israel. Though the combined Egyptian–Syrian force lost the war, Israel recognized the threat, which opened the door to eventual negotiations between Egypt and Israel. Sadat had become so popular as a result of the limited initial success of the war (the 1967 war was completely one-sided) that he gained the political space to seek peace with Israel. In 1978, during the Camp David Accords hosted by President Jimmy Carter, Sadat, and Israeli prime minister Menachem Begin reached a peace agreement whereby Egypt would recognize Israel and Egypt would return the Sinai Peninsula to Egypt. The United States, as part of the peace process, agreed to a generous military aid package with Egypt, making the country the second-largest recipient of U.S. aid. Sadat paid for the peace treaty with his life. He was assassinated by members of the Islamic Jihad in 1981.

During the period from 1981–2011, Hosni Mubarak ruled as president of Egypt. For the most part, the United States and Egypt enjoyed positive relations during this time period, irrespective of whether Democrats or Republicans controlled Congress and the White House. During the Cold War, having Egypt and Israel as allies served as a useful hedge against Soviet influence in places like Syria. Even after the Cold War, having Egypt as an ally was a key to U.S. foreign policy in the Middle East. It was an article of U.S. foreign policy faith that without Egypt, no conceivable array of Arab states would dare attack Israel, a situation that satisfies a key U.S. foreign policy goal. In addition, Egypt's secular dictatorship, while not unique in the region, was much preferred by the United States to the prospect of either a popularly elected Islamist government or, worse, an Islamic Republic similar to Iran. Egypt was the fourth-largest troop contributor to Operation Desert Storm, the U.S.-led effort to liberate Kuwait from Iraq. Egypt also provided the United States with valuable intelligence related to Islamist terrorism both before and after the terrorist attacks of September 11, 2001.

In January 2011, however, Mubarak's government began to come crashing down. Following the example of protesters in Tunisia, thousands of Egyptians took to the streets to rail against high unemployment, government corruption, and repressive governance under Mubarak. Egyptian police and military units cracked down on the protesters, and also arrested members of several Western prodemocracy non-government organizations, including over a dozen Americans (Loveluck 2013). Initially, the U.S. response to the protests was muted. The Obama administration was wary of calling for Mubarak's resignation for a variety of reasons, including the potential for significant harm to the relationship between the United States and Egypt if the protests failed. Over the course of January and the beginning of February 2011, though, the U.S. government began to increase the pressure on the regime step down. Mubarak resigned from office on February 11, 2011.

Egypt had its first free and fair elections in 2011 (for parliament) and 2012 (for the presidency). Mohamed Morsi of the Freedom and Justice Party (FJP) narrowly won the latter election. The FJP had already come to control parliament. For the United States, these results posed a significant problem. The United States supported the idea of democracy in Egypt in theory. However, the FJP, controlled mostly by the Muslim Brotherhood, has a history of mistrust toward the United States, in part because of its Islamist tendencies and in part because of U.S. support of the secular-autocratic Mubarak regime. The Muslim Brotherhood is an Islamist organization (one that favors the integration of Islam into political and social structures) formed in 1928 in Egypt. In 2012, President Obama referred to Egypt as neither an ally nor an enemy, a definitive change from the U.S. relationship with Egypt under Mubarak. On September 11, 2012, Egyptian protesters attacked the U.S. Embassy in Cairo, pulling down the American flag. No embassy staff or officials were injured. After increased protests over abuses of power by Morsi and the FJP, the Egyptian military launched a coup and removed Morsi from power in July 2013, just over a year after he took power. General Abdul Fatah al-Sisi (often referred to simply as Sisi) became president. The United States originally reacted by calling for a return to constitutional governance but has since softened its stance and restored most military aid to Egypt.

Republicans on U.S. Relations with Egypt

Most of the contemporary partisan battles concerning U.S. foreign policy toward Egypt related to the period before and immediately after the Egyptian Revolution in 2011 and the period after the 2013 coup. The 2012 Republican Party platform is not very instructive with regard to the Republican position on Egypt during this period. In part, this is due to focus on other geostrategic issues such as terrorism and the U.S. relationships with China and Russia. In addition, the full implications of the 2012 Egyptian Revolution were not clear at the time when the platform was written. In this context, the platform stops short of taking a direct position, and simply calls on the new Egyptian government to honor its peace treaty with Israel (Republican National Committee 2012). In August 2012, when the Republican platform was being drafted and finalized, Morsi had yet to make an official statement regarding Egypt's intentions vis-à-vis Israel. On August 28, coincidentally at the time of the Republican National Convention, Morsi announced to Western media that Egypt intended to honor its peace treaty with Israel (Blomfield 2012). The 2016 platform praised the al-Sisi government for protecting Coptic Christians from Islamist groups in Egypt. The Coptic Church is an orthodox branch of Christianity that exists primarily in Egypt.

Whether it is because the public has less intense or less informed opinions about Egypt, or because of the paucity of survey data, there is little available evidence on the attitudes of Republican voters regarding U.S. foreign policy toward Egypt. We do know that American public opinion regarding Egypt was historically negative in the immediate aftermath of the 2011 revolution. According to one poll taken during that time, Republicans dropped 21 percentage points in their opinion of Egypt, from 57 percent favorable to 36 percent favorable (Jones 2011). We also know that self-identified Republicans within the general public are more likely to argue that President Obama has not been tough enough on the Egyptian military in the wake of its 2013 military coup than are Democrats (Pew Research Center 2013). According to the same study, slightly more Republicans than Democrats favored cutting military aid to Egypt in the wake of the coup.

The Congressional Republican response to the situation in Egypt has been mixed. In the immediate aftermath of the 2011 protests that triggered Mubarak's downfall, Republican members of Congress largely deferred to the president. Former House Speaker John Boehner and current Senate majority leader Mitch McConnell both issued statements to the effect that Republicans and Congress would help U.S. government "speak with one voice" on the issue (Sidoti 2011). In 2013, after the coup that ousted Morsi, Republicans became much more critical of the president.

The main issue on which the GOP focused its criticisms concerned U.S. military aid to Egypt. Under the terms of America's Foreign Assistance Act of 1961, all foreign aid save humanitarian assistance must be suspended if the president makes the determination that a coup has occurred. In spite of the fact that the military takeover in Egypt in 2013 met the textbook definition of a coup (an extra-constitutional seizure by a person or group outside of the government), Obama was hesitant to declare the situation a coup for a variety of reasons, including the geostrategic importance of Egypt to the United States. Republicans were initially highly critical of this decision. Senators Lindsey Graham and John McCain, two

Republican Senators Reverse Position on Denial of Military Aid to Egypt

As the 2013 debate over whether to cut off military aid to Egypt intensified, Republican senators Lindsey Graham of South Carolina and John McCain of Arizona wrote an opinion article for the *Washington Post* in which they made the case for denying military aid to Egypt:

> Not all coups are created equal, but a coup is still a coup. Morsi was elected by a majority of voters, and U.S. law requires the suspension of our foreign assistance to "any country whose duly elected head of government is deposed by military coup d'état or decree ... in which the military plays a decisive role." We find it hard to describe the situation in Egypt any other way. Congress should review this law to determine whether it serves our national interests, but at this time we believe the United States must suspend assistance to Egypt. This is a difficult decision, but if we expect Egypt and other countries to abide by their laws, then we must abide by ours.

But when given the chance to vote for their desired policy, both Graham and McCain changed positions. When Republican senator Rand Paul introduced a measure that would have diverted all aid to Egypt into U.S. infrastructure projects, both Graham and McCain objected on the grounds that it would increase political instability in the Middle East. According to Graham:

> The cataclysmic effect of a failed state in Egypt would be the biggest booster to radical Islam I could think of and would do a lot of damage to our national security and our best friend in the region, Israel . . . Maybe one day I will be with Senator Paul, saying we have to sever our ties with the Egyptian military and the Egyptian people . . . All I can tell you if that day ever comes, it would be one of the saddest days of my life because that means Egypt is gone, and if Egypt is gone, all hell is going to break loose.

McCain also spoke out against Paul's proposal:

> I think it's important for us to send a message to Egypt that we're not abandoning them, but what we are doing is trying to caution them to try to modify their behavior . . . The most important nation in the Arab world descending into chaos is going to be a threat to the United States of America, and I urge my colleagues and I urge my friend from Kentucky with respect to realize that this amendment would send the wrong message at the wrong time.

In the end, Paul's measure was easily defeated.

Sources:

"Floor Updates—Senate Floor THUD Appropriations bill (S. 1243)." Republican.Senate.Gov. Last modified July 31, 2013. http://www.republican.senate.gov/public/index.cfm/floor-updates?ContentRecord_id=3deac014-4830-4a47-b5d9-850156104b6d.

McCain, John, and Lindsey Graham. "John McCain and Lindsey Graham: Cut Off Aid to Egypt." *Washington Post*. Last modified July 12, 2013. https://www.washingtonpost.com/opinions/john-mccain-and-lindsey-graham-cut-off-aid-to-egypt/2013/07/12/5850a1f4-eb19-11e2-a301-ea5a8116d211_story.html.

prominent Republican voices on foreign policy issues, called the president's inaction contrary to American values and called for an immediate suspension of aid (McCain and Graham 2013).

A month after publishing their joint editorial, however, both Graham and McCain voted against an amendment sponsored by fellow GOPer Rand Paul that would have cut off military aid to Egypt (the amendment failed by a vote of 86–13).

The issue of U.S. relations with Egypt did not play a significant role in the Republican presidential primary of 2016. However, it was possible to discern the positions of several of the leading candidates on the issue. Texas senator Ted Cruz, for example, voted for the Paul amendment to cut aid to Egypt in 2013. Cruz argued that cutting aid to Egypt would be the best way to signal to the military dictatorship that the United States is serious about the need for democratic reform (Cruz 2013). However, Cruz has also praised the al-Sisi government for its willingness to counter Islamic terrorism, arguing that al-Sisi is an example of a "Muslim that we ought to be standing with" (Weichert 2016). Businessman Donald Trump, who ultimately won the Republican nomination and the presidency in 2016, did not take a specific position on U.S.–Egypt relations or America's continued provision of military aid to the country. In 2012, however, Trump did claim on Twitter that "Egypt is a total mess. We should have backed Mubarak instead of dropping him like a dog" (Trump 2012). Ohio governor John Kasich, meanwhile, simply stated that the United States needs to stand with Egypt as it fights terrorists (Kasich 2016).

Democrats on U.S. Relations with Egypt

The 2012 Democratic Party platform mentioned Egypt four times. Like its Republican counterpart, the document mentioned Egypt in the context of its peace treaty with Israel. Unlike the Republican platform, however, the Democratic platform also refers to the Egyptian Revolution in two ways. First, the platform attempted to strengthen the credibility of the Obama administration by highlighting the fact that Obama called for the military and president Mubarak to respect the desire of the Egyptian people for a transition away from dictatorship and toward democracy. The platform also referred to the Arab Spring as a whole and spoke of America's willingness to work with elements of civil society in countries like Egypt, Libya, Syria, and Tunisia, to encourage more inclusive governance (Democratic National Committee 2012). At the time, the fact that only Tunisia would serve as a successful example of a transition to more democratic governance was not apparent. Egypt is not mentioned by name in the 2016 Democratic Party platform.

Polls indicate that the American public's attitudes toward Egypt darkened somewhat in the aftermath of the 2011 revolution and the 2013 coup against the government of President Morsi. Still, Democrats retained higher favorability toward Egypt than Republicans according to one 2011 poll, which found a 6 percentage point difference (Jones 2011). Two years later, a majority of Democrats responded that President Obama was either being too tough on Egypt after the 2013 coup or "about right" (Pew Research Center 2013). According to the same survey, Democrat respondents were slightly less likely to favor cutting off military aid to Egypt than Republicans. Overall, replacement of the stable, though repressive, Mubarak regime with a popularly elected government less friendly to the United States created a lot of uncertainty among the public, regardless of political affiliation. The 2013 military coup, which replaced the elected government with a more traditional military dictatorship, created further uncertainty among Americans of all political orientations.

President Obama's initial reaction to the situation in Egypt was one of caution. Given Egypt's status as a linchpin in U.S. foreign policy in the Middle East, the United States could not afford to push too quickly for Mubarak's resignation, lest he survive the uprising politically and turn his attention to the perceived betrayal. On the other hand, not backing the prodemocracy protesters would have been contrary to American values and would risk alienation if the protests did succeed (which they initially did). Therefore, Obama did not immediately ask Mubarak to step down as president. Secretary of State Clinton and other Democratic advisers urged Obama not to call for President Mubarak's departure too early, for fear of causing instability in Egypt and the Middle East. Eventually, however, the president and most of his advisers unified around the idea that Mubarak's response to the protests had been insufficient, and he would have to leave office to avoid chaos. Obama personally spoke with Mubarak on February 1, 2011, and called on him to resign (Cooper and Worth 2012). Later the same day, Obama delivered a public speech calling for a transition to a new government. On February 11, Mubarak stepped down as president of Egypt.

President Obama's reaction to the 2013 coup in Egypt was also cautious. Had the Obama administration labeled the takeover a coup, the United States would have had to immediately cut all nonhumanitarian aid to Egypt. In addition, in the event the coup was successful, which it was, the United States needed to be in a position to work with the al-Sisi regime on issues such as terrorism. In October 2013, the State Department announced that it was "recalibrating" Egyptian foreign aid away from military assistance and toward humanitarian assistance (United Press International 2013). Some humanitarian aid remained part of the aid package, but most of the $1.5 billion in annual aid was suspended. In March 2015, after it became clear that the cut in aid was not going to result in a restoration of democracy in Egypt, the military aid package was restored. Many of the president's national security advisers also supported the restoration of aid as a means to ensure Egyptian stability and to maintain U.S. influence in the country.

Democrats in Congress have had a mixed reaction to the president's policies toward Egypt. For the most part, Democrats have offered support and, when necessary, votes. For example, Democrats voted, against the 2013 amendment by Republican Rand Paul to cut aid to Egypt. For the most parts, Democrats also deferred to the president on the initial administration response to the 2011

President Obama Hails the Egyptian Revolution of 2011

The Obama administration had mixed feelings about the prospect of an Egypt ruled by someone other than Hosni Mubarak, who had been a reliable U.S. partner in the region for decades. However, once Obama decided to call for Mubarak to resign, it was incumbent on him to commemorate the occasion of Mubarak's ouster. On February 11, 2011, Obama addressed the American people on events in Egypt:

> There are very few moments in our lives where we have the privilege to witness history taking place. This is one of those moments. This is one of those times. The people of Egypt have spoken, their voices have been heard, and Egypt will never be the same.
>
> By stepping down, President Mubarak responded to the Egyptian people's hunger for change. But this is not the end of Egypt's transition. It's a beginning. I'm sure there will be difficult days ahead, and many questions remain unanswered. But I am confident that the people of Egypt can find the answers, and do so peacefully, constructively, and in the spirit of unity that has defined these last few weeks . . . The United States will continue to be a friend and partner to Egypt. We stand ready to provide whatever assistance is necessary—and asked for—to pursue a credible transition to a democracy.

Less than two years later, however, Obama's hopes that democracy would sweep across Egypt were dashed. Protesters returned to the streets, the military stepped in and arrested Mohamed Morsi (Mubarak's democratically elected successor), and Egypt returned to military rule.

Source:

"Remarks by the President on Egypt." White House: Office of the Press Secretary. Last modified February 11, 2011. https://www.whitehouse.gov/the-press-office/2011/02/11/remarks -president-egypt.

Revolution in spite of the fact that Democrats were more likely to see the revolt as a prodemocracy uprising than were Republicans. However, there have also been areas of division between Obama and House and Senate Democrats. For example, Senator John Kerry, who later became Obama's secretary of state, called for Mubarak to step down before Obama publicly made that determination, a breach of conventional party protocol and issues related to foreign policy. Senator Bill Nelson, a Democrat from Florida, made a similar argument at a time when, at least publicly, the Obama administration and Democrats were calling for reforms within the Mubarak regime and an end to the violence (Chaddock 2011).

The situation among Democrats and Congress was also mixed with regard to the cutting and ultimate restoration of military aid to Egypt. Democratic senators such as Patrick Leahy, who praised the decision to cut military aid to Egypt, temporarily blocked the president from restoring aid. As the chairperson of the Subcommittee on Foreign Operations at the time (2014), Leahy had the power to prevent consideration of that portion of the foreign operations budget, which is the source of U.S. aid to Egypt (Zengerle 2014). Other Democrats, like Representative Eliot Engle, ranking member of the House Foreign Affairs Committee, criticized the president's decision to cut off aid in the first place. Engle claimed that "during this fragile period we should be rebuilding partnerships in Egypt that enhance our bilateral relationship, not undermining them" (Hudson 2013). Engle's concern, one shared by some Republicans, was that cutting aid to Egypt would reduce its stability, as well as opening the door for other countries, such as Russia, to increase their influence in Egypt. Once again, the classic tension between the promotion of democracy and human rights and that of maintaining close ties with a key ally regardless of regime type were on full display.

The issue of Egypt was not a prominent one in the 2016 Democratic presidential primary. Both former secretary of state Hillary Clinton (who ultimately won the nomination) and Senator Bernie Sanders focused more on ISIS and other national security issues of particular interest to the public. However, the position of each candidate is discernable. Clinton, for example, was much slower to embrace the idea that the 2011 protests should result in the ouster of Mubarak and appears more willing to deal with the regime. She has also made the argument that the United States must be prepared to work with military dictators in the region (Tau 2015). Senator Sanders did not lay out a specific position on U.S. foreign policy on Egypt. However, he did vote against the 2013 Paul amendment, which would have cut all aid to the military dictatorship. Sanders also argued during the debates that pushing for regime change without a credible plan for what to do in the case of success can lead to the type of power vacuums, such as those in Libya and Iraq, that allow extremists to flourish.

Further Reading

Blomfield, Adrian. "Mohammed Morsi Vows to Respect Egypt-Israel Peace Treaty—Telegraph." Telegraph.co.uk. Last modified August 28, 2012. http://www.telegraph.co.uk/news/worldnews/africaandindianocean/egypt/9504601/Mohammed-Morsi-vows-to-respect-Egypt-Israel-peace-treaty.html.

Chaddock, Gail R. "In Congress, GOP Backs Obama's Egypt Stance, Dems Not So Much." *Christian Science Monitor.* Last modified February 1, 2011. http://www.csmonitor.com/USA/Foreign-Policy/2011/0201/In-Congress-GOP-backs-Obama-s-Egypt-stance-Dems-not-so-much.

Cooper, Helene, and Robert F. Worth. "Arab Spring Proves a Harsh Test for Obama's Diplomatic Skill." *New York Times.* Last modified September 24, 2012. http://www.nytimes.com/2012/09/25/us/politics/arab-spring-proves-a-harsh-test-for-obamas-diplomatic-skill.html?_r=0.

Cruz, Ted. "Sen. Cruz Statement on Egypt." Ted Cruz | U.S. Senator for Texas. Last modified August 16, 2013. https://www.cruz.senate.gov/?p=press_release&id=84.

Democratic National Committee. "2012 Democratic Platform." Democrats.org. Last modified 2012. https://www.democrats.org/party-platform.

Glass, Andrew. "Dulles Announces U.S. Withdrawal of Egypt Dam Offer, July 19, 1956." Politico. Last modified July 9, 2012. http://www.politico.com/story/2012/07/this-day-in-politics-078678.

Hudson, John. "Top Democrat Slams Obama for Cutting Egypt Aid." *Foreign Policy*. Last modified October 9, 2013. http://foreignpolicy.com/2013/10/09/top-democrat-slams-obama-for-cutting-egypt-aid/.

Jones, Jeffrey. "Americans' Views of Egypt Sharply More Negative." Gallup.com. Last modified February 8, 2011. http://www.gallup.com/poll/146003/americans-views-egypt-sharply-negative.aspx.

Kasich, John. "National Security Plan." Kasich for America. Last modified 2016. https://www.johnkasich.com/nationalsecurity/.

Loveluck, Louisa. "Egypt Convicts US NGO Workers." *The Guardian*. Last modified June 4, 2013. http://www.theguardian.com/world/2013/jun/04/egypt-convicts-us-ngo-workers-sam-lahood.

McCain, John, and Lindsey Graham. "John McCain and Lindsey Graham: Cut Off Aid to Egypt." *Washington Post*. Last modified July 12, 2013. https://www.washingtonpost.com/opinions/john-mccain-and-lindsey-graham-cut-off-aid-to-egypt/2013/07/12/5850a1f4-eb19-11e2-a301-ea5a8116d211_story.html.

Pew Research Center. "Public Backs Cutoff of Military Aid to Egypt." U.S. Politics & Policy. Last modified August 19, 2013. http://www.people-press.org/files/legacy-pdf/08-19-13%20Egypt%20Release.pdf.

Republican National Committee. "2012 Republican Platform." Last modified 2012. https://cdn.gop.com/docs/2012GOPPlatform.pdf.

Republican.Senate.Gov. "Floor Updates—Senate Floor THUD Appropriations Bill (S. 1243)." Last modified July 31, 2013. http://www.republican.senate.gov/public/index.cfm/floor-updates?ContentRecord_id=3deac014-4830-4a47-b5d9-850156104b6d.

Sharp, Jeremy. "Egypt–United States Relations." Congressional Research Service. Last modified June 15, 2005. http://www.au.af.mil/au/awc/awcgate/crs/ib93087.pdf.

Sidoti, Liz. "GOP Divided over Obama Response to Egypt." TODAY.com. Last modified February 3, 2011. http://www.today.com/id/41413954/ns/today-today_news/t/gop-divided-over-obama-response-egypt/#.VwW09pwrLIU.

Tau, Brian. "Debate over U.S. Intervention Abroad Crosses Party Lines." *Wall Street Journal*. Last modified December 21, 2015. http://blogs.wsj.com/washwire/2015/12/21/candidates-debate-over-u-s-intervention-abroad-crosses-party-lines/.

Trump, Donald. Twitter Post. Twitter. Last modified December 12, 2012. https://twitter.com/realdonaldtrump/status/278949442999181312.

Weichert, Stefan. "US Presidential Candidate Praises Al-Sisi as 'Shining Example.'" Daily News of Egypt. Last modified March 12, 2016. http://www.dailynewsegypt.com/2016/03/12/us-presidential-candidate-praises-al-sisi-shining-example/.

United Press International. "U.S. State's Psaki Says U.S. 'recalibrating' Egypt Aid." Last modified October 9, 2013. http://www.upi.com/Top_News/US/2013/10/09/Psaki-US-recalibrating-assistance-to-Egypt/11051381348974/?spt=su.

Zengerle, Patricia. "Senior U.S. Lawmaker Blocks Aid for Egyptian Military." Reuters. Last modified April 29, 2014. http://www.reuters.com/article/us-usa-egypt-military-idUSBREA3S0NY20140429.

Energy Policy

At a Glance

The search for new sources of energy to satisfy energy demand in the United States has had a significant impact on U.S. foreign policy dating as far back as the "black gold" rush of the 1860s. The desire to maintain U.S. access to foreign oil while simultaneously working toward greater energy independence has had foreign policy implications that go beyond the resources themselves. A partisan divide has emerged in U.S. foreign policy in terms of access to resources such as oil, renewable energy cooperation and competition with other countries, and international environmental agreements. In addition, energy policy is a classic "intermestic" policy issue—one with both domestic and international dimensions. Securing access to energy abroad, energy independence, decreasing consumption of fossil fuels, international and domestic environmental standards, and trade policy are all interrelated and interdependent.

According to many Republicans . . .

- The United States must continue to decrease its dependence on foreign oil by increasing domestic drilling;
- The United States must be willing to use domestic coal in order to increase energy independence;
- The United States should pursue an "all-of-the-above" energy strategy that combines access to foreign energy resources, renewables, and increased exploration/exploitation of U.S. resources;
- The United States should not enter into international cap and trade schemes because they hurt economic growth and require more sacrifices from the United States than other countries;
- The United States should support the Keystone oil pipeline system between the United States and Canada; and
- The military should not be required to meet energy demands from renewable resources.

According to many Democrats . . .

- The United States should become part of international cap and trade agreements to decrease carbon emissions in order to combat global warming;
- The U.S. should focus on the development of renewable energy at home in order to foster energy independence;
- The Keystone Pipeline is too risky based on the possibility of leaks as well as increased greenhouse gas emissions;
- The U.S. military should meet 25 percent of its energy needs through renewable resources; and
- Renewable energy will increase U.S. international market share in renewable energy technology.

Overview

The most obvious connection between U.S. energy policy and foreign policy relates to the export and especially the import of fossil fuels, especially oil. The United States consumes approximately 19.4 million barrels of petroleum products (much of it refined petroleum products such as gasoline) per day (U.S. Energy Information Administration 2016). The United States imports about 300 million barrels of oil per month, with the largest international source being Canada, which supplies about one-third of the monthly total. The United States also produces significant amounts of its own oil, reaching the point where domestic production has outstripped foreign imports. Higher energy prices from 2001–2008, as well as more domestic development-friendly policies during the George W. Bush administration, catalyzed domestic production, which increased through 2014. In the past two years, falling prices have decreased the amount of hydraulic fracking. This, in turn, has decreased production in 2015–2016. The amount of Middle Eastern oil, often associated with U.S. geopolitics, has fallen significantly, with most Middle Eastern oil now exported to developed Asian countries such as China. A majority of U.S. imports come from the Western hemisphere including countries such as Canada, Mexico, Ecuador, and Venezuela.

In spite of the fact that significant amounts of U.S. oil come from outside of the Middle East, U.S. foreign policy continues to focus on protecting the free flow of Middle Eastern oil for a variety of reasons. First, previous disruptions in the supply of oil from the Middle East, especially the Persian Gulf Region, has caused severe price spikes in the various oil markets. Events in the United Arab Emirates or in Qatar, two countries that export more oil to China than to the United States, still have an impact on U.S. prices. Second, the Middle East still has a majority of the world's proven oil reserves, meaning that access to oil in the future is likely to mean continued diplomatic relations with Middle Eastern nations. Third, the United

States does not enjoy positive relations with all of its oil suppliers outside of the Middle East. Venezuela, which has more proven oil reserves than any country in the world, and is one of the largest suppliers of U.S. oil, is a prime example in this regard. Access to Middle Eastern oil serves as a hedge against potential oil shipment disruptions from such countries.

In his 1980 State of the Union Address, Democratic president Jimmy Carter proclaimed: "An attempt by any outside force to gain control of the Persian Gulf region will be regarded as an assault on the vital interests of the United States of America. Such an assault will be repelled by any means necessary, including military force" (Carter 1980). Much of the world's supply of oil (including oil upon which America has been dependent) passes through the Persian Gulf via the Strait of Hormuz. The Soviet threat to which Carter was referring in the speech has disappeared. However, the Carter Doctrine, as it became known, has guided subsequent U.S. foreign policy in the region. Iran mined the strait in the 1980s and threatened to close it all together in 2011. Each time, the United States has responded by deploying additional military assets to the region to guide commercial ships or to keep the strait open. When Iraq invaded Kuwait in 1990, the U.S. led a coalition of international forces operating under United Nations auspices to free Kuwait. The United States also took steps to protect Saudi Arabia, at the time the country with the largest proven oil reserves, from Iraqi attack.

The politics of energy has also played a role in efforts to combat international terrorism. The Islamic State of Iraq and Greater Syria (ISIS) finances portions of its operations using oil seized in territory it controls. At one point in late 2015, ISIS had been selling up to 40,000 barrels of oil a day, generating over a million dollars in income. The United States was initially reticent to use airstrikes against oil infrastructure, fearing that it would cripple other areas economically and make it more difficult for oil production to begin again after the territory was liberated from ISIS. A combination of factors, including territorial gains against ISIS and increased intelligence gathering, convinced the Obama administration to authorize increased airstrikes against oil refining and production infrastructure in mid-2015. The result appears to have cut ISIS revenue, though exact estimates are not currently available.

Even purely domestic energy policies have foreign policy implications. As part of the Paris Climate Agreement of 2015, the United States has agreed to cut its carbon emissions over time (see below). The Obama administration and most climate scientists believe that this is a necessary step in minimizing the impact of climate change. However, the international agreement will require the United States to generate increased amounts of energy from renewable sources, such as solar and wind. This will create increased economic opportunity in some regions and sectors, especially those subsidized by the government. However, it will also create economic dislocations in regions of the country that have traditionally been economically dependent on heavy fossil fuel production, including coal and oil-rich areas.

Democrats on Energy Policy

Generally, Democrats are known for being more in favor of environmental protection, even if there are some economic dislocations, than are Republicans. This is, in part, due to the belief among most Democrats that protecting the environment provides public health and other economic benefits that outweigh the impact of potential dislocations. Democrats are also somewhat less likely to favor military intervention in other countries than are Republicans. In this context, Democrats favor more significant decreases in fossil fuel production and use, both because such decreases are likely to help combat climate change and because decreased dependence on imports decreases the need have a more interventionist foreign policy. Energy policy is a significant priority in the 2016 Democratic Party platform, which mentioned the issue 43 times. The very first mention provides a partisan foreign policy contrast with Republicans, touting the development over the two terms of the Obama administration to more clean energy sources, thus reducing U.S. reliance on fossil fuels from overseas. The platform also mentions the related belief that energy independence will enhance U.S. security, presumably by subjecting the country to fewer foreign energy shocks, a concern shared by Republicans. The platform also makes a connection between renewable energy and trade, arguing that investing in clean energy at home will improve the trade balance by increasing U.S. exports. The Democratic Party position has long been that the United States must compete with China in emerging markets such as the one that exists for lower cost, more durable, and more readily deployable solar panels. Finally, the platform asserts that continued energy policy reform is a key to international cooperation to combat global climate change. Specifically, Democrats believe that the United States needs to become a party to global agreements that limit the emission of greenhouse gases such as carbon dioxide.

One interesting omission from the Democratic Party platform was the reference to an "all-of-the-above" energy policy, an area of previous bipartisan agreement. Democrats have traditionally supported an energy policy that privileges renewable energy but recognizes the need to continue to expand domestic production of fossil fuels as a "bridge to the future." In June 2016, the Democratic Platform Drafting Committee announced that it was "moving beyond" the all of the above approach to in order to emphasize climate change as a more urgent concern (Democratic National Convention 2016). The argument had been that reducing dependence on foreign energy sources, and the foreign trade and potential military obligations that come with them, would require more domestic production until renewables are able to meet demand in the future. In 2016, the party platform shifted to the left on energy, in part because of increased concerns about climate change (an intermestic issue) and in part because of a strong reaction against the practice of hydraulic fracking (a more strongly domestic issue). Fracking involves drilling into the ground, then injecting water, sand, and other chemicals into the crack in order to release oil and/or natural gas from the rocks beneath. Most Democrats believe that fracking cannot be conducted in an environmentally sound matter.

There are clear partisan divides on several issues related to U.S. energy policy, most of which have at least indirect foreign policy ramifications. A 2014 survey conducted by the Hart Center for American Progress, a left-leaning think tank using standard polling methodology, found that 58 percent of Democrats favor developing renewable resources as the key strategy to U.S. energy independence (Hart Research Associates 2014). Only 23 percent of Democrats believe that the development of fossil fuels in the United States is the best strategy. It is worth noting that both Democrats and Republicans believe that U.S. energy independence from foreign sources is a worthy goal. In 2016, a majority of Americans (60 percent) believe that conservation is a better approach than increased domestic production of energy when it comes to the issue of U.S. energy problems (Gallup 2016). Within the general public, 82 percent of Democrats also believe that state governments should set renewable energy standards that require a set portion of energy to come from non–fossil fuel sources (Center for Local, State, and Urban Policy 2015).

The last significant piece of legislation related to energy policy that passed Congress and was signed into law was the American Recovery and Reinvestment Act of 2009. The act, which was passed over Republican objections by a Democratic-controlled Congress and signed into law by President Obama, is also known as "The Stimulus" or "The Recovery Act" due to its passage as a result of the Great Recession that began in late 2007. The Recovery Act included billions of dollars in grants and tax credits designed to stimulate the production of renewable energy and modernize the nation's electricity grid. Approximately $30 billion was allocated specifically to the development of renewable energy in order to, according to the Obama administration and most Democrats in Congress, decrease dependence on foreign sources of energy and to combat global climate change by reducing U.S. emissions. In the House of Representatives, 244 of 255 Democrats voted for the legislation (Govtrack.us 2009). All 56 Senate Democrats voted for the legislation.

In 2016, an energy bill called the North American Energy Security and Infrastructure Act of 2016 passed the House and Senate by significant margins. The act would require an energy security evaluation by the secretary of energy in consultation with several congressional committees, including the House and Senate Committee on Foreign Relations. Though the bill would adopt new incentives for renewable energy, and energy efficiency, both considered important foreign policy goals undertaken at the domestic level, the Senate version of the legislation does not take a position on climate change or on energy exploration. As a result, both conservative think tanks like the Heritage Foundation, which believes that the legislation would provide for more government interference in the economy, and more liberal environmental groups such as the Sierra Club, which believes that the legislation does not do enough to protect the environment, have lobbied against the bill. In the Senate, the bill passed by a vote of 85–12, with all Democrats voting in favor of the legislation (U.S. Senate 2016).

The 2016 House and Senate versions of the legislation are significantly different, a fact that will require Senate and House conferees to agree on a unified piece of legislation that can pass both chambers of Congress. The House version of the legislation contains more proposals from previous Republican-sponsored legislation, such as a provision to make it easier to approve oil and gas pipeline construction in the United States. The House version also contains less language on renewable energy sources and energy efficiency standards for buildings. As a result, the House version of the legislation passed by a mostly party-line vote of 241–178, with only 8 Democrats voting in favor (Clerk.house.gov 2016). For his part, President Obama has supported the Senate version of the legislation while expressing the desire for it to go further on renewables. He has opposed the House legislation for the same reason most Democratic Representatives oppose the measure. Assuming that the conference committee does not act until after the 2016 elections, the results of those elections may well determine the final content of the legislation.

At the executive level, both President Obama and 2016 Democratic presidential nominee Hillary Clinton support expanded production of renewable energy and decreased carbon emissions for power plants, manufacturing facilities, and automobiles. In 2007, the U.S. Supreme Court ruled in *Massachusetts v. EPA* that the Environmental Protection Agency (EPA) must regulate greenhouse gas emissions in the event that the EPA declared them harmful. The EPA has declared that carbon dioxide and other greenhouse gases are indeed harmful. In 2015, President Obama, unable to pass climate change legislation through Congress, used the *Massachusetts v. EPA* ruling to justify the unveiling of the Clean Power Plan for existing power plants via executive order. New power plants were already covered by 2013 EPA regulations. Auto emissions are covered under a separate set of regulations as well. With respect to power plants, the largest source of carbon emissions, the goal is to lower emissions to 32 percent below 2005 levels by the year 2030 (U.S. Environmental Protection Agency 2015). The constitutionality of the Clean Power Plan is currently in dispute within the federal court system. The U.S. Supreme Court has issued an injunction against carrying out the plan until the legal issues are resolved.

President Obama has also supported internationally negotiated agreements to address climate change via changes in energy efficiency standards. In November 2014, for example, the United States and China issued a joint statement on climate change in which the United States committed to reducing its carbon emissions to 26–28 percent below 2005 levels by 2025, largely by pursuing renewable energy and increased efficiency paths (White House 2014). In September 2016, China and the United States announced that they would ratify the Paris Climate Agreement, which encourages states to adopt emissions reduction targets designed to limit global temperature increases to two degrees Celsius. Clinton has expressed support for both the Paris Agreement and the Clean Power Plan. It is worth noting, however, that President Obama continues to use the "all-of-the-above" language on energy policy that has now been rejected as part of the Democratic Party platform. Clinton has not announced opposition to the policy. However, it is customary for the party nominee to have disproportionate influence in crafting the party platform, raising a strong possibility of a policy difference between Obama and Clinton.

Republicans on Energy Policy

Generally, Republicans are known for the same commitment to energy independence exhibited by Democrats. However, Republicans believe that energy independence is best achieved, as a foreign and domestic policy goal, through the development of U.S. fossil fuel resources, including increased exploration in federally protected areas like national parks and offshore. Republicans also tend to be much more skeptical of anthropogenic climate change, making them less likely to support increased carbon emissions standards as part of domestic or foreign energy policy.

The 2016 Republican platform mentions energy policy 44 times. It insists that American workers will suffer in the event that Democratic Party renewable energy policies and energy standards are enacted. The platform also focuses on existing domestic sources of mineral wealth, calling for increased exploration in the United States and its exclusive economic zones off the coast. Unlike the 2016 Democratic Party platform, which removed its "all-of-the-above" energy strategy language, the Republican platform introduced the phrase, albeit with a different meaning. In the Republican Party, such a strategy means continued support for all fossil fuel industries and the removal of burdensome regulations that hinder those industries (Republican National Committee 2016). Finally, Republicans believe that a more modern electricity grid and pipeline system would enhance the U.S. position in international trade by facilitating exports and lowering the cost of imports.

In the realm of public opinion, Republicans and Democrats are mirror images of each other when it comes to energy policy. According to one 2014 poll, 60 percent of Republicans favored the development of domestic fossil fuels as the main route to energy independence (Hart Research Associates 2014). Only 30 percent of Republicans believed that the development of renewables is the best direction. As mentioned above, for Democrats, those numbers were reversed. Interestingly, though, a 2015 poll found that 60 percent of Republicans joined 82 percent of Democrats in the belief that states should require a set percentage of energy to be produced from renewable sources (Center for Local, State, and Urban Policy 2015). The level of agreement is even closer when one examines the subgroup of Republicans who believe that the Earth is warming. Generally, Republicans are more likely to favor regulations at the state level (whether or not the issue is energy related) than at the national level, which potentially accounts for the agreement in this area. It is also the case that the survey instrument does not ask respondents to react to a proposed level renewable power generation, meaning that Republicans and Democrats may well possess vastly different ideal regulatory points even if they agree with the basic premise.

The partisan gap in public opinion on energy policy extends into Congress. Republicans opposed the 2009 stimulus package as wasteful and unlikely to create jobs in any sector, including energy. When the American Recovery and Reinvestment Act of 2009 passed in the House of Representatives, it did so without a single assenting Republican vote (Govtrack.us 2009). Three Republican senators did vote in favor of the legislation (37 voted no): Senators Susan Collins and Olympia Snow, two moderate Republicans representing Maine, as well as former senator Arlen Specter, who voted for the legislation just before switching parties from Republican to Democrat. Republicans also opposed Democrats on the North American Energy Security and Infrastructure Act of 2016. In the Senate, where the bill was crafted more vaguely to appeal to both parties, all 12 no votes came from Republicans (U.S. Senate 2016). Senators Rand Paul and Marco Rubio, both of whom opposed the legislation, argued that the proposed regulations on energy infrastructure and renewables requirements would distort the impact of the free market on energy production. In the House, where the legislation contained several proposals related to deregulation, only six Republicans voted no (Clerk.house.gov 2016). As mentioned above, the contrast between the bipartisan Senate approach and the partisan House approach will make the status of the bill highly susceptible to changes in the balance of power within Congress, as well as between Congress and the executive branch.

The 2016 Republican Party presidential nominee Donald J. Trump has declared his opposition to renewable energy requirements, the Clean Power Plan, the U.S.–China Joint Statement on Climate Change (which contains U.S. renewable energy commitments), and the Paris Climate Agreement. In May 2016, Trump delivered a speech in North Dakota in which he announced the "America First Energy Plan." After enumerating ways in which federal environmental regulations and lawsuits hurt the energy industry, U.S. energy independence, and American jobs, Trump argued that a new framework was necessary. Trump called for making American "energy dominance"—a term not specifically defined in the speech—an enumerated domestic and foreign policy goal based on the presence of significant oil, coal, and natural gas reserves in the United States (Trump 2016). Trump also stated that under his administration, the government would stop picking "winners and losers," a reference to tax breaks, grants, and subsidies provided to renewable energy companies. Republicans are generally critical of these practices, pointing in particular to the hundreds of millions of dollars in Recovery Act stimulus funds that went to the solar company Solyndra prior to its bankruptcy. Trump also promised to rescind the Clean Power Plan, "cancel" the Paris Climate Agreement, and cut U.S. payments to UN environmental programs dealing with global warming. Trump has also harshly criticized the U.S. Joint Climate Statement with China. Like other Republicans, Trump contended that the Paris agreement ties the United States to specific emissions reductions and energy policy reforms without corresponding Chinese commitments.

Further Reading

Carter, Jimmy. "State of the Union Address 1980." Jimmy Carter Presidential Library and Museum. Last modified March 30, 2016. http://www.jimmycarterlibrary.gov/docu ments/speeches/su80jec.phtml.

Center for American Progress. "Public Opinion on US Energy and Environmental Policy." Last modified December 2014. https://cdn.americanprogress.org/wp-content/uploads /2015/01/Public-Opinion-on-US-Energy-and-Environmental-Policy_slides.pdf.

Center for Local, State, and Urban Policy. "Widespread Public Support for Renewable Energy Mandates Despite Proposed Rollbacks." Last modified June 2015. http://closup .umich.edu/files/ieep-nsee-2015-renewable-portfolio-standards.pdf.

Clerk.house.gov. "Final Vote Results for Roll Call 250." Office of the Clerk of the U.S. House of Representatives. Last modified May 25, 2016. http://clerk.house.gov/evs/2016 /roll250.xml.

Democratic National Convention. "Democratic Platform Drafting Meeting Concludes." 2016. Last modified June 25, 2016. https://www.demconvention.com/news/democratic -platform-drafting-meeting-concludes/.

Gallup.com. "Energy: Gallup Historical Trends." Last modified March 12, 2016. http:// www.gallup.com/poll/2167/energy.aspx.

GovTrack.us. "H.R. 1 (111th): American Recovery and Reinvestment Act of 2009." Last modified January 28, 2009. https://www.govtrack.us/congress/votes/111-2009/h46.

Hart Research Associates. "Public Opinion on US Energy and Environmental Policy." Last modified December 2014. http://www.climateaccess.org/sites/default/files/Hart _Public%20opinion%20US%20energy%20policy.pdf.

Republican National Committee. "Republican Platform 2016." Last modified 2016. https:// prod-static-ngop-pbl.s3.amazonaws.com/media/documents/DRAFT_12_FINAL[1]-ben _1468872234.pdf.

Trump, Donald J. "An America First Energy Plan." Donald J. Trump for President. Last modified May 26, 2016. https://www.donaldjtrump.com/press-releases/an-america-first -energy-plan.

U.S. Energy Information Administration. "How Much Oil Is Consumed in the United States?" Last modified March 8, 2016. https://www.eia.gov/tools/faqs/faq.cfm?id=33&t=6.

U.S. Environmental Protection Agency. "Fact Sheet: Clean Power Plan by the Numbers." Last modified 2015. https://www.epa.gov/cleanpowerplan/fact-sheet-clean-power-plan -numbers.

U.S. Senate. "U.S. Senate: Roll Call Vote: An Original Bill to Provide for the Modernization of the Energy Policy of the United States, and for Other Purposes." Last modified April 20, 2016. http://www.senate.gov/legislative/LIS/roll_call_lists/roll_call_vote_cfm.cfm? congress=114&session=2&vote=00054.

White House. "U.S.–China Joint Announcement on Climate Change." Whitehouse.gov. Last modified November 11, 2014. https://www.whitehouse.gov/the-press-office/2014 /11/11/us-china-joint-announcement-climate-change.

Foreign Aid

At a Glance

In terms of constant dollars (dollars adjusted for inflation by year) the United States normally contributes $20–$40 billion in foreign aid to other countries on an annual basis. Most Americans believe that this is a significant portion of overall government spending, but in actuality, U.S. foreign aid is one of the most misunderstood areas of the federal budget. Generally, less than 1 percent of the total U.S. budget is spent on foreign assistance in any given year. However, the average American believes that the number is closer to 25 percent (DiJulio, Firth, and Brodie 2015). The consistent overestimation of the foreign aid budget makes it more difficult to gauge public opinion, regardless of its partisan components, on this issue. For example, when a survey respondent opines that the U.S. spends too much on foreign aid, it is possible that the answer would be different if the respondent knew the percentage of the U.S. budget actually allocated to foreign aid.

The partisan divide between Republicans and Democrats is clear and fairly wide on issues related to foreign aid provision and allocation. What is less clear is the way that these divisions translate into actual policy outcomes in terms of the amount and distribution of foreign aid.

According to many Republicans, U.S. foreign aid policy . . .

- Should be based on lower total amounts of foreign aid;
- Should focus on foreign aid for security in a way that enhances U.S. national interests;
- Should be based on the recognition that state-to-state foreign aid can lead to corruption;
- Should be based on public–private partnerships rather than state-to-state giving; and
- Should provide aid to faith-based groups and other nongovernmental organizations (NGOs) that act in a manner consistent with conservative principles.

According to many Democrats, U.S. foreign aid policy . . .

• Should be based on higher total amounts of aid, especially to more vulnerable populations;
• Should focus on increasing food security in developing countries;
• Should include debt relief for developing countries;
• Is a critical part of the effort to project "smart power"; and
• Can benefit the U.S. economy by cultivating markets for American goods.

———————

Overview

Although the provision of foreign aid has been an important part of U.S. foreign policy for more than a century, the first large-scale foreign aid program undertaken by the United States was the Marshall Plan, also known as the European Recovery Program, which was designed to help Europe rebuild from World War II. From 1947 through 1952, the United States provided more foreign aid, in constant dollar and as a percentage of gross domestic product (GDP) than at any point in its history (Tarnoff and Lawson 2011). Initial Marshall Plan aid was humanitarian in nature, and included food, fuel, and other basic supplies. Later, funds were used for investments in reindustrialization in 16 European nations. Although the plan was not without its critics, it passed both the House and the Senate with bipartisan support in 1948. The Marshall Plan was popular not only because of its humanitarian basis, but also because the rebuilding of Europe was seen as a developmental bulwark against communism.

In 1961, Congress passed and President Kennedy signed the Foreign Assistance Act of 1961. The act was designed to shape the provision of developmental assistance to developing countries, including the large number of countries that began to gain independence after World War II. Specifically, the act provided for the creation of the U.S. Agency for International Development (USAID), which continues to be a linchpin of U.S. developmental assistance efforts today. Although the vote on the 1961 act was closer than the vote on the European Recovery Program, the Foreign Assistance Act passed comfortably with bipartisan support in both the House and the Senate (Udall 1961). The Foreign Assistance Act itself was popular. However, foreign aid as a whole was not a budget priority. Foreign aid in constant dollar terms (adjusted for inflation) peaked in the Marshall Plan years, and then fell significantly. Since the late 1960s, the amount of foreign aid as a percentage of all federal spending has never risen above 1.5 percent.

The United States will spend $37.9 billion on foreign assistance in 2016 (ForeignAssistance.gov 2016). Although this is a larger amount, in dollar terms, than any other country, it falls below the target level of 0.07 percent of gross national income to development assistance established by the United Nations and the Organization for Economic Cooperation and Development in 1970.

John F. Kennedy Argues for the Creation of USAID

In March 1961, President Kennedy delivered a message to Congress concerning foreign aid. The message was both an argument for foreign aid as a critical tool of U.S. foreign policy and an argument for the development of a unified program for the provision of such aid. This program became the U.S. Agency for International Development (USAID), which continues to stand as the primary department through which American foreign aid is managed. Following is an excerpt from Kennedy's address:

> For no objective supporter of foreign aid can be satisfied with the existing program—actually a multiplicity of programs. Bureaucratically fragmented, awkward and slow, its administration is diffused over a haphazard and irrational structure covering at least four departments and several other agencies. The program is based on a series of legislative measures and administrative procedures conceived at different times and for different purposes, many of them now obsolete, inconsistent and unduly rigid and thus unsuited for our present needs and purposes. Its weaknesses have begun to undermine confidence in our effort both here and abroad.
>
> We live at a very special moment in history. The whole southern half of the world—Latin America, Africa, the Middle East, and Asia—are caught up in the adventures of asserting their independence and modernizing their old ways of life. These new nations need aid in loans and technical assistance . . . There is no escaping our obligations: our moral obligations as a wise leader and good neighbor in the interdependent community of free nations—our economic obligations as the wealthiest people in a world of largely poor people . . . and our political obligations as the single largest counter to the adversaries of freedom.

Source:
"John F. Kennedy: Special Message to the Congress on Foreign Aid." American Presidency Project. Last modified March 22, 1961. http://www.presidency.ucsb.edu/ws/?pid=8545

Foreign aid is classified by the U.S. government both by sector and by recipient. At the sectoral level, health aid receives the largest portion of spending ($9.3 billion for fiscal year 2016). The government will provide aid to over 60,000 programs in this sector over the course of the year, many of them designed to combat the spread of diseases such as HIV/AIDS and malaria. Often, the government provides the aid to local, national, and global nonprofit organizations that provide expertise in a particular area. For example, the largest single health project in FY 2015 was an antimalaria campaign in Mali where the funds were distributed to John Snow Inc., a nonprofit public health management and consulting organization (John Snow Inc. 2016).

The second-largest sector of foreign aid is "peace and security" ($8.8 billion for FY 2016). Security aid includes counterterrorism efforts in troubled countries such as Iraq and Afghanistan. Humanitarian assistance is the third-largest sector, receiving $5.6 billion for FY 2016 (ForeignAssistance.gov 2016). Currently, the largest single humanitarian assistance project is occurring in Syria, where a crisis relating to civil war, drought, and other factors has resulted in millions of refugees and displaced persons.

Israel is the largest single recipient of U.S. aid. Israel is scheduled to receive $3.1 billion in security aid in FY 2016. The United States has long been committed to helping Israel maintain a qualitative military edge (QME) in the Middle East based on perceived U.S. security interests and on the special historic relationship between the United States and Israel (U.S. Department of State 2011). Although partisan differences have emerged in recent years with regard to the U.S. relationship with Israel, the amount of foreign aid, to this point, has not been affected.

Over $1.5 billion in American foreign aid will be spent in Afghanistan in 2016, making the country the second largest recipient of U.S. foreign aid. Much of this aid is concentrated on the security sector, on projects related to counterterrorism, improvement of basic security infrastructure, and combating narcotics trafficking. Though the United States has ended its formal combat role in Afghanistan, the need for foreign assistance for Afghan security operations is anticipated to remain high for the foreseeable future. The third largest recipient of U.S. foreign aid is Egypt. Although the relationship between the United States and Egypt has become strained by issues related to the Arab Spring and the countercoup in its aftermath, the United States has been committed to providing significant foreign aid to Egypt ever since the country agreed to make peace with Israel in 1978. As long as the government of Abdel Fattah el-Sisi (also known simply as Sisi) continues to honor its peace and mutual recognition treaty with Israel, it is likely that high levels of U.S. aid will continue.

Republicans on U.S. Foreign Aid Policy

Although wide partisan gaps exist within certain areas of the debate about foreign aid, there are also areas of relative partisan consensus. For example, as noted above, security aid to Israel has remained at similar levels regardless of which party controls Congress or the presidency. Whether the source of the consensus is agreement on the geostrategic importance of Israel, the strength of the pro-Israel lobby in the United States, cultural or political similarity, or some combination, at present, foreign aid to Israel is not a salient partisan issue. In the same sense, aid to Afghanistan and Iraq, two countries occupied for a time by the United States after the terrorist attacks of 9/11, is also not a partisan issue. In spite of concerns about corruption, there exists a basic agreement that foreign aid, especially security aid, is required if there is to be any hope of stabilization in the two countries. The resurgence of the Taliban in Afghanistan and the rise of the Islamic State in Iraq will likely result in continued high levels of security aid to these parts of the world without a significant amount of partisan debate.

Despite these areas of consensus, however, Republicans are more likely than Democrats to oppose other foreign aid, both conceptually and operationally. In the

2012 Republican Party platform, for example, the GOP explicitly stated that "limiting foreign aid spending helps keep taxes lower, which frees more resources in the private and charitable sectors, whose giving tends to be more effective and efficient" (Republican National Committee 2012). The 2012 and 2016 platforms also call for foreign aid to be based on the Millennium Challenge Corporation (MCC) model. Under this model, countries compete for foreign aid based on transparency and good governance. The goal is to decrease corruption by holding developing states accountable for achieving measurable goals. The model also introduces the private sector into the process by placing corporate leaders onto the MCC board. The MCC normally receives funding of between $800 million and $1 billion per year.

Within the general public, the partisan gap related to foreign aid policy is even larger. According to a 2013 Pew Research Center poll, 70 percent of Republicans favor decreasing the total amount of foreign aid while only 7 percent favor increasing aid. By contrast, 25 percent of self-identified Democrats favor decreasing foreign aid while one-third favor increasing foreign aid to the world's needy (Pew Research Center 2013). In addition, only 7 percent of Republicans within the general public believe that foreign aid to developing countries is a very effective way to achieve U.S. foreign policy goals (Chicago Council on Global Affairs 2015). Overall, public opinion among Republicans is closely tied to broader public opinion on foreign aid. During the 2012–2013 debate over budget sequestration, most Americans favored cutting the budget. However, Americans also opposed cutting most specific areas of the budget. During this debate, the only area of the budget that over 40 percent of Americans agreed should be cut was foreign aid (Pew Research Center 2013).

Tracking Republican and Democrat congressional positions on foreign aid can be difficult. Most foreign aid is considered under the Foreign Operations Bill. However, this bill is normally passed as part of a consolidated appropriations process, and the specific issue of foreign aid is often considered at the committee level via voice vote. In 2015 the House Appropriations Committee proposed a cut of 13.6 percent to the Foreign Operations budget. However, the 2015 Foreign Operations budget, passed as part of the Bipartisan Budget Act of 2015, contained a 10 percent increase in foreign aid over FY 2014, which brought the amount of foreign aid to 2011 levels in constant dollar terms (though overall aid fell slightly as a result of cuts in oversees contingent operations such as Iraq and Afghanistan). The Bipartisan Budget Act of 2015 passed in the House by a vote of 266–167. All Democrats voted yes on the measure. They were joined by 79 Republicans, who crossed party lines and voted yes (govtrack.us 2015). Most Republicans (167) voted against the bill. A similar pattern occurred in the Senate with unanimous Democratic supported added to minority Republican support to pass the bill. As part of the budget process, Republican senator Rand Paul proposed an amendment that would have cut the foreign aid budget by 50 percent and added this money to the defense budget. The amendment failed by a bipartisan vote of 4–96 (U.S. Senate 2015).

Republicans Ted Cruz and Donald Trump Call for Sweeping Changes to Foreign Aid

In 2016, Republican presidential candidates Senator Ted Cruz and real estate executive Donald Trump sharply criticized American allocations of foreign aid. In his announcement of his candidacy, Trump argued that "it is necessary that we invest in our infrastructure, stop sending foreign aid to countries that hate us and use that money to rebuild our tunnels, roads, bridges and schools—and nobody can do that better than me." For his part, Senator Cruz claimed that "we need to stop sending foreign aid to nations that hate us. Just two weeks ago President Obama cancelled White House tours and sent $250 million to Egypt with no conditions, no strings attached, nothing focused on U.S. national security—simply wrote a check." From the perspective of both candidates, U.S. foreign aid should be reserved for close allies such as Israel.

Sources:

"CPAC 2013 Ted Cruz Keynote Address Transcript." P2016 Race for the White House—by Democracy in Action. Last modified 2015. http://www.p2016.org/photos13/cpac13/cruz031613spt.html.

Trump, Donald J. "Donald J Trump Presidential Announcement." Make America Great Again! Donald J. Trump for President. Last modified June 16, 2015. http://www.donaldjtrump.com/media/donald-j-trump-presidential-announcement.

Senator Marco Rubio differs from many of his Republican colleagues in that he is a proponent of foreign aid, even to countries such as Syria and Egypt. In a 2012 press release on foreign policy priorities, Rubio argued that foreign aid to Syria would help weaken Iran and provide a basis for U.S. influence in the event that the Assad regime is successfully deposed (Rubio 2012). Rubio is also a sponsor of the Senate version of the Foreign Aid Transparency and Accountability Act of 2015, which would require benchmarking of goals related to the provision of foreign aid, as well as more readily available information online in a form accessible to the general public. The bill is cosponsored by Democratic senator Ben Cardin of Maryland.

Democrats on U.S. Foreign Aid Policy

The 2012 Democratic Party platform only mentioned foreign aid once, in the context of combating human trafficking (Democratic National Committee 2012). The sections of the 2012 Democratic Party platform devoted to international issues are focused instead on ending the wars in Iraq and Afghanistan, as well as promoting trade and avoiding economic crises in the developing world. The lack of prioritization of foreign aid is consistent with the 2008 platform, which only mentioned aid twice—once in the context of streamlining USAID and once in the context of

Senator Marco Rubio Makes the Conservative Case for Foreign Aid

In a 2012 speech at the Brookings Institution, Republican senator Marco Rubio defended the use of foreign aid as a valuable tool of statecraft:

> Faced with historic deficits and dangerous national debt, there's been increasing talk of reducing our foreign aid budget, but we need to remember that these international coalitions that we have the opportunity to lead are not just military ones, they can also be humanitarian ones. In every region of the world, we should always search for ways to use US aid and humanitarian assistance to strengthen our influence, the effectiveness of our leadership, and the service of our interests and ideals.
>
> When done so effectively, in partnership with the private sector, with faith-based organizations and with our allies, foreign aid is a very cost-effective way, not only to export our values and our example, but to advance our security and our economic interests. One of the programs that I am proudest of is the effort that began under President George W. Bush with robust congressional support, and it's continued under President Obama, and that's to combat AIDS in Africa.

Source:

Rubio, Marco. "Is the American World Order Sustainable and Necessary in the 21st Century?" Brookings Institution, April 25, 2012. http://www.brookings.edu/~/media/events/2012/4/25-rubio/20120425_rubio.pdf%5C.

making sure that foreign assistance includes measures to ensure accountability. Coupled with Republican Party concerns about the value and effectiveness of government spending on foreign aid, and lower taxes, the lack of emphasis on foreign aid in the Democratic Party platform may partially explain why the U.S. foreign aid budget has been flat or slightly declining for decades. The 2016 Democratic Party platform does not mention foreign aid at all. However, it mentions developmental and humanitarian assistance to a variety of contexts, including protecting refugees, promoting LGBT rights, and providing access to safe and legal abortion services (Democratic National Committee 2016).

The lack of emphasis on foreign aid within the Democratic Party platform is at least partially in line with public opinion on foreign assistance among self-identified Democrats. As mentioned above, far fewer Democrats than Republicans are interested in cutting foreign aid. It is also the case, however, that a majority of Democrats are not in favor of increasing the amount of foreign aid provided to developing countries (Pew Research Center 2013). It is also worth noting that, though the gap is smaller for Democrats than for Republicans, Democrats are more likely to believe that maintaining U.S. military superiority is a more effective way to achieve international policy goals than is foreign aid (Chicago Council on Global Affairs 2015).

One of the widest partisan gaps related to foreign aid spending relates to health policy. Twice as many Democrats as Republicans believe that the United States spends too little promoting public health in developing countries (Kaiser Family Foundation 2013). Overall, it appears that both Democrats and Republicans support foreign aid for international public health purposes. Majorities of both Democrats and Republicans believe that the amount of spending in this area is either too little or about right (Kaiser Family Foundation 2013). This partial convergence of public opinion may explain why the United States spends more on foreign aid related to public health projects than it does on any other sector.

The difficulty in tracking partisan gaps in Congress concerning foreign aid has already been noted. The position of the executive branch, including President Obama and Secretary of State John Kerry, is much easier to isolate. President Obama and Secretary Kerry have been consistent defenders of foreign aid. They have defended foreign aid as an effective tool to address global problems before they escalate to the point that they necessitate more costly U.S. military spending in the future. Obama has also argued that cuts to foreign aid, which makes up about 1 percent of the U.S. budget, would not be an effective way to cut the deficit (Holden 2010). During 2013 remarks at the National Defense University, Obama argued that foreign aid should not be viewed as charity. Instead, the president posited that it was "fundamental to our national security. And it's fundamental to any sensible long-term strategy to battle extremism" (White House 2013). For his part, Secretary of State John Kerry noted before the House Appropriations Committee on Foreign Relations that foreign policy expenditures account for only about 1 percent of the entire federal budget: "That's what we put into foreign policy. Between USAID and the State Department in our general operations you're talking about $50.3 billion, and that 1 percent, my friends, I promise you will account for more than 50 percent of the history of this era when it's written" (U.S. Department of State 2015).

Both of the major candidates for the 2016 Democratic Party presidential nomination, Senator Bernie Sanders and former Secretary of State Hillary Clinton, count themselves as proponents of foreign aid. In a 2014 interview, Clinton stated that foreign aid should make up closer to the 25 percent of the budget that the average American thinks it does than to the 1 percent of the budget that is actually spent on foreign aid programs (Realclearpolitics.com 2014). Of course, Clinton never requested a foreign aid budget that large while serving as secretary of state, suggesting that the 25 percent figure was designed more to highlight the utility of aid than to push for such a significant increase in funding. Clinton also backed the creation of the International Aid Transparency Initiative, designed to better track aid flows and assistance outcomes. Senator Sanders, while more known for his initiatives on domestic policy, is also an advocate for increased foreign aid to developing countries. He has sponsored legislation to increase food aid to sub-Saharan Africa and to help meet the United Nations Millennium Development Goals. Both Clinton and Sanders have pledged that, if elected, they would overturn a ban on the use of foreign aid for abortions in the developing world. Sanders had argued that the ban should be removed altogether, while Clinton has argued that the ban should be lifted in cases of rape, incest, or the life of the mother (Bassett and Grim 2016).

Although there is a clear partisan gap in overall support for foreign aid, it is unclear if actual aid levels are responsive to the gap. As President Obama has pointed out, foreign aid is not a popular part of the budget, among the general public or within the legislature. While the data points to more popularity among Democrats, a majority of Americans appear opposed to increasing the foreign aid budget. Once adjusted for inflation, foreign aid had very rarely exceeded $35 billion at any point since the end of Marshall Plan. One of these exceptions occurred during the Reagan administration. A second exception occurred during the George W. Bush administration, after the invasion of Iraq and Afghanistan in the wake of the terrorist attacks of September 11, 2001. Foreign aid during the Obama administration, in part because of the sequestration process, has remained largely flat. One would expect that, if partisanship and the level of foreign aid were related, the level of foreign aid would be higher during Democratic administrations or periods of Democratic congressional control. That fact that this is not the case would seem to indicate, that, while foreign aid is more popular among Democrats than Republicans, the issue is not salient enough for periods of partisan control to translate into major increases in foreign aid.

Further Reading

Bassett, Laura, and Ryan Grim. "Hillary Clinton and Bernie Sanders Make Major Pledge on Abortion Policy." Huffington Post. February 11, 2016. http://www.huffingtonpost.com/entry/hillary-clinton-bernie-sanders-helms-amendment-abortion_us_56bcabdfe4b08ffac124143b.

Chicago Council on Global Affairs. "America Divided: Political Partisanship and US Foreign Policy." Last modified 2015. http://www.thechicagocouncil.org/sites/default/files/CCGA_PublicSurvey2015.pdf.

"CPAC 2013 Ted Cruz Keynote Address Transcript." P2016 Race for the White House—by Democracy in Action. Last modified 2015. http://www.p2016.org/photos13/cpac13/cruz031613spt.html.

Democratic National Committee. "The 2012 Democratic Platform." Last modified 2012. https://www.democrats.org/party-platform.

Democratic National Committee. "2016 Democratic Party Platform." Last modified July 21, 2016. https://www.demconvention.com/wp-content/uploads/2016/07/Democratic-Party-Platform-7.21.16-no-lines.pdf.

DiJulio, Bianca, Jamie Firth, and Mollyann Brodie. "Data Note: Americans' Views on the U.S. Role in Global Health." Kaiser Family Foundation. Last modified February 23, 2015. http://kff.org/global-health-policy/poll-finding/data-note-americans-views-on-the-u-s-role-in-global-health/.

ForeignAssistance.gov. "ForeignAssistance.gov." Last modified 2016. http://beta.foreignassistance.gov/.

Gharib, Malaka. "President Obama Defends Foreign Aid in Google+ Hangout." ONE. Last modified February 1, 2012. http://www.one.org/us/2012/02/01/president-obama -defends-foreign-aid-in-google-hangout/.

GovTrack.us. "H.R. 1314: Trade Act of 2015." Last modified 2015. https://www.govtrack .us/congress/votes/114-2015/h579.

"Hillary Clinton: I Would Have 'Loved' A 20-Fold Increase in Foreign Aid Budget." *RealClearPolitics—Opinion, News, Analysis, Video and Polls.* April 3, 2014. Accessed March 8, 2016. http://www.realclearpolitics.com/video/2014/04/03/hillary_clinton_i_would _have_loved_a_20-fold_increase_in_foreign_aid_budget.html.

Holden, Donna. "CNN Fact Check: Obama Discusses Foreign Aid and Pork Projects— CNN Political Ticker—CNN.com Blogs." CNN Political Ticker. Last modified February 3, 2010. http://politicalticker.blogs.cnn.com/2010/02/03/cnn-fact-check-obama-discusses -foreign-aid-and-pork-projects/.

John Snow Inc. "Who We Are—About Us." Last modified 2016. http://www.jsi.com/JSIIn ternet/About/who-we-are.cfm.

Kaiser Family Foundation. "2013 Survey of Americans on the U.S. Role in Global Health." Last modified November 7, 2013. http://kff.org/global-health-policy/poll-finding/2013 -survey-of-americans-on-the-u-s-role-in-global-health/.

Pew Research Center. "Wide Partisan Gap Exists over U.S. Aid to World's Needy." Last modified March 13, 2013. http://www.pewresearch.org/daily-number/wide-partisan-gap -exists-over-u-s-aid-to-worlds-needy/.

Pew Research Center for the People and the Press. "As Sequester Deadline Looms, Little Support for Cutting Most Programs." Last modified February 13, 2013. http://www .people-press.org/2013/02/22/as-sequester-deadline-looms-little-support-for-cutting -most-programs/.

Republican National Committee. "2012 Republican Platform." Last modified 2012. https:// prod-static-ngop-pbl.s3.amazonaws.com/docs/2012GOPPlatform.pdf.

Rubio, Marco. "Press Releases—Newsroom—U.S. Senator for Florida, Marco Rubio." Rubio.senate.gov. Last modified April 25, 2012. http://www.rubio.senate.gov/public /index.cfm/press-releases?ID=d422e875-c1b9-4193-a0ab-9e09a7287d4f.

Shapiro, Andrew J. "Ensuring Israel's Qualitative Military Edge." U.S. Department of State. Last modified November 4, 2011. http://www.state.gov/t/pm/rls/rm/176684.htm.

Tarnoff, Curt, and Marian L. Lawson. "Foreign Aid: An Introduction to U.S. Programs and Policy." Federation of American Scientists. Last modified February 10, 2011. https:// www.fas.org/sgp/crs/row/R40213.pdf.

Trump, Donald J. "Donald J Trump Presidential Announcement." Make America Great Again! | Donald J. Trump for President. Last modified June 16, 2015. http://www .donaldjtrump.com/media/donald-j-trump-presidential-announcement.

Udall, Morris K. "Special Report: The Foreign Assistance Act of 1961." University of Arizona Libraries. Last modified 1961. http://www.library.arizona.edu/exhibits/udall/special /foreign.html.

U.S. Department of State. "Budget Hearing for the Department of State." Last modified February 25, 2015. http://www.state.gov/secretary/remarks/2015/02/237917.htm.

U.S. Senate. "U.S. Senate: Roll Call Vote 97." Last modified 2015. http://www.senate.gov /legislative/LIS/roll_call_lists/roll_call_vote_cfm.cfm?congress=114&session=1&v ote=00097.

White House. "Remarks by the President at the National Defense University." Whitehouse.gov. Last modified May 23, 2013. https://www.whitehouse.gov/the-press-office/2013/05/23 /remarks-president-national-defense-university.

Human Rights

At a Glance

Democrats and Republicans have historically shared a great deal in common when it comes to promoting human rights as a component of U.S. foreign policy. In the realm of public opinion, Democrats and Republicans place a similar, though not identical, emphasis on the issue. Recent presidents have acted similarly, though, once again, not identically, when it comes to trade-offs between the promotion of human rights and other geostrategic considerations. Even Congress, where party polarization is perhaps most evident, has been relatively unified on recent issues related to human rights. Partisan differences do exist, however, especially when it comes to which human rights are most worthy of promotion, as well as the relative priority of the issue.

According to many Republicans . . .

- The most important human rights are those that relate to civic and political activity, such as the right to vote and freedom from arbitrary detention;
- Although it is important to promote human rights, other concerns, such as protecting U.S. interests abroad, are often more important;
- The United States should use economic leverage to improve human rights in places like China, Cuba, and Iran;
- Foreign aid should be directly tied to the promotion of human rights unless there is an overriding strategic interest associated with the aid in question; and
- Promoting human rights as a matter of U.S. foreign policy should not focus on LGBTQ issues.

According to many Democrats . . .

- Economic rights, such as the right to adequate shelter and health care, are of critical importance;
- Protecting the rights of refugees under international and domestic law is a key foreign policy priority;

- Diplomacy should be used to promote human rights; economic coercion may be appropriate, but it is not the superior first option;
- Foreign aid should be directly tied to the promotion of human rights unless there is an overriding strategic interest associated with the aid in question, or there is a significant humanitarian crisis in the country in question; and
- Promoting the fundamental rights of LGBTQ individuals should be an important part of U.S. foreign human rights policy.

Overview

The United States has had a complex, and often contradictory, history with respect to the promotion of human rights as a part of its foreign policy. On one hand, the United States played a significant role in the development of the post–World War II human rights order. First Lady Eleanor Roosevelt, for example, coordinated the effort that ultimately led to the adoption of the Universal Declaration of Human Rights (UDHR) in 1948. The UDHR enumerates traditional individual-level civil and political rights, such as life, liberty, security, and equality before the law. The UDHR also mentions several rights that would be somewhat more controversial (at least in practice) if proposed today, such as protections against unemployment, equal pay for equal work, favorable remuneration, and the right to join a labor union (United Nations 2016). The UDHR has been influential in the creation of subsequent, more binding, human rights law, including the European Convention on Human Rights.

At the same time, international human rights concerns have often been subordinated to other U.S. geopolitical concerns. During the Cold War, for example, the United States was generally more concerned with preventing the spread of Communism than it was with promoting human rights. This led the country into "uncomfortable" international human rights positions, such as supporting the Apartheid government in South Africa on the grounds that the opposition, led by the African National Congress, had too many ties to the global Communist movement. Even as dissatisfaction with Apartheid grew, and the U.S. Congress passed the Comprehensive Anti-Apartheid Act over the veto of Republican president Ronald Reagan in 1986, the United States never fully implemented its provisions for fear of destabilizing the South African government to the advantage of the Soviet Union. The United States was also known for supporting authoritarian regimes in Latin American countries such as Brazil and Argentina in order to forestall possible experimentation with popular (though not always democratic) socialist governance. In addition, the United States supported a dictatorial regime in its battle with a popular, though also dictatorial, regime in Vietnam in the 1950s–1970s, and was willing to forgo a push for democracy in the Korean Peninsula in the early 1950s in order to avoid Communist rule over all of Korea. All of these actions, whether justified by strategic reality or not, fly in the face of the UDHR's commitment to "democratic society."

The United States has also been slow to ratify a variety of international human rights instruments. For example, the United States did not ratify the International Covenant on Civil and Political Rights, which was opened for signature in 1966 and entered into force in 1976, until 1992. Even then, the United States ratified the treaty with several reservations (areas where the terms of the treaty will not apply) that limited the practical impact of the agreement. The United States is the only country not to ratify the Convention on the Rights of the Child. Opponents of the agreement in the United States argue that the convention would violate U.S. sovereignty by forcing key changes to domestic law. For example, the treaty would hypothetically prevent children from being tried and sentenced as adults, something that is allowed in the United States under state and federal law.

Although U.S. hesitance to sign many international human rights agreements has no direct impact on U.S. promotion of human rights, there are several indirect effects. For example, countries that are known to regularly violate individual human rights can claim that the United States lacks the moral authority to pressure countries to respect the rights of children when it refuses to accede to the relevant international treaty. The most common American response to such lines of attack is that U.S. federal and state law provide protections that in many (though not all) cases exceed those provided under international law.

In the post 9/11 era, the United States has had a mixed record when it comes to promoting international respect for individual human rights. In 2010, the National Security Strategy of the United States was revised to include the promotion of fundamental human rights. In some cases, the United States, consistent with the Foreign Assistance Act of 1961, has withheld some foreign aid from countries, including significant allies such as Mexico, and, for a brief period, Egypt. At the same time, the United States continues to provide aid to, and is generally hesitant to pressure, countries with poor or questionable human rights records in cases where those countries are seen as strategically important in the struggle against international terrorism or in other policy realms. For example, the United States continues to provide aid and other forms of diplomatic support to Saudi Arabia, an autocratic state with a variety of limits on individual human rights based on gender, sexual orientation, and legal-religious status. Critics of U.S. policy point out that the United States is willing to levy sanctions against Iran, a country involved in many of the same activities because it is not an ally of the United States. Proponents of separating human rights promotion from other decisions point out that Iran is a U.S. designated state sponsor of terror, making it, in the eyes of U.S. policy makers, qualitatively different from Saudi Arabia.

There are also cases where human rights concerns have been presented as a justification for military action in service of a larger goal. Such was the case in 2003, when the administration of Republican president George W. Bush carried out a military invasion of Iraq. The invasion was primarily based on administration claims that Iraq possessed weapons of mass destruction and had ties to Al Qaeda, but it was also justified with reference to Saddam Hussein's treatment of

Shia Muslims and Kurds in the country. The human rights justification became more prominent as it became apparent that Iraq no longer possessed weapons of mass destruction.

The United States also has an ambiguous human rights relationship with China. In the period after the Tiananmen Square incident (some sources refer to the incident as a massacre, while others do not) of 1989, in which peaceful protests in China were forcibly put down by the Chinese military, the United States began to apply more pressure to China to improve its human rights record. Estimates of the number of protesters who died in Tiananmen Square and the immediate aftermath vary from a few hundred to over 2,000 (Faison 1999). Human rights organizations such as Amnesty International place the estimated death toll much closer to 10,000. China's most favored nation status, now known as permanent normal trade relations (PNTR), was revoked by the administration of Republican president George H. W. Bush, resulting in more expensive and less competitive Chinese imports in certain sectors. However, the United States eventually established PNTR with China and has had little success pushing a human rights agenda with the world's second largest economy (by purchasing power).

Democrats on Human Rights

The 2016 Democratic Party platform mentions human rights 12 times. The first mention refers directly to LGBT rights, a relatively new focus for Democrats. The call for integration of LGBT rights into U.S. foreign policy decisions coincides with the earlier decision by Democrats, as a party, to push for marriage equality and equality of opportunity for transgender Americans. The platform applauds the Obama administration for offering refugee status to people claiming a legitimate fear of persecution based on sexual orientation. Operationalization of this platform plank can be difficult, as illustrated below. The platform also calls out individual countries for abuses of human rights, including Iran and North Korea. In the case of Iran, the platform is careful to differentiate between sanctions relief that Iran received as a result of its nuclear agreement (see Iran entry) and sanctions levied as a result of human rights abuses and Iranian sponsorship of terrorism. On North Korea, the platform attempts to draw a distinction between Democrats, who condemn and sanction North Korean human rights abuses, and Republican nominee Donald J. Trump, who, in the words of the platform "praises North Korea's Dictator" (Democratic National Committee 2016). Finally, the party platform ties the promotion of democracy and good governance to human rights promotion. Democrats promise to help bolster civil society (voluntary organizations that seek to enhance the public good) in countries around the world.

Democrats in the general public tend to place a higher priority on promoting human rights in the context of foreign policy than do Republicans. However, the gaps are not always significant. It is also the case that survey results in this area appear to vary depending on the context of the survey. In 2016, for example, the

Kaiser Family Foundation found that promoting human rights was the second-most important foreign policy priority, behind combating terrorism (Kaiser Family Foundation 2016). Beyond terrorism, however, the survey tended to focus on social and humanitarian issues, which is intuitive given the Kaiser Family Foundations' focus on humanitarian issues. The survey, however, did follow conventional sampling and statistical inference techniques. During the last Pew foreign policy priorities survey in 2013, only 33 percent of Americans identified promoting human rights in other countries as a top priority (Stokes 2013). A Gallup poll from the same year found that, among Democrats, promoting human rights is a significant priority. Sixty-four percent of Democrats considered promoting and defending human rights in other countries to be a "very important" U.S. foreign policy goal (Saad 2013). The 2015 Pew Global Attitudes survey found that a majority of Democrats (51 percent) are specifically concerned about human rights in China (Pew Research Center 2015).

One of the most difficult aspects of promoting human rights abroad is the operationalization of what seems to be a worthy goal. As a nonparty to many international human rights treaties, the U.S. has difficulty using the measures in such instruments to promote human rights. One way to promote human rights, and one of the few means available to Congress, is to withhold foreign aid or impose sanctions on countries with significant human rights abuses. For example, Congress has cut security aid to Mexico in recent years in part because of concerns about repressive human rights practices. It is virtually impossible to determine, however, what portion of the aid cut is due to human rights concerns and what portions may be due to other factors. It is also virtually impossible to examine partisanship as it related to human rights voting in the context of foreign aid because most of the foreign aid budget is passed in a single resolution rather than country by country. What we do know is that Congress has expressed concerns about recent human rights practices in Mexico and that it has voted for foreign aid resolutions that have provided less foreign security aid to Mexico (Planas 2015). In 2016, Congress passed, and President Obama signed, the North Korean Sanctions and Policy Enhancement Act. The act includes stronger primary sanctions (those directly against North Korea and the Kim Regime), as well as secondary sanctions against businesses working with North Korea. One of the rationales provided for the legislation is North Korea's poor human rights record. However, there are other reasons cited, such as North Korea's nuclear and ballistic missile programs, making it difficult to refer to the act as human rights legislation. The act did pass 96–0 in the Senate and 418–2 in the House (Congress.gov 2016).

Also in 2016, the Senate passed, by acclamation, the Global Magnitsky Human Rights Accountability Act. The act allows the president to impose sanctions on individuals and countries that commit serious human rights abuses, such as torture. The act provides for mostly targeted sanctions, which are designed to punish leaders and force compliance with human rights norms without hurting ordinary people within the target state. Although the implementation language is broad, the act is aimed specifically at government officials who target human rights advocates for abuse as the advocates investigate abuses within a given country. The legislation is also designed to allow the United States to punish states for targeting domestic whistle-blowers highlighting corruption among government officials. The act is named after Sergei Magnitsky, who was imprisoned and mysteriously died in custody after being convicted of tax fraud in Russia. Most external observers, including many human rights groups, viewed the charges as fabricated. Magnitsky, an auditor by trade, had discovered what he believed was massive government fraud, including embezzlement and tax fraud, among government officials at multiple levels. An earlier version of the legislation, only applying to Russia, passed Congress and was signed into law in 2012. The current broader legislation is making its way through the House of Representatives.

Congressional Democrats have at times been critical of what they perceive as a willingness by the Obama administration to sacrifice some human rights concerns in order to advance other foreign policy priorities. For example, after a 2009 coup in Honduras resulted in the ouster of duly elected president Manuel Zelaya, Democrats in Congress, including former Congressional Black Caucus Chair Barbara Lee, called on the president to withhold economic aid until the human rights situation that accompanied the coup improved. Obama was hesitant to officially declare the event a coup, which would have required withholding most financial aid under U.S. law. Ultimately, the United States withheld some aid, but not all of what would have been withheld had an official coup finding been rendered.

For his part, President Obama has defended U.S. human rights policy as one that pursues engagement over punishment. For example, in May 2016, Obama visited Vietnam, where the U.S. fought and lost a war designed to prevent the spread of Communism, but not to promote fundamental civil and political rights. Though Vietnam continues to deny these rights, the Obama administration announced the decision to lift the arms embargo against the country, which has been in effect since the Vietnam War. Obama was criticized for what some perceived as providing a reward for continued human rights abuses, including arbitrary detention. Obama argued, however, that the move would pay future human rights dividends by promoting a closer relationship between Vietnam and the United States. Obama faced similar criticism when he announced the resumption of diplomatic relations with Cuba in December 2014. For this part, President Obama believes that opening diplomatic relations with Cuba is a more productive way to pressure the country to improve its human rights record. Indeed, Obama did mention the importance of universal human rights, including the right to vote, the speech he delivered in Havana in 2016.

The 2016 Democratic presidential nominee (and former secretary of state) Hillary Clinton has made similar arguments, while also speaking out on the importance of guaranteeing human rights for people regardless of gender, race, or sexual orientation. In 1995, at the United Nations Conference on Human Rights in Beijing, China, Clinton delivered her oft-quoted "Women's Rights Are Human Rights" speech. Clinton has also argued that the United States needs to push more force-fully for the full integration of LGBTQ rights into the global human rights frame-work. However, Clinton has drawn criticism from the right and the left on human rights issues. Republicans have argued that Clinton did not advocate forcefully enough for persecuted Christians in Iraq and Syria during her tenure as secretary of state. She also faced criticism during her tenure at the State Department for not doing enough to combat human rights abuses in states such as Saudi Arabia, which has a close relationship with the United States.

Republicans on Human Rights

The 2016 Republican Party platform mentions human rights eight times, begin-ning with the call to "adopt a whole of government approach to protect funda-mental freedoms globally, one where pressing human rights and rule of law issues are integrated at every appropriate level of our bilateral relationships and strategic decision making" (Republican National Committee 2016). The platform goes on to commend Taiwan for its progress on human rights, a stance taken in part to draw a contrast between the democratic government of Taiwan, with which the U.S. has informal relations, and the government of China, which has a poor human rights record. Republican also place priority on continuing improvement of the human rights situation in sub-Saharan Africa, and promise continued economic devel-opment assistance, a bipartisan stance that was a source of foreign policy unity between Democrats and Republicans during the George W. Bush administration (see sub-Saharan Africa entry).

Republicans also use the platform to criticize multilateral institutions, espe-cially the United Nations, in the context of human rights. The platform criticizes the UN Human Rights Council for allowing member states (countries) with poor human rights records to serve. Republicans are also critical of the UN Popula-tion Fund, which promotes family planning services, including abortion. Repub-licans also criticize Democratic Party nominee Hillary Clinton for arguing that human rights concerns at the time have to be subordinated to economic and security concerns. Republicans attempt to create a contrast in this area, arguing that human rights concerns, including adequate protection of civil liberties, are part of the promotion of economic development, environmental protection, and human security.

Among the general public, the promotion of human rights as part of U.S. for-eign policy is not a high salience issue. Most Americans are more concerned with domestic economic issues than they are with foreign policy issues. Within the realm of foreign policy, security issues, especially terrorism, are more salient to most Americans than are "soft-power" issues like the environment and the promo-tion of human rights. There are exceptions, however. For example majorities of both Democrats (51 percent) and Republicans (55 percent) are concerned about the human rights situation in China (Pew Research Center 2015). Delving further into the numbers, however, reveals an interesting partisan difference even in an area of relative similarity. For Democrats, human rights are the third-rated (out of eight) areas of concern. Only U.S. debt held by China and U.S. jobs moving to China are more worrisome to Democrats. To Republicans, human rights issues are tied for the second-least important concern, trailed only by China-Taiwan relations. Put another way, Republican are more concerned with Human rights in China than are Democrats, but they are much more concerned, relatively speaking, with other issues in U.S. – China relations. A minority of Republicans (44 percent) list promoting human rights in other countries as a "very important" U.S. foreign policy objective (Saad 2013).

As stated above, congressional Republicans and Democrats have been unified in their condemnation of human rights abuses in North Korea and Russia. These are not "costly" human rights condemnations in the sense that the United States currently has no relationship with North Korea and a poor relationship with Russia. Partisan fault lines do emerge on human rights issues within the halls of Congress, however.

For example, Republicans in Congress have been highly critical of the Obama administration decision to normalize relations with Cuba. Republicans argue that Cuba remains a systematic violator of fundamental human rights and a state sponsor of terrorism (which Republicans group among human rights issues). Several key members of the Republican Party stated their opposition to Obama's normalization of relations with Cuba, his efforts to ease the embargo, and his decision to remove Cuba from the list of state sponsors of terror. Florida Representative Mario Diaz-Balart commemorated the one-year anniversary of President Obama's decision to begin normalization of relations with Cuba by stating:

> And what have the U.S., and the Cuban people, gained from President Obama's policy? Just take a look at the facts. Political arrests totaled 1,447 in November, the highest monthly tally this year, and there have been 7,686 political arrests this year to date. More than half of the Obama-Castro so-called "list of 53" political prisoners have been re-arrested in the past year. Desperate Cuban refugees are fleeing the regime in ever greater numbers. Meanwhile, the Castro regime is sending members of its military to prop up fellow dictator Assad in Syria and smuggling military weapons to rogue international actors. (Diaz-Balart 2015)

Republicans in Congress were also highly critical of the president's 2016 trip to Cuba, arguing that Obama failed to take a significant enough stance on issues related to human rights. President Donald Trump has not articulated an overall human rights policy in the context of broader foreign policy. However, he has been vocal in denouncing human rights abuses in China. Trump has also argued that U.S. security must be prioritized over the rights of refugees, especially Muslim refugees, under U.S. and international law. Trump has argued that it is virtually impossible to vet refugees from some war-torn areas like Syria. Trump has also been criticized for his position on human rights from both the right and the left. His position on refugees, which would bar refugees from entire countries from entering the United States, has been criticized by some Republicans as reactionary and too broad. UN High Commissioner for Human Rights Zeid Ra'ad Al Hussein grouped Trump with the European far-right in a 2016 speech arguing that they tell half-truths and oversimplify issues related to refugees in a way that emboldens the population with xenophobic rhetoric (Beckwith 2016).

Further Reading

Beckwith, Ryan T. "Donald Trump: United Nations Human Rights Official Speech." TIME.com. Last modified September 7, 2016. http://time.com/4481911/donald-trump-united-nations-speech/.

Congress.gov. "Actions—H.R.757—114th Congress (2015–2016): North Korea Sanctions and Policy Enhancement Act of 2016." Library of Congress. Last modified 2016. https://www.congress.gov/bill/114th-congress/house-bill/757/all-actions?overview=closed&q=%7B%22roll-call-vote%22%3A%22all%22%7D.

Democratic National Committee. "2016 Democratic Party Platform." Last modified 2016. https://www.demconvention.com/wp-content/uploads/2016/07/Democratic-Party-Platform-7.21.16-no-lines.pdf.

Diaz-Balart, Mario. "One Year Later: The Results of Obama's Concessions to the Castros." Congressman Mario Diaz-Balart. Last modified December 17, 2015. https://mariodiazbalart.house.gov/media-center/press-releases/one-year-later-the-results-of-obama-s-concessions-to-the-castros.

Faison, Seth. "The Persistent Mystery: How Many Died in 1989?—*The New York Times*." *New York Times*—Breaking News, World News & Multimedia. Last modified June 4, 1999. http://www.nytimes.com/1999/06/04/world/the-persistent-mystery-how-many-died-in-1989.html.

Kaiser Family Foundation. "Terrorism, Human Rights, and Climate Change Top the Public's Priority List for U.S. Engagement in World Affairs; Other Issues, Including Health, Rated Important." Last modified April 21, 2016. http://kff.org/global-health-policy/press-release/terrorism-human-rights-and-climate-change-top-the-publics-priority-list-for-u-s-engagement-in-world-affairs-other-issues-including-health-rated-important/.

Pew Research Center. "Republicans More Concerned Than Democrats About China on Most Issues." Pew Research Center's Global Attitudes Project. Last modified September 8, 2015. http://www.pewglobal.org/2015/09/09/americans-concerns-about-china-economics-cyberattacks-human-rights-top-the-list/problems-battery-by-u-s-party/.

Planas, Roque. "U.S. Security Aid To Mexico Dwindles Amid Human Rights Abuses." Huffington Post. Last modified December 29, 2015. http://www.huffingtonpost.com/entry/mexico-security-human-rights_us_5681c198e4b0b958f65a3e4b.

Republican National Committee. "Republican Platform 2016." Last modified 2016. https://prod-static-ngop-pbl.s3.amazonaws.com/static/home/data/platform.pdf.

Saad, Lydia. "Republicans, Democrats Agree on Top Foreign Policy Goals." Gallup.com. Last modified February 20, 2013. http://www.gallup.com/poll/160649/republicans-democrats-agree-top-foreign-policy-goals.aspx?g_source=human%20rights&g_medium=search&g_campaign=tiles.

Stokes, Bruce. "Americans' Foreign Policy Priorities for 2014." Pew Research Center. Last modified December 31, 2013. http://www.pewresearch.org/fact-tank/2013/12/31/americans-foreign-policy-priorities-for-2014/.

United Nations. "The Universal Declaration of Human Rights." Last modified 2016. http://www.un.org/en/universal-declaration-human-rights/.

Immigration

At a Glance

Immigration is a classic "intermestic" issue. On one hand, issues relating to documentation requirements, provision of social services, and citizenship questions are largely domestic issues. On the other hand, issues such as border control, policies regarding refugees (who are admitted to the United States under separate rules), and deportation are challenges that have both domestic and international consequences. All aspects of immigration thus have both domestic and foreign policy ramifications.

The debate in the United States over the issue of immigration has become so heated that even the terminology used with respect to illegal immigration in particular is controversial. Proponents of immigration reform that includes a path to citizenship prefer to use the term "undocumented immigrant." Opponents tend to use the term "illegal immigrant," which has a longer history of usage. A smaller number of writings on the subject use the term "unauthorized immigrant." The current entry takes no position on the issue of citizenship status. As a result, the terms undocumented immigrant and illegal immigrant (or immigration) are used interchangeably.

According to many Republicans, immigration reform . . .

- Should include a constitutional change to deny birthright citizenship;
- Should include a wall or fence along the entire U.S. border with Mexico;
- Should not include a "path to citizenship" for undocumented/illegal immigrants in the United States;
- Should focus on strategic legal immigration, such as granting an increased number of work/education visas to immigrants with advanced degrees; and
- Should not include amnesty of any kind for undocumented/illegal immigrants.

According to many Democrats, immigration reform . . .

- Should include a path to citizenship for illegal/undocumented immigrants under certain circumstances;
- Should not change the constitutional principal of birthright citizenship;

- Should include a streamlined application and admission process for immediate family members of U.S. citizens;
- Should not include provisions that require legal immigrants who are not yet U.S. citizens (legal aliens) to carry visa paperwork at all times; and
- Should include programs such as the Deferred Action for Parents of Americans (DAPA) and Deferred Action for Childhood Arrivals (DACA) that delay or abandon efforts to deport undocumented parents of children who attain birthright citizenship or deport children who arrive in the United States alone.

Overview

During the period from U.S. independence until after the Civil War, the United States maintained what was, for the most part, an open immigration policy. Although there was a waiting period for citizenship, any person who was able to get to the United States could settle there. In 1798 Congress passed and President John Adams signed the Alien and Sedition Acts. Under the acts, the president was allowed to deport any immigrant deemed a threat to national security. In practice, the acts did little to alter immigration numbers, which were comparatively low at the time. Three of the four acts were repealed during the Jefferson administration. The remaining piece of legislation, the Alien Enemies Act, remains part of the U.S. legal code today. Its most controversial enforcement occurred during World War II, when the act was modified to allow government internment of thousands of Japanese Americans, as well as many Germans and Italians.

Before the mid-19th century, immigration policy was mostly a matter of state law. Because U.S. foreign policy is, with a few exceptions, carried out at the national level, immigration was primarily treated as a domestic issue. States with labor shortages and existing diversity encouraged immigration. States without labor shortages, with better organized labor, or with strong nativist movements, did not encourage immigration. In time, however, the Supreme Court began to more strictly apply Article I, Section 8, Clause 4 of the Constitution, which places responsibility for naturalization laws in the hands of the federal government. The decision of the Court in the *Head Money Cases* (1874) formally established the supremacy of the national government in determining immigration law (Chacón 2014). In 1875, in the case of *Chy Lung v. Freeman*, the Supreme Court ruled specifically that the admission of immigrants should be subject to federal, rather than state, control. From this point on, immigration became a more prominent element of U.S. foreign policy.

Both legal and illegal immigration to the United States continued to grow at an accelerated pace from the 1850s through the early 1900s. While many state and local governments were wary of the earlier wave of European immigration from Ireland, Eastern Europe, and Germany, these groups were not barred from entry by federal law. In 1882, Congress passed, and President Arthur signed, the Chinese Exclusion Act. Democrats, who were at the time more likely to oppose many forms of immigration, overwhelmingly supported the act. A majority of Republicans, who were more open at the time to immigration, also supported the act. However, 34 Republicans voted against the legislation, in part because of a division between Western and New England Republicans, who held differing views on immigration (Seo 2010). Western Republicans were more prone to blocking Chinese immigration because of the perceived labor issues and general anti-Chinese sentiment in the West. The Immigration Act of 1917, passed with an override of President Wilson's veto, resulted in taxes and literacy tests imposed on immigrants. The Immigration Act of 1924 broadened the scope of the literacy tests beyond "Asiatic peoples" and codified the idea of a national origins quota, enabling the national government to restrict immigration to applicants from more "desirable" areas. The quota system was not removed until 1965. The passage of restrictive immigration acts, combined with World Wars I and II, resulted in a drastic decrease in legal immigration that did not begin to recover until the 1970s and 1980s.

It is also during this time period that the architecture of today's Immigration and Nationalization Service (INS) was formed. The number of national laws restricting legal immigration, as well as increasing levels of illegal immigration, required the creation of a federal bureaucracy to implement the law. The 1880s saw the appointment of the first superintendent of immigration. Next, the Bureau of Immigration and the Bureau of Naturalization were created to manage entrance and citizenship issues. The Bureau of Immigration was eventually expanded to include the first U.S. Border Patrol in 1924. These agencies were fused in 1933 to form the Immigration Support Services (ISS). After the terrorist attacks of September 11, 2001, the INS was split into three agencies—U.S. Citizenship and Immigration Services (USCIS), Immigration and Customs Enforcement (ICE), and Customs and Border Protection (CBP)—as part of a wide-ranging government reorganization aimed at improving national security. All of these agencies were placed under the newly created Department of Homeland Security (DHS).

The rise of illegal immigration in the United States largely corresponds with the passage of federal immigration law. That is to say that illegal immigration is only possible once immigration has been made illegal. Passage of the Chinese Exclusion Act, for example, led to illegal immigration from China into the United States. Immigration from Mexico has been alternatively encouraged and restricted over time. For example, immigration from Mexico, which had been legal and encouraged by the U.S. government during the World War II era, was eventually restricted under the quota system.

As legal immigration of Mexicans became more restricted, the number of undocumented immigrants fleeing impoverished circumstances in search of a better life in the United States steadily grew. In the mid-2000s, the population of unauthorized immigrants peaked at just over 12 million. Estimates indicate that the number of undocumented immigrants has since leveled and declined to around 11.3 million (Krogstad and Passel 2015). Legislation such as the Immigration Reform and Control Act of 1986 and the 1990 Immigration Act provided a path to citizenship for undocumented immigrants under certain circumstances. The 1996 Illegal Immigration Reform and Immigrant Responsibility Act created more strict penalties, including lengthy bans on reentry, for illegal immigrants. Each of these pieces of legislation, given the divided government that existed when each was passed, required bipartisan cooperation.

Democrats on Immigration

The 2012 Democratic Party platform mentioned immigration 14 times. Chief among the planks in the platform is the call for comprehensive immigration reform in order to bring undocumented immigrants "out of the shadows" (Democratic National Committee 2012). The platform argues that immigrants who are willing to pay taxes and learn English should be provided with a path to citizenship. For Democrats, a path to citizenship would allow undocumented immigrants to apply for citizenship after spending a certain amount of time as tax paying undocumented workers. It would also entail payment of a penalty for illegally entering the United States and passing a background check. Finally, the Democratic Party platform supports the Development, Relief, and Education for Alien Minors (DREAM) Act. The proposed DREAM Act would allow undocumented minors who entered the United States before the age of 16 to become "conditional residents"; avoiding immediate deportation and providing a path to eventual citizenship without the payment of fines.

Overall, public opinion among Democrats echoes and in some ways goes beyond those statements in the Democratic Party platform. For example, Democrats in the general public overwhelmingly reject the idea of amending the Constitution to eliminate birthright citizenship (Pew Research Center 2015). Birthright citizenship is the constitutional principal that anyone born in the United States, regardless of the status of their parents, immediately becomes a citizen of the United States. Changing the legal status of children born in the United States to undocumented immigrants would require an amendment to the Constitution. Only 23 percent of Democrats favor this type of amendment. A significant majority (77 percent) of Democrats also believe that a path to citizenship should be available to undocumented immigrants (Kafura and McElmurry 2015). There is a divide within self-identified Democrats on the number of hurdles that should exist on the path to citizenship. A plurality of Democrats believes that there should be no hurdles (i.e., immigrants should be able to keep working and apply for citizenship without delay). However, a large minority of Democrats (29 percent) believe that there should be a waiting period and fines required of undocumented workers seeking citizenship (Kafura and McElmurry 2015). Overall, only 17 percent of Democrats believe that illegal immigrants should not be allowed to stay in the United States legally (Pew Research Center 2015).

Overall, Democrats in Congress have remained relatively unified, and in close proximity to public opinion, on issues related to immigration. For example, 208 out of 216 Democrats supported the Dream Act when it passed the House of

A Bipartisan Bill for Immigration Reform

In April 2013, Republican senator Marco Rubio of Florida cosponsored the Border Security, Economic Opportunity, and Immigration Modernization Act. Rubio argued as follows:

> Our immigration system is broken, and the status quo of having 11 million undocumented people living under de facto amnesty will only continue if we do nothing to solve this problem. This bill marks the beginning of an important debate, and I believe it will fix our broken system by securing our borders, improving interior enforcement, modernizing our legal immigration to help create jobs and protect American workers, and dealing with our undocumented population in a tough but humane way that is fair to those trying to come here the right way and linked to achieving several security triggers.

Senator Bob Menendez, one of the Democrat cosponsors of the bill argued that:

> This bipartisan bill represents a significant milestone in our nation's efforts to fix our broken immigration system," said Menendez, a chief architect of the legislation and a member of the bipartisan Gang of 8. "It is the product of months of negotiations and is the most comprehensive immigration reform initiative in three decades. And it accomplishes something the American people have been asking for—true bipartisan compromise.

Overall, the "gang of eight" senators that introduced that act, which included both a path to citizenship and increased security at the border, hoped that the bipartisan sponsorship would make it possible to pass comprehensive immigration reform.

Sources:

Menendez, Bob. "Press Release U.S. Senator Bob Menendez of New Jersey." U.S. Senator Bob Menendez of New Jersey. Last modified April 17, 2013. http://www.menendez.senate.gov /news-and-events/press/menendez-bipartisan-gang-of-8-introduce-common-sense -immigration-reform.

Rubio, Marco. "Press Releases—Newsroom—U.S. Senator for Florida, Marco Rubio." Marco Rubio, U.S. Senate, Senator for Florida. Last modified April 17, 2013. http://www.rubio .senate.gov/public/index.cfm/press-releases?ID=85a7f16e-7b91-4f44-8c68-129ebd25a865.

Representatives in 2010. Senate Democrats were also unified on the Dream Act in 2010. However, the bill did not pass due to the inability of Democrats to overcome a Republican filibuster or the act, which had been tied at the time to the repeal of "don't ask, don't tell" legislation within the defense appropriations bill (Barrett and Bash 2010).

In 2013, the Senate passed the Border Security, Economic Opportunity, and Immigration Modernization Act. In this case Democratic senators were completely unified in their support of the legislation, introduced by a group of four Democrats

Mitch McConnell Issues a Call for Increased Border Security

During Senate debate on the Border Security, Economic Opportunity, and Immigration Modernization Act in 2013, Senate minority leader (and future majority leader) Mitch McConnell (R-Ky.) spoke against the act:

> If you cannot be reasonably certain the border is secure as a condition of legalization, there is no way to be sure millions more will not follow the illegal immigrants who are already here. As others have rightly pointed out, you also cannot be sure that further Congresses will not just reverse whatever assurances we make today that border security will occur in the future. In other words, in the absence of a very firm results-based border security trigger, there is no way I can look at my constituents, look them in the eye and tell them that today's assurances will not become tomorrow's disappointments.

McConnell's arguments against the act failed to win the day in the Democrat-controlled Senate, which passed the bill. But the proposal ran aground in the Republican-controlled House of Representatives, which killed the bill.

Source:
Congressional Record—Senate. June 27, 2013, 1–3.

---

and four Republicans commonly called the "gang of eight." The bill provided for a path to citizenship as defined above, plus the addition of thousands of new border patrol agents. Every Senate Democrat voted in favor of the legislation, which passed by a margin of 68–32. However, the bill was never taken up in the Republican-controlled House. After Republicans gained control of the Senate in the 2014 mid-term elections, hopes for passage of the bill effectively ended. Democrats argued that the bill represented a reasonable compromise. Many Republicans argued that the bill would encourage more illegal immigration by providing amnesty to current illegal immigrants.

President Obama's position on immigration reform is consistent with public opinion among Democrats as well as with existing action by congressional Democrats. In 2014, after the previous failure of the DREAM Act and the path to citizenship legislation mentioned above, the president took executive action on the immigration issue by announcing the Deferred Action for Parents of Americans (DAPA) and Deferred Action for Childhood Arrivals (DACA) policies. These executive orders called for an end to efforts to deport undocumented parents of children who attain birthright citizenship (in the case of DAPA) or children who arrived in the United States alone (in the case of DACA).

Although a path to citizenship was not part of the DAPA, the program did provide renewable work permits for parents while the deferral was in effect. The president's political calculation was that, in the interim, Congress would pass comprehensive immigration reform. DACA would provide a two-year work permit and deferral from deportation for unauthorized immigrants who entered the country before their 16th birthday.

Almost immediately after the announcement of these executive orders, however, several states led by conservative governors and legislatures filed suit against the president in an effort to block implementation of DAPA and DACA. The U.S. Fifth Circuit Court of Appeals has ruled that a previous lower-court injunction against the implementation of the executive orders will be allowed to stand pending appeal. For its part, the Obama administration has promised to take the issue to the U.S. Supreme Court.

Both of the Democratic Party candidates for president in 2016 expressed strong support for comprehensive immigration reforms that provide for a path to citizenship. Hillary Clinton has promised to defend DAPA and DACA, and expand both orders in ways that make them more accessible to those who would have benefited from the DREAM Act (Hillary for America 2016). Clinton was also a sponsor of one of the many versions of the DREAM Act that have appeared before Congress over the past decade. Senator Bernie Sanders shares many of the same views as Secretary Clinton. His self-described "fair and humane" immigration policies would include passage of a comprehensive immigration reform bill with a path to citizenship as well as passage of the DREAM Act. Sanders also promised to expand DACA and DAPA to benefit more undocumented individuals and families.

Republicans on Immigration

In many ways, Republicans and Democrats act as mirror images of each other on issues related to immigration. Though a certain amount of partisan rancor is common on many foreign policy issues, it is rare to find a foreign policy issue where the parties are so diametrically opposed.

The 2012 Republican Party platform mentioned immigration seven times. The crux of the argument contained in the platform is that illegal immigration harms American workers by driving down wages. Republicans argue that the Obama administration, by filing suit against states that attempt to pass their own immigration legislation, further erode the value of American labor and the value of the legal immigration process (Republican National Committee 2012). The solution, the GOP argues, is to strengthen enforcement of existing laws, including those that related to workplace enforcement and building a double-layered fence along the border. The main item added to the platform was the construction of a wall along the entire length of the U.S. border with Mexico (see below). The Republican platform ended its discussion of immigration by saluting legal immigrants, especially those willing to serve in the U.S. military.

Those platform planks are very much in step with public opinion among rank-and-file Republicans. For example, one 2015 poll found that 73 percent of Republicans favor the construction of a fence along the entire border with Mexico to halt illegal immigration from that nation (Pew Research Center 2015). Another survey found that 63 percent of Republicans view large numbers of immigrants as a critical threat to the United States; by contrast, only 30 percent of self-described Democrats polled agreed with that perspective (Kafura and McElmurry 2015). On the issue of birthright citizenship, numerous polls have indicated that a majority of Republicans favor changing the Constitution to eliminate automatically conferring citizenship on anyone born in the United States, regardless of the citizenship status of their parents. The goal of such an amendment would be to discourage the practice of illegally crossing the border into the United States in order to have a child, in the hopes that the rights conferred on the child will extend to the parent(s) or that the child will reap advantages later in life from being a U.S. citizen.

There is, however, some emerging evidence of public support among Republicans for options other than mass deportation of illegal immigrants currently living and working in the United States. For example, majorities of both Democrats and Republicans believe that there should be a legal way for undocumented immigrants to remain in the United States under certain circumstances, normally related to work status (Pew Research Center 2015). In other words, although Republicans are unlikely to favor a path to citizenship, significant numbers of them are skeptical that deportation will work as a strategy for the millions of undocumented immigrants who are already in the United States. The percentage of Republicans who believe that there should be some sort of path to citizenship for illegal immigrants has also grown incrementally over time (Kafura and McElmurry 2015). Overall, however, Republicans remain much more likely than Democrats to view reducing illegal immigration as a key domestic and foreign policy goal.

Republicans in Congress have remained fairly unified against both a path to citizenship, which many Republicans term "amnesty" because it purportedly excuses breaking the law. With respect to the DREAM Act, Republicans were even more unified than their Democratic counterparts. Only eight Republican representatives voted in favor of the act, compared to 38 Democrats who voted against it. Republicans argued that the act, as written, would amount to amnesty for millions of illegal immigrants, including some with criminal backgrounds. Many Republicans also argued that the act should have gone further to address concerns related to border security. Ultimately, the DREAM Act passed in the House of Representatives but stalled in the Senate due to a Republican filibuster.

The Border Security, Economic Opportunity, and Immigration Modernization Act faced the opposite fate, passing the Senate in 2013 but dying in the House of Representatives, where the bill was not considered due to opposition from the GOP leadership. In the Senate, all 32 "nay" votes came from Republicans. However, roughly one-third of Senate Republicans voted with Democrats in favor of the legislation. Republican senators who favored the legislation argued that the enhanced provisions for border security represented an improvement over the previous path to citizenship legislation. Republicans who opposed the legislation argued both that amnesty would encourage further illegal immigration and that the border security provisions of the legislation were inadequate to prevent further illegal immigration. In the House, Speaker John Boehner originally expressed hope that a compromise could be reached. However, an informal rule often referred to as the "Hastert Rule" after former Republican Speaker Dennis Hastert, ultimately made this impossible. Under the Hastert Rule, a Republican Speaker of the House will not bring a piece of legislation to the floor for a vote unless it has majority support from the majority party. In other words, if a piece of legislation could only pass with a minority of Republicans joining a majority of Democrats, the Speaker will not allow the bill to come to the floor. After an attempt to whip votes in favor of an amended version of the act failed, Speaker Boehner was forced to pull the Senate bill from consideration. The House did pass a bill that would have increased border security and addressed some humanitarian concerns at the border, but did not include a path to citizenship. As a result, the Senate, which was controlled at the time by Democrats, declined to consider the House bill. This set the stage for the battle over executive orders described above.

In 2016, the field of candidates for the Republican presidential nomination spoke with virtual unanimity against most tenets of comprehensive immigration reform supported by Democrats. Senator Marco Rubio, an original member of the "gang of eight," withdrew his support for a path to citizenship and focused on increase border security. However, Rubio does not call directly for the deportation of any illegal immigrants other than those who have committed crimes. Donald Trump, meanwhile, declared that he would end illegal immigration from Mexico by constructing a massive wall along the entire U.S.–Mexico border—to be paid for by Mexico. He has also called for the creation of a deportation force to capture and deport illegal immigrants in the United States. In response to criticism of the deportation force approach, Trump has argued that if the number of ICE agents was increased, it would be possible, as an interim step, to ensure more illegal immigrants, especially those who have committed crimes in the United States, would be rapidly deported. Former Florida governor Jeb Bush, by contrast, argued for a "path to earned legal status" and dismissed Trump's wall idea as impractical. Senator Ted Cruz of Texas, who has previously voted against a path to citizenship in the Senate, called for a tripling of border security, deportations, and a wall (Cruz for President 2016). Ohio governor John Kasich, viewed by many as the most moderate Republican candidate in the primary, was the only candidate who refused to rule out a path to citizenship—although he also did not endorse the concept (LoBianco 2015). The emergence of Trump as the Republican Party nominee has worried other Republicans that a more muscular stance on immigration will alienate voters from immigrant communities in the United States.

Further Reading

Barrett, Ted, and Dana Bash. "Senate Halts 'Don't Ask, Don't Tell' Repeal." CNN. Last modified September 22, 2010. http://www.cnn.com/2010/POLITICS/09/21/senate.defense .bill/index.html?hpt=T1.

Chacón, Jennifer. "Who Is Responsible for U.S. Immigration Policy?" *Insights on Law and Society* 14 (Spring 2014). http://www.americanbar.org/publications/insights_on_law _andsociety/14/spring-2014/who-is-responsible-for-u-s--immigration-policy-.html.

"*Chy Lung v. Freeman*: 92 U.S. 275 (1875): Justia U.S. Supreme Court Center." Justia Law. Last modified 2015. https://supreme.justia.com/cases/federal/us/92/275/case.html.

Cruz for President. "Cruz Immigration Plan." Cruz for President. Last modified 2016. https://www.tedcruz.org/cruz-immigration-plan/.

Democratic National Committee. "The 2012 Democratic Platform." Last modified 2012. https://www.democrats.org/party-platform.

Ford, Matt. "The Fifth Circuit Court of Appeals Rules against Obama's Executive Actions on Immigration." *The Atlantic*. Last modified November 10, 2015. http://www.theatlantic .com/politics/archive/2015/11/fifth-circuit-obama-immigration/415077/.

Hillary for America. "Immigration Reform | Issues | Hillary for America." Last modified 2016. https://www.hillaryclinton.com/issues/immigration-reform/.

"Immigration Reform." Make America Great Again! | Donald J. Trump for President. Last modified 2016. https://www.donaldjtrump.com/positions/immigration-reform.

Kafura, Craig, and Sara McElmurry. "Growing Partisan Divides on Immigration." Home | Chicago Council on Global Affairs. Last modified September 8, 2015. http://www .thechicagocouncil.org/publication/growing-partisan-divides-immigration?utm _source=Informz&utm_medium=Email&utm_campaign=Council.

Krogstad, Jens M., and Jeffrey S. Passel. "5 Facts about Illegal Immigration in the U.S." Pew Research Center. Last modified November 19, 2015. http://www.pewresearch.org /fact-tank/2015/11/19/5-facts-about-illegal-immigration-in-the-u-s/.

LoBianco, Tom. "Kasich Leaves Door Open on Immigration, Supports Abortion Exceptions Politics.com." CNN. Last modified August 12, 2015. http://www.cnn.com/2015/08/12 /politics/john-kasich-immigration/.

New York Times. "Congressional Bills and Votes: House Vote 625—Approves DREAM Act." Last modified December 8, 2010. http://politics.nytimes.com/congress/votes/111/house /2/625.

Pew Research Center. "On Immigration Policy, Wider Partisan Divide over Border Fence Than Path to Legal Status." Pew Research Center for the People and the Press. Last modified October 8, 2015. http://www.people-press.org/2015/10/08/on-immigration -policy-wider-partisan-divide-over-border-fence-than-path-to-legal-status/.

Republican National Committee. "Republican Platform." Last modified 2012. https://prod -static-ngop-pbl.s3.amazonaws.com/docs/2012GOPPlatform.pdf.

Rubio, Marco. "How Marco Will Start Securing Our Border on Day One." Last modified 2016. https://marcorubio.com/issues-2/marco-rubio-immigration-plan-border-security -legal/.

Seo, Jungkun. "Wedge-Issue Dynamics and Party Position Shifts: Chinese Exclusion Debates in the post-Reconstruction US Congress, 1879–1882." *Party Politics* 17, no. 6 (2010): 823–847.

U.S. Senate. "U.S. Senate: Roll Call Vote on Passage of the Bill (S. 744 as Amended)." Last modified June 27, 2013. http://www.senate.gov/legislative/LIS/roll_call_lists/roll_call _vote_cfm.cfm?&congress=113&session=1&vote=00168.

Iran

At a Glance

Since the discovery of a clandestine Iranian nuclear weapons program in 2002, and the declaration of noncompliance with its nuclear safeguards agreement by the International Atomic Energy Agency (IAEA) in 2005, the Iranian nuclear program has dominated debates over U.S. foreign policy toward Iran. Partisan differences that have emerged during these debates rise in sharp contrast to the relative, though by no means absolute, bipartisanship that characterized U.S. foreign policy toward Iran from the time of the U.S.-supported coup in 1953, through the Iranian Revolution and into the early part of the new millennium.

Most support for diplomacy and cooperation with Iran on issues related to nuclear disarmament, as well as some aspects of the "war on terror," comes from within the Democratic Party. The Joint Comprehensive Plan of Action (JCPOA), designed to limit Iran's ability to develop nuclear weapons, has been supported by most, though not all, Democrats. Advocates of this approach argue that sanctions levied by the international community against Iran created an opportunity for unprecedented negotiations. Those negotiations, involving the P5+1 (United States, Russia, China, Great Britain, France, Germany) and Iran resulted in an agreement that limits the Iranian ability to enrich uranium for use in nuclear weapons, subjects the country to IAEA inspections, and ties the success of those inspections to United Nations and certain bilateral sanctions relief.

Much of the opposition to the current rapprochement with Iran is from the Republican Party. The Republican Party argues that the JCPOA does not go far enough in securing Iranian nuclear disarmament. Republicans argue that sanctions against Iran created the opportunity for a better deal than the one that was ultimately negotiated, and that premature sanctions relief will enable Iran to strengthen its destabilizing role in the Middle East. Republicans in Congress, with some support from Democrats, mounted a failed effort to reject the JCPOA as counter to U.S. interests. Several 2016 Republican presidential candidates subsequently promised to withdraw from the JCPOA if elected president.

According to many Democrats, the JCPOA agreement with Iran will . . .

- Make it significantly more difficult for Iran to develop nuclear weapons;
- Make it possible to cooperate with Iran on issues of mutual concern such as the resurgence of the Taliban and ISIS; and
- Increase overall stability in the Middle East.

According to many Republicans, the JCPOA agreement with Iran will . . .

- Make it easier for Iran to develop nuclear weapons;
- Increase the ability of Iran to support militant groups such as Hezbollah; and
- Decrease the probability of political reform within Iran.

Overview

Until the end of World War II, the United States was willing to take a back seat to British interests on Iran. Although not a formal colony, Iranian financial and military interests were largely controlled by Great Britain under a series of unequal treaties. The prospect of increased Soviet influence in Iran after the war was unacceptable to the United States, however. The subsequent provision of technical and logistical assistance to the new Shah, Mohammad Reza Pahlavi, was part of a bipartisan consensus that a close relationship with Iran was vital to U.S. interests in the emerging Cold War. The United States secured the withdrawal of both British and Soviet troops from Iran after World War II in an effort to avoid the country being separated into spheres of interest (Little 2011). The British retained a great deal of influence over Iran as a result of the control of oil resources in the country.

In 1953, the United States, in cooperation with Shah Mohammad Reza Pahlavi, the monarch of Iran, and the United Kingdom, orchestrated a coup that led to the fall of democratically elected Prime Minister Mohammed Mossadeh, who was in the process of nationalizing Iran's oil resources. President Truman's Point IV Program, designed to provide economic, industrial, and technical assistance to developing countries, had already established a basis for U.S. economic and political influence in Iran after World War II (St. Marie and Naghshpour 2011, 120). The United States supported the coup because it believed that the emerging constitutional monarchy under Mossadeh was overly prone to Soviet influence. The Soviet Union, for its part, had courted Iran extensively in the period after World War II. Iranian attempts to chart a nonaligned course between the two superpowers failed.

The transition in the White House from Republican Dwight Eisenhower to Democrat John F. Kennedy in 1961 witnessed the emergence of a partisan divide of sorts between Democrats and Republicans on the issue of Iran. Republican advisers under Eisenhower tended to view any instability in Iran as a part of the Cold War and provided support for the regime's secret police and domestic security organization known as *Sāzemān-e Ettelā'āt va Amniyat-e Keshvar* (SAVAK). SAVAK, which translates roughly in English to Organization of National Security and Information (or alternatively, Intelligence), in coordination with the CIA, worked to silence all domestic opposition in Iran, and was known for using brutal tactics to achieve its goal. From the perspective of many Republicans, including those with the most influence of Eisenhower's foreign policy, SAVAK operations were necessary to quell potential Soviet and Islamist influence in Iran. SAVAK operations did result in the arrest of many political dissidents. However, the organization failed to prevent the proliferation of Marxist and Islamist political organizations (Curtis and Hooglund 2008, 46).

Democratic advisers within the Kennedy administration were more likely to view Iran's internal instability as an artifact of poor domestic governance (Little 2011). From their perspective, corruption and a basic lack of economic opportunity set the stage for the formation of political opposition groups. Many Democrats felt that economic modernization and prosperity, coupled with increased respect for political freedom and other human rights, held the key to keeping nascent Islamist and Communist organizations in check. For its part, the Iranian regime came to see the focus on human rights by Democrats as unhelpful, and gravitated toward support for, and advice from, Republicans on issues related to internal security (Parsi 2007, 70). It is worth noting, however, that the partisan differences between Democrats and Republicans on this issue were not large enough to be insurmountable. Neither party, for example, pressured Iran in a significant way to move toward the constitutional monarchy that many thought would emerge in the early 1950s. Both Democrats and Republicans were broadly supportive of top-down economic reforms designed to improve economic and social conditions.

Ultimately, Islamic revolution came to Iran in 1979 in spite of the efforts of the Shah and the United States to stop it. In the early 1970s, the administration of Republican president Richard Nixon allowed Iran to become a significant regional military power through the purchase of U.S. arms. Although Democratic president Jimmy Carter exhibited some concern at Iran's human rights record after taking office in 1977, the United States did not exert sufficient pressure to create genuine political reform. Demonstrations against the Shah and the government at large began and quickly expanded in 1977 and 1978. Ayatollah Ruhollah Khomeini, a religious scholar who was exiled from Iran in the 1960s after criticizing economic and social reforms under the Shah, helped to marshal further opposition both domestically and abroad. Secular protesters joined the Islamists in opposition. Economic stagnation after over a decade of growth played a role in overall dissatisfaction. The Iranian government cracked down on protesters in 1978, further fueling the instability. The Iranian opposition, encouraged by the belief that the Carter administration would not intervene militarily, ramped up the level of protest, ultimately forcing the Shah to abdicate (Amuzegar 1991, 290). On February

11, 1979, the old regime and its provisional replacement fell, paving the way for the establishment of the Islamic Republic of Iran.

The Iranian hostage crisis, which began on November 4, 1979, created a second period of relative partisan unity on U.S. foreign policy toward Iran. After the revolution, President Carter permitted the Shah, who was suffering from lymphoma, to seek treatment in the United States. The escape of the Shah prompted a large group of Iranian students to storm and occupy the U.S. embassy in Tehran, taking over 60 hostages in the process. The Ayatollah used the event to rally the opposition, which showed signs of fragmentation after the revolution, around the formulation of a theocratic republic (Sick n.d.). The United States attempted a military rescue operation on April 24, 1980. The operation, which failed, added additional fervor to Iranian outrage toward the United States, which the Ayatollah termed "the Great Satan."

Though the hostage crisis was eventually resolved with the release of the American prisoners during the opening hours of Ronald Reagan's presidency, the damage to the relationship between the United States and Iran was significant. Opposition to Western cultural ideas became the cornerstone of Iranian domestic and foreign policy. Opposition to the theocracy was central to U.S. policy in the region.

During the Iran–Iraq War of the 1980s, the United States supported both sides at different periods of time, but overall lent more support to Iraq. The Reagan administration also arranged for the United States to secretly sell arms to Iran in order to secure the release of a group of hostages in Lebanon held by Hezbollah and to fund the anti-Communist Contras in Nicaragua, contrary to U.S. law. This so-called "Iran-Contra Scandal" did little to ease the relationship between the United States and Iran, which continued to sour into the George H. W. Bush and Clinton administrations. Even the election of a proreform president, Mohammed Khatami, did not lead to a significant thaw (Little 2011). In January 2002, President George W. Bush gave his famous "Axis of Evil" speech in which he labeled Iran, Iraq, and North Korea as brutally repressive sponsors of terrorism and developers of weapons of mass destruction. The speech, coupled with the rise of Iranian president Mahmoud Ahmadinejad in 2005, cemented the status of the relationship.

During the U.S. presidential election campaign in 2008, Barack Obama signaled a willingness to engage with Iran in order to cultivate an improved relationship on areas of mutual concern. Obama insisted that Iran would remain on the U.S. list of state sponsors of terror, and that progress on nuclear disarmament would be necessary. However, the president-elect also indicated that the United States and Iran shared some common goals, such as the desire to prevent the resurgence of the Taliban in Afghanistan. The 2008 Republican candidate for president, Senator John McCain of Arizona, denounced these views as naïve.

The initial years of the Obama administration exhibited continuity with past presidential administrations in their attempt to isolate Iran. Iran, for its part, added to the attention by restarting its nuclear weapons program, a process that began in the late 1980s with the development of a nuclear energy program with assistance from several foreign governments. Ultimately, the United States imposed its harshest economic sanctions on Iran in 2010 with passage of the Comprehensive Iran Sanctions, Accountability, and Divestment Act. Coupled with various economic sanctions by other countries, and by the United Nations, the sanctions regime ultimately led to talks aimed at securing Iranian nuclear disarmament between the P5+1 and the Iranian government. The resulting JCPOA forms the primary basis of the partisan divide that has recently opened between Republicans and Democrats on the Iranian issue.

The JCPOA is not technically a law in that it was nether passed by Congress nor established as a treaty with the advice and consent of the Senate. However, the existence of the JCPOA is tied directly to existing sanctions against Iran, which are established in both domestic and international law. In addition, the JCPOA is designed to ensure that Iran fulfills its obligations under the nonproliferation of nuclear weapons treaty (NPT), which is a well-established part of international law of which both the United States and Iran are parties.

The JCPOA contains several key provisions, including:

- An agreement by Iran to reduce its number of centrifuges (used for the enrichment of uranium (by two-thirds);
- Reduction of Iranian stockpiles of low-enriched uranium;
- No new construction of facilities for the enrichment of uranium;
- IAEA access to all Iranian enrichment facilities for inspection;
- Access to the IAEA for inspection of "suspicious" facilities;
- UN sanctions against Iran will be lifted upon verification of compliance with the JCPOA; and
- Automatic reimposition of sanctions in the event that a dispute relating the JCPOA cannot be resolved.

Democrats on Iran

On issues related to Iranian nuclear disarmament, the position of a plurality of members of the Democratic Party is to support the JCPOA. Democrats have coalesced around the idea that the JCPOA is the best deal that could have been negotiated given the parties involved and the current level of development of the Iranian nuclear program. Iran has a right under existing international law to develop nuclear technology for peaceful purposes, such as nuclear energy, which limits the ability of the United States to degrade the entire Iranian Nuclear Program.

Currently, the Democratic Party enjoys less political unity concerning its position on Iran than does the Republican Party. In part, this is due to the ambitious nature of the JCPOA. Negotiation of the JCPOA not only involves a number of ambitious proposals for sanctions relief in exchange for Iranian cooperation on its nuclear weapons program, it is also the product of negotiations between the

United States and a variety of partners with varying domestic and international agendas. As a result, while the JCPOA survived a congressional challenge, the debate over the framework highlighted significant divisions within the Democratic Party. Those divisions were highlighted during debate on the JCPOA in Congress. The JCPOA is not a treaty, and hence not subject to the advice and consent of the U.S. Senate. However, Congress did have the opportunity to reject the JCPOA by voting against it. In the Senate, Democrats were able to successfully filibuster the attempt to vote against the JCPOA by mustering 42 votes against bringing the resolution to the floor (Steinhauer 2015). In the House of Representatives, 25 Democrats crossed party lines and voted against the JCPOA.

Several Democratic representatives spoke out against the JCPOA. Representative Alcee Hastings of Florida, for example argued that "the goal of the recently concluded negotiations was to prevent Iran from obtaining a nuclear weapon. The negotiators worked diligently, but in the end, the JCPOA allows Iran to remain a nuclear threshold state while simultaneously reaping the benefits of relief from international sanctions" (Hastings 2015). Representative Nita M. Lowey of New York joined many members of the New York Democratic congressional delegation in rejecting the JCPOA. Lowey posits that "in my judgment, sufficient safeguards are not in place to address the risks associated with the agreement. Relieving UN sanctions on conventional arms and ballistic missiles and releasing billions of dollars to the Iranian regime could lead to a dangerous regional weapons race and enable Iran to bolster its funding of terrorists" (Lowey 2015).

Many Democrats also expressed their overall support for the JCPOA. Representative John Conyers Jr. of Michigan, for example, stated "President Obama Administration's determined diplomatic efforts have yielded one of the great international agreements of our time: a verifiable deal to prevent Iran from obtaining a nuclear weapon" (Conyers 2015). Senator Brian Schatz of Hawaii agreed, stating "after multiple readings, numerous briefings with officials, discussions with experts outside of government, consultations with my constituents and colleagues, I am satisfied that the Joint Comprehensive Plan of Action is the best approach to deny Iran a nuclear weapon and places its nuclear program under strict international supervision" (Schatz 2015). In the end, while many Democrats expressed concern over the JCPOA, a majority were willing to side with President Obama's perspective that the agreement blocks Iran from the pathways that it might use to develop a nuclear weapon in the near future. The maintenance of some level of party unity on the Iranian nuclear issue came after intense lobbying of congressional Democrats by the president and, in the Senate, after Minority Leader Harry Reid announced his support of the deal.

The Democratic Party's position that diplomacy is the preferable means for dealing with Iran extends beyond the nuclear issue. Secret communications with Iran, with Oman as an intermediary, date back to the early days of the Obama administration (Solomon 2015). The United States appears to have made minor concessions to Iran related to Iranians detained in the United States. Oman also acted

Two Prominent Democrats Debate the Iran Nuclear Deal

One of the keys to the survival of the JCPOA in the U.S. Senate was the support of Senate minority leader Harry Reid. Reid's support provided political cover for more hesitant Democratic senators to assist with the filibuster that ended the Republican attempt to derail the nuclear agreement. Ironically, the main Democratic opposition to the JCPOA among Senate Democrats came from Chuck Schumer. Reid had endorsed Schumer as his replacement for minority leader. In his statement opposing the JCPOA, Schumer raised concern that:

- "First, inspections are not 'anywhere, anytime'; the 24-day delay before we can inspect is troubling.
- Even more troubling is the fact that the U.S. cannot demand inspections unilaterally.
- After fifteen years of relief from sanctions, Iran would be stronger financially and better able to advance a robust nuclear program."

For his part, Senator Reid argued that:

- "This nuclear agreement is consistent with the greatest traditions of American leadership.
- If America walks away from this agreement and loses the support of our allies in the sanctions regime, Iran could have enough fissile material to make a nuclear bomb in a matter of months.
- Throughout all of these deliberations, critics of the agreement failed to articulate a viable alternative."

Sources:

Reid, Harry. "U.S. Senate Democratic Leader Harry Reid—Reid Statement on the Joint Comprehensive Plan of Action." U.S. Senate Democratic Leader Harry Reid. Last modified August 13, 2015. http://www.reid.senate.gov/press_releases/2015-08-23-reid-statement-on-the-joint-comprehensive-plan-of-action.

Schumer, Chuck. "My Position on the Iran Deal." medium.com. Last modified August 7, 2015. https://medium.com/@SenSchumer/my-position-on-the-iran-deal-e976b2f13478#.p3t1j17er.

as a backchannel for negotiations that led to the release of three American hikers who were being held in Iran on charges of espionage. These informal communications eventually gave way to more direct talks centering on Iranian enrichment of uranium. However, even as a candidate for the Democratic Party nomination for president, Barack Obama indicated that he was willing to negotiate with Iran without conditions on a variety of issues. At the time, Hillary Clinton, also a candidate for the Democratic Party nomination, suggested that negotiations with the Iranians, without conditions, would be counterproductive. At the time, more hawkish members of the Democratic Party argued that direct negotiations would confer legitimacy on the Iranian government without increasing the probability of a positive result. In the wake of the Iran Nuclear Deal, however, most Democrats have expressed support for the Obama administration's handling of the issue as well as the agreement itself. The two frontrunners for the 2016 Democratic Party nomination for president, Secretary of State Hillary Clinton and Senator Bernie Sanders, both endorsed the JCPOA.

The Democratic Party has also been quick to condemn Iran on a variety of issues unrelated to the JCPOA. For example, in spite of some reports to the contrary, Democrats have strongly supported keeping Iran on the Department of State list of state sponsors of terrorism. Iran has been on the list since 1984. Iran is currently on the list due to its support for Hezbollah, Palestinian terrorist groups in the Gaza Strip, Shia militias in Iraq, and terrorist groups in Syria fighting against ISIS (U.S. Department of State 2014). Iran is also a supporter of the Assad regime in Syria. Democrats and Republicans have, to this point been unified in calls for the removal of Assad as head of the Syrian government.

Republicans on Iran

Republicans appear to be united around the idea that negotiations with Iran without preconditions were a mistake. In addition, Republicans argue that the JCPOA is a foreign policy disaster. The fact that Iran has hidden its nuclear facilities from the IAEA before, in spite of having ratified the Treaty on the Non-Proliferation of Nuclear Weapons, is advanced by Republicans as evidence that only the strictest of inspections regimes is capable of ensuring Iranian compliance with any new agreement. Republicans also argue that the sanctions relief provided to Iran under the JCPOA, coupled with the potential for a clandestine nuclear weapons program, represents a more grave threat to the Middle East, especially Israel, than the status quo.

Republican members of Congress replied quickly and critically to the JCPOA. John Boehner, Speaker of the House when the JCPOA came up for debate, promised to do "everything we can to stop it" (Boehner 2015). Boehner scheduled a vote on a resolution supporting the JCPOA in order to get Democrats onto the record supporting the proposal. The Bill, H.R. 3461 to approve the Joint Comprehensive Plan of Action, signed at Vienna on July 14, 2015, relating to the nuclear program of Iran, failed 162–269. The impact of the vote was partially nullified by the aforementioned inability of Senate Republicans to overcome a Democrat-led filibuster of a bill rejecting the JCPOA. However, by forcing a vote in the House of Representatives, former Speaker Boehner fulfilled his pledge to allow Republicans to vote against the bill. The vote also brings the partisan divide on Iran into sharp contrast as the 2016 election approaches.

Other Republican members of the House and Senate also condemned the P5+1 Agreement. Senator Marco Rubio, a 2016 candidate for the Republican Party nomination for president, argued that "based on what we know thus far, I believe that

Republican House Speaker John Boehner on the Iran Nuclear Deal

While serving in his capacity as Speaker of the House, John Boehner delivered an official statement concerning nuclear negotiations with Iran. The statement is noteworthy in that it set many of the basic parameters of the argument against the JCPOA once the details of the agreement became public.

The president says negotiators have cleared the basic threshold needed to continue talks, but the parameters for a final deal represent an alarming departure from the White House's initial goals. My longtime concerns about the parameters of this potential agreement remain, but my immediate concern is the administration signaling it will provide near-term sanctions relief. Congress must be allowed to fully review the details of any agreement before any sanctions are lifted.

After visiting with our partners on the ground in the Middle East this week, my concerns about Iran's efforts to foment unrest, brutal violence and terror have only grown. It would be naïve to suggest the Iranian regime will not continue to use its nuclear program, and any economic relief, to further destabilize the region.

In the weeks ahead, Republicans and Democrats in Congress will continue to press this administration on the details of these parameters and the tough questions that remain unanswered. We will stand strong on behalf of the American people and everyone in the Middle East who values freedom, security, and peace.

Source:

Boehner, John. "Speaker Boehner Statement on Iran Nuclear Talks." Speaker.gov. Last modified April 2, 2015. http://www.speaker.gov/press-release/speaker-boehner-statement-iran-nuclear-talks.

this deal undermines our national security" (Rubio 2015). Senator James Risch from Idaho claimed that "this deal falls disastrously short of what the Obama administration originally promised and gives the Iranian government what it desires" (Risch 2015). Senator Risch also expressed concern that the JCPOA represents a danger to Israel, a sentiment echoed by conservative Israeli prime minister Benjamin Netanyahu, who referred to the accord as an "historic mistake."

The 2016 Republican candidates for president were heavily critical of the Iranian nuclear agreement, although Governor John Kasich of Ohio refused to promise to withdraw the United States from the JCPOA if he became president (Weigel 2015). However, he was part of a group of governors that expressed opposition to the deal in principal. All of the other Republican candidates indicated that they would terminate the deal if elected president. Given the fact that the JCPOA is not a treaty, it would be hypothetically possible for any president to withdraw the United States from the agreement without action by Congress. However, the status of sanctions levied by other members of the P5+1 is less clear. Some Republicans have argued, along with Israel, that countries like Germany, the United Kingdom,

France, and possibly China would follow the lead of the United States, given the size of the U.S. economy and the potential for economic incentives to be used as leverage, to impose new sanctions until a better deal is reached.

On issues related to Iran beyond nuclear nonproliferation, Republicans enjoy a similar level of unity to that of Democrats. There are also areas of bipartisan agreement. For example, both Republican and Democrats believe that Iran is a state sponsor of terror. Republicans and Democrats tend to agree that the Assad regime in Syria must go, though they disagree on the methods that should be employed in pursuit of that goal. In the ongoing cold war between Saudi Arabia and Iran for hegemony in the Middle East, Republicans and Democrats are both likely to support the Saudis. Although both Saudi Arabia and Iran are theocratic governments, the government of Saudi Arabia has enjoyed strong relations with the United States, in part because of its willingness to work with secular Arab dictatorships in the region. In spite of some areas of bipartisan agreement, it can be reasonably concluded that Republicans are both more unified in their condemnation of Iran than are Democrats and are more willing to entertain the use of force as an option.

Further Reading

Amuzegar, Jahangir. *The Dynamics of the Iranian Revolution: The Pahlavis' Triumph and Tragedy*. Albany: State University of New York Press, 1991.

Boehner, John. "Boehner on Iran: 'We'll Do Everything We Can to Stop' a Bad Deal." Speaker.gov. Last modified July 14, 2015. http://www.speaker.gov/press-release/boehner-iran-we-ll-do-everything-we-can-stop-bad-deal.

Conyers, John. "Conyers: Iran Agreement Is Historic Win for Peace." Congressman John Conyers. Last modified July 13, 2015. https://conyers.house.gov/media-center/press-releases/conyers-iran-agreement-historic-win-peace.

Curtis, Glenn E., and Eric J. Hooglund. *Iran: A Country Study*. Washington, D.C.: Federal Research Division, Library of Congress, 2008.

Gary, Sick. "The Carter Administration." United States Institute of Peace. Accessed January 10, 2016. http://iranprimer.usip.org/resource/carter-administration-0.

Hastings, Alcee L. "Hastings to Vote against Iran Deal." U.S. Congressman Alcee Hastings. Last modified August 13, 2015. http://alceehastings.house.gov/news/documentsingle.aspx?DocumentID=398464.

Little, Douglas. "Frenemies: Iran and America since 1900." *Origins: Current Events in Historical Perspective*. Last modified May 2011. http://origins.osu.edu/article/frenemies-iran-and-america-1900.

Lowey, Nita M. "Lowey Opposes P5+1 Iran Agreement." Representative Nita Lowey. Last modified August 4, 2015. https://lowey.house.gov/media-center/press-releases/lowey-opposes-p51-iran-agreement.

Parsi, Trita. *Treacherous Alliance: The Secret Dealings of Israel, Iran, and the United States*. New Haven, CT: Yale University Press, 2007.

Risch, James. "Risch Statement on Nuclear Deal with Iran James E Risch, U.S. Senator for Idaho." James E. Risch U.S. Senator for Idaho. Last modified July 14, 2015. http://www.risch.senate.gov/public/index.cfm/pressreleases?ID=7ec3e8f1-7a22-42e6-8ba4-d48b718a16bc.

Rubio, Marco. "Marco Rubio Statement on Obama's Dangerous Iran Deal." Marco Rubio for President. Last modified 2015. https://marcorubio.com/news/marco-rubio-statement -on-obamas-dangerous-iran-deal/.

Schatz, Brian. "Schatz Statement on Iran Nuclear Agreement." U.S. Senator Brian Schatz of Hawaii. Last modified August 10, 2015. http://www.schatz.senate.gov/press-releases /schatz-statement-on-iran-nuclear-agreement

Solomon, Jay. "Secret Dealings with Iran Led to Nuclear Talks." *Wall Street Journal*. Last modified June 28, 2015. http://www.wsj.com/articles/iran-wish-list-led-to-u-s-talks -1435537004.

St. Marie, Joseph J., and Shahdad Naghshpour. *Revolutionary Iran and the United States Low-Intensity Conflict in the Persian Gulf*. Farnham, Surrey, England: Ashgate, 2011.

Steinhauer, Jennifer. "Democrats Hand Victory to Obama on Iran Nuclear Deal." *New York Times*. Last modified September 10, 2015. http://www.nytimes.com/2015/09/11/us /politics/iran-nuclear-deal-senate.html?_r=0.

U.S. Department of State. "Country Reports on Terrorism 2014 State Sponsors of Terrorism Overview." Last modified 2014. http://www.state.gov/j/ct/rls/crt/2014/239410.htm.

U.S. Department of the Treasury. "Comprehensive Iran Sanctions, Accountability, and Divestment Act of 2010." Accessed January 10, 2016. https://www.treasury.gov/resource-cen ter/sanctions/Documents/hr2194.pdf.

Weigel, David. "John Kasich Stakes Out Room in the Center on Iran Deal," *Washington Post*, September 2, 2015. https://www.washingtonpost.com/news/post-politics/wp /2015/09/02/john-kasich-stakes-out-room-in-the-center-on-iran-deal-kentucky-clerk-protest/.

White House. "Parameters for a Joint Comprehensive Plan of Action Regarding the Islamic Republic of Iran's Nuclear Program." Whitehouse.gov. Last modified April 2, 2015. https://www.whitehouse.gov/the-press-office/2015/04/02/parameters-joint-compre hensive-plan-action-regarding-islamic-republic-ir.

White House. "The Historic Deal That Will Prevent Iran from Acquiring a Nuclear Weapon." Accessed January 12, 2016. https://www.whitehouse.gov/issues/foreign-policy/iran -deal.

Iraq

At a Glance

Since the United States invaded Iraq in March 2003 under the direction of Republican president George W. Bush, the successes and failures of U.S. foreign policy have been tied in significant ways to the relationship between the two countries. Although the Second Gulf War formally ended with the withdrawal of U.S. troops in 2011, the rise of the Islamic State of Iraq and Syria (ISIS), often referred to as the Islamic State of Iraq and the Levant (ISIL) by U.S. government officials, has reignited partisan debates over the direction of U.S. foreign policy in Iraq. In addition, the continuation of sectarian conflict creates the constant potential for further destabilization.

According to many Republicans, U.S. foreign policy toward Iraq . . .

- Should be based on a willingness to put boots on the ground to defeat ISIS;
- Should be based on the recognition that the United States is at war with ISIS and global terrorism in general;
- Should recognize that withdrawing most troops from Iraq in 2011 was a mistake; and
- Should be based on a willingness to detain ISIS and Al Qaeda terrorists indefinitely, either in Iraq or in facilities like Guantanamo Bay, Cuba.

According to many Democrats, U.S. foreign policy toward Iraq . . .

- Should be based on a recognition that terrorists captured in Iraq should be tried in the Iraqi judicial system, rather than being held in facilities like Guantanamo Bay;
- Should not include any U.S.-run military bases, though U.S. training personnel at Iraqi bases are a possibility, as is additional security assistance;
- Must focus on consolidating a more inclusive government in Iraq; and
- Should not include any conventional combat troops in the effort to stabilize the country and combat ISIS. Special Forces and training specialists, in addition to air strikes, should be the limit of U.S. involvement.

———————————

Overview

The United States has a long diplomatic and foreign policy history with Iraq, which was first recognized by the U.S. government as an independent state in 1930. However, the roots of the current relationship can be traced to the Iraqi invasion of Kuwait in 1990. Kuwait was liberated relatively easily by an international force led by the United States, whose president at the time, Republican George H. W. Bush, orchestrated the creation of a military coalition with troops from 28 countries. Under the terms of surrender, Iraq was forced to destroy all of its chemical weapons under strict international verification, abandon its nuclear weapons program, and submit all suspect facilities to International Atomic Energy Agency (IAEA) inspections. The United States, France, and Great Britain also established two no-fly zones in Iraq; one to protect the Kurdish minority in the north, and one to protect the Shia majority in the South. Iraq was placed under comprehensive economic sanctions and was only permitted, at times, to sell oil for humanitarian purposes and to pay reparations.

In 1998, Iraq ended its cooperation with the United Nations Special Commission (UNSCOM), which was monitoring Iraqi compliance with the mandate to rid itself of weapons of mass destruction. Great Britain and the United States subsequently initiated a bombing campaign against Iraqi targets that enjoyed broad bipartisan support in the United States. In 1999, Iraq rejected the mandate of the UN commission created to replace UNSCOM, further heightening tensions. By 2001, the United States and Great Britain had stepped up bombing runs over the northern no-fly zone in response to what the George W. Bush administration characterized as increased Iraqi aggression in the area (Dao and Myers 2001). The terrorist attacks of September 11, 2001, in the United States caused a momentary shift in focus to Al Qaeda, Afghanistan, and Osama Bin Laden.

By late December 2001, the United States was making plans for a potential invasion of Iraq (Hamilton 2004). The United States believed at the time that Iraq under Saddam Hussein had a cooperative relationship with Al Qaeda, an assertion later disputed by the bipartisan 9/11 Commission. The Bush administration also believed that there was potential for increased cooperation in the future, based on shared grievances with the United States and with Shia Muslims. Saddam Hussein and Osama bin Laden were both Sunni Muslims (the largest group within Islam, but a minority group within Iraq). The Bush administration also asserted that Iraq retained significant weapons of mass destruction (mainly chemical weapons) stockpiles and that it possessed a mobile clandestine biological weapons program. The Hussein regime had previously used chemical weapons on the Shia Muslims and Kurds.

In October 2002, the House and Senate passed an authorization for the use of military force (AUMF) against Iraq. The resolution passed with nearly unanimous Republican support. Democratic support was mixed. In the Senate, a slim majority of Democrats (29–21) supported the AUMF on the grounds that Iraq had significant weapons of mass destruction capability, was actively seeking nuclear capability, had attempted to assassinate a sitting president, and had attacked innocent members of its own population. In the House of Representatives, a majority of Democrats voted against the resolution, with most arguing that it gave President Bush too much power over the decision to go to war or that it enabled the United States to go to war without specific authorization from the United Nations. In November 2002, the United Nations passed Security Council Resolution 1441, which specified "serious consequences" if Iraq was found in "material breach" of its obligations to declare all of its weapons programs and allow access to inspectors (S/RES 1441 2002).

In response to U.S./UN demands, Iraq allowed weapons inspectors access to Iraq for the first time in several years. Iraq also turned over the required declaration to the UN inspectors. However, Hans Blix, the chief weapons inspector found "gaps" in the declaration, though he reported that inspectors had been granted access to relevant facilities. The United States and the United Kingdom argued that the gaps represented a material breach of Security Council Resolution 1441. Other council members, including France, Russia, and China, argued that the inspectors should be given more time. The United States claimed that it had legal authorization to strike Iraq under the terms of Resolution 1441. Other council members claimed that only the council could make a determination as to the existence of a material breach of the resolution. On March 20, 2003, after failing to gain UN approval, the United States led a multinational "coalition of the willing" as the Bush administration called it, in an invasion of Iraq. Critics argue that the idea of a coalition was essentially window dressing for what was, for the most part, a unilateral invasion.

A history of the U.S-led war in Iraq is beyond the scope of the entry. The conventional military phase of the war only lasted about a month and led to the ouster of Saddam Hussein. Hussein was captured in December 2003. As the conventional phase of the war ended with a decisive U.S. victory, however, a new and more dangerous phase began. The removal of important Baath Party officials from positions in the bureaucracy, including the military and police forces, left a power vacuum. Soon insurgents representing both Sunni and Shia Muslims began doing battle with coalition forces, who they viewed as occupiers and human rights abusers. The growing number of civilian deaths in Iraq and scandals over the treatment of military prisoners by U.S. forces fed this narrative. The United States returned sovereignty to a new Iraqi government in June 2004. Iraq drafted a new constitution and held parliamentary elections in 2005. However, the violence intensified and became full-scale civil war. It is during this time that Abu Musab al-Zarqawi pledged his loyalty to Al Qaeda and announced the formation of Al Qaeda Iraq (AQI).

The United States attempted several measures to control the insurgency. The Iraqi-led, U.S.-fostered Sunni Awakening succeeded in weakening AQI for a time, as did the 2007 U.S. troop surge. However, the exclusionary politics of Nouri al-Maliki provided the fuel the insurgency needs to survive. In 2006, AQI was renamed as the Islamic State of Iraq.

During the 2008 presidential election, Barack Obama promised to withdraw combat troops from Iraq. The withdrawal was completed as promised, thus satisfying most members of the American public, but Iraq continued to be beset by violence, political and economic instability, and sectarian strife. In 2013, the Islamic State of Iraq became the Islamic State of Iraq and Syria, after taking advantage of the civil war in Syria to expand its influence. By 2014, ISIS had gained control of large amounts of territory in northern and central Iraq, including the city of Falluja, which is only about 35 miles from the capital of Bagdad. Though ISIS has since lost significant portions of the territory formerly under its direct control, it continues to conduct operations in significant portions of Iraq. Currently, U.S. foreign policy toward Iraq is intertwined with the goal of defeating ISIS. Promoting good governance and general internal stability are also critical concerns.

Democrats on U.S. Relations with Iraq

The 2012 Democratic Party platform mentioned the word "Iraq" 20 times. However, since at the time the platform was written, ISIS had not yet grown to the point where the United States considered it a top-level threat, the platform focused on the withdrawal of U.S. troops in Iraq and the broader effort to defeat Al Qaeda, which had not become separated from ISIS. The platform emphasized the fact that the U.S. withdrawal plan was approved by the Iraqi government, which had previously negotiated a status of forces agreement with the Bush administration (Democratic National Committee 2012). The platform also promised that military disengagement from Iraq will not end diplomatic and economic engagement and that the departure of U.S. troops will enable the United States to focus on global counterterrorism efforts. The Democratic authors of the platform did not envision that these counterterrorism efforts would cause the United States to reengage in Iraq in significant ways just two years later. The 2016 platform primarily mentions Iraq in the context of ISIS/ISIL, humanitarian assistance for those displaced by ongoing conflict, and the need for good governance. The platform does not directly mention the contentious issue of Special Forces troops in Iraq to combat ISIS.

Surveys of the American public show that most people supported the decision to go to war with Iraq in 2003. But although majorities of both parties supported the war, the partisan gap was still significant. Sixty-one percent of Democrats supported the decision to go to war according to one poll, while 96 percent of Republicans contacted in the same poll favored military action (Newport, Moore, and Jones 2003). In 2013, after the war had ended, 58 percent of Republicans still believed that going to war was the right thing according to one Pew poll. By comparison, only 33 percent of self-identified Democrats held the same view (Pew Research Center 2013). As one might expect, according to the same survey, the percentage of Democrats who believe that the war in Iraq either had already succeeded or would succeed has increased since President Obama took office. It is common in opinion polling to find that the public focuses as much or more on

Status of Forces Agreement between the United States and Iraq

In the waning days of his presidency, George W. Bush joined with Prime Minister al-Malaki of Iraq to sign a status of forces agreement (SOFA) that would bind the United States to withdraw all troops from Iraq by the end of 2011. Significant provisions of the SOFA included:

> While conducting military operations pursuant to this Agreement, it is the duty of members of the United States Forces and of the civilian component to respect Iraqi laws, customs, traditions, and conventions and to refrain from any activities that are inconsistent with the letter and spirit of this Agreement (Article 3, Section 1).
>
> All the United States Forces shall withdraw from all Iraqi territory no later than December 31, 2011 (Article 24, Section 1).
>
> All United States combat forces shall withdraw from Iraqi cities, villages, and localities no later than the time at which Iraqi Security Forces assume full responsibility for security in an Iraqi province, provided that such withdrawal is completed no later than June 30, 2009 (Article 24, Section 2).
>
> In the event of any external or internal threat or aggression against Iraq that would violate its sovereignty, political independence, or territorial integrity, waters, airspace, its democratic system or its elected institutions, and upon request by the Government of Iraq, the Parties shall immediately initiate strategic deliberations and, as may be mutually agreed, the United States shall take appropriate measures, including diplomatic, economic, or military measures, or any other measure, to deter such a threat (Excerpted from Article 27).

Source:

New York Times. "Agreement Between the United States of America and the Republic of Iraq on the Withdrawal of United States Forces from Iraq and the Organization of Their Activities during Their Temporary Presence in Iraq." Last modified November 17, 2008. http://graphics8.nytimes.com/packages/pdf/world/20081119_SOFA_FINAL_AGREED_TEXT.pdf.

the party or person setting a given policy than the policy itself. As such, it is not shocking to find Democrats finding that events in Iraq are developing more favorably under a Democratic Party president.

When President Obama took office in 2008, he did so having made the promise to responsibly end the war. Although he was not able to meet the goal of removing combat troops within 16 months of taking office, he did remove all U.S. troops by December 2011. President George W. Bush had signed a status of forces agreement (SOFA) with the Iraqi government with December 31, 2011, as the deadline for troop withdrawal.

Several Republicans criticized Obama's decision to remove troops from Iraq, arguing that the president should include a new SOFA that would provide for a residual force of U.S. troops based on continuing threats to Iraq. While this appears to be allowed under Article 27, the Obama administration maintained

President Obama's Announcement on Ending the War in Iraq

As a candidate for president, Barack Obama pledged to end the war in Iraq responsibly, and on a specific timetable. Upon taking office, the president instructed his military advisers to develop plans for the withdrawal of U.S. troops. On October 21, 2011, President Obama delivered a speech in which he announced that the war would formally end by the end of December of that year:

> Today, I can report that, as promised, the rest of our troops in Iraq will come home by the end of the year. After nearly nine years, America's war in Iraq will be over.
>
> Over the next two months, our troops in Iraq—tens of thousands of them—will pack up their gear and board convoys for the journey home. The last American soldiers will cross the border out of Iraq with their heads held high, proud of their success, and knowing that the American people stand united in our support for our troops. That is how America's military efforts in Iraq will end.
>
> But even as we mark this important milestone, we're also moving into a new phase in the relationship between the United States and Iraq. As of January 1st, and in keeping with our Strategic Framework Agreement with Iraq, it will be a normal relationship between sovereign nations, an equal partnership based on mutual interests and mutual respect.

On December 18, 2011, the last U.S. troops departed Iraq. While the U.S. effort to defeat ISIS has resulted in the reintroduction of U.S. Special Forces and military advisers, combat troops had not been redeployed there as of August 2016.

Source:

White House. "Remarks by the President on Ending the War in Iraq." Whitehouse.gov. Last modified October 21, 2011. https://www.whitehouse.gov/the-press-office/2011/10/21/remarks -president-ending-war-iraq.

that the Iraqi leadership desired the withdrawal of all U.S. troops. Obama also emphasized that he was honoring the agreement made by the previous president— a Republican—and that it was time for Iraq to take greater responsible for its own security (White House 2011).

President Obama also argued that ending the war in Iraq would enable the United States to focus more on the terrorist threat from Al Qaeda. ISIS, for its part, had yet to formally split from Al Qaeda.

Two main factors have forced the president to reevaluate U.S. foreign policy toward Iraq in the postwar era. First, the rise of ISIS, including their control of major Iraqi cities, has been cause for reevaluation. Second, former Iraqi prime minister al-Maliki and his government made decisions that according to some experts, made it more difficult for Iraq to stabilize. The two conditions were related in that al-Maliki's refusal to accommodate the needs and political desires of Sunni Muslims and Kurds in Iraq, including in the security forces, provided fertile ground for ISIS, a Sunni group. As ISIS began to sweep through and claim territory in Iraq, the security forces collapsed. Obama made the decision in 2014 to refuse to intervene in Iraq to help check ISIS until al-Maliki resigned from power. Maliki resigned in the face of both U.S. pressure and rising discontent within his own government. His successor, Haider al-Abadi, was viewed as more moderate and willing to set up a unity government that included more Sunnis and Kurds. Shortly after, Obama ordered the beginning of airstrikes against ISIS targets in Syria and Iraq. The United States has since deployed hundreds of troops to Iraq to engage in training of Iraqi personnel against ISIS. Special Forces were also deployed to both Iraq and Syria to target ISIS directly.

For the most part, Democrats in Congress have been supportive of President Obama's policies related to Iraq. Democrats applauded the decision to end the war in Iraq. In 2015, when the president advanced a plan to close the prison where many suspected terrorists are held at Guantanamo Bay in Cuba, many Democrats agreed that sites like Guantanamo Bay were counterproductive because their very existence was utilized as an effective recruiting tool by terrorist groups like ISIS. In 2014, when the president ordered air strikes against ISIS positions in Iraq and Syria, Democrats agreed that it was the correct policy—though some expressed trepidation at the prospect of widening the war. House minority whip Steny Hoyer argued that no further action, especially deploying ground troops, should be considered without further consultations with Congress (Lillis 2014). When Republican leaders, including Bush-era officials, charged that Obama's policies in Iraq were at least part of the reason for ISIS's growing strength, Congressional Democrats countered that ISIS had grown out of Al Qaeda Iraq, an organization they say would never have come into being were it not for the decision by the Bush administration to bar members of the Baath Party from service in key positions, including the armed forces and the police.

Both former secretary of state Hillary Clinton and Senator Bernie Sanders, the two main candidates for the Democratic Party presidential nomination, focused their positions concerning Iraq on containing and defeating ISIS. Secretary Clinton, who ultimately won the nomination after a grueling primary, argued that it will be necessary to continue to help to build the military and to govern capacity of Iraq in order to stabilize the country and contain ISIS. In contrast to her support for the 2003 invasion of Iraq, however, Clinton has promised not to send U.S. troops into "another misguided ground war" in that country.

Republicans on U.S. Relations with Iraq

Given the intense criticism of the Obama administration's first-term actions and policies regarding Iraq from some members of the Republican Party, especially Republican presidential nominee Mitt Romney, it would not have been surprising to see a 2012 Republican Party platform that echoed many of these sentiments. Instead, however, the five mentions of Iraq in the platform were remarkably muted. The first three mentions of Iraq in the platform related to situations outside of Iraq, specifically the need to attend to soldiers wounded in various ways during the conflicts in Iraq and Afghanistan and the need to ensure stability within Pakistan (Republican National Committee 2012). The platform also saluted European countries for their role in the conflicts in Iraq in Afghanistan. The only specific account of the situation in Iraq in the platform refers to the ability of Iraqis to build their own secure and democratic society, bearing in mind the need to "protect and preserve the ethnic and religious diversity of their nations" (Republican National Committee 2012). In terms of foreign policy issues, the 2012 Republican platform was much more focused on Iran, Russia, and China. In this fashion, the Republican platform shared with its Democratic Party counterpart a desire to move beyond Iraq and focus on other key foreign policy issues. The 2016 Republican platform only mentions Iraq four times, primarily in the context of fighting ISIS (and criticizing the Obama administration for not doing enough to protect vulnerable communities in Iraq from ISIS).

As noted above, while both parties favored the original decision to go to war with Iraq, Republicans in the general public were even more convinced that the decision was the right one. As with Democrats, however, Republican support for the war decreased over time as the country fell into violent chaos and American casualties mounted. Even in 2013, however, one poll found that a majority of Republicans (58 percent) believed that going to war was the right decision. By contrast, only 33 percent of Democrats polled felt that way (Pew Research Center 2013). In terms of ISIS, the main focus of American foreign policy in both Iraq and Syria, Republicans and Democrats agree that the group is a significant threat to U.S. interests. For Republicans, ISIS, and groups like it ranked as the number one threat to the United States, at least within the realm of U.S. foreign policy (Chicago Council on Global Affairs 2015).

Republicans have taken aim at Democrats, especially the president, on decision making with respect to the situation in Iraq. In 2011, Governor Mitt Romney, the eventual Republican presidential nominee, used the occasion to argue that the president had been short sighted to not conclude a status of forces agreement with Iraq to allow for the maintenance of a residual force of 10,000 to 30,000 troops in Iraq (BBC News 2011). South Carolina Republican senator Lindsey Graham claimed that the withdrawal would put in jeopardy everything that the United States had worked for and gained in Iraq (O'Brien 2011). House Speaker John Boehner, striking a more conciliatory note, stated that, while he was concerned about the withdrawal, he was hopeful that Iraq and the United States would be able to continue to work together to consolidate the gains that both sides fought for (Boehner 2011).

As ISIS has become more powerful in Iraq and Syria, the Republican narrative has sharpened. For example, in an interview on CBS News' *Face the Nation*, Cheney advanced the idea that blame for the rise of ISIS lay with the decision by President Obama to neither leave a residual force in Iraq nor provide for adequate training upon the departure of U.S. troops (CBS News 2015). Republicans also point to an interview in which Obama appears to refer to ISIS as Al Qaeda's "jayvee team" as an indication that the president lacks a coherent strategy for dealing with the terrorist group. Former Florida governor Jeb Bush, who ultimately withdrew from the race to succeed Barack Obama as president of the United States, expressed the belief in an interview that the decline of Iraq is primarily due to the decision by the president to withdraw as early and completely as possible (Nagourney 2015).

The current Republican candidates for president are, like the Democratic candidates, much more focused on ISIS as a transnational actor than they are on U.S.-Iraq relations. Among the Republican presidential candidates, only Senator Ted Cruz mentioned Iraq on the national security section of his Web site, and only then in the context of barring refugees from any country with substantial territory controlled by a terrorist organization (Cruz 2016). With regard to ISIS, Ohio governor John Kasich appears to have the most aggressive strategy, in that he is willing to commit to putting "boots on the ground" as part of the effort to defeat ISIS (Kasich 2016). Kasich has not directly committed to engaging U.S. combat brigades in a battle with ISIS during the Republican debates. Instead, he has argued for a coalition force with a U.S. presence, in addition to arming moderate rebels in Syria and building government capacity in Iraq. Businessman Donald Trump at one point in the debates suggested that he had always been opposed to the Iraq War, a position that would have put him at odds with other Republican candidates, but in line with the populist wing of the Republican Party. The fact-checking organization Politifact found this statement false (Carroll 2016).

Further Reading

BBC News. "Romney Attacks Obama over US Troop Withdrawal from Iraq." Last modified December 18, 2011. http://www.bbc.com/news/world-us-canada-16237428.

Boehner, John. "Statement by Speaker Boehner on President Obama's Iraq Announcement." Speaker.gov. Last modified October 21, 2011. http://www.speaker.gov/press-release /statement-speaker-boehner-president-obama%E2%80%99s-iraq-announcement.

Carroll, Lauren. "Donald Trump Was Not 'Loud and Clear' in Iraq War Opposition | Politifact." @Politifact. Last modified February 13, 2016. http://www.politifact.com/truth-o-meter /statements/2016/feb/13/donald-trump/donald-trump-says-his-early-opposition-iraq -war-wa/.

CBS News. "Former VP Cheney and Daughter on Iran Nuclear Deal, Rise of ISIS—Videos— CBS News." August 31, 2015. http://www.cbsnews.com/videos/former-vp-cheney-and -daughter-on-iran-nuclear-deal-rise-of-isis/.

Chicago Council on Global Affairs. "America Divided: Political Partisanship and US Foreign Policy." Last modified 2015. https://www.thechicagocouncil.org/sites/default/files /CCGA_PublicSurvey2015.pdf.

Cruz, Ted. "Defend Our Nation." Ted Cruz for President. Last modified 2016. https://www .tedcruz.org/issues/defend-our-nation/.

Dao, James, and Steven L. Myers. "Attack on Iraq—The Overview—U.S. and British Jets Strike Air-Defense Centers in Iraq—NYTimes.com." *New York Times—Breaking News,*

World News & Multimedia. Last modified February 17, 2001. http://www.nytimes .com/2001/02/17/world/attack-iraq-overview-us-british-jets-strike-air-defense-centers -iraq.html?pagewanted=all.

Democratic National Committee. "2012 Democratic Platform." Democrats.org. Last modified 2012. https://www.democrats.org/party-platform.

Hamilton, William. "Bush Began to Plan War Three Months after 9/11." *Washington Post*. Last modified April 17, 2004. http://www.washingtonpost.com/wp-dyn/articles/A17347 -2004Apr16.html.

Kasich, John. "John Kasich: We Need Boots on the Ground to Defeat ISIS." TIME. Accessed April 9, 2016. http://time.com/4119069/isis-john-kasich.

Lillis, Mike. "Key Democrats Offer Obama Support on Iraq." *The Hill*. Last modified August 12, 2014. http://thehill.com/policy/international/214948-key-democrats-offer -obama-support-on-iraq-and-a-warning.

Nagourney, Adam. "Jeb Bush Blames Hillary Clinton and Obama for Iraq's Decline." *New York Times*. August 11, 2015. http://www.nytimes.com/2015/08/12/us/politics/jeb-bush -blames-us-policies-for-isis-rise.html.

"National Security | Issues | Hillary for America." Hillary for America. Last modified 2016. https://www.hillaryclinton.com/issues/national-security/.

Newport, Frank, David W. Moore, and Jeffrey M. Jones. "Special Release: American Opinion on the War." Gallup.com. Last modified March 21, 2003. http://www.gallup.com /poll/8068/special-release-american-opinion-war.aspx.

O'Brien, Michael. "Republicans Criticize Obama over Iraq Withdrawal." NBC News. Last modified October 21, 2011. http://firstread.nbcnews.com/_news/2011/10/21/8433344 -republicans-criticize-obama-over-iraq-withdrawal.

Pew Research Center. "A Decade Later, Iraq War Divides the Public." Pew Research Center for the People and the Press. Last modified March 18, 2013. http://www.people-press .org/2013/03/18/a-decade-later-iraq-war-divides-the-public/.

Republican National Committee. "2012 Republican Platform." Last modified 2012. https:// cdn.gop.com/docs/2012GOPPlatform.pdf.

United Nations. "Resolution 1441 (2002) S/RES/1441 2002." Last modified November 8, 2002. http://www.un.org/Depts/unmovic/documents/1441.pdf.

White House. "Remarks by the President on Ending the War in Iraq." Whitehouse.gov. Last modified October 21, 2011. https://www.whitehouse.gov/the-press-office/2011/10/21 /remarks-president-ending-war-iraq.

ISIS/ISIL

At a Glance

The Islamic State of Iraq and Syria (ISIS), often called the Islamic State of Iraq and the Levant (ISIL) by the U.S. government, or the Islamic State (IS) by members of the terrorist organization itself, has been consistently rated by both the public and political elites as a significant threat to U.S. domestic and foreign policy interests. The 2016 mass shooting at the Pulse Nightclub in Orlando, which was partially inspired by ISIS, coupled with direct ISIS attacks in Africa, Europe, the Middle East, and Asia, has raised the profile of the organization. Under the Obama administration, the official policy of the United States toward ISIS has been to contain and degrade the organization through a mixture of airstrikes, support for ISIS opponents, and the use of airstrikes on territory controlled by the organization. Republicans have argued the Obama administration response has been too late, too limited in scope, and generally ineffective.

According to many Democrats, U.S. foreign policy toward ISIS . . .

- Should not include the involvement of U.S. ground troops with the exception of Special Operations forces;
- Should be based on supporting more moderate insurgents and other political/military actors in countries such as Syria, Iraq, and Libya;
- Must include airstrikes to target areas held by ISIS; and
- Should not include a moratorium on the acceptance of refugees or other immigrants from countries with high levels of ISIS activity.

According to many Republicans, U.S. foreign policy toward ISIS . . .

- Should include the option of sending more ground troops into countries such as Syria and Iraq to combat ISIS;
- Should include a moratorium on the acceptance of refugees and other immigrants from countries with high levels of ISIS activity;

- Should focus on a more rapid time frame for the destruction of the organization using more aggressive techniques; and
- Should equate ISIS terrorist activity with radical Islam.

Overview

Though the history of ISIS can be traced as far back as the late 1980s, the rise of the organization is more directly tied to the Sunni insurgency in Iraq that arose after the 2003 U.S. invasion of that country. In 2004, a group of insurgents led by Abu Musab al-Zarqawi declared its loyalty to Osama bin Laden, leader of the Al Qaeda terrorist organization responsible for the September 11, 2001, terrorist attacks against New York City and Washington, D.C. This group took on the name Al Qaida Iraq (AQI). In 2006, al-Zarqawi was killed by a U.S. airstrike and ultimately replaced by Abu Ayyub al-Masri, who subsequently renamed AQI the Islamic State in Iraq (ISI). This rebranding was part of an effort to draw more recruits by calling for the development of a theocratic Sunni State in Iraq. However, the rise of nationalism among Iraqi Sunnis (an event sometimes referred to as the Sunni Awakening) coupled with the "surge" of U.S. troops into Iraq further weakened ISI. By time the United States began withdrawing troops from Iraq, ISI was decimated to the point where most of its forces had either been killed or imprisoned. Al-Masri died by his own hand in 2010 during a joint attack by U.S. and Iraqi forces.

Several factors enabled Al-Masri's successor, Abu Bakar al-Baghdadi, to resuscitate the organization. During his campaign for president, Barack Obama promised a timely withdrawal from Iraq according to the timeline negotiated in the waning days for the George W. Bush administration. The withdrawal, however, opened space for ISI to gain ground against Iraqi troops of police forces that still lacked numbers and key training in critical areas. More importantly, the regime of Prime Minister Nouri al-Maliki focused on the isolation of Sunni Muslims in Iraq, in part as retribution for the marginalization of Shia Muslims during the rule of Saddam Hussein. Maliki cracked down on Shia protesters, stripped Shia Muslims of key government and military positions, and instituted several other practices incompatible with good governance (Al-Ali 2014). ISI spread into Syria amid the chaos that resulted from the Arab Spring protests, and more specifically, the brutal crackdown on civilian protesters by Syrian forces under Bahir al-Assad. In 2011, al-Baghdadi sent key surrogates into Syria to establish the al-Nursa Front. In 2013, ISI insurgents in Syria merged with the al-Nursa and became the Islamic State of Iraq and greater Syria (ISIS).

In 2013, ISIS and Al Qaeda officially separated over strategic, tactical, and power-sharing differences. ISIS was able to increase its momentum, however, taking control of the cities of Mosul and Falluja in Iraq, as well as large portions of eastern Syria. In 2014 Al-Baghdadi declared the territory under ISIS control to be a caliphate (an Islamic caliphate consists of an area ruled by a successor to the

Prophet Muhammed). The successor would be the leader of all Muslims in a transnational empire, ruled in accordance with the principles of Islamic Law.

ISIS has used a mixture of extortion, oil sales, kidnapping, and "taxation" schemes in order to finance its activities. As a terrorist organization that is also attempting to hold territory in furtherance of its political goals, ISIS requires more money to operate than a typical terrorist group. Payments to ISIS fighters, transfer payments to the families of suicide bombers, equipment maintenance, and the provision of social services within its area of control all weigh heavily on the ISIS budget.

In the beginning, the United States appeared to focus more on what remained of the Al Qaeda network than the relatively newly formed ISIS. In a 2014 interview with the *New Yorker*, Obama appeared to compare ISIS to a jayvee basketball team (Remnick 2014). In addition, the repressive policies of the al-Maliki regime, which the United States blamed along with Assad's repression in Syria for most of the renewed sectarian violence in the region, made the Obama administration hesitant to devote resources to combating ISIS when the underlying conditions for violence had not been addressed. Only after al-Maliki agreed to step down in August 2014 did the United States begin airstrikes against ISIS positions in Iraq and Syria. After some hesitation, the Obama administration, with congressional support, began to train and equip more moderate rebels, especially in Syria, in their efforts to combat both Assad and ISIS. U.S. Special Forces troops are also active in both Iraq and Syria.

ISIS began to lose control of territory in Iraq and Syria in early 2015. A combination of U.S. airstrikes, increasing effectiveness of Iraqi security operations, independent Kurdish operations in Syria and parts of Iraq, Russian airstrikes, and Syrian military action have all taken their toll on the terrorist group. As ISIS has begun to lose territory in the region, it has expanded its overall area of operations and changed strategies to a degree by initiating more attacks on foreign soil. The most infamous of these attacks were the Paris attacks of November 2015, which left more than 100 dead and hundreds wounded, and the Brussels attacks of March 2016, which killed over 30. However, ISIS attacks in Bangladesh, Egypt, Indonesia, Iraq, Libya, and Saudi Arabia have killed hundreds more. These attacks represent a projection of power beyond traditional ISIS strongholds, but they may also be a symptom of a group resorting to more traditional tactics as their ability to take and hold territory diminishes.

ISIS has also focused on using social media in an effort to inspire sympathizers who are not actual members of the organization to carry out attacks against its enemies, including the United States. In June 2016, an American citizen named Omar Mateen shot and killed 49 patrons (and wounded 53 others) at the Pulse Nightclub in Orlando. In a 9-1-1 call that he placed during the attack, Mateen pledged allegiance to ISIS. Amaq News Agency, which issues press releases on behalf of ISIS referred to Mateen as an "ISIS Fighter" (Politico 2016). Mateen, however, was not trained by ISIS nor is there evidence that he coordinated his attack with ISIS leadership at any level. A similar loyalty pledge was discovered on a social media account for Tashfeen Malik, one two perpetrators of the 2015 San Bernardino attack, which killed 14 and injured 22. Attacks on U.S. soil such as these have heightened partisan tensions concerning use of the term "radical Islam" as well as refugee and immigration policy.

Democrats on ISIS/ISIL

The 2016 Democratic Party platform mentioned ISIS seven times in its section on combating terrorism. The platform, in essence, represents a defense and rationale for continuing current U.S. policy by emphasizing the destruction of ISIS strongholds in Iraq and Syria, the need for countries in their region to "carry their weight" and the desire to pursue multilateralism in all phases of the existing conflict (Democratic National Convention 2016). In continuity with its 2012 platform, Democrats avoid the use of global war on terror language, focusing instead on stances and strategies toward individual terrorist organizations. Democrats also argue that Republicans are far too quick to vilify Muslims in general, rather than the terrorist organizations that preach a perverted form of Islam rejected by mainstream Muslims. Democrats assert that such rhetoric from the GOP actually makes it easier for ISIS to recruit members, both within its area of direct territorial control and within target states, to its cause.

Within the realm of public opinion, Democrats and Republicans are united around the idea that ISIS is a significant threat to the United States. Seventy-nine percent of Democrats and 93 percent of Republicans view ISIS as a major threat according to a poll by the Pew Research Center (Doherty and Smith 2015). Once one moves beyond the basic agreement that the organization poses a threat, however, the partisan gap rapidly opens. For example, a majority of Democrats believe that too much military force creates more terrorism by groups such as ISIS, while a majority of Republicans believe that employing overwhelming military force is the best way to defeat ISIS (Doherty and Smith 2015). In addition, a majority of Democrats (58 percent) opposed the use of U.S. ground troops to fight ISIS in Iraq and Syria, according to a poll conducted by CNN (Agiesta 2015).

Overall, opinion polling provides a murkier picture regarding public opinion about the overall merits of using U.S. ground troops to combat ISIS (especially in Iraq and Syria). It is possible to find both narrow support and narrow opposition to the use of U.S. ground troops. The fact that the margin between support and opposition normally falls within a given poll's margin of error suggests a heavily divided public, largely on partisan lines. As more attacks occur (both of the "inspired" and "direct" nature) the salience of this issue is likely to increase. In a poll conducted after the partially ISIS-inspired Orlando nightclub attack, respondents overall found former secretary of state and 2016 Democratic presidential nominee Hillary Clinton to be more trustworthy with regard to terrorism in general by an overall margin of 11 percentage points than GOP nominee Donald Trump (ABC News/

Washington Post 2016). That poll indicated that Democrats and Democrat-leaning independents were more likely to trust Clinton on the issue of terrorism than Republicans (and Republican-leaning independents) were to trust Trump.

Democrats in Congress have been mixed in response to President Obama's approach to ISIS. On one hand, a majority of Democrats voted for the president's "train and equip" proposal, which has resulted in arming insurgents in Syria to fight both against the regime of Bashar al-Assad and ISIS. A majority of Democrats have also supported the president in the aggressive use of airstrikes against ISIS positions and resources, as well as the effort to cut off various avenues of financing for the organization. In addition, congressional Democrats have supported Obama's position that the proper response to potential ISIS-inspired mass shootings in the United States is to avoid the vilification of Muslims in general and to focus on measures to reduce American vulnerability to such attacks, such as through enhanced background checks for firearms purchases and bans on military-style assault rifles (a term that is also the subject of significant debate). Senator Christopher Murphy of Connecticut, for example, argued that the Orlando attack was an example of a mass shooting of the type that happens at an alarming rate in the United States due to inadequate gun control laws (Murphy 2016).

Conversely, many congressional Democrats have been critical, at least in part, of the president's approach. For example, the train and equip resolution passed the House by a vote of 273–156 in 2014. Eighty-five Democrats supported the legislation, while 71 voted against it. Democratic leadership, especially Minority Leader Nancy Pelosi, favored the provision to arm Syrian rebels, claiming that the decision was "hard, but necessary" (Roll Call 2014). Several antiwar Democrats voted against the amendment that allowed continued funding of the program over concerns that arming the rebels would be a prelude to further U.S. involvement in another war in the Middle East. Representative Jackie Speier of California asserted that "we should be frank with ourselves and the American people. We are not facing a limited engagement, but a new war that will only escalate" (Marcos 2014). A similar debate occurred in the Senate, where the measure passed by a vote of 78–22 in September 2014. Senate leadership, as well as Democrats likely to be vulnerable in the 2014 midterm elections, tended to support the train and equip program, while antiwar Democrats warned that arming the rebels might create a slippery slope toward full U.S. military involvement.

Some Democrats in Congress, though, have been critical of the president for not going far enough in the effort to defeat ISIS, especially in the wake of attacks since 2015 in Europe and the United States. California representative Adam Schiff, for example, indicated that he expected the president to propose new elements to the strategy to defeat ISIS in the wake of the Paris attacks. Senator Diane Feinstein argued that the president's response may not be "robust enough" to counter the threat posed by the terrorist organization (Steinhauer and Shear 2015). Secretary of State and 2016 Democratic presidential nominee Hillary Clinton has argued that ISIS needs to be defeated, not merely contained. Language suggesting the need for

ISIS's defeat also has a prominent place in the 2016 Democratic Party platform. At the same time, antiwar Democrats, many of whom voted against the equip and train program, are concerned that the presidential request for an authorization for use of military force (AUMF) against ISIS in 2015 potentially left the door open to another protracted conflict in the Middle East. Coupled with concerns expressed by Republicans that the AUMF would not go far enough, the conflict with ISIS remains justified by previous AUMF resolutions related to Afghanistan and Iraq.

Republicans on ISIS/ISIL

Generally, Republicans contend that Democrats, especially President Obama and Secretary of State Hillary Clinton, have acted too slowly and indecisively with respect to ISIS. For example, they seized on President Obama's apparent reference to ISIS as Al Qaeda's "jayvee team" in 2014 to underscore their assertion that he underestimated the severity of the threat that ISIS posed. Republicans have also mocked and condemned Obama's refusal to use the term "radical Islam" in describing the belief system of ISIS. For the president, this refusal originates in the belief that ISIS is not an Islamic organization, given its willingness to indiscriminately kill Muslims and engage in other violent actions forbidden according to mainstream understandings of the Islamic faith. Obama's contention is that using the term "radical Islam" to describe ISIS in effect slanders the faith of millions of peaceful Muslims around the world. "We are not at war with Islam. We are at war with people who have perverted Islam," Obama said in February 2016. "These terrorists are desperate for legitimacy. And all of us have a responsibility to refute the notion that groups like ISIL somehow represent Islam because that is a falsehood that embraces the terrorist narrative."

For Republicans, though, the refusal of Obama to employ the term represents a basic failure "to understand the enemy—a key component of which, they argue, is the radical Islamic ideology that is fueling terrorist attacks in the Middle East and increasingly in the West. Terrorists who perpetrated the most recent attacks in Europe and the United States—like the shootings in San Bernardino, California, and Paris—all subscribed to radical Islamic ideologies. The White House, Republicans say, shouldn't be afraid to call out the source of this violence" (Diamond and Gaouette 2016).

Within the general public, polls indicate that Republicans are more likely to support the use of ground troops against ISIS than are Democrats or independents. Overall, 57 percent of self-identified Republicans and 61 percent of conservative Republicans in one 2015 Pew poll favor the use of ground troops against ISIS in Iraq and Syria (Pew Research Center 2015). As one might expect in a partisan environment, Republicans are more likely than Democrats to believe that President Obama has handled the conflict with ISIS poorly and that the United States lacks a coherent plan to deal with the terrorist group. It is worth noting, however, that both Democrats and Republicans have become more likely to express the view that the conflict with ISIS is going poorly over time (Agiesta 2015). The rising number of ISIS attacks outside of Syria and Iraq likely play a significant role in this finding.

The 2015 ISIS attacks in Paris, as well as the 2016 attacks in Brussels, coupled with the Orlando mass shooting have intensified Republican criticism of President Obama's ISIS policy. After the Brussels attack, for example, Republican senators John McCain and Lindsey Graham, who often speak in tandem on foreign policy issues, argued that "the Administration still has no plausible strategy to destroy ISIL on anything close to an acceptable timeline" (McCain and Graham 2016). Republicans such as McCain and former vice president Dick Cheney, joined by Democrats such as Leon Panetta, have consistently argued that the United States withdrew combat troops from Iraq too early, causing instability and providing breathing space to a beleaguered ISIS. Finally, Republicans, especially in the House of Representatives, have been critical of perceived hesitance on the part of the Obama administration to label ISIS terrorist acts, especially against Christians, as acts of genocide. In 2016, Republicans advanced a bill to make such a determination and call on the president to do the same. The resolution passed 393–0 in the House and was not taken up by the Senate. As a "sense of the House" resolution, the bill did not go to the Senate. Three days later, Secretary of State John Kerry referred to ISIS atrocities as acts of genocide against Christians, Yazidis (a small ethno-religious minority in Iraq), and Shia Muslims.

It is less clear, however, how the Republican critique translates to the world of policy. Republicans have advocated for airstrikes against ISIS positions, but this is not a position that is qualitatively or quantitatively different from Obama administration policy. Republican leaders have also called for the use of ground troops to fight ISIS, but as of mid-2016 Republicans had not rallied behind any single proposal or bill that would increase the American ground presence in Iraq, Syria, and Libya. At times during the 2016 presidential campaign, Republican nominee Donald Trump has argued for a troop surge of between 20,000 and 30,000 in Iraq and Syria to fight ISIS (Gaouette and Starr 2016). Earlier in the campaign, however, Trump expressed skepticism about sending additional ground troops, especially to Syria, to combat the terrorist group. Trump has also suggested seizing oil fields in Iraq and Syria in order to deny those resources to ISIS. But any such action would require major American ground operations in both countries.

The ambivalence among leaders in both parties can been seen in the debate over President Obama's request for an AUMF against ISIS. Originally, the Obama administration argued that the AUMF passed after 9/11 provided the necessary authorization for military action against ISIS. Republicans, including then Speaker of the House John Boehner, argued that a new AUMF would be needed to strike ISIS, since the organization did not exist at the time of the original AUMF in 2001. Other Republicans, including Senator Marco Rubio, argued that the existing AUMF was sufficient. When the president did submit a request for an AUMF in February 2015, further divisions arose. Republicans argued that the prohibition on "enduring offensive ground combat operations" would be too limiting on the current president and his successor (Berman 2015). Democrats, joined by more libertarian-minded Republicans such as Ron Paul argued that the AUMF would provide the president with too much flexibility in containing ISIS. In the end neither the House nor the Senate voted on the measure. The budget for overseas contingent operations, which includes money used in operations against ISIS was set at $58.6 billion in 2016 (Rogers 2016). In effect, operations against ISIS continue to be funded without specifically being approved. This legal and budgetary ambiguity is likely to continue into the next presidential administration, whether it is a Democrat or a Republican in the Oval Office.

Further Reading

ABC News/*Washington Post*. "Vast Support for a Watch-List Gun Ban; Clinton Prevails in Response to Orlando." Last modified June 28, 2016. http://www.langerresearch.com/wp-content/uploads/1178a2GunsandTerrorism.pdf.

Agiesta, Jennifer. "Poll: Most Say Send Ground Troops to Fight ISIS." CNN. Last modified December 7, 2015. http://www.cnn.com/2015/12/06/politics/isis-obama-poll/.

Al-Ali, Zaid. "How Maliki Ruined Iraq." *Foreign Policy*. Last modified June 19, 2014. http://foreignpolicy.com/2014/06/19/how-maliki-ruined-iraq/?wp_login_redirect=0.

Allen, Ron. "After Brussels Terror Attack, Obama Says No Need for a 'Plan B' against ISIS." NBC News. Last modified March 23, 2016. http://www.nbcnews.com/politics/barack-obama/after-brussels-terror-attack-obama-says-no-need-plan-b-n544586.

Berman, Russell. "Congress Won't Approve Obama's Authorization of Force against ISIS." *The Atlantic*. Last modified April 15, 2015. http://www.theatlantic.com/politics/archive/2015/04/the-war-against-isis-will-go-undeclared/390618/.

Boyer, Dave. "Obama Confesses: 'We Don't Have a Strategy Yet' for Dealing with Islamic State." *Washington Times*. Last modified August 28, 2014. http://www.washingtontimes.com/news/2014/aug/28/obama-admits-isil-dilemma-we-dont-have-strategy-ye/?page=all.

Democratic National Convention. "2016 Democratic Platform Draft." 2016 Democratic National Convention. Last modified July 1, 2016. https://demconvention.com/wp-content/uploads/2016/07/2016-DEMOCRATIC-PARTY-PLATFORM-DRAFT-7.1.16.pdf.

Diamond, Jeremy, and Nicole Gaouette, "Does It Matter if Obama Uses the Term 'Islamic Terrorism'?" June 13, 2016. http://www.cnn.com/2016/06/13/politics/islamic-terrorism-trump-obama-clinton/

Doherty, Carroll, and Samantha Smith. "Republicans and National Security: 5 Facts." Pew Research Center. Last modified December 15, 2015. http://www.pewresearch.org/fact-tank/2015/12/15/5-facts-about-republicans-and-national-security/.

Gaouette, Nicole, and Barbara Starr. "Trump Wants 30,000 Troops. Would That Defeat ISIS? Politics.com." CNN. Last modified March 11, 2016. http://www.cnn.com/2016/03/11/politics/donald-trump-30000-troops-isis/.

Marcos, Cristina. "85 Democrats Buck Obama in ISIS Vote." *The Hill*. Last modified September 17, 2014. http://thehill.com/blogs/floor-action/house/218102-85-democrats-buck-obama-on-syria.

McCain, John, and Lindsey Graham. "Mccain & Graham on Terrorist Attacks in Brussels Press Releases United States Senator John McCain." John McCain U.S. Senator: Arizona. Last modified March 22, 2016. http://www.mccain.senate.gov/public/index.cfm/press-releases?ID=72644D94-A453-4855-AC8E-CD8E3F4775D4.

Murphy, Chris. "Murphy Statement on Orlando Shooting." U.S. Senator Chris Murphy of Connecticut. Last modified June 12, 2016. https://www.murphy.senate.gov/newsroom/press-releases/murphy-statement-on-orlando-shooting.

Pew Research Center. "Growing Support for Campaign against ISIS—and Possible Use of U.S. Ground Troops." Pew Research Center for the People and the Press. Last modified February 24, 2015. http://www.people-press.org/2015/02/24/growing-support-for-campaign-against-isis-and-possible-use-of-u-s-ground-troops/.

Politico. "ISIL Takes Credit for Mass Shooting in Orlando." Last modified June 12, 2016. http://www.politico.com/story/2016/06/isil-takes-credit-for-mass-shooting-in-orlando-224242.

Remnick, David. "Going the Distance: On and Off the Road with Barack Obama." *New Yorker*. Last modified January 27, 2014. http://www.newyorker.com/magazine/2014/01/27/going-the-distance-david-remnick.

Rogers, Hal. "FY 2016 Omnibus—Department of Defense Appropriations." The U.S. House of Representatives Committee on Appropriations. Last modified 2016. http://appropriations.house.gov/uploadedfiles/12.15.15_fy_2016_omnibus_-_defense_-_summary.pdf.

Roll Call. Sanchez, Humberto. "Paul and Rubio Spar over Foreign Policy, ISIS AUMF." Last modified December 12, 2014. http://www.rollcall.com/wgdb/paul-and-rubio-spar-isis-aumf-foreign-policy/?dcz=.

Steinhauer, Jennifer, and Michael D. Shear. "Obama's Plans to Stop ISIS Leave Many Democrats Wanting More" *New York Times*, Last modified December 5, 2015. http://www.nytimes.com/2015/12/09/us/politics/obamas-plans-to-stop-isis-leave-many-democrats-wanting-more.html.

Wolfgang, Ben. "Obama Admits: We Don't Have a Complete Strategy to Fight Islamic State," *Washington Times*. Last modified June 8, 2015. http://www.washingtontimes.com/news/2015/jun/8/obama-admits-we-dont-have-complete-strategy-fight-/.

Israel

At a Glance

For decades, U.S. foreign policy toward Israel has been characterized by bipartisan consensus. The consensus had been centered on a close, generally supportive relationship with Israel since the early 1970s. In recent years, however, a partisan gap has opened between Democrats and Republicans on the issue of U.S.–Israel relations. Although this gap has not had a significant impact on policy outcomes to this point, it is notable that the gap appears both in public opinion and in increased presidential criticism of Israeli policies.

Democrats are more likely than Republicans to . . .

- Be critical of Israeli policy in the occupied territories, including the West Bank, the Gaza Strip, and the Golan Heights;
- Favor a two-state solution with a viable Israeli and Palestinian state;
- Believe that Israel bears some responsibility for the explosive political tensions it has with its Arab neighbors in the Middle East; and
- Oppose the Israeli position on the Iran nuclear issue.

Republicans are more likely than Democrats to . . .

- Sympathize with Israel more than the Palestinians;
- View the current lack of a two-state solution as the fault of the Palestinians;
- Believe that Israel has a positive impact on the overall political situation in the Middle East; and
- Favor the Israeli position on the Iran nuclear issue.

Areas of relative partisan agreement between Republicans and Democrats . . .

- Republicans and Democrats are more likely to sympathize with Israel over the Palestinians (though Republicans tend to be more sympathetic);
- Both parties favor a two-state solution; and
- Both parties continue to see Israel as a key ally in the Middle East.

Overview

It is possible to trace the relationship between the United States and Israel to a time before modern Israel declared independence in 1948. Although originally ambivalent about Zionism (the drive to establish a Jewish state in Palestine), Woodrow Wilson came to support the Balfour Declaration by the British, who held control over much of the area as a trusteeship territory. The Balfour Declaration expressed support for the idea of a Jewish state in Palestine and acted as a catalyst in convincing increasing numbers of Jews to immigrate into the area. As it became clear that Turkey would be defeated in World War I, Wilson's reservations about supporting the declaration—and angering Turkey—decreased (Lebow 1968, 523). Congress passed a concurrent resolution supporting the establishment of the state of Israel in 1922. Succeeding presidents also acquiesced to the Balfour Declaration, though the formation of a Jewish homeland in Palestine was not a high priority for the United States.

World War II and the Holocaust provided a spark for further Jewish immigration into the region. The Holocaust also increased international sympathy for the creation of a Jewish state in Palestine. In 1947, the newly formed United Nations developed a partition plan for Palestine that would have split the territory into Jewish and Palestinian States. Jews in the region widely accepted the plan. Palestinians, who believed that the plan amounted to the theft of Palestinian land, rejected the proposal. In addition, all of the Middle Eastern countries that were members of the United Nations at the time voted against the partition plan. As the British withdrew from the region, Israel unilaterally declared independence on May 14, 1948. On the same day, the United States became the first country to provisionally recognize Israel (National Archives 2006).

The Israeli declaration of independence led to an immediate war between the new State of Israel and its Arab neighbors, who believed the declaration was illegal. For its part, the United States, in cooperation with the United Nations, maintained an arms embargo over the region and did not intervene directly. Ultimately, Egypt, Iraq, Jordan, Lebanon, and Syria declared war and fought alongside troops from Saudi Arabia, Yemen, and Palestinian militias (Office of the Historian n.d.). Israel ultimately won the war and gained a small amount of territory as a result. In 1956, during the Suez Canal crisis, in which Israel worked with Great Britain and France to gain control of the canal zone, the United States sided with the Soviet Union and forced a withdrawal of foreign forces from Egypt.

The United States began to sell arms to Israel in the 1960s under President Kennedy. However, the United States did not take sides in the 1967 war, in which Israel launched what it claimed were preemptive strikes against Egypt and Syria, which had built up their military forces along their borders with Israel. By the close of the so-called Six-Day War, which also pulled in Jordan on the side of its Arab neighbors, Israel had gained control over what are now called the occupied territories, including the West Bank of the Jordan River, the Gaza Strip, the Sinai Peninsula, and the Golan Heights, and began allowing Jewish settlement of some of these lands. Though the United States was critical of the Israeli practice of building settlements within the occupied territories, the relationship between the two countries rapidly improved at the end of the 1960s and the beginning of the 1970s. The United States supported Israel during the 1973 Yom Kippur War with military aid. In 1974, the United States made its first military grants to Israel. Overall, the initial cool relationship, as well as the later improvement, occurred across partisan lines.

Relations between the United States and Israel continued to improve over time. The Camp David Accords of 1978, which brought peace between Egypt and Israel, resulted in large outflows of U.S. aid to both countries. In 1979, for example, Israel received nearly $5 billion in U.S. aid (Sharp 2015, 30). The relationship continued to deepen during the Reagan years, though the Israeli invasion of Lebanon caused some alarm in the United States and the U.S. sale of Airborne Warning and Control Systems (AWACS) to Saudi Arabia raised alarms in Tel Aviv. During the administration of George W. Bush, the relationship between the United States and Israel cooled a bit as the United States withheld certain loan guarantees as leverage against the construction of Israeli settlements in the West Bank (Lasensky 2002). However, in no year during the 1990s did U.S. aid drop below $3 billion.

In 1995, Israel and the Palestinian Authority (PA) signed the Oslo Accords, designed to bring peace between Palestinians and Israelis based ultimately on the creation of a Palestinian state. For a variety of reasons, including the failure to resolve the key issue of control over Jerusalem and the right of return for Palestinian refugees, the peace process ultimately failed. Although disappointed in the outcome, the United States continued to maintain positive relations with Israel. Members of both parties generally laid the blame for the failure of the Oslo process on the Palestinian Authority than on Israel. The Clinton administration relaunched peace efforts in the late 1990s. These efforts also failed, though, due to Clinton's political weakness in the wake of his impeachment, the Israeli belief that the PA would not keep its end of the bargain to help prevent Palestinian attacks against Israel, the precarious position of Yasser Arafat (leader of the Palestinian Authority), and the unwillingness of the PA to accept what it viewed as less than was offered in Oslo. Any hopes for a peace brokered by Clinton ended at the beginning of the Second Intifada (uprising) which began in September 2000. The uprising resulted in a period of increased violence between Israelis and Palestinians between 2000 and 2005.

Overall, the U.S. relationship with Israel remained positive during the administration of Republican President George W. Bush. Aid levels to Israel remained high, and the United States, in spite of some disagreement, was willing to take a hard line on Syria, a position favored by Israel, in spite of the potential adverse implications for the war on terror in the wake of the terrorist attacks of September 11, 2001. The election of Democrat Barack Obama as president in 2008, coupled with the election of Benjamin Netanyahu as prime minister of Israel in 2009, has resulted in the emergence of a partisan element to U.S.–Israel relations. Specifically, the gap between Democrats and Republicans in terms of the level of favorability toward Israel has begun to widen, in some cases significantly.

Israeli Prime Minister Benjamin Netanyahu

Benjamin Netanyahu, the ninth prime minister of Israel, was born in 1949, the year after Israel declared independence. Netanyahu, sometimes referred to as "Bibi" grew up in Jerusalem, but also spent a number of years in the United States, where his father taught history. After serving in the Israeli Defense Force (IDF), Netanyahu returned to the United States and earned a degree from MIT. His political career began in Washington working in the Israeli embassy to the United States. By 1988, Netanyahu was elected to the Knesset (the Israeli Parliament) as a member of the conservative Likud Party. In the 1970s, Likud had become the first right-wing party to govern Israel. In 1993, Netanyahu became the leader of Likud. When Likud returned to power in 1996, Netanyahu became prime minister of Israel. After a period of political retirement, Netanyahu once again became prime minister of Israel in 2009. In spite of a strong electoral challenge, Netanyahu was able to form successive governments in 2013 and 2015.

Netanyahu's life experiences have formed the basis of his hawkish stance on the Israeli conflict with the Palestinians. In the 1970s, Netanyahu was part of a commando unit that rescued hostages from the Palestinian terrorist group Black September. His brother was killed on a hostage rescue operation in Uganda. He spent a great deal of his subsequent career leading international counterterrorist efforts. He is known for his willingness to use Democratic–Republican political tensions to seek political leverage on issues relating to the relationship between the United States and Israel.

As prime minister, Netanyahu has spoken out against the U.S. nuclear deal with Iran and has argued that the Palestinian Authority is not currently a viable partner in the peace process. However, after winning reelection in 2015, Netanyahu reiterated his support for the principle of a two-state solution to the conflict. This claim is viewed with some skepticism by Democrats in the United States as well as proponents of a two-state solution in Israel.

Sources:

"Benjamin Netanyahu." Israel Ministry of Foreign Affairs. Accessed January 19, 2016. http://www.mfa.gov.il/mfa/aboutisrael/state/pages/benjamin%20netanyahu.aspx.

"Benjamin Netanyahu Biography." Biography.com. Accessed January 19, 2016. http://www.biography.com/people/benjamin-netanyahu-9421908#political-success.

Doyle, John. "Always at War—A Hard Look at Benjamin Netanyahu." *The Globe and Mail*, January 4, 2016. http://www.theglobeandmail.com/arts/television/john-doyle-always-at-war-a-hard-look-at-benjamin-netanyahu/article27996154/.

Democrats on Israel

Overall, Democrats are broadly supportive of Israel. The 2012 Democratic Party platform referred to an "unshakable commitment to Israel's security," and despite clashes with Netanyahu on a variety of Middle East policy issues, Obama and other members of his administration have repeatedly declared their dedication to ensuring Israel's safety and continued existence.

President Obama's Speech at the 2012 AIPAC Annual Conference

During the 2012 presidential campaign, Barack Obama addressed the annual AIPAC. What follows are excerpts from the speech related to the Israel–Palestine dispute. These remarks provide an interesting contrast to remarks made by eventual Republican nominee Mitt Romney to the same conference.

Of course, there are those who question not my security and diplomatic commitments, but rather my administration's ongoing pursuit of peace between Israelis and Palestinians. So let me say this: I make no apologies for pursuing peace. Israel's own leaders understand the necessity of peace. Prime Minister Netanyahu, Defense Minister Barak, President Peres—each of them have called for two states, a secure Israel that lives side by side with an independent Palestinian state. I believe that peace is profoundly in Israel's security interest.

But as hard as it may be, we should not and cannot give in to cynicism or despair. The changes taking place in the region make peace more important, not less. And I've made it clear that there will be no lasting peace unless Israel's security concerns are met. That's why we continue to press Arab leaders to reach out to Israel and will continue to support the peace treaty with Egypt. That's why—just as we encourage Israel to be resolute in the pursuit of peace—we have continued to insist that any Palestinian partner must recognize Israel's right to exist and reject violence and adhere to existing agreements. And that is why my administration has consistently rejected any efforts to short-cut negotiations or impose an agreement on the parties.

Source:

Obama, Barack. "Text of Obama's AIPAC Speech." Politico, March 4, 2012. http://www.politico .com/story/2012/03/text-of-obamas-aipac-speech-073588.

Aid to Israel, in the form of grants and loan guarantees, is higher during the Obama administration than it was during the George W. Bush administration. In addition, the Obama administration continued, and in some cases intensified, Bush administration policies related to intelligence and security cooperation. In the United Nations, the United States continues to vote with Israel on questions related to the Arab–Israeli conflict in the Middle East. In 2014, the United States voted against a resolution in the UN Security Council that would have called for the establishment of a Palestinian State by 2017 (the United States wields a veto on the UN Security Council that enables it to block resolutions with a single vote). In spite of partisan variation in support for Israel, people who identify with the Democratic Party in the United States are still much more likely to sympathize with Israel more than with the Palestinians (Pew Research Center 2014).

Still, there exists an evident division between progressive Democrats, who are more likely to criticize Israel for some of its policies relating to its Arab neighbors, and moderate/conservative Democrats, who are less critical. The gap between liberal and more moderate Democrats, however, is smaller than the gap between Democrats and Republicans as a whole (Pew Research Center 2014). Traditionally, the Democratic Party platform has contained language stating that Jerusalem is and will remain the capital of Israel. Originally, the party's 2012 platform was passed without this language. The Romney campaign reacted quickly, criticizing Democrats for betraying Israel. Under pressure from President (and Democratic Party nominee) Barack Obama, the Democrats reinserted the Jerusalem language into the platform in a series of contentious voice votes (Chaggaris and Montopoli 2012). The issue of the Israeli capital among Americans is often highlighted as a key test of support for Israel. Most governments do not recognize Jerusalem as the capital of Israel, referring back to the UN partition plan, which declared Jerusalem to be an international city pending final status negotiations between Israel and Palestine. Instead, most governments recognize Tel Aviv, the locus of government. Israel, however, considers its capital to be Jerusalem.

It is the case, however, that the Democrats, especially during the Obama administration, have been more critical of Israel than have Republicans. In the 1990s, the partisan gap in support for Israel was relatively narrow. By 2014, the percentage of Democrats sympathizing with Israel has fallen to nearly 30 points below the percentage of Republicans sympathizing with Israel, according to the Pew Research Center for People and the Press. A similar, though not as wide, gap has opened between Jews in the United States identifying as Democrats versus those who identify as Republicans. Democrats are also more likely than Republicans to favor leaning toward neither side in the conflict. Finally, Democrats are more likely to be critical of Israeli settlements in the occupied territories than are Republicans, though majorities of both parties are critical of Israeli settlement policy overall (Telhami 2014)

The emerging partisan gap between Democrats and Republicans on matters related to U.S.–Israeli relations extends beyond public opinion and into debates between elected officials. For example, in 2010 the Obama administration pressed Netanyahu to agree to a moratorium on new Israeli settlements in the occupied West Bank. Netanyahu ultimately complied, but once the moratorium expired, construction on settlements began anew. It is also worth noting that the United States still vetoed a 2011 resolution that declared Israeli settlements illegal. In December 2016, the United States failed to veto a similar resolution, allowing international condemnation of settlement activity by the Security Council.

The perception among many Democrats and other political observers that Netanyahu indirectly campaigned for Republican candidate Mitt Romney in the 2012 election campaign nonetheless increased the level of tension between Israel's leadership and the Obama White House. Romney visited Israel and met with Netanyahu as part of his campaign. Both Romney and Netanyahu are conservatives, the two know each other well, and they have several political connections in the United States in common (Marquardt 2012). For his part, Netanyahu denies taking anything other than a neutral position on the campaign. However, there is speculation that a 2011 speech where Obama promoted the idea of a return to pre-1967 war boundaries in the region served as a catalyst for Netanyahu's support of a Republican in the 2012 election. Traditionally, both the United States and Israel have taken great strides to appear neutral in electoral contests. From the Israeli perspective, this policy dovetails well with the desire that the U.S.–Israeli relationship not vary due to partisanship.

Another source of the partisan gap at the executive level is the debate over U.S. policy toward the Iranian nuclear program. The Obama administration, as well as most Democrats, favor the Joint Comprehensive Plan of Action (JCPOA). The JCPOA trades international and U.S. sanctions relief for Iranian concessions on its nuclear weapons program, including an agreement not to enrich uranium beyond the level required to generate nuclear power. The Israeli government has supported the Republican position that the JCPOA does not do enough to verify Iranian compliance and that it leaves too much of the Iranian nuclear program intact. In January 2015, the controversy came to a head when Republican Speaker of the House John Boehner invited Netanyahu to speak before a joint session of Congress concerning the Iran negotiations. Democrats opposed the invitation, which was extended without the knowledge of the Obama administration, and decried it as shockingly disrespectful. Obama refused to meet with Netanyahu while he visited Washington (though the two did meet in November 2015) and several Democratic lawmakers boycotted the speech (CBS News 2015). As expected, Netanyahu opposed the Obama administration approach to Iranian nuclear negotiations. Republicans lauded Netanyahu's speech, while Democrats were more likely to criticize it. Democrat and House Minority Leader Nancy Pelosi, for example, referred to the speech as an "insult to the intelligence of the United States" (French 2015).

Republicans on Israel

The Republican Party, like the Democratic Party, tends to support Israel to a significant degree. Most Republicans, in fact, view support for Israel as a critical component of U.S. national security interests. Like Democrats, Republicans have generally expressed support for a two-state solution to the Israeli–Palestinian conflict. Unlike Democrats, however, Republicans appear to condition their support for the two-state solution on the idea that Palestine will be a political democracy. Finally, the Republican Party platform of 2012 specifically mentioned the goal of military cooperation with Israel in order to make sure that the country maintains a "qualitative advantage" over potential adversaries. The Democratic Party platform that year did not contain this language in its plank on Israel. In practice, however, military grants and loan to Israel have remained relatively level across Republican and Democratic presidential administrations.

As a matter of general public opinion, Republican voters also tend to be more supportive of Israel than do Democrats. For example, 64 percent of self-described moderate Republicans support Israel over the Palestinians, while 48 percent of Democrats have the same opinion (Pew Research Center 2014). The gap between self-identified conservative Republicans and liberal Democrats shows an even wider gap in perspective. Seventy-seven percent of conservative Republicans support Israel, compared to 39 percent of liberal Democrats (Pew Research Center 2014). It is worth noting, however, that the Pew survey measures levels of support for both Israel and the Palestinians vis-à-vis the other group. More Democrats and Republicans favor Israel than favor the Palestinians. The gap is, however, much smaller (39 percent Israel/21 percent Palestinians) for liberal Democrats than it is for Conservative Republicans (77 percent Israel/4 percent Palestinians). Republicans are also more likely to say that, in its role as a mediator, the United States should lean toward Israel rather than the Palestinians. A majority of Republicans believe this, while a majority of Democrats want the United States to lean toward neither side (Telhami 2014). Over three times as many Republicans as Democrats favor U.S. use of its veto in the UN Security Council as a means to prevent passage of a resolution promoting Palestinian Statehood (Telhami 2014). Both Republicans and Democrats are more likely to favor a two-state solution than other approaches to the Israel–Palestinian conflict.

Telhami and Kishi (2014) have also noted that elites, including elected officials, in the Republican Party, are more in harmony with public opinion among Republicans with regard to the U.S.–Israel relationship than are Democratic Party elites. For Republican elected officials, a policy that heavily favors Israel is in step with the way most Republicans feel about the relationship. Members of the public that identify as Democrats are likely to be more critical of Israeli policy than are Democrats serving as elected officials.

Organizations such as the American Israel Public Affairs Committee (AIPAC), which serves at the vanguard of the pro-Israel lobby in the United States, are one potential source of this disconnect. Elected officials from both parties recognize the power of AIPAC, which is often ranked as one of the top three most powerful interest groups in the United States. Both Republicans and Democrats make a point of addressing the AIPAC Annual Conference in order to demonstrate continued U.S. support for Israel. The point is that the average Democrat may be more critical of Israel than the average Republican. However, unless U.S.–Israel relations are a salient issue for Democrats, there is little cost for Democratic Party elites to take positions that are closer to Republicans (and the AIPAC position) on U.S.–Israel relations. As a result, the partisan gap in criticism does not become a partisan gap in policy in most cases.

One area where the policy gap between Republicans and Democrats did manifest itself was on the debate over the JCPOA. As mentioned above, Democrats generally lined up behind Obama to support the JCPOA. By contrast, every Republican in the House of Representatives and the U.S. Senate voted against the nuclear deal with Iran. Both the Israeli government and most of the pro-Israel lobby in the United States also pushed heavily for Congress to reject the agreement. From the perspective of the Republican policy makers, the nuclear accord with Iran was good for neither the United States nor Israel. With regard to the United States, Republicans argue that Iran will be able to do more harm to U.S. interests in the

Middle East, including in Iraq and Syria if the country is able to operate under conditions of sanctions relief. Republican policy makers charged that the Iran deal was fundamentally incompatible with the desire to protect Israel from a country that denies its legitimacy and has stated a desire to eliminate it. Many Democrats, however, scoffed at these claims and insisted that much of the GOP opposition was due to nothing more than the usual knee-jerk obstructionism from Republicans to Obama administration policies and goals.

The Iran issue, however, is an exception to the general rule when it comes to policy. Whether the reason is strategic convergence, common polity type, cultural affinity, or interest group influence or some combination of these, Republican and Democratic Party policy makers are likely to make decisions that reinforce the strong bond between the United States and Israel. Patterns of voting in the United Nations on issues related to Israel are similar between Republican and Democrats. Levels of aid provided to Israel are also similar. Even on the Iranian issue, the decision by the Obama administration in January 2016 to levy additional sanctions against Iran, even as some international sanctions were being lifted in response to the International Atomic Energy Agency finding of Iranian compliance, represents a convergence between Republicans and Democrats on an issue of importance to U.S.–Israeli relations. Overall then, on issues related to U.S. foreign policy toward Israel, the Republican Party and the Democratic Party continue to experience more convergence than divergence.

Further Reading

CBS News. "5 Things to Know about Netanyahu's Speech to Congress—CBS News." Last modified March 3, 2015. http://www.cbsnews.com/news/five-things-netanyahu-speech-congress/.

Chaggaris, Steve, and Brian Montopoli. "Democrats Reinstate 'God' and Jerusalem Language in Party Platform—CBS News." Breaking News, U.S., World, Business, Entertainment & Video—CBS News. Last modified September 5, 2012. http://www.cbsnews.com/news/democrats-reinstate-god-and-jerusalem-language-in-party-platform/.

Democratic National Committee. "The 2012 Democratic Party Platform." Last modified 2012. https://www.democrats.org/party-platform.

Freedman, Robert Owen. *Israel and the United States Six Decades of US–Israeli Relations.* Boulder, CO: Westview Press, 2012.

French, Lauren. "Pelosi: Netanyahu Speech 'Insulting to the Intelligence of the United States.'" Politico. Accessed January 18, 2016. http://www.politico.com/story/2015/03/nancy-pelosi-benjamin-netanyahu-speech-react-115701.

Lasensky, Scott. "Underwriting Peace in the Middle East: U.S. Foreign Policy and the Limits of Economic Inducements." Middle East Review of International Affairs. Last modified March 2002. www.rubincenter.org/2002/03/lasensky-2002-03-07/.

Lebow, Richard N. "Woodrow Wilson and the Balfour Declaration." *The Journal of Modern History* 40, no. 4 (1968): 501–523. doi:10.1086/240237.

Marquardt, Alexander. "Israel's Netanyahu Takes Heat after Obama Victory." ABC News. Last modified November 8, 2012. http://abcnews.go.com/blogs/headlines/2012/11/israels-netanyahu-takes-heat-after-obama-victory/.

National Archives. "Teaching with Documents Lesson Plan: The U.S. Recognition of the State of Israel." Last modified August 23, 2006. https://www.archives.gov/education/lessons/us-israel/.

Office of the Historian. "The Arab–Israeli War of 1948—1945–1952—Milestones." U.S. Department of State. Accessed January 13, 2016. https://history.state.gov/milestones/1945-1952/arab-israeli-war.

Pew Research Center. "As Mideast Violence Continues, a Wide Partisan Gap in Israel-Palestinian Sympathies." Pew Research Center for the People and the Press. Last modified July 15, 2014. http://www.people-press.org/2014/07/15/as-mideast-violence-continues-a-wide-partisan-gap-in-israel-palestinian-sympathies/.

Republican National Committee. "Republican Party Platform 2012." Last modified 2012. https://prod-static-ngop-pbl.s3.amazonaws.com/docs/2012GOPPlatform.pdf.

Schoenbaum, David. *The United States and the State of Israel*. New York: Oxford University Press, 1993.

Sharp, Jeremy M. "U.S. Foreign Aid to Israel." Congressional Research Service. Last modified June 10, 2015. https://www.fas.org/sgp/crs/mideast/RL33222.pdf.

Telhami, Shibley. "American Public Attitudes toward The Israeli–Palestinian Conflict." Center for Middle East Policy: The Brookings Institution. Last modified December 5, 2014. http://www.brookings.edu/~/media/research/files/reports/2014/12/05-american-opinion-poll-israeli-palestinian-conflict-telhami/israel_palestine_key_findings_telhami_final.pdf.

Telhami, Shibley, and Katayoun Kishi. "Widening Democratic Party Divisions on the Israeli–Palestinian Issue." *Washington Post*. Last modified December 15, 2014. https://www.washingtonpost.com/blogs/monkey-cage/wp/2014/12/15/widening-democratic-party-divisions-on-the-israeli-palestinian-issue/.

UN News Service Section. "United Nations News Centre—United States Vetoes Security Council Resolution on Israeli Settlements." Last modified February 18, 2011. http://www.un.org/apps/news/story.asp?NewsID=37572#.Vp0RgZorLIU.

Latin America

At a Glance

As a region, Latin America can be defined as North and South American countries, including adjacent islands where languages derived from Latin predominate. In political speech, Republican and Democrats refer to "the Americas," which includes Canada and non-Latin countries in the Western hemisphere as part of a single region. The U.S. State Department manages relationships with Latin American countries as part of its Bureau of Western Hemisphere Affairs, which includes a subsection for Latin America and the Caribbean. Due to geographic proximity, patterns of colonialization and independence, and strategic considerations, Latin America has been a critical focus of U.S. foreign policy since the early days of the republic. Since the 1990s, the rise of oil imports from the region (the United States now imports more oil from Latin America than from any other region) has added to the geopolitical importance of Latin America. The region is also a growing outlet for U.S. exports. Republicans and Democrats have converged on common policies with respect to the region. Partisan differences do exist, however, especially on immigration, as well as on issue prioritization.

According to many Republicans . . .

- The United States has not done enough to deter radical socialism and secure basic human rights in countries such as Cuba and Venezuela;
- Immigration policy should focus on securing the U.S. border against illegal entry from Latin American immigrants;
- U.S. policy must focus on preventing drug production and transport, as well as associated organized crime, in Latin America;
- U.S. trade policy, including NAFTA and CAFTA, should be renegotiated to provide more protections for American workers; and
- The United States should not renew diplomatic relations with Cuba until the Castro regime is no longer in power.

According to many Democrats . . .

- The United States must engage Cuba with direct diplomacy in order to open the country and improve human rights standards;
- U.S. policy must focus on preventing drug production and transport, as well as associated organized crime, in Latin America;
- U.S. immigration policy, especially toward Mexico and Central America, should be based on engagement and economic reality, as opposed to strictly border security;
- U.S. trade policy with the region should be based on protecting American workers, as well as the environment and human rights; and
- The U.S. Army School of the Americas should be closed in light of its subversion of democratic principles in the region.

Overview

On December 2, 1823, President James Monroe delivered his seventh message to Congress. These messages, now called "State of the Union" addresses as a result of language in Article II, Section 3 of the U.S. Constitution, were designed to help the president set an agenda of important measures before Congress. In this particular message, Monroe stated that:

> In the discussions to which this interest has given rise and in the arrangements by which they may terminate the occasion has been judged proper for asserting, as a principle in which the rights and interests of the United States are involved, that the American continents, by the free and independent condition which they have assumed and maintain, are henceforth not to be considered as subjects for future colonization by any European powers. (History of Congress 1823)

The Monroe Doctrine, as it became known, became a significant basis for U.S. foreign policy toward Latin America through at least the end of the Cold War in 1991. The Monroe Doctrine became a justification for direct intervention in Latin America, especially after the proclamation of the so-called Roosevelt Corollary to the Monroe Doctrine in 1904. That year, President Theodore Roosevelt argued that the United States, as a civilized nation, had a moral obligation to intervene in the Western hemisphere to correct "chronic wrongdoing." The Roosevelt Corollary was used to legitimize U.S. intervention in Latin American countries such as the Dominican Republic (1916), Cuba (1906 and 1917), and Haiti (1915).

During the Cold War, U.S. policy toward Latin America centered on checking the potential spread of Communism. In many ways, this was not a significant departure from previous U.S. willingness to intervene in Latin America to advance its national interests. As the Cold War deepened, the United States interceded, both directly and indirectly, in Latin American politics on several occasions in order to support authoritarian but anti-Communist rulers over pro-Soviet, broadly Socialist governments, even in instances when the Socialist governments enjoyed popular support (though they were also generally not democratically elected).

For example, the United States supported the Batista Regime in Cuba in part because of its ties to U.S. business interests and in part because it was stridently anti-Communist. When Fidel Castro launched his Communist peoples' revolution (see Cuba entry) it gained a great deal of popular support as a reaction against government corruption and U.S. interference. Similar movements developed in a number of other Latin American countries.

In Argentina, the Nixon administration gave approval for the Argentine military to overthrow the leftist populist government of Isabel Perón in 1976. The new government, which was headed by a military junta, took Secretary of State Henry Kissinger's back-channel approval of the coup as a "green light" to launch harsh reprisals against their potential enemies, including arbitrary detentions and summary executions of leftists and accused leftists (*New York Times* 2016). As many as 30,000 people died during what came to be known as the "Dirty War." The United States also provided arms, at times in contravention of U.S. law to the anti-Communist Contras in Nicaragua in the mid-1980s. In what became known as the Iran–Contra Scandal, the United States provided arms to Iran (which was under an arms embargo). Proceeds from these arms sales were diverted to the Contras in Nicaragua. Overall, U.S. foreign policy toward Latin America during the Cold War placed strategic concerns over both partisanship and the promotion of democratic norms. In fact, the United States supported a coup against the first democratically elected Socialist in Latin America (Salvador) in 1973.

The end of the Cold War did not necessarily alter the complex relationship between the United States and Latin America. The United States continued to take steps, including tightening economic sanctions, to dislodge the Castro regime in Cuba from power. These measures failed. The United States also provided its tacit approval for an unsuccessful attempt in 2002 against leftist president Hugo Chavez. In other cases, such as in Brazil, which began to open politically before the end of the Cold War, and Mexico, which experienced a more rapid transition after years of authoritarian rule, the United States was able to develop a positive relationship with a democratizing country. The overall influence of the United States over the region also began to decrease over time. A combination of economic growth in countries such as Brazil and Argentina, coupled with increased cooperation with other large developing economies such as China and India, has challenged U.S. primacy in the region.

Another theme of late Cold War/post–Cold War U.S. foreign policy toward Latin America relates to the war on drugs. The United States has devoted billions of dollars in military aid to curtail coca production in places such as Columbia, but many observers believe that these efforts have cost thousands of human lives without a discernable impact on overall narcotics production and trafficking. The United States has also made the war on drugs a significant component of its foreign policy toward Mexico, providing billions in assistance to police and military forces fighting against organized criminal activity related to the drug trade. The United States sees moving against the narcotics industry in Latin America as essential in reducing the market for illicit drugs in the United States.

Immigration issues have also informed U.S. foreign policy toward Latin America, both historically and recently. The overall size and prosperity of the U.S. economy make a certain amount of immigration from poorer countries inevitable. This immigration takes both legal and illegal forms. In both 2014 and 2016, for example, thousands of undocumented child immigrants arrived in the United States from Central America (often via Mexico). Immigration, both legal and illegal, from Mexico, has decreased somewhat in recent years. In spite of the decrease, there are still approximately six million undocumented immigrants from Mexico living in the United States (Krogstad, Passel, and Cohn 2016). Both as a matter of domestic and foreign policy, immigration has created significant partisan divides in U.S. policy.

Republicans on U.S. Foreign Policy toward Latin America

The 2016 Republican Party platform mentions Latin America in the context of "the America's" three times. In addition, it contains numerous mentions of specific countries such as Cuba, Mexico, Colombia, and Venezuela. Interestingly, especially given recent debates over free trade within the Republican Party, as well as concerns that environmental protection trades off with job creation, the first mention relates to shared trade and environmental interests. These shared interests are not enumerated, which is common in platform language, especially where there might be agreements about how such common interests would be operationalized. More traditional Republicans tend to favor free trade, for example. However, more populist Republicans, who are more likely to support Republican presidential nominee Donald Trump, are less likely to favor free trade out of concerns over manufacturing jobs in the United States. On immigration, another issue related both directly and indirectly to foreign policy with Latin America, the Republican platform posits that the attempt by the Obama administration to use executive orders to allow certain undocumented immigrants to remain in the United States is illegal (see Immigration entry). The 2016 GOP platform also advocates for the construction of a wall along the entire length of the U.S. border with Mexico in order to stop illegal immigration of Mexicans and others.

In terms of specific Latin American countries, the Republican platform draws the greatest distinction with Democrats on the subject of Venezuela. The Democratic Party platform refers broadly to the need to push Venezuela to respect basic human rights. The Republican platform, by contrast, argues that "the current chief executive has allowed that country to become a narcoterrorist state, an Iranian outpost threatening Central America, and a safe haven for the agents of Hezbollah" (Republican National Committee 2016). The 2016 Report of Overseas Advisory

Security Council (OASC), a public–private partnership between the State Department and several U.S. industries or agencies, has declared Venezuela to be one of the most dangerous countries in the world, in part because of narcoterrorism (Overseas Security Advisory Council 2016). Though there have been periods of friction, Iran and Venezuela have enjoyed relatively warm relations both during and after the administration of Hugo Chavez. Current president Nicolas Maduro welcomed Iranian representatives to his inauguration and has visited Iran. Recent revelations have also suggested a link between Venezuela and the Iranian-backed terrorist organization Hezbollah (Nagel 2015). Venezuela is not on the official list of state sponsors of terror maintained by the State Department.

Public opinion polls geared toward tracking American public opinion about issues related to Latin America are quite rare. However, we can discern what Republicans within the general public believe on issues related, at least in part, to Latin America. Free trade is one such issue. Traditionally, Republicans of all socio-economic stripes have favored free trade more than have Democrats. However, the rise of the Tea Party movement, associated with a rejection of mainstream Republicanism, as well as Donald Trump's identification of free trade as a key source of blue-collar economic woe, has changed this calculus. A poll released in September 2016, for example, found that 61 percent of all Republicans believe that free trade with Mexico hurts the United States (American Views on Current Trade and Health Policies 2016). As recently as 2009. Republicans were more likely to favor the North American Free Trade Agreement (NAFTA) than oppose it. The overwhelming majority of the shift in Republican Party public opinion on NAFTA came from within the Tea Party, 63 percent of which opposes NAFTA (Pew Research Center 2010). Generally, free trade is viewed by populist Republicans as part of the overall trend of globalization, which is strongly opposed by many of Trump's supporters. A poll taken during the 2016 Republican Primary indicated that supporters of Donald Trump were at least 20 percent more likely than Ted Cruz or John Kasich supporters to view free trade in a negative light (Stokes 2016). Only Kasich supporters exhibited net-positive views of free trade, suggesting a weakening in the position of moderate Republicans relative to Tea Party Republicans on this issue. Republicans within the general public also tend to oppose the Trans-Pacific Partnership, a comprehensive trade agreement favored by some Democrats as well as by Mexico (see entry on the Trans-Pacific Partnership).

With regard to immigration, Republicans within the general public appear to agree with the strong Republican platform stance against any liberalization of current immigration policy. For example, one 2015 poll found that 73 percent of Republicans favor the construction of a fence along the entire border with Mexico to halt illegal immigration from that nation (Pew Research Center 2015). Another survey found that 63 percent of Republicans view large numbers of immigrants as a critical threat to the United States; by contrast, only 30 percent of self-described Democrats polled agreed with that perspective (Kafura and McElmurry 2015). On the issue of birthright citizenship, numerous polls have indicated that a majority of

Republicans favor changing the Constitution to eliminate the automatic conferring of citizenship on anyone born in the United States, regardless of the citizenship status of their parents. The goal of such an amendment would be to discourage the practice of illegally crossing the border into the United States in order to have a child, in the hopes that the rights conferred on the child will extend to the parent(s) or that the child will reap advantages later in life from being a U.S. citizen.

Among elected officials, Republicans and Democrats enjoy some areas of bipartisanship with regard to U.S. foreign policy toward Latin America. For example, Republicans and Democrats have agreed to increased foreign aid to Mexico under the Mérida Initiative, which is designed to combat drug production and trafficking, and the organized crime that often accompanies it. Republicans and Democrats have also agreed, for the most part on broader counternarcotics policies as they related to Latin America, as well as other regions. Republicans also broadly agreed with the 2015 decision to withhold a portion of U.S. foreign aid to Mexico based on human rights concerns that the Mexican government was violating civil liberties as part of the effort to stop drug trafficking. Although it is difficult to argue empirically that U.S. drug interdiction policy has been successful, it does appear, especially with regard to Latin America, to be an area of relative U.S. foreign policy consensus.

Republicans in Congress have been much more critical of other areas of U.S. foreign policy toward Latin America. For example, Republicans strongly denounced the decision by the Obama administration to restore diplomatic relations with Cuba and to relax some travel restrictions to the country in 2014. Senator Marco Rubio, for example, argued that President Obama's visit to Cuba provided a propaganda tool for the repressive Cuban government to make it appear that it was winning its standoff with the United States. Several Republican senators have also vowed to block the confirmation of President Obama's nominee for U.S. Ambassador to Cuba, Jeffrey DeLaurentis. Although public opinion has moved in a direction that favors normalization of U.S. relations with Cuba, Republicans in Congress have a strong hand on this issue, given their ability to directly regulate sanctions against the country and the general logjam that has existed on ambassador confirmations in the Senate since Republicans gained control of the body in 2014.

Republicans also strongly oppose Democrats on issues related to immigration. Republicans in the House of Representatives, for example, have been able to successfully block passage of the USA DREAM Act, which would provide a path to citizenship for some undocumented immigrants in the United States (see Immigration entry). When President Obama announced executive orders that would have implemented parts of the DREAM Act without congressional approval, 17 states with Republican governors sued in federal court to block the order. The lawsuit was later joined by several other states. The order would have allowed some individuals brought to the United States as undocumented children to stay in the country. It would have also allowed some parents of U.S. citizens, including undocumented parents who gave birth on U.S. soil, to stay in the country.

The twin orders, Deferred Action for Parents of Americans and Lawful Permanent Residents (DAPA) and Deferred Action for Childhood Arrivals (DACA) have been enjoined (prevented from taking full effect) by a federal district court. Ultimately, the case made it all the way to the U.S. Supreme Court of the United States (SCOTUS). A 4–4 deadlock on the case by SCOTUS means that the original injunction against DACA and DAPA remain in effect. To be sure, the twin orders would have an impact on immigration from outside of Latin America. However, in the 2016 election year, the implementation of DACA and DAPA was tied primarily to immigration from Mexico and Central America.

2016 Republican presidential nominee Donald Trump expressed opposition to both DACA and DAPA, and he is the nation's best-known proponent of building a wall along the entire U.S. border with Mexico. In addition, Mr. Trump favors the creation of a domestic deportation force to remove illegal immigrants from the United States. When the initial idea of a wide-ranging deportation force met with criticism from both Republicans and Democrats, Trump modified the proposal to create a force that would focus its efforts on undocumented immigrants who committed crimes in the United States. The idea of a deportation force of any type remains a controversial issue for a variety of reasons. It is unclear whether Trump has the political support to implement the plan if elected. Trump also has voiced opposition to the TPP and called for a renegotiation of NAFTA on the grounds that free trade costs jobs in America as a result of cheap goods entering the United States from other countries and from U.S. companies locating in other countries.

Democrats on U.S. Foreign Policy toward Latin America

Like its Republican counterpart, the 2016 Democratic Party platform contains a foreign policy subsection on "the Americas" as well as mentions of specific Latin American countries. The priorities with respect to Latin America diverge significantly, though not completely, from the Republican platform. The first mention of foreign policy toward Latin America relates to immigration. Specifically, Democrats argue that the Republican plan to build a wall along the entire border with Mexico would alienate Mexico, which the platform characterizes as "a valuable partner" (Democratic National Committee 2016). Also related to immigration, the Democratic Party platform specifically mentions the Temporary Protected Status (TPS) applied to Haiti. TPS allows people in countries adversely affected by natural disasters and complex humanitarian emergencies to remain in the United States regardless of immigration status. TPS is not a path to citizenship, and as a result, it is less controversial than other proposed protections for undocumented immigrants and asylum-seekers. Like Republicans, Democrats express concerns about drugs and transnational organized crime in Latin America and pledge to continue efforts to combat the twin phenomena. The platform does not, however, mention Venezuela specifically in the context of the drug trafficking and production issues.

Another major area of contrast between the two platforms exists with respect to Cuba. The Democratic Party platform supports the decision by the Obama administration to reopen diplomatic ties and to drop the travel ban. As recently as the early 2000s, maintenance of the Cuban embargo was a matter of relative national consensus, due in part to human rights concerns, anti-Communist sentiment, and the political influence in electoral vote-rich Florida of the Cuban American lobby (which has been historically anti-Castro). As perceptions about the embargo have changed, in part due to younger Cuban Americans being less supportive of the embargo and the end of the Cold War, Democrats have been first to call for changes in the relationship between the two countries. It is worth noting, however, that interest groups that traditionally support Republicans, such as the U.S. Chamber of Commerce, also favor lifting the embargo.

Historically speaking, Democrats have been less likely than Republicans to favor free trade agreements. Organized labor, a traditional Democratic Party constituency, has opposed free trade on the grounds that it costs American jobs. Recently, however, Democrats have been somewhat more favorable toward free trade than Republicans. For example, while Republican favorability toward NAFTA has significantly declined since the rise of the Tea Party in 2010, Democrats have only become moderately less favorable toward the agreement. In 2010, one poll found 40 percent of Democrats favored trade agreements like NAFTA, while 35 percent opposed such agreements (Pew Research Center 2010). A 2016 survey conducted by Internet polling firm YouGov, found that a plurality of Democrats (41 percent) believe that the United States should stay in NAFTA (Vianovo.com 2016). By contrast, a plurality of Republicans (44 percent) asserted that the United States should withdraw from the agreement. A 2016 tracking poll by Morning Consult revealed that more Democrats (40 percent) than Republicans (31 percent) support the TPP (Morning Consult 2016). One must always approach results related to the TPP with a bit of caution since individuals often report not knowing a great deal about the agreement. In the case of the Morning Consult poll, pluralities of Democrats and Republicans expressed the view that they did not know enough about the TPP to make a decision.

Overall, public opinion among Democrats echoes and in some ways goes beyond those statements in the Democratic Party platform. For example, Democrats in the general public overwhelmingly reject the idea of amending the Constitution to eliminate birthright citizenship (Pew Research Center 2015). Birthright citizenship is the constitutional principle that anyone born in the United States, regardless of the status of their parents, immediately becomes a citizen of the United States. Changing the legal status children born in the United States to undocumented immigrants would require an amendment to the Constitution. Only 23 percent of Democrats favor this type of amendment. A significant majority (77 percent) of Democrats also believe that a path to citizenship should be available to undocumented immigrants (Kafura and McElmurry 2015). There is a divide within self-identified Democrats on the number of hurdles that should exist on the path to citizenship. A plurality of Democrats believes that there should be no hurdles (i.e., immigrants should be able to keep working and apply for citizenship without delay). However, a large minority of Democrats (29 percent) believe that there should be a waiting period and fines required of undocumented workers seeking citizenship (Kafura and McElmurry 2015). Overall, only 17 percent of Democrats believe that illegal immigrants should not be allowed to stay in the United States legally (Pew Research Center 2015).

As mentioned above, there are areas of bipartisanship on issues related to narcotics interdiction and human rights in Latin America. Democrats diverge from Republicans in several areas as well. For example, Democrats in Congress have supported the decision by the United States to reopen diplomatic relations with Cuba and to hold new high-level talks with Venezuela (the United States already has partial diplomatic relations with Venezuela). In fact, several Democrats have called on President Obama to rescind sanctions that the Obama administration imposed on Venezuela in 2015 in response to a crackdown by the military on political dissidents after a series of arbitrary arrests and detentions. The letter argues that the sanctions "may actually hinder human rights and dialog inside of Venezuela" (Huffington Post 2015). Most Democrats have also expressed support of the Obama administration decision to renew diplomatic relations with Cuba. Some intraparty discord exists, mostly among Democrats who serve in Florida, where Cuban Americans who favor continuance of the embargo and oppose significant diplomatic opening, have their greatest political influence.

On the issue of immigration, Democrats have been unified around the idea of a path to citizenship for undocumented immigrants. In 2013, the Senate passed the Border Security, Economic Opportunity, and Immigration Modernization Act. In this case, Democratic senators were completed unified in their support of the legislation, introduced by a group of four Democrats and four Republicans commonly called the "gang of eight." The bill provided for a path to citizenship as defined above, plus the addition of thousands of new border patrol agents. Every Senate Democrat voted in favor of the legislation, which passed by a margin of 68–32. However, the bill was never taken up in the Republican-controlled House. After Republicans gained control of the Senate in the 2014 midterm elections, hopes for passage of the bill effectively ended. Democrats argued that the bill represented a reasonable compromise. Many Republicans argued that the bill would encourage more illegal immigration by providing amnesty to current illegal immigrants. Democrats have also supported President Obama in his efforts to use executive orders to change immigration policy by fiat. The Texas State Democratic Party, for example, referred to the Supreme Court decision to maintain the injunction against DACA and DAPA and "anti-family ruling" (Texas Democratic Party 2016).

For her part, 2016 Democratic Party presidential nominee Hillary Clinton has maintained a unified position with other Democrats on the issues of immigration, Cuba, and Venezuela. On issues related to trade, though, Clinton's position diverges somewhat from that of Obama, some Democrats in Congress, and portions of public opinion. Specifically, Clinton has expressed opposition to the TPP, an agreement that would contain three Latin American countries (Chile, Mexico, and Peru) among its 12 member countries. Clinton has expressed concern that the agreement compromises U.S. sovereignty on issues related to administrative adjudication (resolution of disputes without direct input from elected officials). Clinton also favors the renegotiation of NAFTA to provide for increased labor and environmental protection, a position at least partially shared by Donald Trump. Trump has taken the issue a step further, arguing that the United States should withdraw from the agreement in the event that renegotiation fails.

Further Reading

"American Views on Current Trade and Health Policies." Politics, Policy, Political News—Politico. Last modified September 2016. http://www.politico.com/f/?id=00000157-58ef-d502-ad5f-dbef0b4f0000.

Democratic National Committee. "2016 Democratic Party Platform." Last modified July 26, 2016. https://www.demconvention.com/wp-content/uploads/2016/07/Democratic-Party-Platform-7.21.16-no-lines.pdf.

History of Congress: President's Annual Message. American Memory: Library of Congress, 1823. Accessed October 2, 2016. https://memory.loc.gov/cgi-bin/ampage?collId=llac&fileName=041/llac041.db&recNum=4.

Huffington Post. "Letter to the Honorable Barack Obama, President of the United States." Last modified May 15, 2015. http://big.assets.huffingtonpost.com/vzletter.pdf.

Kafura, Craig, and Sara McElmurry. "Growing Partisan Divides on Immigration." Chicago Council on Global Affairs. Last modified September 8, 2015. http://www.thechicagocouncil.org/publication/growing-partisan-divides-immigration?utm_source=Informz&utm_medium=Email&utm_campaign=Council.

Krogstad, Jens M., Jeffrey S. Passel, and D'Vera Cohn. "5 Facts about Illegal Immigration in the U.S." Pew Research Center. Last modified September 20, 2016. http://www.pewresearch.org/fact-tank/2016/09/20/5-facts-about-illegal-immigration-in-the-u-s/.

Morning Consult Intelligence. "Morning Consult National Tracking Poll." Last modified August 10, 2016. https://morningconsultintelligence.com/media/mc/160804_crosstabs_Topicals_v2_AP.pdf.

Nagel, Juan C. "Something Is Rotten in the State of Venezuela." *Foreign Policy.* Last modified April 28, 2015. http://foreignpolicy.com/2015/04/28/something-is-rotten-in-the-state-of-venezuela-chavez-maduro-cabello-salazar-farc/.

New York Times. "America's Role in Argentina's Dirty War." Last modified March 17, 2016. http://www.nytimes.com/2016/03/17/opinion/americas-role-in-argentinas-dirty-war.html.

Overseas Security Advisory Council. "Venezuela 2016 Crime & Safety Report." Last modified 2016. https://www.osac.gov/pages/ContentReportDetails.aspx?cid=19065.

Pew Research Center. "Americans Are of Two Minds on Trade." Last modified November 9, 2010. http://www.pewresearch.org/2010/11/09/americans-are-of-two-minds-on-trade/.

Pew Research Center. "On Immigration Policy, Wider Partisan Divide over Border Fence Than Path to Legal Status." Pew Research Center for the People and the Press. Last modified October 8, 2015. http://www.people-press.org/2015/10/08/on-immigration-policy-wider-partisan-divide-over-border-fence-than-path-to-legal-status/.

Republican National Committee. "Republican Platform 2016." Last modified 2016. https://prod-static-ngop-pbl.s3.amazonaws.com/media/documents/DRAFT_12_FINAL[1]-ben_1468872234.pdf.

Stokes, Bruce. "Republicans, Especially Trump Supporters, See Free Trade Deals as Bad for U.S." Pew Research Center. Last modified March 31, 2016. http://www.pewresearch.org/fact-tank/2016/03/31/republicans-especially-trump-supporters-see-free-trade-deals-as-bad-for-u-s/.

Texas Democratic Party. "Texas Democrats on Anti-Family DACA/DAPA Supreme Court Hearing." Last modified April 18, 2016. http://www.txdemocrats.org/press/texas-democrats-on-anti-family-dacadapa-supreme-court-hearing.

Theodore Roosevelt's Corollary to the Monroe Doctrine (1905). ourdocments.gov, 1904. https://www.ourdocuments.gov/doc.php?doc=56.

Vianovo.com. "Mexico's Brand in the U.S.: National Survey Results." Last modified June 2016. http://www.vianovo.com/assets/uploads/news/U.S.-Attitudes-About-Mexico-June-2016-final-release.pdf.

Libya

At a Glance

Significant tensions between the United States and Libya predate the Arab Spring protests that erupted in 2011. When that political unrest swept into Libya, however, longtime Libyan leader Muammar Qaddafi was ousted from power and ultimately killed, thus changing the U.S.–Libya relationship in profound, still-evolving ways. The civil war in Libya has created chaotic conditions that have enabled the rise of both conventional and terroristic violence. Most notably, the power vacuum created by the fall of Qaddafi—a fall that was aided by American military involvement—resulted in the rise of Islamic State of Iraq and Greater Syria (ISIS) in Libya, though the amount of territory that ISIS controls in Libya is less than in Iraq or Syria. In addition, rival Libyan governments each claim to be the authority in the country, which has ignited a second civil war. Democrats and Republicans are united in support of the United Nations–backed unity government. The unity government, or Government of National Accord (GNA) is based in Tripoli and contains a mix of tribal and militia leaders designed to soothe sectarian tensions. They are also united in obvious opposition to ISIS. However, a partisan divide exists over how much blame the Obama administration should shoulder for the current state of affairs in Libya, as well as the correct strategy going forward.

According to many Democrats, U.S. foreign policy toward Libya . . .

- Must be based on supporting the internationally recognized government in its efforts to combat ISIS;
- Should not include the involvement of U.S. ground troops, with the exception of Special Operations Forces;
- Should be based on a willingness to work with the United Nations and the North Atlantic Treaty Organization (NATO) to supply the legitimate U.S. recognized government with weapons; and
- Must include airstrikes and other military operations to target ISIS leaders and strongholds.

According to many Republicans, U.S. foreign policy toward
Libya . . .

- Should recognize that the original 2011 U.S. intervention in Libya was not
  authorized by Congress as it should have been;
- Has been marked during the Obama years by poor decisions that have
  enabled ISIS to thrive in Libya;
- Should recognize that the ouster of Qaddafi was positive but was not
  accompanied by a plan to secure the country; and
- Should not commit U.S. ground troops, with the exception of Special
  Operations Forces, to coordinate attacks against ISIS and other Islamist
  forces in Libya.

Overview

After a period of colonial rule by Italy, Libya became fully independent in 1951.
The United States supported Libyan independence and generally enjoyed a positive relationship with Libya, which functioned as a kingdom from 1951–1969.
Oil was discovered in 1959, and the U.S. oil companies were granted concessions
in Libya, resulting in a large inflow of hard currency into the Libyan economy. In
1969, a 27-year-old captain in the Libyan armed forces named Muammar Qaddafi
(alternatively Gaddafi/Gadhafi) led a successful coup against the monarchy, putting in place a revolutionary Socialist government. Domestically, Qaddafi began
large developmental building projects and significantly expanded the social safety
net. Qaddafi also nationalized the Libyan oil industry, which angered the United
States and Great Britain.

A combination of factors resulted in the further deterioration of relations
between the United States and Libya during the Qaddafi era. Qaddafi closed all
foreign military bases in Libya, which the United States saw as a blow to its strategic interests in the Middle East/North Africa region. Libya also began to support terrorism and other forms of political subversion in Africa and elsewhere. In
response, the United States withdrew its ambassador from the embassy in Tripoli,
Libya's capital. In 1979, the United States withdrew its remaining diplomatic staff
from Libya.

Over time, Libya also developed a close relationship with the Soviet Union,
much to the consternation of the United States. In addition, Libya's support of Palestinian nationalist groups, including those engaged in terrorism, angered American lawmakers on both sides of the aisle. After Libya fired on U.S. aircraft over
international waters in the Gulf of Sidra in 1981, the United States imposed various types of economic sanctions on Libya. In 1986, the United States launched
airstrikes against Libya in response to the targeted killing of two U.S. servicemen
in Berlin. Qaddafi's adopted daughter was killed in the bombing, and two of his
sons were injured. Then came the infamous Lockerbie bombing of 1988, in which

Libyan nationals, acting with government assistance, used a bomb to blow up a commercial airliner on a transatlantic flight from Europe to the United States. This terrorist attack, coupled with revelations about Libya's development of a nuclear weapons program, led to the imposition of comprehensive economic sanctions by the United States and, later, by the United Nations. The Lockerbie bombing was a terrorist attack on an international flight from Scotland to New York. Two Libyan nationals were tried for the bombing, which killed 270 people, including 189 U.S. citizens. One of the alleged bombers, Abdelbaset al-Megrahi, was convicted. The United States and the United Nations tied the bombing to the Libyan government.

In the late 1990s and early 2000s, relations between the United States and Libya improved somewhat as Qaddafi sought to decrease Libya's, and his own, isolation from the international community. Libya surrendered two of the suspected masterminds of the Lockerbie bombing in 1999, agreed to pay reparations to the victims' families in 2003, and later that year renounced its nuclear weapons program. In response, the United States allowed some UN sanctions against Libya to be lifted, specifically those related to the Libyan nuclear program. Some sanctions related to terrorism were maintained until 2007 when then secretary of state Condoleezza Rice announced that Libya would be removed from the State Department list of state sponsors of terrorism (Kaplan 2007). The United States also began the process of restarting full diplomatic relations with Libya. Rice visited Libya in 2008. As a sign of Qaddafi's rehabilitation in Africa, Libya was elected chair of the African Union in 2009.

In 2011, popular protests and revolts collectively referred to as the Arab Spring rocked several countries in the Middle East and North Africa, including Libya. Qaddafi's response, much like that of the al-Assad regime in Syria, was to use violence to crush the nascent protests. Instead, the protests grew into an armed rebellion. In response to what it characterized as brutal suppression tactics by the Libyan government, the Obama administration enacted targeted sanctions against Libyan leaders, including freezing their financial assets when possible, and withdrew America's diplomatic representation. In part due to the United States' history of tense relations with Libya, and in part due to estimates about the weakness of the Qaddafi regime, the Obama White House was more willing to act directly in Libya than it was in Egypt or Syria. The United States pushed for the United Nations to authorize military intervention in the conflict, a move that the UN Security Council granted when China and Russia agreed not to veto the authorizing resolution. Amid significant political debate about the legitimacy of U.S. intervention, President Obama brought the United States into the conflict by providing air support to the rebels. North Atlantic Treaty Organization (NATO) allies also played a significant role in the conflict. Tripoli fell to the rebels in August 2011. Qaddafi, who fled the capital, was killed in October of the same year.

As of mid-2016, Libya is in a renewed state of civil war. The coalition that toppled Qaddafi and formed an interim government was not able to remain unified. Local Islamist militias have taken control of areas of the country, especially in areas outside of the capital region around Tripoli. It is against this backdrop that Islamist militants stormed the U.S. consulate in Benghazi, killing Ambassador Christopher Stevens and three other Americans, on September 11, 2012. Ultimately, the United States advised all Americans to leave the country.

The General National Council (GNC) made up of Islamists and secularists, refused to disband after elections in 2014 where secularists picked up seats in the Council of Deputies, which was to replace the GNC. The situation resulted in two rival governments in Libya, both of which claimed to be legitimate. The UN brokered an agreement to create a unity government, the Government of National Accord, which is now the main internationally recognized government in Libya. However, rival groups still control significant portions of the country. Against this backdrop, ISIS has gained a foothold in Libya, with approximately 5,000–8,000 fighters in the country (Walsh 2016). The United States has responded with air-strikes against ISIS positions as well as the deployment of Special Forces troops to combat the terrorist group.

Democrats on Libya

The 2016 Democratic Party platform does not mention Libya at all. This is in contrast to the 2012 platform, which mentioned the situation in Libya four times. The change between platforms can be attributed to two primary factors. First, the U.S. intervention began in 2011, so it is more proximate to the 2012 platform. However, the United States continues to intervene in Libya today, especially as it relates to targeting ISIS, so this is not a complete answer. Second, in 2012, it made more political sense, given the inherently political nature of party platforms, to talk about the intervention in Libya. At the time, the intervention was broadly viewed as an exercise of "smart power," where the United States made a relatively small, calculated intervention with a significant potential reward. In 2016, it has become clear that many Democrats, including President Obama, view the decision to intervene in Libya as a mistake. With regard to ISIS, which is the main current focus of U.S. intervention in Libya, the Democratic platform focuses understand-ably on Iraq and Syria, where ISIS is at its most powerful. However, the platform does mention ISIS more generally in terms of crushing its financial and supply networks in the broader Middle East and North Africa. The 2016 platform also mentions specific limits on anti-ISIS efforts by pledging to work toward a new Authorization for the Use of Military Force (AUMF) that does not employ "large scale combat deployment of American troops" (Democratic National Committee 2016). It is worth noting that, hypothetically, an AUMF worded in such a manner would allow smaller-scale deployments beyond the deployment of small numbers of Special Forces troops.

Much of the public opinion data relating to U.S. intervention in Libya relates to 2011. In spite of the fact that the United States has currently intensified its efforts to target ISIS in Libya, and in spite of the regular invocation of Libya in the 2016 presidential election, the issue was more salient to the public during the first weeks and months of the intervention. At the time of the original intervention, one poll found that a majority (51 percent) of self-identified Democrats in the general public supported direct U.S. military action against the Qaddafi regime in Libya (Jones 2011). By June, support had grown to 54 percent, according to the same poll. With respect to the rise of ISIS in Libya due to the power vacuum left by the fall of Qaddafi and the inability of rival factions to reach a governing accord, public opinion is more ambiguous. However, we can perhaps infer opinion about the use of U.S. ground troops to fight ISIS in Libya from relative support for the same measures in Syria and Iraq. In this regard, one 2016 poll found nearly two-thirds (63 percent) of Democrats opposed the use of combat ground troops in Syria and Iraq (CNN/ Opinion Research Corporation 2016).

Democratic support for the 2011 intervention in Libya on Capitol Hill was mixed. Most of the House and Senate Democratic Party leadership, including figures like House minority leader Nancy Pelosi and Senate majority whip Dick Durbin, supported the intervention as a means to end humanitarian abuses and remove Qaddafi from power. Other rank and file members were more skeptical. Representatives Barbara Lee, Mike Honda, and Lynn Woolsey of California, joined by Arizona representative Raul Grijalva, issued a statement in which they argued that "the United States must immediately shift to end the bombing in Libya" (Grijalva, Lee, Honda, and Woolsey 2011). These Democratic critics argued that the Obama administration was rushing to war in Libya, which could lead to a prolonged military engagement of the type that occurred in Afghanistan and Iraq. They also emphasized that Congress had not been consulted on the decision to intervene militarily before the intervention occurred, a point that was repeatedly raised by congressional Republicans.

With congressional Republicans and some congressional Democrats arguing that the Obama administration needed authorization under the War Powers Resolution of 1973 to intervene in Libya, Congress held two votes on the Libya issue in 2011. First, the House of Representatives voted 295–193 against authorizing U.S. military intervention in support of the NATO mission in Libya. Overall, 115 Democrats voted "aye" while 70 voted "nay" on the resolution (Pro Publica 2011). Most of the no votes among the Democrats came from antiwar stalwarts such as Dennis Kucinich of Ohio and Barbara Lee of California. Most of the yes votes came either from more moderate Democrats, members of the Democratic leadership team in the House and/or Representatives known for fierce loyalty to President Obama, who supported the intervention as a means to simultaneously pursue an important humanitarian goal (protection of civilians), while achieving a long-standing, though recently more muted, political goal (the removal of Qaddafi from power). A "sense of the Congress" resolution was introduced in the Senate, which also would have condemned the intervention. However, the measure never reached voting procedure due to lack of support among most Democrats and a few Republicans who supported the idea of toppling Qaddafi. An attempt in the House to withdraw funding from most aspects of the intervention in Libya also failed by a vote 238–180, providing President Obama with a more limited victory. Democrats were more unified on this vote, with only 36 out of 149 House Democrats voting in favor of the GOP-sponsored bill.

For his part, at least in 2011, Obama strongly defended the decision to intervene in Libya. Obama specifically argued that the United States had a moral and strategic responsibility to act in Libya after the brutal reprisals of the Qaddafi regime. He also advanced the proposition that, since the United States had taken the time to assemble an international coalition of actors, U.S. ground forces would not be required, thereby limiting the risk to U.S. armed forces. Obama also promised that the engagement would be of limited duration, in contrast to the longer-term commitments in Afghanistan and Iraq. On the issue of whether the president exceeded his authority under the War Powers Resolution by initiating a conflict without congressional approval, the president argued that the intervention occurring in Libya is "distinct from the kinds of hostilities contemplated by the [War Powers] resolution" (Wilson 2011).

Currently, there are two broad partisan trends in the debate over U.S. foreign policy toward Libya. One is the continuing debate over responsibility for the consulate attack in the eastern city of Benghazi. The House of Representatives held hearings in October 2015 on the attack as they relate to lapses in embassy security, as well as the accusation that former secretary of state Hillary Clinton had misled the public and the victim's families about the nature of the attack. Democrats on the select committee argued that the work of the committee itself had already been done during previous investigations and that the current investigation was a politically motivated effort to damage Obama's presidency and discredit the front-runner for the 2016 Democratic Party presidential nomination. Democrats also argued that it would have been impossible to dispatch additional support to the embassy in time to save those under attack, that decreases in embassy security funding could be traced directly to Republican spending cuts, and that the motivations for the attack were at least partially unclear in the immediate aftermath of the attacks.

The second issue relates to the decision to intensify airstrikes against ISIS positions in Libya. President Obama, while defending the initial decision to intervene in Libya, later stated during an interview that his greatest mistake was "probably failing to plan for the day after what I think was the right thing to do in intervening in Libya" (Fox News 2016). In this context, Obama essentially admitted that the failure to plan for the future of Libya created a power vacuum that has led to civil war and the rise of ISIS. The Obama administration, with the backing of most Democrats, including Democratic nominee Hillary Clinton, decided to begin airstrikes against ISIS positions in Libya in 2015. In August 2016, the United States began an intensified series of airstrikes around ISIS strongholds such as the city of Sirte (also referred to as Surt). These airstrikes, which were ordered in specific response to requests for military assistance from the internationally backed government in Libya, appear to have resulted in initial gains of Libyan forces against ISIS positions.

Republicans on Libya

The 2016 Republican Party platform mentions Libya once, in the context of the terrorist attack in Benghazi. Nonetheless, the Republican National Committee, which plays a role in creating the platform, and the great majority of Republicans in Congress have been vociferous in their criticism of the Obama administration's handling of the situation in Libya, including the role played by Hillary Clinton, who was Obama's secretary of state when Qaddafi's regime fell (September 2011) and when a mob attacked the U.S. embassy in Benghazi, killing four Americans (September 2012). For example, in March 2016, the RNC used the social media platform Twitter to tweet a video in which Secretary Clinton stated that the United States "did not lose a single person in Libya" (Merica 2016). For its part, the Clinton campaign argued that the quote was taken out of context and that Clinton was referring to the fact that no U.S. combat troops were killed over the course of the 2011 intervention. The RNC has also argued that the tragedy in Benghazi cannot be blamed on a decrease in the embassy security budget, insisting that many precautions could have been taken at little or no cost to the State Department.

At the onset of the 2011 U.S. military intervention in Libya, at least one poll indicated that more Republicans (57 percent) than Democrats (51 percent) favored military action against the Qaddafi regime (Jones 2011). By June of the same year, according to the same poll, a significant gap had opened between Republicans and Democrats, with 54 percent of Democrats supporting military action and 39 percent of Republicans coming to the same conclusion. Several factors have been cited for this widening partisan divide. First, the period between March and June of 2011 saw increased partisan rancor related to both the wisdom of military intervention in Libya and to the legality of intervention in light of the War Powers Resolution. It is often the case in U.S. politics that public perceptions on foreign policy issues change once political elites have weighed in the on the subject. Second, the fact that Democratic elites were still bullish on the intervention led to a slight increase in support among Democrats, further widening the gap. It is worth noting, however, that self-identified independents, who had always been the most skeptical of military intervention, experienced a seven-point erosion in support from March to June, according to the Gallup poll cited above. On the balance, then, the American public was becoming more skeptical the Libyan intervention in a relatively short period of time. The prospect of new military engagement to replace the conflicts in Afghanistan and Iraq is another likely reason for the relatively rapid erosion of support, especially among independents.

Republicans in Congress strongly opposed the 2011 intervention, raising objections on both strategic and legal grounds. Former Speaker of the House John Boehner, for example, argued that the mission lacked clarity and was undertaken without regard to its potential costs. Many Republicans expressed skepticism over whether it was possible to identify and differentiate between forces fighting for Qaddafi, secular rebels, and Islamist rebels working against U.S. interests. By far, however, the most widely voiced criticism related to the legality of the intervention. In an opinion piece in the *Washington Times,* for example, Kentucky senator Rand Paul advanced the argument used by many Republicans. First, he argued that only Congress has the power to declare war. Second, he argued that military intervention within the confines of the War Powers Resolution is limited to cases not applicable to the situation in Libya. Third, Senator Paul argued that President Obama had failed in his obligation to notify Congress of the military action (Paul 2011). Specifically, Paul argued that:

> The administration's complete disregard for the Constitution has bothered many Americans, for the Constitution clearly states that it is Congress that has the power to declare war, not the president. The War Powers Act also clearly states that U.S. armed forces are to engage in immediate hostilities only if the circumstances are "pursuant to (1) a declaration of war, (2) specific statutory authorization, or (3) a national emergency created by attack upon the United States, its territories or possessions, or its armed forces." (Paul 2011)

One former Reagan administration attorney began the process of drafting articles of impeachment over the perceived constitutional impropriety, a move that was partially supported by antiwar Democrat Dennis Kucinich. However, the effort to formally begin the impeachment process never achieved critical mass in the House of Representatives, where the process would have to have begun under the procedure outlined in the Constitution. Republicans reasoned that the impeachment process would not survive the Senate where a two-thirds supermajority would be required to convict the president. In addition, it is not clear that Republicans in the House of Representatives had the votes to impeach the president. Moderate Republicans would have been difficult to persuade on this issue, especially after the last attempt to impeach a president (President Clinton) led to an increase in his popularity.

When the GOP-controlled House of Representatives initiated—at President Obama's request—an authorization process for the intervention in Libya, an overwhelming percentage of Republican representatives opposed the intervention. Of the 233 Republicans who voted on the resolution, only eight voted in favor of intervention. The eight Republicans who cast votes to authorize tended to argue that, since Congress had earlier failed to deny funding for the intervention, a limited authorization for military action made sense. But while House Republicans were more unified against authorization than Democrats, the opposite was the case on the issue of funding. As mentioned earlier, roughly 20 percent of Democrats in the House voted in favor of immediately withdrawing funding from most aspects of the U.S. intervention in Libya. By contrast, nearly 40 percent of Republicans voted against the cut in funding (House of Representatives 2011). There are few discernable patterns in the Republican vote, other than the fact that the party leadership was unified in favor of cutting funding that would be used for the intervention.

On the issue of the 2015 Benghazi hearings, Republicans have been unified in their condemnation of the response of the Obama administration and, by extension, of Hillary Clinton. South Carolina representative Trey Gowdy, who chaired the select committee, claimed that the committee uncovered evidence that requests for increased security directly from Ambassador Chris Stevens, who was killed in the attack, countered claims from Clinton and the broader Obama administration about the lack of demand for increased security from sources on the ground in Libya. Republicans were also highly critical of the use by Clinton of a private e-mail server for State Department business, arguing that it could compromise security and result in sharing classified information. Two Republican members of the committee, Ohio representative Jim Jordan and Kansas representative Mike Pompeo, took a harder line, arguing that "she (Clinton) missed the last clear chance to defend her people" (Demirjian 2016). Ultimately, the e-mail server issue was referred to the Federal Bureau of Investigation (FBI) for review. Although the director of the FBI found evidence of significant carelessness in the handling of classified information, the investigation did not find enough evidence to recommend an indictment of Clinton by the Department of Justice.

The issue of Libya became a significant part of the 2016 election campaign of businessman Donald Trump. Trump's essential argument is that Hillary Clinton was the chief architect of the 2011 intervention in Libya, which in turn created a power vacuum that enabled ISIS to rise in Libya. This argument is consistent with Trump's position on ISIS in Syria and Iraq as well, though in those cases the argument is more difficult to make given the historical development of ISIS, especially in Iraq (see ISIS/ISIL entry). On the issue of Benghazi, Trump has been even more critical, arguing that Ambassador Chris Stephens was "left helpless to die as Hillary Clinton slept in her bed" (Schwartz 2016). Clinton has offered in her defense that the attacks occurred during the day in the Eastern time zone and that she worked late into the night. However, the issue has had some resonance, especially when tied to the line of attack concerning Clinton's e-mail server arrangement. A July 2016 poll by the *Washington Post* revealed that, as one might expect, 88 percent of Republicans disagree with the decision of FBI Director James Comey's decision not to recommend an indictment against Clinton (Sargent 2016). Nearly one-third of Democrats have the same view, which explains, in part, Trump's use of the Libya and e-mail arguments in concert in an effort to win over wavering Democrats in the 2016 election.

Further Reading

CNN. "CNN/Opinion Research Corporation International Poll." Last modified May 5, 2016. http://i2.cdn.turner.com/cnn/2016/images/05/05/rel6c.-.isis.pdf.

Demirjian, Karoun. "Trey Gowdy Defends Two-Year Benghazi Probe That Was Riddled with Partisan Conflict." *Washington Post*. Last modified June 28, 2016. https://www.washingtonpost.com/news/powerpost/wp/2016/06/28/house-benghazi-report-reveals-little-new-information-about-hillary-clinton/.

Democratic National Committee. "2016 Democratic Party Platform." Last modified July 21, 2016. https://www.demconvention.com/wp-content/uploads/2016/07/Democratic -Party-Platform-7.21.16-no-lines.pdf.

Fox News. "Exclusive: President Barack Obama on 'Fox News Sunday.'" Last modified April 10, 2016. http://www.foxnews.com/transcript/2016/04/10/exclusive-president -barack-obama-on-fox-news-sunday/.

Grijalva, Raul M., Barbara Lee, Mike Honda, and Lynn Woolsey. "Representatives Grijalva, Lee, Honda, Woolsey Issue Joint Statement on the Situation in Libya." Congressman Raul Grijalva. Last modified March 22, 2011. https://grijalva.house.gov/common/popup /popup.cfm?action=item.print&itemID=890.

Jones, Jeffrey M. "Americans Shift to More Negative View of Libya Military Action." Gallup. Last modified June 24, 2011. http://www.gallup.com/poll/148196/americans-shift -negative-view-libya-military-action.aspx.

Kaplan, Eben. "How Libya Got Off the List." Council on Foreign Relations. Last modified October 16, 2007. http://www.cfr.org/libya/libya-got-off-list/p10855.

Merica, Dan. "Clinton Campaign Defends Libya Comment in Face of RNC Attacks." CNN. Last modified March 15, 2016. http://www.cnn.com/2016/03/15/politics/hillary-clinton -republicans-benghazi/.

Paul, Rand. "PAUL: Obama's Unconstitutional Libyan War." *Washington Times*. Last modified June 15, 2011. http://www.washingtontimes.com/news/2011/jun/15/obamas-uncon stitutional-libyan-war/.

Pro Publica. "House Vote 493—Rejects Authorization of Limited Military Involvement in Libya." Last modified June 24, 2011. https://projects.propublica.org/represent/votes /112/house/1/493/?nyt=true.

Sargent, Greg. "This New Poll Shows That Even a Lot of Democrats Worry about Clinton's Emails." Washington Post. Last modified July 11, 2016. https://www.washingtonpost .com/blogs/plum-line/wp/2016/07/11/this-new-poll-shows-that-even-a-lot-of-dems -worry-about-hillarys-emails/?utm_term=.cc4f65d92c5e.

Schwartz, Ian. "Trump Hits Clinton on Benghazi: When the Phone Rang at 3AM, She Was Sleeping." RealClearPolitics. Last modified June 22, 2016. http://www.realclearpolitics .com/video/2016/06/22/trump_hits_clinton_on_benghazi_when_the_phone_rang _at_3am_she_was_sleeping.html.

U.S. House of Representatives. "House Roll Call Vote 494: To Limit the Use of Funds Appropriated to the Department of Defense for United States Armed Forces in Sup- port of North Atlantic Treaty Organization Operation Unified Protector with respect to Libya, Unless Otherwise Specifically Authorized by Law." Office of the Clerk of the U.S. House of Representatives. Last modified June 24, 2011. http://clerk.house.gov /evs/2011/roll494.xml.

Walsh, Declan. "A Slow, Steady Siege on an ISIS Stronghold in Libya." *New York Times*. Last modified June 29, 2016. http://www.nytimes.com/2016/06/30/world/africa/a-slow -steady-siege-on-isis-stronghold-in-libya.html?_r=0.

Wilson, Scott. "Obama Administration: Libya Action Does Not Require Congressional Approval." *Washington Post*. Last modified June 15, 2011. https://www.washington post.com/politics/obama-administration-libya-action-does-not-require-congressional -approval/2011/06/15/AGLttOWH_story.html.

Mexico

At a Glance

Overall, the United States enjoys a positive but complicated relationship with Mexico. The two neighboring countries cooperate on a variety of issues, including narcotics interdiction, border security, terrorism prevention, trade promotion, and immigration. At the same time, the fact that the United States is the more economically developed of the two countries (though both Mexico and the United States are economically developed by international standards) creates economic incentives for immigration, both legal and illegal, between the two countries. In addition, Mexico acts as both a producer and transit state for several illegal drugs bound for U.S. markets. Finally, Mexico's comparative economic advantage in the realm of cheap labor, coupled with the United States' comparative advantage in capital, creates the classic economic conditions for some U.S. companies to produce products in Mexico for sale in America and other parts of the world. During election season, especially presidential election season, each of these items is prone to politicization. Under the somewhat unique circumstances of the 2016 election, the politicization of the U.S.–Mexico relationship has become more intense and somewhat more partisan.

According to many Democrats . . .

- Mexico and its people have been vilified by Republicans on issues related to immigration;
- Trade with Mexico should do more to accommodate U.S. concerns about labor and environmental standards within Mexico's borders;
- Undocumented immigrants from Mexico and other states should have a path to citizenship in the United States provided that they meet certain conditions; and
- There should not be a border wall along the entire U.S. border with Mexico.

According to many Republicans . . .

- Mexico has been a valuable ally in the war on drugs;
- There should be a border wall along the entire U.S. border with Mexico;

- Mexico must do more to prevent illegal immigration into the United States; and
- Undocumented immigrants from Mexico or other states should not have a path to U.S. citizenship under most conditions.

Overview

The State Department characterizes current U.S. relations with Mexico in 2016 as "strong and vital" (U.S. Department of State 2016). The very nature of the 2,000-mile shared border between the two countries necessitates cooperation in a variety of areas. Within the realm of border security cooperation, multiagency cooperation occurs through the U.S.-Binational Group on Bridges and Border Crossings (BBBXG). With regard to economics, Mexico and the United States are part of both the North American Free Trade Agreement (NAFTA) and High-Level Economic Dialog (HLED). The two countries have institutionalized educational and cultural exchanges as well. Finally, the United States provides assistance to Mexico in training and equipping local, state, and national law enforcement in order to combat organized crime, including drug trafficking. Each of these areas of cooperation involves a detailed set of economic, political, and social relationships examined briefly in the paragraphs that follow.

In 1994, NAFTA came into force as a trilateral agreement between the United States, Canada, and Mexico. Mexico is the second-largest export market for the United States (after Canada), which provided an incentive for the United States to seek reciprocal tariff elimination with both countries. Mexico is also the second-largest source of U.S. imports behind only China. Beyond the tariff reduction and elimination provisions, the NAFTA regime consists of side agreements related to environmental protection and labor standards. At the time NAFTA passed Congress as an executive-legislative agreement (as opposed to a conventional treaty), most opponents of the agreement were Democrats. Democrats feared that NAFTA would lead to job losses, lower wages, and, potentially fewer protections for workers, especially within their organized labor base. Majorities of Democrats voted against the agreement in both chambers of Congress, though the vote was closer in the Senate. Republicans in both chambers favored the measure by significant margins. President Clinton, however, favored the measure as a means to increase U.S. market access to Mexico and Canada. As a result, NAFTA entered into force in 1994. That same year, Clinton used Treasury Department stabilization funds to provide loan guarantees to Mexico, whose economy was on the verge of collapse.

Border cooperation between the United States and Mexico creates many logistical challenges. In addition to the length of the border, the United States and Mexico must manage over 200 million border crossings per year, most of which are perfectly legal (Bonner and Rozental 2011). The BBBXG, which contains both national and state-level delegates from the United States and Mexico, meets in different states and deals with logistical and technical issues related to different crossing points along the border. One of the greatest challenges to temporary migration between the United States and Mexico, which occurs in both directions, is crowding and congestion at the border. Wait times at the border make it difficult for workers and tourists to cross between the two countries, which has an adverse economic impact on both the United States and Mexico. The development of new border crossings, however, must be done with both security and ease of movement in mind. Local-level meetings of the BBBXG are designed to strike the proper balance between security and freedom of movement that is key to the economic vitality of the large border region.

With regard to security, including illegal crossings for the purpose of narcotics trafficking or terrorism, the amount of cooperation between the U.S. Border Patrol and its Mexican counterpart has also increased, as has cooperation between the two nations' military forces. The Mérida Initiative, initiated in 2007 and backed by over $2.5 billion in U.S. aid, has increased the amount of border security between the United States and Mexico while also providing needed resources and training to the Mexican government to combat organized crime (Seelke and Finklea 2016).

Significant challenges still remain. For example, corruption at border crossings, especially in Mexico, often leads to increased numbers of undocumented border crossings. Poorly paid border agents in Mexico are subject to bribes by organized narcotics trafficking cartels, which makes it difficult to stem the flow of illicit drugs into the United States. Mérida Initiative funds have been used for justice system reform, both to decrease the amount of corruption and to introduce adversarial reform designed to ensure the rights of the accused. Significant demand for narcotics in the United States, coupled with economic inequality and pockets of extreme poverty in Mexico, however, limit the efficacy of reform.

In part because of border security cooperation and in part because of the so-called great recession that hit the United States in December 2007, the number of undocumented immigrants from Mexico living in the United States has decreased markedly in recent years. While undocumented immigration is difficult to track for obvious reasons, the nonpartisan Center for Migration studies and the Pew Research Center produce estimates that are widely used by policy makers. According to the Center for Migration studies, the Mexican-born undocumented immigrant population in the United States fell by about 600,000 between 2010 and 2014 (Center for Migration Studies 2016). For the first time ever, in 2014, more non-Mexicans than Mexicans were apprehended on immigration-related violations (Gonzalez-Barrera and Krogstad 2015). Undocumented immigrants of Mexican origin, however, still make up the largest group of undocumented immigrants in the United States. Mexican citizens also make up the largest group of legal migrants to the United States, though the number of legal migrants from India and China has outpaced the number from Mexico in recent years. Finally, a 2014 surge in the number of unaccompanied minors attempting to illegally cross the border has raised the salience of illegal immigration in the United States. Most of these children were born in Central America, not Mexico. However, it is still the case that the American public tends to associate most immigration from the south with Mexico.

Currently, a combination of economic populism and nationalism has increased the salience of U.S.–Mexico relations, especially as it related to border control. Proponents of increased border enforcement believe that undocumented or illegal immigration from Mexico costs jobs in the United States and leads to increases in crime. Proponents of a stronger U.S. anti-illegal immigration policy also argue that Mexico is not doing enough to discourage illegal immigration. Opponents argue that, while the border must be kept secure, basic economic differences between the United States and Mexico will always present immigration challenges. Opponents tend to argue that illegal or undocumented immigration can only be confronted by promoting economic development, especially in poorer regions of Mexico. In the interim, immigration policy must address the impracticality of apprehending and deporting the 5.6 million undocumented immigrants from Mexico living in the United States (Gonzalez-Barrera and Krogstad 2015). There is also a difference in vernacular between the two groups. Proponents of stronger border enforcement tend to refer to unauthorized immigrants in the United States as "illegal immigrants" or simply "illegals." Opponents of the more nationalist perspective, who generally favor pathways to citizenship for unauthorized immigrants living in the United States, tend to use the term "undocumented immigrants."

Democrats on U.S. Foreign Policy toward Mexico

The 2016 Democratic Party platform only mentions Mexico specifically once. In the platform, Democrats argue that Republican presidential nominee Donald Trump's preferred policy of building a wall along the entire southern border in order to halt illegal immigration has alienated Mexico. The platform does, however, refer to several facets of the U.S. relationship with Mexico indirectly. For example, Democrats promise, in general terms, to combat organized crime, narcotics production and trafficking, and corruption in Latin America. These are all issues that can be applied to the U.S. relationship with Mexico specifically. The platform also argues that global free trade has resulted in economic dislocations for American workers, a classic Democratic Party position even in the age of NAFTA and the Trans-Pacific Partnership (TPP; see associated entries "Trans-Pacific Partnership" and "Trade Policy"). Democrats posit that older free trade agreements, without mentioning NAFTA by name, need to be reviewed and updated to include increased protections for workers and improved environmental protection standards. Of course, integrating increased trade or environmental protections into almost any trade agreement, especially one that involves the developing world, would increase American worker competitiveness by forcing developing countries to partially forgo their comparative advantage in unskilled labor. Finally, the Democratic Party platform advocates the development of a "path to citizenship" for undocumented immigrants, many of whom are from Mexico, in order to reunite families, increase economic growth, and expand the income tax base.

Within the realm of public opinion, most opinion polls handle issues related to Mexico indirectly via questions about immigration, free trade, and other issues. A 2016 Gallup poll indicated that overall, more Americans (59 percent) view Mexico favorably than unfavorably (38 percent) (Gallup 2016). However, partisan data on general U.S. feelings toward Mexico are lacking. Partisan data exist on more specific issues. However, it is important to recognize that the results do not apply exclusively to Mexico. For example, a 2016 Pew Research Center poll found that an overwhelming majority (88 percent) of Democrats believe that undocumented immigrants, under certain circumstances, should be offered a path to U.S. citizenship (Jones, B. 2016). A 2015 Pew poll, meanwhile, found that a majority of Democrats (62 percent) believe that immigration, illegal and legal, strengthens the United States (Goo 2015). According to Gallup, the vast majority of Democrats (88 percent) opposed the construction of a wall along the entire U.S.–Mexican border (Jones, J. 2016). With regard to NAFTA, 2016 survey data from Rasmussen Reports suggests that a minority of Democrats (38 percent) believe that the agreement needs to be negotiated to provide more protections for U.S. workers (Rasmussen Reports 2016). Mexico would also be party to the Trans-Pacific Partnership, an even larger trade agreement involving 12 countries. A narrow majority (51 percent) of Democrats favored that agreement according to one 2015 poll (Poushter 2015).

Political elites within the Democratic Party are overwhelmingly positive about U.S. relations with Mexico. President Obama, for example, has referred to Mexico as "a critical partner" and "critically important to our well-being" (Somander 2016). In 2011, after former Mexican president Calderón argued that the United States was not committed enough to fighting drug-related organized crime in Mexico, President Obama reaffirmed the U.S. security commitment to Mexico, offered additional high-level meetings, and increased some of the aid available under the Mérida Initiative. In 2016, a congressional delegation consisting of mostly Democrats visited Mexico, Peru, and Chile to discuss security cooperation and the Trans-Pacific Partnership. Each of the delegation members reiterated the strong bilateral relationship between the United States and Mexico as part of their individual press releases.

As we move from the general to the specific, however, we find varying degrees of support among Democrats for policies relating to Mexico. On immigration, 208 of 246 House Democrats supported the Dream Act, which would have provided a path to citizenship for undocumented immigrants, when the measure came up for a vote in 2010. The measure failed in the Senate due to a Republican-led filibuster, which prevented a final vote on the legislation. Five Democrats, all from conservative states where they would be vulnerable on the issue of immigration, voted with Republicans to sustain the filibuster. In 2013, the Senate passed the Border Security, Economic Opportunity, and Immigration Modernization Act. In this case,

Democratic senators were completely unified in their support of the legislation, introduced by a group of four Democrats and four Republicans commonly called the "gang of eight." The bill provided for a path to citizenship as defined above, plus the addition of thousands of new border patrol agents. Every Senate Democrat voted in favor of the legislation, which passed by a margin of 68–32. However, the bill was never taken up in the Republican-controlled House. Democrats in Congress, as well as President Obama, have also been highly critical of proposals from Republicans to build a wall along the entire U.S. border with Mexico, arguing that such measures would undermine the U.S. relationship with Mexico, in addition to being practically unworkable. 2016 Democratic presidential nominee Hillary Clinton has also heavily criticized the notion of building a comprehensive border wall, though she voted for the development of a shorter border wall (approximately 700 miles) as part of an immigration reform package while serving as a senator from New York.

On the TPP, which is also favored by Mexico, Democratic support is more mixed. In 2015, a majority of Senate Democrats voted against Trade Promotion Authority (TPA), a provision designed to give the president more flexibility in negotiating trade agreements. TPA expiration would have effectively killed the TPP in the United States. Ultimately, TPA passed with mostly Republican support in the Senate. Senator Elizabeth Warren, one of the most outspoken critics of the agreement, argued that the TPP would hurt U.S. workers, damage the environment, and weaken U.S. sovereignty in the realm of international trade disputes. Democrats have also been inconsistent in their support of NAFTA. President Obama ran for president in 2008 promising to renegotiate NAFTA, a move opposed by Mexico. Hillary Clinton has made a similar pledge. It is important to recognize that renegotiation of the agreement would require Mexico's support as well as significant unity in Congress. Experts also caution that lowered levels of support for NAFTA reflect a basic division between Democrats on trade-related issues—not hesitance or unhappiness about America's relationship with its southern neighbor.

Republicans on U.S. Foreign Policy toward Mexico

As is the case with the Democratic Party, the 2016 Republican Party platform is sparse in terms of specific mentions of Mexico. The platform commits Republicans to working closely with Mexico on trade and environmental issues and applauds Mexico for its assistance in combating terrorism and drug-related organized crime (Republican National Committee 2016). On immigration, the Republican platform accuses the Obama administration of bullying states, primarily through the use of executive orders (see the entry on Immigration). In essence, Republicans believe that the decision of President Obama to defer deportation proceedings for undocumented parents of children born in the United States and undocumented immigrants who were children when they arrived in the United States ties the hands of states that wish to take a stronger stance on illegal immigration. Republicans also advance the argument that illegal immigration results in job losses for American workers, necessitating greater enforcement at and protection of the U.S. border with Mexico. In addition to harming the American worker, Republicans believe that illegal immigration increases the crime rate and contributes to the proliferation of illegal drugs in the United States. Finally, the platform supports the position that a wall ought to be built along the entire U.S. border with Mexico. Although most Republicans favor enhanced monitoring of the border, the specific reference to an all-encompassing border wall is new and broadly reflective of the position of Republican presidential nominee Donald Trump. On issues related to trade, the Republican platform mentions walking away from trade negotiations that do not advance the interests of the United States. This is more or less a direct reference to the TPP, which is supported by many Republicans, but not its 2016 presidential nominee.

As mentioned above, public opinion in the United States related to Mexico is generally positive. Partisan gaps emerge quickly on specific issues, however. For example, 62 percent of Republicans expressed a belief in one 2015 poll that immigrants are an overall burden, as opposed to strength, for the United States (Goo 2015). Republicans are also more likely than Democrats to favor a change in the Constitution to prevent the children of undocumented immigrants from automatically attaining U.S. citizenship ("birthright" citizenship). Republicans who identify with the more conservative Tea Party movement are even more likely to oppose birthright citizenship. With regard to trade, a plurality of Republicans joins a majority of Democrats in supporting the TPP. Forty-three percent of Republicans support the TPP while 34 percent oppose the agreement (Poushter 2015). On NAFTA, the partisan gap is much wider. Sixty-two percent of Republicans, as opposed to 38 percent of Democrats, believe that NAFTA needs to be renegotiated (Rasmussen Reports 2016). There is, of course, a pure partisan impact at play here. Both NAFTA and the TPP are widely viewed as Democratic Party trade deals, though the real picture is much more complicated and bipartisan. In this context, it is intuitive that Republicans would be leerier of these two trade deals, while Democrats may be more apt to support them. In addition, Republicans, at least in the general public, have become more skeptical of free trade, especially since the rise of the Tea Party movement, which is more economically nationalistic than more mainstream Republicans.

Elected Republicans have generally opposed legislation that would grant undocumented immigrants a path to citizenship, a measure favored by Mexico. In 2010, the DREAM Act passed the House with only eight Republican votes in favor (Pro Publica 2010). Thirty-six Republican senators joined five Democrats in a successful filibuster of the DREAM Act in the Senate. With regard to the 2013 Border Security, Economic Opportunity, and Immigration Modernization Act, 32 Republicans voted against the act, while 14 voted in favor. Republicans from more liberal states, as well as from states with large numbers of Hispanic immigrants such as Arizona and Florida, were more likely to support the proposal. Consideration of the bill ended when the House of Representatives failed to take up the legislation.

Overall, Republicans in Congress have been more supportive of the TPP, of which Mexico is a member than Democrats. When the Senate passed trade promotion authority, for example, 47 of 52 Republicans voted in favor of the resolution which strengthened the president's hand to negotiate the TPP by making it so that Congress would be unable to offer amendments to the final agreement (*New York Times* 2015). In the House, 190 of 240 Representatives voted in favor of TPA. The higher percentage of Republican no votes in the House can be attributed to two main factors. First, Republicans in states that have lost large numbers of manufacturing jobs, such as Michigan and New York, were more likely to vote against TPA in an effort to prevent final negotiation of the TPP. Second, Tea Party Republicans, while not unified on the TPP, were more likely to vote against the measure. Overall, Tea Party Republicans are more likely to believe that free trade hurts American workers.

With regard to presidential politics, Republican businessman Donald Trump opposes the TPP, of which Mexico is a party, and favors the construction of a wall along the entire U.S. border with Mexico. Trump has argued that the United States is not tough enough in negotiating trade agreements in general, creating the conditions for expanded trade deficits with countries like Mexico with lower labor costs. This position is generally contrary to that of most Republicans seeking office. However, Trump has, to a degree, locked on to a more recent anti–free trade trend among Republicans, especially in the rust belt, which has lost a large number of manufacturing jobs (though the empirical evidence that the job losses are related to free trade is mixed at best). On immigration, Trump has made several statements, some of which have caused a great deal of controversy, and all of which strongly oppose any flexibility with regard to the status of undocumented immigrants. Trump's most famous position is that a wall should be built, and financed by Mexico, along the entire border between the two countries. Although this position has also generated controversy, it has endeared Trump to economic and political nationalists who have felt marginalized within contemporary Republican Party politics. Critics of the plan argue that there is no realistic way to force Mexico to pay for the wall, that the rhetoric surrounding the wall alienates Mexico from the United States, and alienates Latino voters from the Republican Party (a significant concern for Republicans).

Further Reading

Bonner, Robert C., and Andres Rozental. "Managing the United States–Mexico Border: Cooperative Solutions to Common Challenges." Wilson Center. Last modified July 7, 2011. https://www.wilsoncenter.org/sites/default/files/PCIP%20Comexi%20Full%20 Report-%20english%20version.pdf.

Center for Migration Studies. "Center for Migration Studies Reports Decline of the US Undocumented Population." Last modified January 20, 2016. cmsny.org/press-release -undocumented-decline/.

Democratic National Convention. "2016 Democratic Party Platform." Last modified July 21, 2016. https://www.demconvention.com/wp-content/uploads/2016/07/Democratic -Party-Platform-7.21.16-no-lines.pdf.

Gallup.com. "Country Ratings | Gallup Historical Trends." Last modified February 7, 2016. http://www.gallup.com/poll/1624/perceptions-foreign-countries.aspx.

Gonzalez-Barrera, Ana, and Jens M. Krogstad. "What We Know about Illegal Immigration from Mexico." Pew Research Center. Last modified November 20, 2015. http://www .pewresearch.org/fact-tank/2015/11/20/what-we-know-about-illegal-immigration-from -mexico/.

Goo, Sara K. "What Americans Want to Do about Illegal Immigration." Pew Research Center. Last modified August 24, 2015. http://www.pewresearch.org/fact-tank/2015/08/24 /what-americans-want-to-do-about-illegal-immigration/.

Jones, Bradley. "Americans' Views of Immigrants Marked by Widening Partisan, Generational Divides." Pew Research Center. Last modified April 15, 2016. http://www.pewresearch .org/fact-tank/2016/04/15/americans-views-of-immigrants-marked-by-widening-par tisan-generational-divides/.

Jones, Jeffrey. "More Republicans Favor Path to Citizenship Than Wall." Gallup.com. Last modified July 20, 2016. http://www.gallup.com/poll/193817/republicans-favor-path -citizenship-wall.aspx?g_source=Election%202016&g_medium=newsfeed&g_campaign =tiles.

New York Times. "Senate Vote 219—Passes Trade Promotion Authority." Last modified June 24, 2015. http://politics.nytimes.com/congress/votes/114/senate/1/219.

Poushter, Jacob. "Americans Favor TPP, but Less Than Those in Other Countries Do." Pew Research Center. Last modified June 23, 2015. http://www.pewresearch.org/fact-tank /2015/06/23/americans-favor-tpp-but-less-than-other-countries-do/.

Pro Publica. "House Vote 625—Approves DREAM Act." Last modified December 8, 2010. https://projects.propublica.org/represent/votes/111/house/2/625.

Rasmussen Reports. "Voters Aren't Happy with NAFTA, Other Free Trade Deals." Last modified July 5, 2016. http://www.rasmussenreports.com/public_content/politics/general _politics/june_2016/voters_aren_t_happy_with_nafta_other_free_trade_deals.

Republican National Committee. "Republican Platform 2016." Last modified 2016. https:// prod-static-ngop-pbl.s3.amazonaws.com/media/documents/DRAFT_12_FINAL[1] -ben_1468872234.pdf.

Seelke, Clare R., and Kristin Finklea. "U.S.–Mexican Security Cooperation: The Mérida Initiative and Beyond." Congressional Research Service. Last modified February 22, 2016. https://www.fas.org/sgp/crs/row/R41349.pdf.

Somander, Tonya. "President Obama on the U.S.—Mexico Relationship." Whitehouse.gov. Last modified July 25, 2016. https://www.whitehouse.gov/blog/2016/07/25/president -obama-us-mexico-relationship.

U.S. Department of State. "Mexico." Last modified July 12, 2016. http://www.state.gov/r /pa/ei/bgn/35749.htm.

Military Intervention

At a Glance

As a global military power with a wide variety of foreign policy goals, the United States has frequently resorted to various types of military intervention during its history. In 2003, for example, the United States invaded Iraq in what is commonly cited by Republicans, especially within the George W. Bush administration, as a preventive—as opposed to preemptive—war (the war was not a response to an imminent territorial threat, hence it was not preemptive). Correctly or incorrectly, the Republican administration of President George W. Bush viewed Iraq as a threat to the United States. The Bush administration decided that acting first would be the most effective way to counter the potential future threat posed by Iraqi weapons of mass destruction, which the administration believed to exist in various stages of development. Critics argue that the intelligence that existed was oversold and undersourced. A partisan gap does exist on issues related to military intervention. However, there is also a strong degree of intraparty disagreement on the circumstances under which military intervention is an appropriate tool of foreign policy. The current entry focuses on cases of military intervention where the United States initiates the use of military force in pursuit of some foreign policy goal, regardless of its perceived justification.

According to many Republicans . . .

- Military intervention is often a more reliable instrument of foreign policy than diplomacy;
- The threat of military intervention makes other, less forceful options more effective;
- It is acceptable to consider preventive military action when doing so reduces risks and threats in the future; and
- Military strength is the best way to promote peace.

According to many Democrats . . .

- Military intervention should almost always be the last foreign policy option;
- Diplomacy is often a superior instrument of foreign policy than is the use of force;

- Military intervention, especially for humanitarian purposes, is sometimes unavoidable and is at times a responsibility of powerful countries; and
- Diplomacy is more likely to promote peace than military intervention.

Overview

The United States has used military action as a tool of foreign policy ever since President John Adams engaged in the "Quasi-war," an undeclared naval war with France in the 1790s. The Quasi-war, however, was a response to French seizure of U.S. merchant ships and is hence not a classic case of preemptive military intervention. In 1818, General Andrew Jackson invaded areas of Spanish-controlled Florida to attack Seminole Indians gathering near Pensacola. Jackson's invasion was a classic military intervention in that it was designed to advance the foreign policy interests of the United States—in this case, the safety of white settlers in adjacent U.S. territory—rather than a response to aggression by Spain against the United States. The Monroe Doctrine, announced in 1823, became the basis for U.S. military intervention in the Western hemisphere for well over a century. The Monroe Doctrine stated that European powers must refrain from intervention in the Western hemisphere.

As the United States grew in power, so did its penchant for military intervention. The United States added several territories, including Guam, the Philippines, and Puerto Rico, during the Spanish-American War of 1898. The United States initiated the conflict, which it framed as an honorable effort to secure Cuban independence from Spain, after the mysterious sinking of an American battleship USS Maine in the waters off of Havana. The United States did not directly annex Cuba after its successful invasion of the island. Instead, it established a protectorate over the island while reserving the right to intervene militarily if such an intervention was necessary to protect U.S. interests. The United States also intervened in the Dominican Republic in 1905 after a financial crisis in order to protect its interest in denying European powers a path to influence in the Western hemisphere. Perhaps most famously, the U.S. navy intervened on the side of Panamanian separatists in 1903 as they fought for independence from Columbia. Once Panama became independent, the United States was able to secure the treaty rights necessary to build the Panama Canal. Localized military intervention continued as a part of U.S. policy through World War I, after which a period of isolationism set in.

After World War II, which was partially a direct military intervention and partially a reaction to the Japanese attack on Pearl Harbor, the Cold War between the United States and the Soviet Union led to more direct military intervention from the United States. The Korean War and the Vietnam War were both examples of direct U.S. military intervention, at times taken under international auspices, designed to prevent the spread of Communism, which the United States feared would expand by contagion if left unchecked. The United States also undertook several military interventions in Africa, Asia, and Latin America, all for the purpose of halting Communist expansion in those areas. After Vietnam, Congress attempted to limit the authority of the president to send troops into harm's way by passing the War Powers Resolution in 1973. Generally speaking, however, the War Powers Resolution, while it has strengthened the norm of congressional–executive consultation, has not limited the practice of direct military intervention.

At the end of the Cold War, many observers expected the realization of a "peace dividend" whereby wars would become less necessary and military budgets could be reduced. Continued direct military intervention after the Cold War, however, erased most hope for the realization of a significant peace dividend. In 1990, the United States led an international coalition to reverse the Iraqi annexation of Kuwait. The resulting Operation Desert Storm was widely viewed as an archetype for the legitimate use of force in furtherance of international law. The United States also engaged in humanitarian interventions of various sorts in areas such as the Balkans (1992–1995) and Somalia (1993). The Battle of Mogadishu in Somalia left 18 U.S. soldiers, and over a thousand civilians, dead. The debacle in Somalia did not prevent further U.S. military intervention in other areas. However, it did increase public and political skepticism about humanitarian crises as a justification for U.S. intervention.

The U.S. invasion of Afghanistan is not properly viewed as a direct military intervention in that it occurred in response to an aggressive act by nonstate actors (Al Qaeda) provided a safe haven and partial sponsorship within another state. However, the Bush administration's invasion of Iraq in 2003 was a direct military intervention, taken under the argument that the concept of preemption should be expanded to include cases where a direct threat to the United States is not imminent but is foreseeable based on the best intelligence available. The National Security Strategy of 2002 became the basis for expanding the concept of preemptive war to include fighting terrorism, including state sponsorship. U.S. direct military intervention in states such as Iraq (after the rise of the Islamic State of Iraq and Greater Syria, commonly known as ISIS), Libya, Syria, and Yemen that have occurred since the original invasion of Iraq, are properly viewed as part of this most recent pattern of intervention.

Republicans on Military Intervention

Neither the Republican nor the Democratic Party platform mentions military intervention as a general topic. A party platform is much more likely to examine specific policies and actions, such as the Obama administration's decision to intervene in Libya in 2011, than it is to mention general foreign policy concepts. With regard to specific interventions, Republicans tend to be critical of what they perceive as the unwillingness of the Obama administration to confront threats quickly, decisively, and with a plan for what to do in the aftermath of the intervention. The GOP platform is critical, for example of the Obama administration decision to draw down troops in Iraq, which Republicans view as one of the primary conditions leading to the reemergence of ISIS. Although the 2016 platform does not call for further military intervention in Iraq, it is critical of the Obama administration for what it characterizes as a lack of support for endangered Christian communities in Iraq, as well as an unwillingness to more strongly support the Kurdish region of Iraq. The platform is also highly critical of the U.S. handling of the Arab Spring, which led to uprisings in several Middle Eastern and North African states. The Republican platform advances the argument that American weakness in Syria enabled the regime of Bashir al-Assad to brutally murder its own people while providing breathing space for ISIS.

The closest that the 2016 Republican platform comes to directly examining the issue of direct military intervention occurs in its introduction, where the platform takes President Obama to task for not consulting Congress before taking action overseas. The primary reference, in this case, is to Libya, where the United States provided air support to forces resisting dictator Muammar Qaddafi. Republicans have generally been critical of the intervention in Libya on both procedural and practical grounds. In the aftermath of the fall of Qaddafi, Libya has fallen into civil war, ISIS has gained a foothold in the country, and the U.S. consulate in Benghazi was attacked, resulting in the deaths of two U.S. diplomats and two security contractors. Republicans believe that these events all stemmed from a failure on the part of the administration to adequately plan for events in the post–Qaddafi era.

Within the general public, self-identified Republicans and Democrats share a belief in the idea that the United States must maintain its military superiority in order to deal with various threats to U.S. interests. A 2015 survey by the Chicago Council on Global affairs found that 86 percent of Republicans and 83 percent of Democrats believe that maintaining U.S. military superiority is at least somewhat effective in advancing U.S. foreign policy goals (Chicago Council on Global Affairs 2015). According to the same survey, 69 percent of Republicans believe that maintaining U.S. military superiority worldwide is, in itself, a major foreign policy goal. In addition, a majority of Republicans polled expressed support for military intervention in Iran in the event that the 2015 diplomatic deal negotiated by the Obama administration to stunt Iran's nuclear weapons program fails to achieve its desired goal. A majority of Republicans also favor U.S. military intervention to defend Israel from attack and to fight ISIS in the Middle East and North Africa.

With regard to specific interventions, though, Republican public opinion is mixed. For example, when the United States originally intervened in Libya to help topple the Qaddafi regime, 51 percent of Republicans favored military action (Jones 2011). By June of the same year, however, Republican support had fallen to 39 percent. As we shall see below, the degradation of support may well be related to increasing conservative criticism of the Obama administration's decision to intervene in Libya without seeking authorization from Congress, a fact that angered many congressional Republicans. Republicans also opposed the idea of intervening in Syria when the al-Assad regime used chemical weapons against civilians.

Fifty-one percent of Republicans opposed intervention in this case (Dugan 2013). The rise of ISIS, however, has shifted the calculus somewhat. Republicans are more likely to support the use of ground troops against ISIS than are Democrats or independents. Overall, 57 percent of self-identified Republicans and 61 percent of conservative Republicans favor the use of ground troops against ISIS in Iraq and Syria (Pew Research Center 2015). Intervening with ground troops to combat ISIS would, by definition, require military intervention in Iraq and Syria.

Although Republicans are generally more likely to support direct military intervention than are Democrats, Republicans in Congress have been more mixed in their views of direct military intervention with President Obama in office. In late 2015, Republicans in Congress blocked an Authorization for the Use of Military Force (AUMF) against ISIS. Many Republicans, such as South Carolina senator Lindsey Graham, argued that the AUMF advanced by the president provided him with less authority to intervene in countries such as Iraq, Syria, and Libya than did existing law. Arizona senator John McCain has made a similar argument for a restriction-free AUMF, arguing, "Congress should not be telling the commander-in-chief what to do," McCain says. "If we establish that precedent, he's no longer the commander-in-chief" (Fuller 2015). Overall, Republicans in Congress were disappointed that the Obama administration requested an AUMF that specifically forbade the use of regular ground troops (Special Forces would still be permitted). Republicans do not want to constrain the next president, especially if the next president is a Republican.

Republicans in Congress were more critical of the decision to intervene in Libya. Former Republican Speaker of the House John Boehner, for example, argued that the mission lacked clarity and was not undertaken with sufficient regard to its potential costs. Many Republicans expressed skepticism over whether it was possible to identify and differentiate between forces fighting for Qaddafi, secular rebels, and Islamist rebels working against U.S. interests. By far, however, the most widely heard criticism related to the legality of the intervention. Many Republicans argued that only Congress has the power to declare war and that military intervention within the confines of the War Powers Resolution was not applicable to the situation in Libya.

At the executive level, 2016 Republican presidential nominee Donald Trump was highly critical of the military intervention in Libya, arguing that it has opened space for ISIS to operate in the wake of Qaddafi's ouster. However, in a June 2016 interview, Trump argued that he would have supported a "surgical strike" to remove Qaddafi from power (Cheney 2016). Trump had previously argued that it would have been better for Qaddafi to remain in power. Trump has also expressed the position that other countries are capable of intervening in conflicts in ways that protect U.S. interests. For example, he has argued that Russian action in Syria could help effectively defeat ISIS without risking U.S. lives. However, Trump also argued during a Republican primary debate that he would be willing to deploy up to 30,000 troops in the Middle East to combat ISIS.

Democrats on Military Intervention

The 2016 Democratic Party platform does not speak explicitly about its overarching philosophy toward military intervention. However, like its Republican counterpart, it does include references to times when military intervention has been used. One area where the Democratic platform sends a very clear signal on intervention relates to ISIS. The platform states that "Democrats will seek an updated Authorization for Use of Military Force (AUMF) that is more precise about our efforts to defeat ISIS and that does not involve large-scale combat deployment of American troops" (Democratic National Committee 2016). This is a direct response to Republicans complaints about the level of flexibility the president should be provided in using military intervention to confront ISIS in countries such as Iraq, Libya, and Syria. Generally, Democrats want an AUMF that prevents the executive branch from having authority to deploy regular combat groups abroad in the fight against ISIS. Republicans would like to see more expansive AUMF authority, including the ability to deploy ground troops (beyond Special Forces) if necessary. Notably, the platform does not mention the situation in Libya as a case where the United States has recently undertaken a second military intervention in order to combat ISIS (the first intervention was to aid rebels in toppling Qaddafi). From a political perspective, it makes sense to not mention Libya given President Obama's reflection that the earlier intervention was a mistake, as well as the fact that Democratic Party nominee Hillary Clinton has come under fire from Republicans for issues related to consular security in Libya in the wake of the 2012 attack in Benghazi.

Although Democrats in the general public support a strong military, they are less likely to believe that military superiority, in itself, is the key to U.S. foreign policy success. For example, a minority of Democrats (37 percent) believe that maintaining military superiority is a "very effective" way to achieve U.S. foreign policy goals, according to one 2015 survey (Chicago Council on Global Affairs 2015). When standards are relaxed to include people who believe that military superiority is at least a somewhat effective way to achieve the same goals, Republicans and Democrats are nearly indistinguishable from each other. In addition, public opinion surveys generally find that while maintaining U.S. military superiority is one of the most important policy goals for Republicans, it falls further down the list of Democratic priorities. For Democrats, securing access to clean water and combating world hunger are both more important priorities than military superiority (Chicago Council on Global Affairs 2015).

Though self-identified Democrats appear to favor military intervention less in the abstract than do Republicans, Democrats have been generally supportive of U.S. military interventions when engineered by the Obama administration. For example, when the United States intervened in Libya in 2011, Republican support quickly fell after an initial uptick, as did support among independents. Among self-identified Democrats, however, support climbed from 51 percent to 54 percent over a three-month period (Jones 2011). It is not uncommon to see partisans of all types support the actions of a president from the same party. Only in cases such as Vietnam and Iraq, where wars lasted long periods of time and casualties mounted, have we seen bipartisan disapproval of an intervention. Democrats also strongly oppose the use of ground troops in Syria, a sentiment echoed by President Obama. Sixty-three percent of Democrats oppose ground troops as part of the U.S. intervention in Syria, which is now focused in combating ISIS and lending support to anti-ISIS and anti-Assad forces (Pew Research Center 2015). It is worth noting that Democrats in the general public did not support the decision by President Obama to employ airstrikes in Syria. At the outset of the airstrikes in 2013, only 29 percent of Democrats supported the move (Doherty 2013).

Like Republicans, Democrats in Congress have displayed mixed reactions to military interventions during the Obama administration. Democrats supported the president when he asked Congress for a new AUMF to fight ISIS, which would have required military intervention in several countries. Representative Marcia Fudge of Ohio referred to her Republican colleagues as "cowards" when Republicans decided not to take up the AUMF in the House of Representatives (Fuller 2015). Congressional Democrats were willing to support limited intervention, including airstrikes against ISIS positions. However, they refused to sanction the use of conventional ground troops as part of the strategy. For his part, President Obama argued that the AUMF passed by Congress after the 9/11 terrorist attacks provided sufficient authority for him to launch attacks against ISIS. However, he was willing to pursue a more limiting AUMF. In the face of Republican opposition to the more limited AUMF, some senior congressional Democrats signaled in early 2016 that they might be willing to accept language that would allow the use of ground troops to fight ISIS in the event that Congress voted to provide specific authorization in advance of their deployment. Republicans are unlikely to accept language that significantly limits the flexibility of the president. In this context, an AUMF that allows for intervention in another country for the sake of defeating ISIS is likely a matter for negotiations between Congress and the next president.

Democratic support for the 2011 intervention in Libya was mixed. Most of the House and Senate Democratic Party leadership, including figures like House minority leader Nancy Pelosi and Senate majority (at the time) whip Dick Durbin, supported the intervention as a means to end humanitarian abuses and help the rebels remove Qaddafi from power. Other rank and file members, especially more liberal Democrats, were more skeptical. Representatives Barbara Lee, Mike Honda, and Lynn Woolsey of California, joined by Arizona representative Raul Grijalva, issued a statement in which they argued that "the United States must immediately shift to end the bombing in Libya" (Grijalva, Lee, Honda, and Woolsey 2011). They argued that the Obama administration was rushing to war in Libya, which could lead to a prolonged military engagement of the type that occurred in Afghanistan and Iraq.

With regard to executive-level politics, former secretary of state and 2016 Democratic presidential nominee Hillary Clinton is widely viewed as a foreign policy hawk, implying that she is more likely than most Democrats to support military intervention as a tool of U.S. foreign policy. Clinton voted for the AUMF for Iraq before the 2003 invasion. For her part, Clinton claims that the authorization was designed to provide the Bush administration with the leverage needed to open Iraq to weapons inspections. Clinton was also one of the primary architects of the decision to intervene in Libya to topple the Qaddafi regime. As secretary of state, Clinton was also part of the team that made the decision not to declare the 2009 coup in Honduras, which replaced a democratically elected leader, as a coup for U.S. legal purposes. Although this was not an example of direct military intervention by the United States, it was used during the primary campaign by Senator Bernie Sanders as an example of Clinton's tolerance for military intervention in general. Clinton has argued that the removal of the Honduran president was legal and that it was only the aftermath that created the image of military intervention. Clinton also argued that calling the coup a coup would have required the suspension of aid under U.S. law, which would have hurt the Honduran people.

Further Reading

Cheney, Kyle. "Trump Shifts Position on Libya." Politico. Last modified June 5, 2016. http://www.politico.com/story/2016/06/libya-donald-trump-qadhafi-223911.

Chicago Council on Global Affairs. "America Divided: Political Partisanship and US Foreign Policy." Last modified September 15, 2015. https://www.thechicagocouncil.org/publication/america-divided-political-partisanship-and-us-foreign-policy.

Democratic National Committee. "2016 Democratic Party Platform." Last modified July 21, 2016. https://www.demconvention.com/wp-content/uploads/2016/07/Democratic-Party-Platform-7.21.16-no-lines.pdf.

Doherty, Carroll. "Public Opinion Runs against Syrian Airstrikes." Pew Research Center. Last modified September 3, 2013. http://file:///C:/Users/trubenzer.USCUPSTATE/Downloads/9-3-13%20Syria%20Release.pdf.

Dugan, Andrew. "U.S. Support for Action in Syria Is Low vs. Past Conflicts." Gallup.com. Last modified September 6, 2013. http://www.gallup.com/poll/164282/support-syria-action-lower-past-conflicts.aspx.

Fuller, Matt. "Why Won't Congress Declare War on ISIS?" The Huffington Post. Last modified December 15, 2015. http://www.huffingtonpost.com/entry/congress-isis-war_us_566f47cae4b0fccee16f938b.

Grijalva, Raúl M., Barbara Lee, Mike Honda, and Lynn Woolsey. "Representatives Grijalva, Lee, Honda, Woolsey Issue Joint Statement on the Situation in Libya." Congressman Raul Grijalva. Last modified March 22, 2011. https://grijalva.house.gov/common/popup/popup.cfm?action=item.print&itemID=890.

Jones, Jeffrey M. "Americans Shift to More Negative View of Libya Military Action." Gallup.com. Last modified June 24, 2011. http://www.gallup.com/poll/148196/americans-shift-negative-view-libya-military-action.aspx.

NPR. "What a Downed Black Hawk in Somalia Taught America." NPR.org. Last modified November 5, 2013. http://www.npr.org/2013/10/05/229561805/what-a-downed-black-hawk-in-somalia-taught-america.

Paul, Rand. "PAUL: Obama's Unconstitutional Libyan War." Washington Times. Last modified June 15, 2011. http://www.washingtontimes.com/news/2011/jun/15/obamas-unconstitutional-libyan-war.

Pew Research Center. "Growing Support for Campaign against ISIS—and Possible Use of U.S. Ground Troops." Pew Research Center for the People and the Press. Last modified February 24, 2015. http://www.people-press.org/2015/02/24/growing-support -for-campaign-against-isis-and-possible-use-of-u-s-ground-troops/.

Republican National Committee. "Republican Platform 2016." Last modified 2016. https:// prod-static-ngop-pbl.s3.amazonaws.com/media/documents/DRAFT_12_FINAL[1] -ben_1468872234.pdf.

U.S. Department of State. "The National Security Strategy of the United States of America." Last modified 2002. http://www.state.gov/documents/organization/63562.pdf.

Narcotics and Drug Policy

At a Glance

The integration of antidrug policy into broader U.S. foreign policy dates back to at least 1909, when the United States pushed colonial powers such as Great Britain to limit exports of opium to China. However, what is often known today as the "war on drugs" dates to 1971, when Richard Nixon declared: "America's public enemy number one in the United States is drug abuse. In order to fight and defeat this enemy, it is necessary to wage a new, all-out offensive" (Nixon 1971). Since Nixon issued that declaration, the United States has spent billions of dollars to combat drug production and drug trafficking operations outside of the United States (as well as billions more on drug interdiction efforts inside the United States). Historically, most foreign policy components of the war on drugs have been nonpartisan in implementation, even if Democrats are less likely than Republicans to use the term "war on drugs." Most current partisan differences on drugs exist with regard to domestic policies, such as how to treat state-level marijuana legislation when it conflicts with federal drug laws. However, partisan differences are more pronounced on drug policy beyond America's borders, especially when it comes to the integration of anti–drug trafficking and production efforts into other parts of U.S. foreign policy, such as immigration.

This essay will focus mostly on the direct foreign policy of the war on drugs, examining domestic issues only when they have a clear foreign policy context. As a result, the current entry does not focus on partisan differences related to cannabis legalization or decriminalization, for example, because cannabis interdiction at the border would likely still be a federal policy even in an environment of 100 percent domestic legalization. The supply and demand issues related to legalization are considered currently too indirect for inclusion, especially in an environment where most of these processes occur at the state level.

According to many Republicans . . .

- Narcotics interdiction as part of foreign policy is hindered by a permeable border with Mexico, resulting in drug trafficking by illegal immigrants;
- The United States must expand existing cooperation with Mexico as part of the Mérida Initiative;

- The United States should continue to provide security and military assistance to the governments of other Latin American countries that produce illicit narcotics; and
- The war on drugs as part of U.S. foreign policy has become less salient over time.

According to many Democrats . . .

- The term "war on drugs" is becoming more counterproductive as it takes focus away from demand-based treatment strategies in the United States;
- The United States should continue cooperation with Mexico as part of the Mérida Initiative; however, Mexico must not use security concerns as a pretext for the violation of civil liberties;
- While the border with Mexico should be made as secure as possible, diverting too many resources to this area decreases neither illegal immigration nor drug trafficking, given other potential points of entry into the United States;
- Further research is necessary to determine whether cannabis (also known as marijuana) should continue to occupy the same position as cocaine, heroin, and other narcotics in the war on drugs; and
- The war on drugs as part of U.S. foreign policy has become less salient over time.

Overview

Current U.S. foreign policy related to illicit drugs is multifaceted as a result of the number of concurrent challenges related to the issue. Domestically, the United States must deal with the demand issue, determining what combination of punishment, treatment, and/or legalization is appropriate for drug users and distributors (dealers). As a matter of foreign policy, the United States takes steps to slow or stop the cultivation of a variety of narcotics in foreign countries. In addition, as a matter of both foreign and domestic policy, the United States must combat drug transit (more commonly referred to as drug trafficking outside of the context of U.S. foreign relations law) in order to interrupt supplies of illicit drugs entering the United States.

Each year, under the provisions of the Foreign Relations Authorization Act, the president is required to name major drug producing and drug-transit countries, as well as maintain a separate list of countries that have failed to live up to their obligations under international law related to narcotics production and trafficking. There are 21 countries on the most current list (White House, "Presidential Determination" 2015). All but Afghanistan, India, and Burma are in Latin America. Of those countries, Bolivia, Burma, and Venezuela have been determined to be out of compliance with their international obligations. Under the terms of the law, the president is able to exempt states on the noncompliance list from direct punishment (via the withholding of aid) if the president views such aid as vital to U.S. interests. Burma and Venezuela are currently exempt from the consequences of the law under this provision.

At the bilateral level, the United States has operated under the National Drug Control Strategy, a policy document created by the executive bureaucracy. The strategy is updated periodically, but the last significant rewrite occurred in 2010. The strategy focuses on bilateral cooperation to prevent the cultivation and transit of illicit drugs. The United States provides financial, technical, logistical, and military assistance to counternarcotics programs, mostly in Latin America and Asia (U.S. Department of State 2016). For example, the United States provides military assistance and legal assistance to Colombia to help it combat drug production and prosecute drug-related crime. The United States also provides demand-side assistance to a variety of developing countries to help treat drug addiction at home as a step toward discouraging domestic production.

Under the Mérida Initiative, the United States provides assistance to Mexico to combat organized crime related to narcotics, to support human rights and the rule of law (in order to avoid the war on drugs being used as a pretext for violations in those areas), to increase cross-border cooperation in order to prevent drug transit, and to increase the capacity of civil society in Mexico to combat drug production, transport, and use at the local level. The Mérida Initiative has received bipartisan support under both the George W. Bush and the Obama administrations. The United States also provides assistance to Central American states through the Central American Regional Security Initiative. Central American countries are often transit points between South American countries like Colombia and final transit points such as Mexico.

In some countries, most significantly in Afghanistan, the United States has shifted away from the strategy of crop destruction, which tends to hurt local communities as a result of lost revenue, and toward alternative crop subsidization and development. While illicit drugs are almost always more lucrative than legal alternatives as a cash crop, it is the case that most of the benefits do not accrue to local farmers. The United States hopes that this strategy, coupled with efforts to fight drug-based organized crime and other forms of corruption, will bear more fruit than the traditional strategy of burning/spraying crops of illicit drugs. The United States continues to support eradication strategies in countries like Colombia, but coca plant cultivation has increased in spite of aggressive crop destruction techniques such as aerial spraying (U.S. Department of State 2016). Environmental activists, both in Colombia and the United States are concerned that aerial eradication, which by necessity uses chemical defoliants to kill plants, is harmful to the environment, including natural flora and the water supply.

At the international level, several treaties define the global antinarcotics regime. The oldest of current global treaties is the 1961 Single Convention on Narcotic

Drugs. The convention divides drugs into "schedules" based on their perceived risk and requires countries to adopt domestic measures to prevent the production, trafficking, and supply of these drugs. The convention is currently noteworthy for its inclusion of cannabis as a Schedule I drug (a distinction reserved for the most dangerous or addictive drugs). Current efforts to "reschedule" cannabis under U.S. domestic law may have to take the status of the drug under international law into account. The 1971 Convention on Psychotropic Substances attempts to introduce many of the same provisions for drugs that alter brain function at the chemical level. The most historically famous of these drugs is lysergic acid diethylamide (commonly known as LSD). The 1988 Convention against Illicit Traffic in Narcotic Drugs and Psychotropic Substances requires member states to prevent the transit of the drugs listed in the first two conventions through their territory. The United States is a party to all three conventions, which are widely ratified.

In spite of the wide variety of bilateral and multilateral policies supported by the United States, the war on drugs has been a largely losing, or at least not a winning, proposition. Even as coca production decreases in some states, such as Colombia, the production of other drugs, including opiates and cannabis, has increased in Central Asia and Mexico. The 2015 World Drug Report, for example, stated that opiate production has been increasing for several years and that the market in the United States for opiates is "resurgent" (United Nations Office on Drugs and Crime 2015). Mexico has had to shift resources away from combating production at it seeks to increase stability in areas where rival drug cartels (which have replaced the famous Colombian Cartels of the 1980s and 1990s) have engaged in warfare against each other and the local population. The various escapes and recaptures of Mexican drug lord and leader of the Sinaola Cartel, Joaquin "El Chapo" Guzman, have garnered a great deal of media attention. However, they have not solved the overall problem of market resiliency. There continues to be significant demand for various sorts of drugs in the United States, creating major financial incentives for suppliers to meet that demand.

Most of the criticism of existing foreign policy related to narcotic drugs comes from intergovernmental (international) organizations and nongovernmental organizations (NGOs). These groups tend to argue that the war on drugs has not decreased drug production or transit in developing countries. The nonpartisan Council on Foreign Relations (CFR), for example, has argued that U.S.–Mexico cooperation has failed to decrease narcotics production in Mexico, has resulted in increased human rights abuses in Mexico on the part of the government, and has led to more generalized political violence (Lee 2014). The CFR argues that drug decriminalization, coupled with taking a public health approach to drug addiction will ultimately lower demand, which will, in turn, lower the supply of drugs to the United States. The United Nations has also argued that the U.S.-supported drug war in Mexico has resulted in needless death and other human rights violations.

Republicans on Narcotics Policy

The 2016 Republican Party platform mentions drug policy in the context of foreign policy four times (there are several other mentions of domestic drug policy). The first Republican argument is that current U.S. immigration policy, which the platform characterizes as "executive amnesties," makes it much more difficult to stem the flow of illegal drugs into the United States. Republicans assert that building a wall along the entirety of the southern border would both decrease illegal immigration and decrease the amount of drugs smuggled into the United States. The other mentions of drug policy as part of foreign policy related to providing assistance to countries like Mexico as they struggle with drug production and trafficking and associated corruption and violent crime. Over 15,000 drug-related murders, for example, occur in Mexico each year (Castillo 2016). Finally, the Republican Party continues to use the phrase "war on drugs" in a foreign policy context. To Republicans, efforts to cut drug production and trafficking abroad, place the United States in a state of war in the same sense that the threat of terrorism places the United States in a state of war.

Although polling data on domestic aspects of the war on drugs is very common, very little public opinion data exists related to the foreign policy components of drug interdiction. The "America's Place in the World" Survey conducted by the Pew Research Center contains some useful data; however, they did not ask a drug policy question in their most recent survey in 2015. In 2013, the most recent year where a drug policy question was posed, 57 percent of the overall population believed that combating international drug trafficking should be a top foreign policy priority (Dimock, Doherty, and Horowitz 2013). In the survey, Republicans and Democrats exhibited almost identical levels of support for this priority (59 percent of Republicans; 60 percent of Democrats).

Within Congress, Republicans and Democrats have largely agreed on the foreign policy aspects of the war on drugs. With regard to the Mérida Initiative, for example, Congress has continually funded the program at levels very close to those requested in the budget submitted by Presidents Bush and Obama. Congress has also been generally supportive of increased funding for Coast Guard patrols as well over $500 million in funding received by the Geographic Combatant Commanders (GCC) in their efforts to provide military support to drug producing and transit countries. The GCC consists of each of the geographic areas of command maintained by the U.S. military. USNORTHCOM, for example, covers North America. It should be noted that it is difficult to trace individual positions/votes on funding questions related to foreign policy aspects of the war on drugs because the domestic and international funding packages of the Office of National Drug Control Policy (ONDCP) are approved together as part of the appropriations process. Republicans were less likely to vote for the 2016 appropriations bill than were Democrats, in part due to concerns about excess spending. However, there is no indication that their "no" votes were related to funding of antinarcotics programs in Latin America, Asia, or Africa.

Republicans in Congress, though they have not moved to withdraw funding, have been more critical of U.S. efforts to stamp out the illicit drug trade in Afghanistan than they have been of similar efforts in Latin America. Representative Thomas Massie of Kentucky, for example, has argued that the billions of dollars spent attempting to curtail the production opium in Afghanistan have been wasted (Massie 2016). John F. Sopko, the Special Inspector General for Afghanistan Reconstruction, who can be seen in the Massie 2016 video cited above, asserted as early as 2014 that poppy interdiction efforts in Afghanistan, which cost over $7 billion, had failed to prevent a tripling of poppy cultivation in Afghanistan (Special Inspector General for Afghanistan Reconstruction 2014). To this point, however, both Republicans and Democrats in Congress appear willing to continue funding antiopium efforts in Afghanistan, following the Department of State's argument that poppy cultivation has decreased in areas under effective government control.

The 2016 Republican presidential candidate, businessman Donald J. Trump, did not take a definitive position on the foreign policy aspects of the drug war—with one notable exception. Namely, Trump frequently alleged a direct relationship between drug interdiction and border security on the campaign trail. Trump called for the construction of a wall along the entire southern border with Mexico, in part based on the belief that this will prevent drug traffickers and cartels from penetrating the lucrative U.S. drug market. Trump also argued that a more robust immigration policy would help prevent undocumented immigrants from becoming drug dealers in the United States. Finally, Trump argued that drugs from Mexico are "pouring into the country" and "poisoning our youth," and he asserted that: "the largest suppliers of heroin, cocaine, and other illicit drugs are Mexican cartels that arrange to have Mexican immigrants trying to cross the borders and smuggle in the drugs. The border patrol knows this" (Neate and Tuckman 2015). In response to significant criticism from Republicans and Democrats on his statements concerning the relationship between immigration from Mexico, drugs, and crime, Trump argued that his statements had been taken out of context, and were designed only to apply to illegal immigrants, many of whom, Trump argues, are using the porous border to transport drugs to the United States.

Democrats on Narcotics Policy

The 2016 Democratic Party platform only mentions foreign policy considerations related to illegal narcotics once. The platform highlights the desire of Democrats to assist Latin American countries in combating drug, transnational crime, and corruption, but it does not employ "war on drugs" rhetoric. Democrats eschew the term "war on drugs," arguing that the war has resulted in increased criminal sentencing for nonviolent offenders, especially people of color, without reducing drug abuse or drug production and trafficking (Democratic National Committee 2016).

Once again, however, these differences between the parties in their preferred terminology has not been matched by significant differences in preferred policies.

The Obama administration has, in some ways, increased its level of sensitivity to the human rights implications of the international drug war. For example, in 2015 the United States cut $5 million in Mérida Initiative aid to Mexico in response to human rights concerns. It is worth noting that, while this decision was initiated by a Democratic president, it was not criticized by Republicans.

The Obama administration has also "expressed concern," though it has not cut any anti-drug-related aid, to the Philippines as a result of similar concerns. In July 2016, President Rodrigo Duterte became president of the Philippines. Duterte declared a renewed war on narcotics and launched coordinated police, military, and paramilitary attacks against alleged drug traffickers. During July and August of 2016, approximately 1,800 drug-related killings have occurred (Lema 2016). The United States, as well as the United Nations, are concerned in part by the fact that some of the killings appear to have been extrajudicial executions (executions without trial). NGOs like Human Rights Watch have argued that the United States needs to withdraw antinarcotics aid from the Philippines until the human rights situation improves. The Obama administration has yet to make a decision in this regard.

Current Obama administration policy regarding narcotics is embodied in the 2015 National Drug Control Strategy, which in turn is broadly based on the original strategy document introduced in 2010. Chapters five and six of the strategy deal with foreign policy issues, including drug trafficking and production. The foreign policy section of the Strategy contains a large number of action items related to intelligence sharing, border security, disruption of financial networks, disruption of organized crime, and security cooperation. For the most part, these action items reflect continuity with previous versions of the Strategy and reflect a relatively broad, bipartisan consensus on the nature of drug control as a component of U.S. foreign policy. Domestically, the increased focus on treatment, including treatment for opioid addiction, has been a matter of some partisan debate. The foreign policy components, however, are not, for the most part, contentious.

For the most part, Democrats in Congress have supported the foreign drug control policy of the Obama administration. Democrats in Congress are more likely to favor decriminalization and legalization as a demand-reduction strategy; however, criticism of Obama for allegedly moving too slowly on domestic policy has not spilled over into the foreign policy realm. Democrats also tend to support immigration reform, including a path to citizenship for undocumented immigrants in the United States (especially those who came to the United States as children). In this context, Democrats have supported the decision by the Obama administration to focus on intelligence sharing and police/military cooperation with Mexico at the border, rather than completing a physical wall. Overall, however, the vast majority of criticism of Obama administration foreign policy as it relates to illicit drugs comes not from with the Democratic or Republican Parties, but from various components of civil society such as the Council on Foreign Relations. Civil society refers to voluntary organizations and other groups that undertake collective action to further their vision of the public good.

For the most part, 2016 Democratic Party presidential nominee and former secretary of state Hillary Clinton represents continuity with the Obama administration on foreign drug control policy. Although Clinton did not negotiate the original Mérida Initiative, she did support it as secretary of state. Clinton was also broadly supportive of the effort to stem the tide of drug trafficking and production in Central America, Africa, and Central Asia. At the domestic level as well, Clinton represents continuity with the Obama administration. Clinton is not an advocate of full decriminalization or legalization of cannabis, for example. Clinton has indicated the desire to move further toward a treatment model, rather than a punishment model, of dealing with drug addiction. However, individuals and groups within civil society who believe that the foreign policy portion of the war on drugs can only be won by focusing on demand in the United States will not, based on policy statements, find an ally in Trump or Clinton.

Further Reading

Castillo, Mariano. "Drugs, Money and Violence: The Toll in Mexico." CNN. Last modified February 15, 2016. http://www.cnn.com/2016/02/15/world/mexico-drug-graphics/.

Democratic National Committee. "2016 Democratic Party Platform." Last modified July 21, 2016. https://www.demconvention.com/wp-content/uploads/2016/07/Democratic-Party-Platform-7.21.16-no-lines.pdf.

Dimock, Michael, Caroll Doherty, and Juliana M. Horowitz. "America's Place in the World 2013." Pew Research Center: U.S. Politics & Policy. Last modified December 3, 2013. http://www.people-press.org/files/legacy-pdf/12-3-2013%20APW%20VI.pdf.

Lee, Brianna. "Mexico's Drug War." Council on Foreign Relations. Last modified March 5, 2014. http://www.cfr.org/mexico/mexicos-drug-war/p13689.

Lema, Karen. "Philippines Drug War Deaths Climb to 1,800; U.S. 'Deeply Concerned.'" Reuters. Last modified August 23, 2016. http://www.reuters.com/article/us-philippines-duterte-un-killings-idUSKCN10X0IS.

Massie, Thomas. "Rep. Massie Investigates Infrastructure Projects Afghanistan 3/16/16." Congressman Thomas Massie. March 16, 2016. Accessed September 19, 2016. https://massie.house.gov/newsroom/videos/rep-massie-investigates-infrastructure-projects-afghanistan-31616.

Neate, Rupert, and Jo Tuckman. "Donald Trump: Mexican Migrants Bring 'Tremendous Infectious Disease' to US." The Guardian. Last modified July 6, 2015. https://www.theguardian.com/us-news/2015/jul/06/donald-trump-mexican-immigrants-tremendous-infectious-disease.

Nixon, Richard M. "Richard Nixon: Remarks about an Intensified Program for Drug Abuse Prevention and Control." American Presidency Project. Last modified June 17, 1971. http://www.presidency.ucsb.edu/ws/?pid=3047.

Special Inspector General for Afghanistan Reconstruction. "Poppy Cultivation in Afghanistan: After a Decade of Reconstruction and Over $7 Billion in Counternarcotics Efforts, Poppy Cultivation Levels Are at an All-Time High." Accessed October 14, 2014. https://www.sigar.mil/pdf/Special%20Projects/SIGAR-15-10-SP.pdf.

U.S. Department of State. "2016 INCSR: U.S. Government Assistance." Last modified 2016. http://www.state.gov/j/inl/rls/nrcrpt/2016/vol1/253218.htm.

White House. "Drug Control Funding Priorities in the FY 2016 President's Budget." Last modified 2015. https://www.whitehouse.gov/sites/default/files/ondcp/press-releases/ondcp_fy16_budget_fact_sheet.pdf.

White House. "Presidential Determination—Major Drug Transit or Major Illicit Drug Producing Countries for Fiscal Year 2016." Whitehouse.gov. Last modified September 4, 2015. https://www.whitehouse.gov/the-press-office/2015/09/14/presidential-determination-major-drug-transit-or-major-illicit-drug.

World Drug Report 2015. United Nations Office on Drugs and Crime, 2015. Accessed September 18, 2016. https://www.unodc.org/documents/wdr2015/World_Drug_Report_2015.pdf.

Nation-Building

At a Glance

After failed nation-building efforts in Afghanistan and Iraq in the wake of U.S. military intervention in both countries, little appetite exists within either major U.S. political party to engage in further nation-building in any other country. However, while nation-building in the comprehensive sense of rebuilding and reshaping infrastructure and political, economic, and social institutions to benefit nations wracked by war, disaster, or impoverishment may have fallen out of fashion, the United States continues to implement nation-building policies in a more limited manner in a variety of different countries around the world. In this context, nation-building has become partially decoupled from direct military intervention, but not entirely from U.S. foreign policy. Partisan differences and similarities related to nation-building relate to these more limited elements of the nation-building process.

According to many Democrats . . .

- Promoting democracy, civil society, and human rights are vital to nation-building, especially in the developing world;
- U.S. military intervention should be limited and not done with nation-building in mind;
- The United States should be willing to provide more foreign aid to developing countries to assist in the process of nation-building; and
- The United States should promote increased funding for the United Nations and its specialized agencies for projects that facilitate nation-building.

According to many Republicans . . .

- Promoting democracy and human rights is vital to nation-building, especially in the developing world;
- U.S. military intervention should not be done with nation-building in mind;
- Providing foreign aid generally won't facilitate nation-building; and
- The United Nations is too inefficient and internally corrupt to facilitate in the process of nation-building.

———————

Overview

It is worth noting at the outset that there is some controversy over what the term nation-building means. In the traditional language of international relations, a nation is a social construct; a group of people who often live in a similar space and share a common history, language, race, ethnicity, or some combination of these cultural attributes. A state, by contrast, is a physical entity including a more or less permanent population living within the recognized borders of a sovereign country. In this context, nation-building was traditionally viewed as the process of convincing the people living within a given state that they are either part of one nation or that they ought to at least interact in ways that promote unity over discord. By contrast, state-building was viewed as being concerned with constructing political, social, and economic institutions required for the state to function. In the recent language of U.S. foreign policy, nation-building is more closely associated with what has traditionally been called state-building or institution-building. In this entry, nation-building is treated as the process of rebuilding (or building for the first time) the political, social, and economic institutions necessary for the state to function with sufficient capacity to remain viable. One of the main goals of recent nation-building efforts for the United States has been the construction of democratic, or at least more pluralist, political institutions in the target country. It is recognized, of course, that some elements of modern state-building, such as developing political institutions that promote unity, fit well under both conceptions of nation-building.

Though not all uses of force are accompanied by nation-building, the history of U.S. military intervention goes hand in hand with its history of nation-building, especially after the Civil War. As Carson and Helis (2003) point out, U.S. interventions in Cuba and the Philippines were taken directly with nation-building in mind. The goals of the United States, not all of them realized, were to create or restore constitutional government (not necessarily democracy) that is supportive of U.S. regional policies, make sure that basic government services existed, and provide economic aid that would catalyze economic growth in both countries. In cases such as West Germany and Japan after World War II, the United States imposed military governments for a time, using these governments as a means to create or re-create the rule of law, and form the basis for a developmental state. The history of these exercises is beyond the scope of this entry; however, both Germany and Japan are advanced as examples of successful nation-building activities. One might argue, of course, that nation-building in more economically advanced states is far less of a challenge than the task might be within the developing world.

In terms of the overall success of nation-building, the results have been decidedly mixed. Social scientists often examine whether the target country ultimately becomes a democracy as one measure of the success of nation-building. One study conducted on U.S. nation-building efforts since 1900 found that only in one-fourth of all cases did the target state become a democracy within 10 years (Pei and Kasper 2003). If one extrapolates forward and adds the results of Afghanistan (which were not determined at the time of this study) and the results from Iraq (which was not part of the study) the number of total successful transitions to democracy remains the same. Overall, the United States appears to have a better record in nation-building when working with a country with a history of strong governmental capacity (democratic or not).

It is impossible, of course, to talk about nation-building in the modern era without discussions of the unsuccessful efforts in Iraq and Afghanistan. Neither country, as of 2016, has become a democracy in even the most expansive sense of the term. In addition, the capacity of the governments of both countries to provide basic public goods such as security and minimal social services has decreased over time (though small pockets of success have emerged at times). Although there are many reasons for the failure of these nation-building efforts, a few are worth highlighting. First, nation-building works better when the occupied country either initially accepts or comes to accept the occupation. The assumption that the United States would be "greeted as liberators" in Iraq and Afghanistan turned out not to be remotely true. Instead, especially in Iraq, new resistance to the occupation arose that made circumstances worse, both for the occupied country and for the United States. Second, as previously stated, economically advanced states are easier to "build" than are less-developed areas. In this sense, Iraq should have had better prospects for nation-building than Afghanistan. However, the imposition of crippling economic sanctions on Iraq after its invasion of Kuwait in 1990 resulted in severe economic contraction and the further concentration of resources in the hands of a small number of political elites. Third, it appears that relative homogeneity in the country targeted for nation-building is positively correlated with the success of nation-building. In this regard, Iraq, and even more so Afghanistan, presented much more heterogeneity (ethnically and religiously) than did more successful cases from decades past, like Panama, West Germany, and Japan.

It appears, at first blush, that the United States has lost the desire to engage in classic nation-building, which normally requires military intervention in advance of attempting to reshape the institutions of government, in the wake of its failures in Afghanistan and Iraq. It is certainly the case that there is less talk of "boots on the ground" in response to crises in places like Syria and Libya. However, the United States still engages in several less direct nation-building activities. In Afghanistan and Iraq, for example, the United States remains engaged in the attempt to build more responsive political institutions, as well as efforts to train police and military forces to provide protection for the populace. The United States is also involved in the conflict in Syria, launching airstrikes and deploying Special Forces in an attempt to deny gains to the Islamic State of Iraq and greater Syria (ISIS) and to encourage the removal of the al-Assad regime from power. The negotiations occurring around these topics are exercises in nation-building, given the fact that Syrian political institutions have no capacity in significant portions of the country. U.S. Special Forces are currently involved in cooperative operations with Libyan troops attempting to combat ISIS. Although one goal of the operation is to deal a blow to ISIS (a U.S. foreign policy goal that at times is only weakly related to nation-building), the United States is also attempting to create political and economic operating space for the nascent unity government in the country. As a result, the politics of nation-building will continue to be politically salient in any discussion of U.S. foreign policy for the foreseeable future, even if the era of classic nation-building via military intervention has faded somewhat.

Democrats on Nation-Building

The 2016 Democratic Party platform does not specifically mention nation-building, nor do any of its recent predecessors. The platform does, however, mention several aspects of nation-building, either directly or indirectly. For example, the document contains several references to promoting and protecting democracy in Africa, Asia, Latin America, and the Middle East. The platform also mentions support for civil society (voluntary associations designed to advance the public good). The development of a healthy civil society is considered a key component of nation-building because it promotes civic activity beyond basic participation in elections. Interestingly, an early draft of the platform did mention the "conclusion of long-term nation-building," specifically in the context of Iraq and Afghanistan (Democratic National Convention 2016). Although it is unclear why the language was removed from the platform, this version seeks to more clearly signal a departure from previous nation-building policies during the George W. Bush and Obama administrations.

With regard to countries such as Cuba and Venezuela, which are not likely to emerge as democracies anytime in the near future, Democrats mention the need to promote "the popular will" and "the rule of law," both elements of nation-building. The platform also mentions assistance to Afghanistan to build its security apparatus and to advance human rights, especially those of women and girls. Both of these elements could be considered part of the broader concept of institution-building that is necessary for nation-building to occur. In no case, however, does the platform suggest the classic nation-building formula where these goals are accomplished in the context of direct military intervention.

Very little public opinion data exists directly on the question of nation-building. A 2016 survey by Rasmussen Reports found, however, that only 28 percent of Americans favored continued nation-building efforts of the type undertaken in Iraq and Afghanistan (Rasmussen Reports 2016). The poll, however, defined nation-building in a fairly narrow context, focusing on the promotion of democracy as opposed to the more general building of political, economic, and social institutions. Among self-identified Democrats solicited in the poll, 45 percent opposed further nation-building efforts whereas 36 percent supported the concept (the remainder are unsure or did not answer). Majorities of Democrats also saw the wars in Iraq (68 percent) and Afghanistan (53 percent) as mistakes, according to a 2015 poll by Gallup (Dugan 2015). It is interesting to note that the percentage of Democrats who believe the wars in Afghanistan and Iraq were a mistake declined somewhat between 2014 and 2015 according to separate poll administrations by Gallup. One must use caution before attributing any of the Gallup results directly to the perceived success (or lack thereof) of nation-building. The larger than expected number of U.S. casualties, the length of both conflicts, and the cost of the intervention and its aftermath could all be factors that might drive public opinion in a negative direction.

It is difficult to track partisan currents on nation-building to specific congressional votes, mainly because resolutions supporting military intervention don't specifically mention nation-building. As a result, the goal of the intervention might dovetail with the goals of nation-building without being *about* nation-building. With this reservation in mind, it is worth noting that a majority of Democrats in Congress voted in favor of the U.S. intervention in Afghanistan. A majority of Democrats in the House of Representatives voted in favor of the Authorization for the Use of Military Force (AUMF) Resolution in Iraq, while a majority of Senate Democrats supported the measure (see entries on Afghanistan and Iraq). A majority of Democrats supported the proposed 2011 AUMF for Libya (which ultimately failed). However, the Libya AUMF limited the potential for nation-building by specifying that the United States would not deploy regular combat troops to the country. Once again, separating the nation-building elements of the missions, especially in Afghanistan and Iraq, from their antiterrorism goals is quite difficult. Republican president George W. Bush believed that promoting democracy in Iraq and Afghanistan would make both countries less likely to support terrorists. However, it is difficult to determine whether the more short-term goal of combating terrorism was more important to elected officials than promoting the long-term goal of consolidated democratic governance.

President Obama ran for office on a platform of ending the wars in Iraq and Afghanistan and shifting the focus back to domestic politics. Contextually, this was an argument for focusing more resources on priorities such as physical infrastructure and economic growth. In reality, however, Obama has been forced by circumstances on the ground, to partially reintensify U.S. military action in Iraq and delay the final drawdown of troops in Afghanistan. In both cases, the administration has come to the conclusion that neither country can provide for the security of its population without continued U.S. assistance. As a result, the process of institution-building continues, though with less military support behind the process. For her part, 2016 Democratic Party presidential nominee Hillary Clinton has pledged to take the advice of the military with respect to Iraq and Afghanistan. Clinton's campaign Web site does not contain a direct position on nation-building, nor has she specifically mentioned the concept on the campaign trail. If Clinton were to pursue the same priorities as president that she pursued as secretary of state, one would expect significant continuity with the Obama policy of not embracing nation-building through intervention and occupation, but using diplomatic, and sometimes limited military, power, to promote democratization and other forms of institution-building.

Republicans on Nation-Building

The 2016 Republican Party platform mentions nation-building once, specifically in the context of its overall undesirability. The platform implies that the military has been forced to spend too much time nation-building and not enough time performing its core function of national defense. Like Democrats, however, Republicans mention numerous foreign policy goals associated at least indirectly with nation-building, such as promoting human rights, democracy, and the rule of law. The Republican platform is more insistent than its Democratic Party counterpart on promoting democracy, arguing that the United States has been too willing to negotiate with dictators in places like Cuba, Iran, and Venezuela. The platform is also critical of what it views as an unwillingness on the part of the Obama administration to take the advice of military commanders and leave a larger residual force in Afghanistan. The GOP platform also argues that the United States, in cooperation with international partners, should set aside a safe haven for persecuted ethnic and religious communities in northern Iraq (Republican National Committee 2016). None of these platform elements is a direct call for nation-building via military intervention. However, many observers assert that they constitute indirect nation-building activities.

Within the general public, Republicans show even less appetite for nation-building than do Democrats. One 2016 poll found that 62 percent of Republicans believe that the United States should not be involved in the type of nation-building (military intervention and the imposition of democracy) engaged in by the administration of George H. W. Bush (Rasmussen Reports 2016). According to the same survey, 59 percent of Republicans believe that nation-building has been a failure, while less than 10 percent view nation-building policies as successful. In spite of a negative view of nation-building, far fewer Republicans (31 percent) than Democrats (68 percent) are likely to say that the war in Iraq was a mistake, according to another poll conducted in 2015 by Gallup (Dugan 2015). The same general trends exist with respect to Afghanistan, where only 27 percent of Republicans believe that U.S. action in Afghanistan was a mistake.

To the extent that the results of two different surveys can be used to demonstrate an overall point, it appears that Republicans may well continue to support the wars in Afghanistan and Iraq for reasons other than the goal of building the types of institutions that would make both countries more resistant to extremism and more likely to take a positive view toward U.S. interests. Especially in the case of Afghanistan, the goal of punishing the state most directly associated with Osama bin Laden (at least at the time of the terrorist attacks of September 11, 2001) may well be viewed as worthy by Republicans even if the nation-building can be said to have objectively failed. There is also likely a partisan effect at play, where Republicans are more likely to defend the actions of a Republican president.

There are some areas of common ground between Republicans and Democrats on the issue of nation-building. For example, the United States spends approximately $200 million annually on democracy promotion in Iraq through the

Human Rights and Democracy Fund (U.S. Department of State 2016). Obviously, the United States is no longer engaged in traditional intervention-based nation-building in Iraq. Republicans also supported the plan by President Obama to leave "residual forces" in Afghanistan until at least 2017. Senate majority leader Mitch McConnell gave the president credit for "finally getting to the right place" on the issue (Youngman 2015). These forces would provide security services and training that are vital to providing breathing space for a functioning state. It is worth nothing that, in this case, Republicans were critical of Obama's decision to set the residual force strength at a lower number (approximately 5,000 in 2017) as opposed to keeping current U.S. force levels (around 10,000) constant. The newly elected president will have to decide in early 2017 whether or not to modify or halt the troop drawdown.

Conversely, Republicans have been quite critical of most nation-building activities supported by Democrats. For example, Democrats, whether seated in Congress or the Oval Office, have tended to support the role of the United Nations in nation-building. The UN has provided security, electoral, and development assistance in a variety of countries since its founding at the end of World War II. In Iraq, for example, the United Nations worked alongside occupation forces to broker agreements that allowed an interim government to form and to set the groundwork for elections at multiple levels of government. Republicans are generally more critical of the UN role in nation-building, arguing that the UN is wasteful, too prone to corruption, and likely to turn a blind eye to severe human rights violations. For its part, the UN has countered that the United States, which is often behind in its assessed payments to the organization, has handicapped the ability of the organization to carry out its mandate.

In August 2016, Republican presidential nominee Donald J. Trump delivered a foreign policy address in the key swing state of Ohio in which he issued an explicit call for an end to U.S. nation-building, and a return to foreign policy "realism." During the speech, Trump argued:

> If I become President, the era of nation-building will be ended. Our new approach, which must be shared by both parties in America, by our allies overseas, and by our friends in the Middle East, must be to halt the spread of Radical Islam.
>
> All actions should be oriented around this goal, and any country which shares this goal will be our ally. We cannot always choose our friends, but we can never fail to recognize our enemies.
>
> As President, I will call for an international conference focused on this goal. We will work side-by-side with our friends in the Middle East, including our greatest ally, Israel. We will partner with King Abdullah of Jordan, and President Sisi of Egypt, and all others who recognize this ideology of death that must be extinguished. (*PBS NewsHour* 2016)

Trump's stance reflected a belief among some foreign policy experts that international relations are inherently conflictual and based on the application of power. In this environment, countries like the United States are best served if they only use their power in pursuit of key national interests such as state security against external threats. Trump has argued, that terrorist groups are a direct territorial threat to the United States. Therefore, intervention should be based not on nation-building, but on destroying terrorist organizations in regions such as the Middle East.

Further Reading

Carson, Jayne A., and James Helis. "Nation-Building, the American Way." Federation of American Scientists. Last modified April 7, 2003. https://fas.org/man/eprint/carson.pdf.

Democratic National Convention. "2016 Democratic Party Platform." Last modified July 21, 2016. https://www.demconvention.com/wp-content/uploads/2016/07/Democratic-Party-Platform-7.21.16-no-lines.pdf.

Democratic National Convention. "2016 Democratic Party Platform Draft." Last modified 2016. https://www.demconvention.com/wp-content/uploads/2016/07/2016-DEMOCRATIC-PARTY-PLATFORM-DRAFT-7.1.16.pdf.

Dugan, Andrew. "Fewer in U.S. View Iraq, Afghanistan Wars as Mistakes." Gallup.com. Last modified June 12, 2015. http://www.gallup.com/poll/183575/fewer-view-iraq-afghanistan-wars-mistakes.aspx.

PBS NewsHour. "Trump to Declare End to Nation Building, if Elected President." Last modified August 15, 2016. http://www.pbs.org/newshour/rundown/trump-declare-end-nation-building-elected-president/.

Pei, Minxin, and Sara Kasper. "Lessons from the Past: The American Record on Nation Building." Carnegie Endowment for International Peace. Last modified May 2003. http://carnegieendowment.org/files/Policybrief24.pdf.

Rasmussen Reports. "Most Voters Say No to Further U.S. Nation-Building Efforts." Last modified August 22, 2016. http://www.rasmussenreports.com/public_content/politics/general_politics/august_2016/most_voters_say_no_to_further_u_s_nation_building_efforts.

Republican National Committee. "Republican Platform 2016." Last modified 2016. https://prod-static-ngop-pbl.s3.amazonaws.com/media/documents/DRAFT_12_FINAL[1]-ben_1468872234.pdf.

U.S. Department of State. "DRL Programs." Last modified 2016. http://www.state.gov/j/drl/p/index.htm.

Youngman, Sam. "After Trip to Afghanistan, McConnell Credits Obama for Leaving Forces | Lexington Herald-Leader." *Lexington Herald-Leader.* Last modified October 18, 2015. http://www.kentucky.com/news/politics-government/article42644964.html.

NATO

At a Glance

The North Atlantic Treaty Organization (NATO), designed primarily as a bulwark against Soviet aggression during the Cold War era, has suffered somewhat of an identity crisis since the early 1990s when the Soviet Union dissolved. Determined to use NATO as a vehicle for European integration, political elites ultimately agreed to expand NATO into Eastern Europe. After the terrorist attacks of September 11, 2001, NATO invoked its mutual defense provisions for the first time and became heavily involved in the conflict in Afghanistan and, more indirectly, in Iraq. Democrats and Republicans in the United States are unified in their overall support for NATO. However, there are important partisan differences in issues related to NATOs ongoing mission, as well as the United States' financial stake in the organization.

According to many Republicans, U.S. NATO policy . . .

- Should focus on making sure that other member states pay their fair share by increasing, where necessary, their military budgets to match NATO guidelines;
- Should recognize that NATO is a benefit to U.S. security and foreign policy goals;
- Should not attempt to placate Russia on issues related to NATO expansion;
- Should be willing to use NATO as a vehicle for arming Ukraine in the face of Russian aggression in Eastern Ukraine; and
- Should recognize that while NATO is important to the United States, it is even more important to other NATO members.

According to many Democrats, U.S. NATO policy . . .

- Should recognize that NATO is a benefit to U.S. security and foreign policy goals;
- Should include targeted sanctions on Russian officials who violate human rights and/or were involved with Crimean annexation;

- Should be based on cooperation in the area of nuclear arms control;
- Should be based on cooperation when interests partially or fully coincide, such as Iran; and
- Should oppose Russian efforts to support the Assad regime in Syria.

Overview

At its founding in 1949, NATO was designed to fulfill three purposes. The first and most famous purpose was to deter further Soviet expansion in the wake of the Soviet Union's famous construction of an "iron curtain" of influence in Eastern Europe. The second purpose of the organization was to prevent the rise of militant nationalism in Europe by providing for mutual defense against any aggressor. Finally, NATO was designed to foster European integration by providing for the common defense and military coordination of member states.

In 1948, a Soviet-sponsored coup in Czechoslovakia converted the formerly democratic country into a "Soviet satellite state"—a nation ruled by a government heavily influenced by the ideology and priorities of Moscow. Coupled with the Soviet Blockade of Berlin, Soviet actions in Czechoslovakia served as a catalyst for the formation of NATO. As the Cold War dragged on, NATO membership gradually expanded to include other Western European countries such as Greece, Spain, and West Germany, as well as Turkey, a nation situated mostly in Asia that came to be seen, in part because of its geographic location, as a key ally against Communist expansion.

In spite of NATO's status as a military alliance, the organization did not conduct military operations during the Cold War. A combination of factors, including nuclear and conventional military deterrence, largely prevented direct conflict between the eastern and western blocs. After the Cold War ended, though, NATO became involved in several military operations around the world. NATO became directly involved in military action in the former Yugoslavia, enforcing a no-fly zone to help stem the genocide in Bosnia and in Kosovo, to protect Kosovar Albanians. After the terrorist attacks of 9/11, NATO invoked Article 5 of the North Atlantic Treaty (sometimes called the Washington Treaty), which states:

> The Parties agree that an armed attack against one or more of them in Europe or North America shall be considered an attack against them all and consequently they agree that, if such an armed attack occurs, each of them, in exercise of the right of individual or collective self-defense recognized by Article 51 of the Charter of the United Nations, will assist the Party or Parties so attacked by taking forthwith, individually and in concert with the other Parties, such action as it deems necessary, including the use of armed force, to restore and maintain the security of the North Atlantic area. (NATO Official Text 2016)

NATO took command of the International Security Assistance Force (ISAF) in 2003 and was directly active in Afghanistan until 2014. NATO is currently acting in an advisory/training role in Afghanistan. One of NATO's most recent military actions was in Libya, where the organization enforced a no-fly zone and arms embargo during the Libyan Civil War and acted in concert with other forces, including the United States, France, and Great Britain, to engineer the ouster of Muammar Qaddafi. Although the NATO portion of the operation was largely successful in the beginning, the death of Qaddafi has not resulted in enduring peace in Libya. Instead, Libya is in the grip of renewed civil war and numerous acts of terrorism by groups such as the Islamic State of Iraq and Greater Syria (ISIS).

NATO also expanded its membership in the post–Cold War era, eventually reaching its current membership of 28 countries. In the United States, the expansion of NATO required the advice and consent of the Senate. Ultimately, the Senate voted 80 to 19 in favor of expansion, with 35 out of 45 Democrats and 45 out of 54 Republicans offering their support (Schmitt 1998). The first expansion in 1999 resulted in the ascension to membership of Poland, Hungary, and the Czech Republic and paved the way for future expansion. The fact that the vote passed with a bipartisan supermajority obscures the fact that there was concern among both Democrats and Republicans about expansion. Democrats worried that NATO expansion would anger Russia and possibly move the country away from democracy. Republicans worried that expanding NATO might dilute the effectiveness of the organization. A "dear colleagues" letter from Democratic senator Joe Biden and Republican senator Jesse Helms helped to sway the Senate by arguing that NATO expansion was a vital and bipartisan part of the U.S. national interest (Asmus 2004).

Currently, the future of NATO has reemerged as an important issue on the U.S. foreign policy landscape. NATO has a defense spending target of 2 percent of gross domestic product (GDP) in order to make sure that all members are capable of contributing to the common defense. As of 2016, only five countries—the United States, Greece, the United Kingdom, Estonia, and Poland (in order of expenditures)—were meeting the target (NATO Defense Expenditures 2016). Although both parties have recently called on NATO members to meet the expenditure goal, the issue has become more partisan as Republicans, particularly Republican nominee Donald Trump, have tied paying a "fair share" to the invocation of Article 5. Specifically, Trump has argued that countries not meeting their NATO expenditure targets should not be able to invoke the mutual defense portion of the treaty. Support for Brexit (the withdrawal of Great Britain from the European Union) has also led a portion of the conservative movement to question U.S. involvement in NATO. In spite of these issues, overall support for NATO and its mission remains strong in the United States.

Republicans on NATO

The 2016 Republican Party platform refers to NATO five times. The first instance highlights the Republican position, which is the subject of some intraparty debate, that the United States should coordinate with NATO to provide assistance to the armed forces of Ukraine in its fight against Russian-backed separatists in the east. The platform plank calling for "assistance" as opposed to "military assistance," or "lethal assistance," represents a departure from previous Republican thought on the issue. Republicans, and to a degree Democrats, had previously supported providing arms to Ukraine in the fight against separatists. The platform also demands that NATO member states permit more military spending in order to meet the 2 percent goal mentioned above. The 2012 version of the GOP platform does not make such a demand, owing largely to the difference between supporters of former Massachusetts governor Mitt Romney on the platform committee in 2012 and supporters of businessman Donald Trump dominating the committee in 2016. The 2016 platform does, however, support the deployment of NATO troops to Poland in response to Russian actions in Eastern Europe. There is no mention of the concurrent troop deployment to the Baltic republics of Estonia, Latvia, and Lithuania.

Public opinion polls relating to U.S. attitudes toward NATO are not as plentiful as polling on issues such as ISIS, conflicts in the Middle East, or free trade. However, it is possible to discern a clear partisan divide within the public on issues related to NATO. For example, 69 percent of self-identified Republicans in the general public believe that the United States should use military force to defend a NATO ally against Russia, according to the 2015 Pew Global attitudes survey (Simmons, Stokes, and Poushter 2015). Republicans are also more likely than Democrats to support Ukrainian membership in NATO, though a majority from both parties favor membership. Polls indicate that a majority of Republicans also support NATO action to arm Ukraine in its efforts to thwart eastern separatists supported by Russia. Finally, Republicans are somewhat more likely than Democrats to believe that NATO is more important to other member states than it is to the United States. Forty-three percent of Republicans believe that NATO is more important to other allies than it is to the United States, while 37 percent believe that the United States benefits as much as other members (Pew Research Center 2016).

Both during and after the Cold War, Republicans in Congress have tended to be very supportive of NATO expansion, and less likely than Democrats to worry about such measures angering Russia. It was Republicans in Congress who first pushed for the expansion of NATO to include Montenegro, a move that has angered Russia and sparked a debate within NATO member states. In spite of the fact that Montenegro does not share a border with Russia, Russia believes that any expansion is part of an effort to further isolate Russia diplomatically and, especially, militarily. Montenegro currently has "invitee" status, meaning it is allowed to participate in NATO as a nonvoting observer until its accession to the Washington Treaty is approved by all member states. Republican representative Mike Turner of Ohio, who is also the current president of the NATO Parliamentary Assembly, argued that "as an increasingly aggressive Russia looks to expand its influence in the Balkans, it's imperative that NATO reaffirm its support for the region" (Barnes 2015).

Traditional support for NATO, in general, has created some intraparty tension between Republican elites in Congress and elsewhere and Republican presidential nominee Donald Trump. Trump has argued that NATO needs to be modernized or potentially abandoned if it cannot successfully make the transition to fighting terrorism. In this context, he has criticized NATO for being obsolete as a result of "not having the right countries in it for terrorism" (Haines 2016). Trump also has asserted that the United States, which spends a greater percentage of its GDP on defense than any other NATO ally, is contributing too much to the organization relative to the potential benefits of membership. In this context, Trump has suggested that U.S. defense of NATO allies should be tied, at least in part, to those countries meeting their obligations to the United States, including spending their fair share. Specifically, Trump argued: "You can't forget the bills. They have an obligation to make payments. Many NATO nations are not making payments, are not making what they're supposed to make. That's a big thing. You can't say forget that" (*New York Times* 2016). Asked about mutual defense assistance to new NATO members, Trump appeared to tie mutual defense to NATO defense spending obligations, saying: "Have they fulfilled their obligations to us? If they fulfill their obligations to us, the answer is yes." Asked about countries that did not fulfill their obligations, Trump stated, "Well, I'm not saying if not. I'm saying, right now there are many countries that have not fulfilled their obligations to us." Although the critique of NATO as an obsolete organization is not new, the idea of conditioning U.S. assistance on meeting NATO spending goals has not been previously suggested by a major party presidential candidate or a party platform. Trump's position has resonated to a degree with his supporters in the public. Republicans who favored Trump during the 2016 primary were almost twice as likely to think that membership in NATO is bad for the United States than are other Republicans (Pew Research Center 2016). However, Trump supporters still believe that membership in NATO is good for the United States by a two-to-one margin.

Republicans in Congress and elsewhere were quick to distance themselves from Trump's position on NATO. Senate majority leader Mitch McConnell, for example, acted quickly to reassure NATO allies that the United States would be there to defend them in the event of an external attack. Republicans also responded positively to Toomas Hendrik Ives, the president of Estonia, when he stated that Estonia would act to defend all NATO allies. Ives's comments and the Republican response is relevant because Estonia is a country that, like the United States, exceeds its NATO defense spending target, in large part because of its proximity to Russia. Striking a more conciliatory tone, Senate Foreign Relations Committee chairman Bob Corker argued that the United States is required by the Treaty of Washington to defend its allies, and that Trump's comments were a "rookie mistake" born from trying to convince other countries to pay their fair share (Fox News 2016). At the same time, many Republicans agree with Trump's view that NATO allies are underspending on defense. Senator Corker has referred to underspending NATO allies as "laggards" while Republican senator John Barrasso of Wyoming insisted after a recent meeting with the secretary general of NATO that spending by most allies was not where it needed to be (Hudson 2016).

Democrats on NATO

For their part, Democrats have seized upon the division between Trump and other Republicans, both in their 2016 platform and in statements issued by lawmakers. The 2016 Democratic Party platform mentions NATO nine times, an increase from the 2012 platform. The platform takes the Republican nominee to task, stating that "Donald Trump would overturn more than 50 years of American foreign policy by abandoning NATO partners—44 countries who help us fight terrorism every day—and embracing Russian President Vladimir Putin instead" (Democratic National Committee 2016). Although it is not rare at all for a platform to attempt to criticize the opposing party's candidate directly, it is rare, at least in recent years, for the Democratic Party platform to call out Republicans for being weak on a national security issue. It is worth noting that the Democratic Party platform, like its Republican counterpart, expresses the view that several NATO allies are not paying their fair share. The Democratic variant of the platform, however, stops short of a demand that NATO allies meet the 2 percent goal. Finally, the platform supports countries such as Georgia and Ukraine, which seek a closer relationship with NATO. The platform, however, does not explicitly call for the expansion of NATO to include Georgia and Ukraine.

Democrats in the general public appear to be somewhat less supportive of potential military action under NATO treaty obligations than their Republican counterparts. For example, only 47 percent of Democrats, compared to the above-mentioned 69 percent of Republicans would favor the use of military force to defend a NATO ally against Russia (Simmons, Stokes, and Poushter 2015). In the same survey, 12 percent fewer Democrats (59 percent total) favored Ukrainian membership in NATO than did Republicans. The fact that a majority of Democrats favor Ukrainian membership is interesting in that Ukrainian membership in NATO could trigger an invocation of Article 5, and hence the requirement for mutual defense, if NATO determined that Russia was responsible for the secession of Crimea. In the presence of strong to overwhelming evidence of direct Russian intervention in Crimea, as well as elsewhere in eastern Ukraine, it would be difficult for NATO members not to support the invocation of Article 5 if Ukraine requested it. In this sense, the response to the first question, concerning military force, could be viewed as being at odds with the second, concerning Ukrainian membership in NATO. Unlike Republicans, where a gap exists between supporters of Donald Trump and those of other candidates, a nearly identical percentage of Hillary Clinton and Bernie Sanders supporters (83 percent and 84 percent, respectively) agreed that NATO membership is good overall for the United States, according to a 2016 Pew poll (Pew Research Center 2016).

According to the same survey, 15 percent fewer Democrats than Republicans believe that NATO is more important to U.S. allies than it is to the United States. Overall, the data suggests that Democrats are more sold on the utility of NATO in general, but less sold on the idea of NATO intervention. This fits the overall pattern of Democrats being more skeptical of military intervention, for almost any reason, than Republicans.

Democrats in Congress and the executive branch have been generally supportive of NATO during the Obama administration. NATO's direct role in Afghanistan and Libya, and its indirect training role in Iraq, has served to decrease the cost and, to a degree, to increase the legitimacy of U.S. intervention. In response to Donald Trump's criticism of NATO, President Obama referred to the organization as a "linchpin" of U.S. and European security (Fabian 2016). Obama has also supported NATO in its decision to stage military exercises in Ukraine in June 2016. The move is seen as a deterrent to further Russian aggression in the region. Rhode Island senator Jack Reed, argued, referring to Trump, that "when it comes to foreign policy he is ill-informed, inexperienced and completely unprepared in every dimension. Much of what he says is contrary to our national interests" (Gould 2016).

For her part, 2016 Democratic presidential nominee Hillary Clinton and her running mate Senator Tim Kaine have primarily used their defense of NATO as a way to draw contrasts with the Trump campaign. The Clinton campaign issued a statement challenging Trump that read, in part: "Ronald Reagan would be ashamed. Harry Truman would be ashamed. Republicans, Democrats, and Independents who help build NATO into the most successful military alliance in history would all come to the same conclusion: Donald Trump is temperamentally unfit and fundamentally ill-prepared to be our commander in chief" (Toosi 2016). In his 2016 convention speech, Kaine accused Trump of being willing to abandon U.S. allies in NATO.

On the issue of defense spending as it relates to NATO funding, there is more room for agreement between Republicans and Democrats in Congress. During his unsuccessful run for the Democratic presidential nomination in 2016, Bernie Sanders argued that other NATO members should be spending more on defense in order to potentially lessen the level of defense spending necessary in the United States. Although congressional Republicans do not favor reducing defense spending, they also believe that most NATO allies need to spend more. During a closed-door meeting with NATO secretary general Jens Stoltenberg, both Democrats and Republicans voiced concerns with "free-riders" among the allies. At present, it appears that the main difference between the parties on the spending issue pertains to their willingness to raise those concerns in public. Republicans, especially those who support Donald Trump, have become more publicly vocal in their critique of those states that have not met the spending goal. Democrats in Congress have, with limited exceptions, remained publicly silent on the issue.

Further Reading

Asmus, Ronald D. *Opening NATO's Door: How the Alliance Remade Itself for a New Era.* New York: Columbia University Press, 2004.

Barnes, Julian E. "Will Montenegro Become NATO's 29th Member?" *Wall Street Journal.* Last modified September 24, 2015. http://blogs.wsj.com/brussels/2015/09/24/will-montenegro-become-natos-29th-member/.

Democratic National Committee. "2016 Democratic Party Platform." Last modified July 21, 2016. https://www.demconvention.com/wp-content/uploads/2016/07/Democratic-Party-Platform-7.21.16-no-lines.pdf.

Fabian, Jordan. "Obama Defends NATO after Trump Criticisms." *The Hill.* Last modified April 4, 2016. http://thehill.com/policy/national-security/275088-obama-defends-nato-after-trump-criticisms.

Fox News. "The Latest: Leading Republicans Reject Trump's NATO Comments." Last modified July 21, 2016. http://www.foxnews.com/us/2016/07/21/latest-leading-republicans-reject-trump-nato-comments.html.

Gould, Joe. "Dems Press GOP on Trump's Fitness to Be President Amid NATO Backlash." Defense News. Last modified July 22, 2016. http://www.defensenews.com/story/defense/2016/07/22/after-nato-comment-dems-press-gop-trumps-fitness-president/87441388/.

Haines, Tim. "Trump: NATO Is Obsolete and Expensive, 'Doesn't Have the Right Countries in It for Terrorism.'" *RealClearPolitics.* Last modified March 27, 2016. http://www.realclearpolitics.com/video/2016/03/27/trump_europe_is_not_safe_lots_of_the_free_world_has_become_weak.html.

Hudson, John. "Senators Slam NATO 'Free-Riders' in Closed-Door Meeting with Secretary General." *Foreign Policy.* Last modified April 6, 2016. http://foreignpolicy.com/2016/04/06/senators-slam-nato-free-riders-in-closed-door-meeting-with-secretary-general/.

NATO. "Defense Expenditures of NATO Countries (2009–2016)." Last modified July 4, 2016. http://www.nato.int/nato_static_fl2014/assets/pdf/pdf_2016_07/20160704_160704-pr2016-116.pdf.

NATO. "Official Text: The North Atlantic Treaty, 04-Apr.-1949." Last modified 2016. http://www.nato.int/cps/en/natolive/official_texts_17120.htm.

New York Times. "Transcript: Donald Trump on NATO, Turkey's Coup Attempt and the World." *New York Times*—Breaking News, World News & Multimedia. Last modified July 21, 2016. http://www.nytimes.com/2016/07/22/us/politics/donald-trump-foreign-policy-interview.html.

Pew Research Center. "Public Uncertain, Divided over America's Place in the World.". Last modified May 5, 2016. http://www.people-press.org/2016/05/05/public-uncertain-divided-over-americas-place-in-the-world/.

Schmitt, Eric. "Senate Approves Expansion of NATO by Vote of 80 to 19—Clinton Pleased by Decision." *New York Times.* Last modified May 1, 1998. http://www.nytimes.com/1998/05/01/world/senate-approves-expansion-nato-vote-80-19-clinton-pleased-decision.html?pagewanted=all.

Simmons, Katie, Bruce Stokes, and Jacob Poushter. "1. NATO Public Opinion: Wary of Russia, Leery of Action on Ukraine." Pew Research Center's Global Attitudes Project. Last modified June 10, 2015. http://www.pewglobal.org/2015/06/10/1-nato-public-opinion-wary-of-russia-leery-of-action-on-ukraine/#major-partisan-split-in-the-u-s.

Toosi, Nahal. "Republicans Rip Trump over NATO Plan." Politico. Last modified July 21, 2016. http://www.politico.com/story/2016/07/trump-nato-new-york-times-225942.

North Korea

At a Glance

The secretive government of the People's Democratic Republic of Korea (PDRK) or North Korea, reinserted itself into the American political consciousness in 2016 with its test of an enhanced nuclear weapon (though probably not a hydrogen bomb as announced) and through its tests of an improved ballistic missile. Overall, Democrats and Republicans are united on U.S. foreign policy toward North Korea. They agree that the government's repression of its people is deplorable and that its dictatorial and unpredictable leadership poses a threat to global stability and peace. That said, there remain areas of partisan disagreement over policy specifics.

According to many Democrats, North Korea should be . . .

- Subject to sanctions and other forms of economic and diplomatic isolation;
- Patiently negotiated with to reduce the danger of its nuclear and missile programs;
- Treated as a critical threat to the United States; and
- Recognized as a potential source of deadly weaponry for terrorist groups.

According to many Republicans, North Korea should be . . .

- Subject to policies that impose economic sanctions and project U.S. military strength;
- Recognized as a potential source of deadly weaponry for terrorist groups;
- Checked by increasing budgetary support for the U.S. military on the Korean Peninsula and throughout the wider region; and
- Better neutralized through the development of a missile defense system capable of intercepting North Korean long-range missiles.

Overview

In the closing days of World War II, the Soviet Union invaded the Korean Peninsula, which was occupied by Japan at the time. The United States invaded in the south. Ultimately, the Soviet Union accepted Japanese surrender in the north and the United States did the same in the south. In response to a proposal by the United States, a temporary division of the territory at the 38th parallel was established. Originally, the division was designed to end with elections in the north and the south supervised by the United Nations. The Soviet Union blocked elections in the north and supported Kim Il Sung. The United States supported Syngman Rhee to take the reins of leadership in the peninsula's southern region. North Korea subsequently became the PDRK and South Korea became the Republic of Korea (ROK). The Soviet-supported North Korean military then invaded South Korea on June 25, 1950.

Prior to the commencement of hostilities, the United States had been withdrawing troops from South Korea. As late as January 1950, in fact, the United States had indicated that it would not protect Rhee's government in the event of a Communist attack. For a variety of reasons, however, including concerns about the spread of Communism and the political reality that the fall of another state to Communism would strengthen the Republican claim of Democratic Party weakness in responding to Soviet aggression, the administration of Democratic president Harry S. Truman decided that it needed to intervene on the Korean Peninsula. The United States brought the invasion before the United Nations Security Council (UNSC). Ultimately, the UNSC passed Resolution 84, which declared the invasion to be a breach of the peace. Under Chapter VII of the UN Charter, a breach of the peace allows the UN to take military measures to stop the breach and restore peace. The United States subsequently joined with 15 other nations in contributing troops to stop North Korea's invasion and restore peace on the peninsula. Nearly two million Americans served in the Korean War, with over 50,000 total deaths.

At the beginning of the war, the partisan dimension that had shaped the original decision by the Truman White House to step in militarily largely disappeared. Congressional Republicans were generally in favor of the war, even though Truman had not taken the step of asking for a formal declaration (Fisher, Hendrickson, and Weissman 2008). However, Republicans became critical of Truman again after the Communist nation of China entered the Korean War on the side of North Korea in late 1950 after the United States crossed into North Korean territory and advanced toward the North Korea–China border. General Douglas MacArthur, who had assured Truman that China would not enter the war, urged Truman to respond with full force, including attacks on China by U.S. and ROK forces. Truman refused and ultimately relieved MacArthur of his command. Republicans embraced MacArthur's address to Congress, where the general argued that the only way to win the war was to use airstrikes north of the Yalu River in China (Public Broadcasting Service 2009). Republicans attacked Truman as someone willing to appease both North Korea and China, a charge that weakened Truman politically for the remainder of his presidency (Miller Center of Public Affairs n.d.). Ultimately, the Korean War ended in an armistice in 1953. The DPRK continued to rule north of the 38th parallel, while the ROK ruled to the south. The United

States and the South Korean government then signed a mutual defense treaty, and approximately 28,000 U.S. troops remain in South Korea to this day.

During much of the remainder of the Cold War, the partisan gap relating to U.S. foreign policy toward North Korea was narrow. Both Democrat and Republican presidential administrations, for example, maintained and strengthened the comprehensive embargo against North Korea that had been instituted at the beginning of the war in 1950. In 1958 under Republican president Dwight Eisenhower, the United States secretly deployed tactical nuclear weapons to the peninsula. These nuclear weapons remained in place during the Kennedy through Carter administrations and were not removed until the end of the Cold War in 1991 (Wertz and Gannon 2015). North Korea initiated several provocations from its side of the Demilitarized Zone (DMZ)—an approximately 150-mile-long border between North and South Korea—during both Republican and Democratic presidencies. The line, at the 38th Parallel, is the ceasefire line from the war. Generally speaking, Republicans were more hawkish on North Korea, with the Nixon administration going as far as the consideration of a nuclear strike after the DPRK shot down a U.S. spy plane in 1969 (Shuster 2010). However, both Republicans and Democrats supported joint military exercises between the United States and the ROK. These exercises were designed to increase preparedness, but also to deter potential aggression by the North Korean military.

The end of the Cold War eventually led to the reemergence of the partisan divide over U.S. foreign policy toward North Korea. However, this did not happen immediately. In 1991, at the very end of the Cold War, George H. W. Bush announced the withdrawal of all tactical nuclear missiles from other countries. This included South Korea. Democrats were broadly supportive of the measure, which helped lead the DPRK and ROK to sign the South–North Joint Declaration on the Denuclearization of the Korean Peninsula. In 1992, North Korea concluded a nuclear safeguards agreement with the International Atomic Energy Agency (IAEA), a first step toward ensuring that the country was not diverting enriched uranium and plutonium from the energy sector to the production of nuclear weapons. The agreement began to break down almost immediately when the IAEA demanded special inspections in response to discrepancies in initial DPRK reports. The North Korean government refused.

In an effort to prevent North Korea from withdrawing from the Nuclear Nonproliferation Treaty (NPT), the United States dispatched former president Jimmy Carter to the DPRK for negotiations. Ultimately, the United States and North Korea signed an "Agreed Framework" whereby North Korea would freeze and ultimately eliminate its nuclear facilities in exchange for temporary supplies of fuel, sanctions relief, and the construction of light-water nuclear reactors, which are less susceptible to the diversion of plutonium, which can be used to build nuclear weapons (Arms Control Association 2016). Republicans were critical of the Agreed Framework, arguing that the Clinton administration had given away too much at the negotiating table without adequate safeguards that an agreement would be kept.

The 1996 Republican Party platform even referred to the Agreed Framework as an example of appeasement.

When Republican president George W. Bush took office in 2001, he was convinced that both the Clinton administration and South Korea had been naive about North Korea's intentions (Matray 2013). In 2002, Bush labeled North Korea as part of the "axis of evil" in his State of the Union Address. For its part, the North Korean government admitted—and then denied that it had admitted—to enriching uranium. The United States claimed that the enrichment violated the Agreed Framework, and suspended fuel shipments to the DPRK. North Korea ultimately responded by withdrawing from the NPT. It then restarted processing plutonium from spent nuclear fuel rods. Both uranium and plutonium are fissile materials, meaning they are capable of sustaining the nuclear reaction necessary to create a nuclear weapon. In 2006, when North Korea tested its first nuclear weapon, Democrats laid the blame squarely at the doorstep of the George W. Bush administration. First, they argued that the administration's diplomatic bungling had set in motion North Korea's decision to withdraw from the NPT. Second, Democrats argued that the Bush administration's focus on the war in Iraq (which had become very unpopular with the American public by 2006) had allowed the North Korean regime to develop a nuclear weapon (Sidoti 2006). Since that time, the partisan divisions between Republicans and Democrats on North Korea have remained wide.

In January 2016, for example, North Korea conducted a nuclear test, detonating what it claimed to be a hydrogen, or fusion, bomb. Such a device would represent a significant advancement for the North Korean nuclear program given the significantly greater explosive yield of fusion weapons. Although nonproliferation experts doubt whether the device was a fusion weapon, Democrats in Congress joined Republicans in universal condemnation of the test. In early February, Congress passed, with only two votes against, the North Korea Sanctions and Policy Enhancement Act of 2016. President Obama signed the bill into law within a week. The act imposes additional primary sanctions on the regime; including individuals accused of money laundering and human rights abuses (Demirijan 2016). All Democratic members of the House and Senate voted for the act, and only two Republicans in the House of Representatives voted against it. But while the two parties were fairly united in condemning the test, they hotly criticized one another, both for their past foreign policy stances toward North Korea and for their proposed responses to the test.

Democrats on North Korea

The 2012 Democratic Party platform mentioned North Korea eight times. As the platform pointed out, the United States joined the international community in levying harsh multilateral sanctions against North Korea as a result of its nuclear and ballistic missile tests (Democratic National Committee 2012). The United

States has imposed sanctions on North Korea for its missile development several times since the 1990s. In this sense, there is a great deal of continuity between Democrats and Republicans in the wake of the 2006 North Korean nuclear test. The platform also raises concerns about the potential for transfers of nuclear and ballistic missile technology between North Korea and nonstate actors, including terrorist groups. In 2006, North Korea provided a prototype nuclear reactor to the Assad regime in Syria. Israel eventually launched airstrikes against the facility that effectively destroyed it; however, the concern remains that the DPRK would consider the transfer of such technology to states seeking to develop nuclear weapons or terrorist groups interested in acquiring and using nuclear weapons or other weapons of mass destruction. Many Democrats have suggested that the key to isolating and applying pressure on the DPRK is cooperation with Russia and, especially, China, both of whom, for historical and contemporary reasons, have demonstrated at least some ability to influence the decision making of North Korea—which is sometimes called the "hermit kingdom" due to its isolation from the international system at large.

Overall, the Obama administration maintained a policy toward North Korea throughout Obama's second term that was largely in step with the 2012 party platform. On the one hand, the Obama administration has repeatedly expressed a willingness to negotiate with North Korean leaders in Pyongyang on issues related to its nuclear weapons program. However, Obama has always made it clear that any talks must begin with the condition that North Korea will abandon the program. To this point, the regime of Kim Jong-Un has been unwilling to meet this condition and has continued to test nuclear devices and ballistic missiles. As a result, the Obama administration has fallen back to a position of "strategic patience" in which it continues to apply pressure through cooperation as part of a so-called six-party process. The six-party talks, first initiated in 2003, are an effort by the United States, Russia, China, Japan, South Korea, and North Korea to negotiate a settlement of the nuclear issue. In 2009, the United States pushed for and gained passage of Security Council Resolution 1874, which permits member states to inspect North Korean ships suspected of carrying nuclear supplies. Relief from the sanctions imposed under Resolution 1874, as well as other UN resolutions, would be used as an incentive to promote North Korean nuclear disarmament.

Although the overall percentage is not as great as it is for Republicans, a majority of Democrats within the general public believe that North Korea is a serious threat to the United States (Pew Research Center 2013). A more significant partisan gap exists on the question of whether the DPRK is willing to follow through on the threats it often has made against the United States of a nuclear strike. A minority of Democrats (37 percent) believe that North Korea will follow through on its threats according to one 2013 poll, while a majority (58 percent) of Republicans believe the same (Pew Research Center 2013).

Most experts agree that, as of 2016, North Korea does not possess a ballistic missile capable of reaching the continental United States. Although North Korea has

United Nations Security Council Resolution 1874

The UNSC passed a variety of resolutions imposing sanctions on North Korea after the country announced its intention to conduct a nuclear test in 2006. North Korea was the first country to ever provide advanced public notice of its first nuclear test. Security Council Resolution 1874, passed under Chapter VII of the UN Charter, which provides enforcement capability in the event of a threat to the peace, breach of the peace, or act of aggression, stood apart from previous UN resolutions based on the intrusiveness of its enforcement provisions. The resolution contained the following key language designed to prevent North Korea from importing new nuclear or ballistic missile technology, as well as to provide a coercive incentive for North Korea to abandon its nuclear weapons program:

Calls upon all States to inspect, in accordance with their national authorities and legislation, and consistent with international law, all cargo to and from the DPRK, in their territory, including seaports and airports, if the State concerned has information that provides reasonable grounds to believe the cargo contains items the supply, sale, transfer, or export of which is prohibited by paragraph 8 (a), 8 (b), or 8 (c) of resolution 1718 or by paragraph 9 or 10 of this resolution, for the purpose of ensuring strict implementation of those provisions;

Calls upon all Member States to inspect vessels, with the consent of the flag State, on the high seas, if they have information that provides reasonable grounds to believe that the cargo of such vessels contains items the supply, sale, transfer, or export of which is prohibited by paragraph 8 (a), 8 (b), or 8 (c) of resolution 1718 (2006) or by paragraph 9 or 10 of this resolution, for the purpose of ensuring strict implementation of those provisions;

Calls upon all States to cooperate with inspections pursuant to paragraphs 11 and 12, and, if the flag State does not consent to inspection on the high seas, decides that the flag State shall direct the vessel to proceed to an appropriate and convenient port for the required inspection by the local authorities pursuant to paragraph 11.

Source:

Security Council Resolution 1874 (2009), S/RES/1874 (2009) available from http://www.un .org/ga/search/view_doc.asp?symbol=S/RES/1874%282009%29.

missiles under development that might be capable of striking Alaska, it is unclear whether such weapons could deliver a nuclear payload. Overall, both Democrats and Republicans place North Korea in their top 10 threats to the United States (Chicago Council on Global Affairs 2015).

During the 2016 Democratic presidential campaign season, both former secretary of state Hillary Clinton and Senator Bernie Sanders (Vt.) described North Korea as a significant threat to the United States. In a February 2016 debate, Sanders argued the North Korea, due to its isolation and nuclear weapons, posed a greater threat to the United States than Iran or Russia. Sanders also asserted that the People's Republic of China, as North Korea's main ally, should be pressured to play a more constructive role in bringing the DPRK back into the community of nations. In the same debate, Secretary Clinton agreed that North Korea and its unpredictable leadership remained a worrisome force on the international stage. As secretary of state, Hillary Clinton had advocated for a policy of strategic patience with North Korea. As a further part of this policy, Clinton has argued that no further incentives should be offered to bring North Korea back to the negotiating table (Hirsh 2016).

Republicans on North Korea

The Republican Party has been harshly critical of Democrats, and especially President Obama, for "leading from behind" on issues related to North Korea. For example, the GOP posits that the Obama administration decision not to pursue a so-called "missile shield" leaves the country vulnerable to attack from rogue states with developing ballistic missile systems such as Iran and North Korea. Republicans have also been united in insisting that North Korean nuclear disarmament be permanent in nature. This suggests a complete abandonment of the nuclear fuel cycle in North Korea, a call not made in the Democratic platform. The nuclear fuel cycle refers to the entire process of creating nuclear power, which involves mining or purchasing uranium and enriching the uranium to the point necessary to sustain a nuclear reaction. Once uranium has been enriched to the point where it can be used for nuclear power, further enrichment could make it possible to use the uranium in an explosive device. It is also possible to remove plutonium from nuclear fuel rods in a uranium reactor and use the plutonium to build a weapon.

Within the general public, Republicans tend to be more concerned than Democrats about the threat posed by North Korea. As mentioned above, a majority of both Democrats and Republicans view North Korea as a significant threat. However, one 2013 poll found a 12-point gap—64 percent Republican to 52 percent Democrat—in the number of people who consider North Korea to be a "very serious threat" (Pew Research Center 2013). According to the same poll, Republicans were also 21 percent more likely to believe that North Korea will follow through on its threats against the United States. To many Republicans, the frequent ballistic missile tests by North Korea, coupled with occasional nuclear weapons tests, represent a direct existential threat to the United States. For most Democrats, the testing represents a significant threat, but also an attempt by North Korea to increase its leverage at the negotiating table.

In addition to general agreement that North Korea is a threat to the United States, Republican and Democrats are also in agreement, at least in the most basic sense, about negotiations. Since 2008, a majority of both Republicans and Democrats have argued that the United States should be willing to engage North Korean leaders directly, should the conditions present themselves (Chicago Council on Global Affairs 2015).

During the 2016 Republican presidential primary, all of the major candidates for the GOP nomination made strong statements concerning North Korea. Senator Marco Rubio of Florida, for example, was critical of both the Bush and the Obama administrations for being unable to reverse North Korean gains in nuclear and ballistic missile technology. He also dismissed the doctrine of "strategic patience" espoused by the Obama administration and by former secretary of state and Democratic Party presidential nominee Hillary Clinton, arguing that it amounted to appeasement of the DPRK (Rubio 2016). Senator Ted Cruz (TX) argued during a debate in February 2016 that the North Korean nuclear program was the direct result of the Clinton administration relaxing sanctions against the country (*Washington Post* 2016). During the same debate, Donald Trump argued that the key to controlling North Korea was by putting increased pressure on China.

Congressional Republicans have been strongly critical of Obama administration policy toward North Korea. Generally, Republicans have used the occasion of North Korea nuclear tests to drive toward reinitiating the U.S. ballistic missile defense program, stalling cuts in the U.S. nuclear stockpile, and increasing the defense budget (Broder 2013). Congressional Republicans have also echoed the argument made by Republican presidential candidates that the Obama administration has appeased North Korea and that what is happening in North Korea will also happen in Iran (Iran will successfully build and test a nuclear weapon if the United States does not act more forcefully). In spite of this criticism, it is not clear that Republicans seek a U.S. policy toward North Korea that is significantly different from that sought by Democrats. Both parties have called for strengthened multilateral and unilateral sanctions. Both parties agreed in 2015 to raise the defense budget to near presequestration levels. Both parties also agreed to the North Korea Sanctions and Policy Enhancement Act of 2016. Any sanctions relief that North Korea received during the Clinton administration has vanished under a wave of new U.S. and UN sanctions. Neither party has called for the initiation of armed hostilities against North Korea in response to its nuclear and ballistic missile tests.

The main salient difference between the two parties, in terms of measurable policy outcomes, is that Republicans are somewhat less likely within the public, and significantly less likely among elected officials, to favor direct U.S. talks with North Korea. Instead, Republicans favor the continued imposition of economic sanctions until North Korea comes to the negotiating table with an offer to completely abandon its nuclear and ballistic missile programs.

Further Reading

Arms Control Association. "Chronology of U.S.–North Korean Nuclear and Missile Diplomacy." February 2016. https://www.armscontrol.org/factsheets/dprkchron.

Broder, Jonathan. "Republicans Blast Obama over North Korean Nuclear Test." Roll Call. Last modified February 12, 2013. http://www.rollcall.com/news/republicans_blast_obama_over_north_korean_nuclear_test-222345-1.html.

Bush, George W. "President Delivers State of the Union Address." Welcome to the White House. Last modified 2002. http://georgewbush-whitehouse.archives.gov/news/releases/2002/01/20020129-11.html.

Chicago Council on Global Affairs. "America Divided: Political Partisanship and US Foreign Policy." Last modified 2015. http://www.thechicagocouncil.org/sites/default/files/CCGA_PublicSurvey2015.pdf.

Demirjian, Karoun. "Congress Sends Obama North Korea Sanctions Bill" *Washington Post.* February 12, 2016. https://www.washingtonpost.com/news/powerpost/wp/2016/02/12/house-poised-to-give-final-go-ahead-to-north-korea-sanctions-bill/.

Democratic National Committee. "The 2012 Democratic Platform." Last modified 2012. https://www.democrats.org/party-platform.

Fisher, Louis, Ryan Hendrickson, and Stephen R. Weissman. "Congress at War." *Foreign Affairs the Magazine*, May/June 2008. https://www.foreignaffairs.com/articles/united-states/2008-05-03/congress-war.

Hirsh, Michael. "Hillary's North Korea Problem." Politico. Last modified January 6, 2016. http://www.politico.com/story/2016/01/hillarys-north-korea-fail-217424.

Matray, James I. "The Failure of the Bush Administration's North Korea Policy: A Critical Analysis." *International Journal of Korea Studies* 17, no. 1 (2013): 140–177.

Miller Center of Public Affairs. n.d. "Harry S. Truman: Foreign Affairs." University of Virginia. Accessed February 21, 2016. http://millercenter.org/president/biography/truman-foreign-affairs#contributor.

National Archives and Records Administration. "US Enters the Korean Conflict." Accessed February 21, 2016. https://www.archives.gov/education/lessons/korean-conflict/.

Pew Research Center. "Public Divided over North Korea's Intentions, Capability." Pew Research Center for the People and the Press. April 9, 2013. http://www.people-press.org/2013/04/09/public-divided-over-north-koreas-intentions-capability/.

Public Broadcasting Service. "American Experience: General MacArthur's Address to Congress." PBS: Public Broadcasting Service. Last modified 2009. http://www.pbs.org/wgbh/amex/macarthur/filmmore/reference/primary/macspeech05.html.

Republican National Committee. "2012 Republican Platform." Last modified 2012. https://prod-static-ngop-pbl.s3.amazonaws.com/docs/2012GOPPlatform.pdf.

Rubio, Marco. "Here Are Four Things Marco Would Do to Take on North Korea." Marco Rubio for President. Last modified 2016. https://.com/news/marco-rubio-north-korea-test-plan/.

Shuster, Mike. "Nixon Considered Nuclear Option against N. Korea." NPR.org. July 6, 2010. http://www.npr.org/templates/story/story.php?storyId=128337461.

Sidoti, Liz. "Democrats Assail Bush's N. Korea Policy." *Washington Post.* October 10, 2006. http://www.washingtonpost.com/wp-dyn/content/article/2006/10/10/AR2006101000182.html.

Snyder, Scott A. "U.S. Policy toward North Korea." Council on Foreign Relations. January 2013. http://www.cfr.org/north-korea/us-policy-toward-north-korea/p29962.

Washington Post. "Sanders–Clinton Debate Transcript: Annotating What They Say." February 4, 2016. https://www.washingtonpost.com/news/the-fix/wp/2016/02/04/sanders-clinton-debate-transcript-annotating-what-they-say/.

Wertz, Daniel, and Chelsea Gannon. "A History of U.S.—DPRK Relations." The National Committee on North Korea. November 2015. http://www.ncnk.org/resources/publications/US_DPRK_Relations.

Pakistan

At a Glance

U.S. foreign policy toward Pakistan in the post-9/11 era has largely been shaped by American efforts to combat international terrorism, specifically Al Qaeda. The Taliban, a political and terrorist organization that is active in both Afghanistan and Pakistan, has also been a focus of the United States. Pakistan's existence as a nuclear power and its tense, often conflict-ridden, relationship with India, have led the United States to promote internal capacity-building, through increased military and police strength and the provision of basic services in order to stabilize the central government. Overall, a strong, stable, and secular Pakistan is seen by both Republicans and Democrats as integral to U.S. efforts to combat international terrorism and bring stability to central Asia. Much of U.S. foreign policy toward Pakistan has been bipartisan, at least with respect to desired policy outcomes.

According to many Democrats, U.S. foreign policy toward Pakistan . . .

- Must be focused on domestic stabilization of Pakistan;
- Should pressure Pakistan to deny terrorists sanctuary;
- Should promote peaceful relations between Pakistan and India; and
- Should not withhold security assistance from Pakistan for jailing Shakil Afridi (the physician who aided the United States in tracking Osama bin Laden).

According to many Republicans, U.S. foreign policy toward Pakistan . . .

- Must focus on securing Pakistan's nuclear arsenal as well as stabilizing the country;
- Should pressure Pakistan to deny terrorists sanctuary with additional pressure on the government to avoid punishments for individuals who provide intelligence to the United States;

- Should promote peaceful relations between Pakistan and India; and
- Should withhold security assistance from Pakistan for jailing Shakil Afridi.

Overview

Relations between the United States and Pakistan have been both complex and shifting over time. During the beginning of the Cold War, the United States counted Pakistan as an ally. To Pakistan, warm relations with the United States provided international legitimacy as well as foreign humanitarian and military aid. In 1953, for example, the United States provided $75 million in emergency food aid to Pakistan (Haqqani 2013). To the United States, a positive relationship with Pakistan provided a check against Soviet expansion in South and Central Asia. In 1954, the two countries signed a mutual defense assistance agreement designed to curtail Soviet influence in the area. Also in the 1950s, the United States began to provide Pakistani scientists with nuclear reactor training under the Atoms for Peace Program (Weiner 1998).

Coupled with a Pakistani nuclear espionage program and with significant assistance from China, U.S. assistance helped pave the way for the emergence of Pakistan as a nuclear power. Pakistan officially declared itself a nuclear weapon state in 1998 after conducting a series of nuclear tests in response to similar tests by India, which first tested a nuclear weapon in 1974. During the 1980s, the United States worked from within Pakistan to provide military aid to the mujahideen, a loosely tied group of Afghan and foreign rebels devoted to fighting the Soviet occupation of Afghanistan.

Toward the end of the Cold War, which formally ended with the collapse of the Soviet Union in 1991, Pakistan lost some of its strategic importance to the United States, at least for a time. In 1985, Congress passed the Pressler Amendment, which would ban most foreign aid to Pakistan unless the president could certify that the country did not have nuclear weapons or was not in the process of developing such weapons. The Pressler Amendment was invoked for the first time in 1990 by President George H. W. Bush. It is probably not a coincidence that the Soviet Union had completed its withdrawal from Afghanistan in 1989. Soviet withdrawal made Afghanistan less strategically important to the United States, which created an opportunity to punish Pakistan for its nuclear weapons program without worrying about the need for Pakistani assistance in providing aid to Afghan rebels. The sanctions were never fully imposed in that Pakistan was still able to procure U.S. arms from commercial sources without U.S. interference. Congress did allow some foreign aid for humanitarian purposes to flow to Pakistan in the mid-1990s. In 1998, however, the United States imposed further sanctions on both India and Pakistan in response to the detonation of nuclear devices by both countries. These sanctions were modified to allow India and Pakistan to purchase food from the United States.

The terrorist attacks of September 11, 2001, against the United States, brought about a reassessment of Pakistan's strategic importance, however. In a short period of time, Pakistan went from a country under U.S. sanctions to the official designation as a major non-NATO ally. Under the Foreign Assistance Act, this designation allows for increased military and nonmilitary aid. Pakistan was equipped to help the United States rout the Taliban in part because Pakistan played a role in the development of the Taliban. In fact, Pakistan had been one of only three countries to recognize the Taliban government in Afghanistan after it assumed de facto control over that country in the mid-1990s (Riedel 2013). The Taliban is a radical Islamist group that seeks to control the government of Afghanistan in order to set up an Islamic state in the country. The Taliban also has territorial ambitions in Pakistan and is a significant source of instability in the country. During the war in Afghanistan, Pakistan received over $10 billion in U.S. aid and had its sanctions lifted by the United States. Pakistan arrested hundreds of members of the terrorist group Al Qaeda, as well as many wanted members of the Taliban.

One reason for the continued complexity of U.S.–Pakistan relations is that portions of the Pakistan security and intelligence services continued to support the Taliban even after 9/11. To Pakistan, the Taliban represents a partial buffer against Indian territorial ambitions in the region. Pakistan is also skeptical of long-term U.S. commitments in the region, which provides an incentive for Pakistan to maintain relations with the Taliban as a power-player in Afghani affairs. The United States is also not politically popular in Pakistan, which means that the government must always balance its interest in receiving aid from the United States with angering the domestic constituency during a time of relative instability.

Like their Democratic counterparts, Republicans have been eager to point out that Pakistan and the United States have a shared interest both in defeating the Taliban and in securing Pakistan's nuclear arsenal. Pakistan, like India, Israel, and North Korea, have developed nuclear weapons after eschewing membership in the Nuclear Non-Proliferation Treaty (NPT). The NPT allows for only five declared nuclear weapons states; China, France, Russia (formerly the Soviet Union), the United Kingdom, and the United States. Pakistan is estimated to possess 110–130 nuclear warheads, which the country maintains are vital as a deterrent against Indian aggression (ICAN 2016).

The United States has carried out a number of drone strikes in Pakistan against suspected terrorist targets. These attacks sometimes kill innocent civilians, which increases resentment toward the United States (as does the idea that Pakistan is not fully sovereign if the United States can freely launch drone strikes inside of its territory). The Obama administration also did not inform Pakistan of the decision to conduct the raid that killed Osama bin Laden in the city of Abbottabad, a relatively short distance from the Pakistani capital of Islamabad. Although this was likely a strategically sound decision based on the possibility that bin Laden would learn about the pending attack from a Pakistani source, it has further cultivated feelings of mistrust between Pakistan and the United States. As a result of all of these factors, Pakistan, especially the Pakistani military, encourages the continued viability of the Taliban on one hand and attempts to prevent them from increasing instability in Pakistan on the other.

As of 2016, U.S. foreign policy toward Pakistan is based on increasing the stability of the country. The United States encourages U.S. companies to invest in Pakistan, and the United States is a significant source of foreign direct investment as a result of these efforts. The United States also provides billions of dollars in civil and humanitarian assistance to Pakistan in order to help provide for nutritional and medical needs in vulnerable areas of the country, including the border region next to Afghanistan (the poorest region of the country). There can be little doubt that some of this assistance falls into the hands of the Taliban. Finally, the United States provides military and security assistance to Pakistan. Designation as a major non-NATO ally provides access to more sophisticated weapons systems, though pressure from Congress (see below) has placed limits on the nature of military aid.

Democrats on U.S. Relations with Pakistan

The 2016 Democratic Party platform mentions Pakistan specifically twice. One mention is in the context of terrorism, where Democrats promise to pressure both Pakistan and Afghanistan to prevent terrorists from finding safe haven along the border. The border between the two countries tends to be porous, which allows terrorist groups to move with relative freedom between the two countries. The border region is also politically unstable, which adds to the problem. The United States will provide over $400 million in security assistance to Pakistan in 2017 (Bearak and Gamio 2016). Second, Democrats pledge to stabilize Pakistan, in part by "building an effective relationship with the predominantly young population of this strategically located, nuclear-armed country" (Democratic National Committee 2016). The median age in Pakistan is 23.4 years old, making Pakistan a young country by comparative standards (Central Intelligence Agency 2016). Pakistan has the lowest median age of any of the nuclear powers, a source of concern given that low median age is often associated with conflict and lower life expectancy.

Very little public opinion data exists concerning U.S. perceptions of Pakistan. In a 2012 Pew survey about U.S. relations with several countries, however, only 10 percent of Americans indicated that they trust Pakistan (Pew Research Center 2012). In fact, Pakistan earned the lowest trust rating of any country in the survey, including China and Russia. It is worth noting that, for the most part, the feeling is mutual. According to one 2015 poll, only 22 percent of Pakistanis have a positive view of the United States and the majority of Pakistanis view the United States as an enemy (Wike, Stokes, and Poushter 2015).

One area where public opinion data does exist on an issue related directly to Pakistan is drone strikes by U.S. forces against terrorist targets in places like Afghanistan, Pakistan, Somalia, and Yemen. Citizens of Pakistan often cite drone strikes—and the civilian casualties from those strikes—as a reason for resentment against the United States. Despite these civilian deaths, though, a 2015 Pew poll found a majority of Democrats (52 percent) supported the continued use of drone strikes against terrorist groups in countries like Pakistan (Pew Research Center 2015). These results reflect general agreement with American authorities who frame drone strikes as a key element in efforts to combat terrorism. In May 2016, for example, a drone attack killed the leader of the Afghan Taliban, Mullah Mansoor, in Pakistan. Pakistan, which did not provide permission for the strike, protested that the attack was a violation of Pakistani sovereignty.

The most recent congressional vote related to Pakistan was an amendment, advanced in 2016, to the 2017 Defense Appropriations bill that would have barred security aid to Pakistan. Proponents of the amendment argued that Pakistan's violation of fundamental human rights, especially the arrest and imprisonment by Pakistan's government of Dr. Shakil Afridi, who played a key role in the CIA effort to pinpoint the location of Osama bin Laden, warranted a punitive response. The vote on the amendment failed by a bipartisan majority of 84–336 (Office of the Clerk 2016). Democrats were more unified in their opposition to the measure than were Republicans, with 171 of 180 Democrats opposing the amendment. A separate amendment that would have reduced aid to Pakistan by $200 million was struck down in a much closer vote (191–230). A majority of Democrats (137) opposed the amendment, while the majority of Republicans supported it. Democrats argued that the security aid was vital both to efforts to combat terrorism and to efforts to improve relations with Pakistan.

Congress was successful in withholding a portion of U.S. aid to Pakistan in response to Pakistani ties to Haqqani Network, an insurgent group that operates in Pakistan and Afghanistan. Portions of the Pakistani security establishment are thought to back the Haqqani Network in an effort to maintain a certain amount of instability in Afghanistan. The House and Senate passed similar legislation in 2015, requiring certification by the Department of Defense that Pakistan is making adequate progress in targeting groups like the Haqqani Network. The failure of the Department of Defense to provide certification in 2015 also resulted in the loss of hundreds of millions of dollars in Coalition Support Funds (CSF). CSF are designed to provide assistance to countries participating in efforts to combat international terrorism and are considered separate from traditional foreign security aid. Democrats and Republicans in Congress are broadly unified around tying CSF to Pakistan to progress in the fight against the Haqqani Network. Democrats and Republicans also were largely unified in an effort to prevent the U.S. government from subsidizing Pakistan's purchase of U.S. F-16 fighter craft. Pakistan has balked at paying the full price for the advanced weapons system and considering buying used F-16s from Jordan.

At the executive level, both President Obama and 2016 Democratic Party presidential nominee Hillary Clinton have promised to maintain a strong relationship with Pakistan. Clinton, however, did not shy away from criticism of the Pakistani government on the campaign trail. Clinton argued, for example, the Pakistan knew that Osama bin Laden was hiding in Pakistan in advance of the raid that ultimately killed him. In an interview in May 2016, Clinton stated that it was "just too much of a coincidence . . . that that house, that unusual-looking house would be built in that community near the military academy, surrounded by retired military professionals, even though we couldn't prove it" (Gaoutte 2016). Clinton has also supported the continued use of drone strikes against terrorist targets, including those in Pakistan. In spite of a potentially tougher stance against Pakistan, Clinton would be unlikely as president to support more than the current reductions in aid to the country. Pakistani assistance, even if it is not complexly forthcoming, remains a key part of the U.S. strategy to stabilize Afghanistan. In addition, the internal stability of Pakistan, which has its own significant Islamist militancy problem, is in the security interests of the United States.

Republicans on U.S. Relations with Pakistan

Pakistan is mentioned four times in the 2016 Republican Party platform. The first mention relates to a general desire to maintain a positive relationship, in spite of significant challenges, with Pakistan as an ally in the global war on terror. The second mention takes on the imprisonment of Dr. Shakil Afridi directly, though without mentioning his name. The platform states that the process of strengthening ties between the United States and Pakistan "cannot progress as long as any citizen of Pakistan can be punished for helping the War on Terror" (Republican National Committee 2016). Republicans believe that President Obama has not done enough to put sufficient pressure on Pakistan to free Dr. Afridi.

As noted above, public opinion polling related to Pakistan is sparse. One area where Democrats and Republicans appear to agree is the issue of drone attacks in countries like Pakistan, where remote terrain and high-risk make conventional air strikes are less effective. Seventy-four percent of Republicans back continued drone strikes, according to one poll (Pew Research Center 2015). One reason why majorities of both Democrats and Republicans may support continued drone strikes is the continued high salience of international terrorism as a foreign policy issue. For Republicans, international terrorism is viewed as the second-most critical threat (behind only terrorism in the United States) to U.S. security. For Democrats (as well as independents) it is the third-most critical threat (Chicago Council on Global Affairs 2015).

During the 114th Congress, Republicans were more supportive than Democrats of ending foreign aid, especially CSF, to Pakistan in response to perceived Pakistani intransigence in the war on terror and the jailing of Dr. Afridi. With regard to the amendment in the House of Representatives to withdraw all aid from Pakistan from the Department of Defense Appropriations Act, 75 of the 84 Representatives who voted yes were Republicans (Office of the Clerk 2016). Representative Dana Rohrabacher, who sponsored the amendment argued, "Unless the Pakistanis prove to us that I'm wrong by simply releasing Dr. Afridi, it is basically—they are insulting us, they are insulting the victims and the families of 9/11 and the fact is they can't even do this" (Brufke 2016). Rohrabacher also implied that many representatives believe that Pakistan is not cooperating in the war on terror. A majority of House Republicans (147) voted for the so-called Poe amendment, which would have cut $200 million in military aid to Pakistan. Many Republicans unwilling to completely cut military aid to Pakistan voted for the Poe measure to signal their dissatisfaction with the Pakistani government. Republican congressman Trent Franks of Arizona, who voted against the total cut but in favor of the $200 million cut, stated "I'm a big defense hawk and a big fiscal conservative, but in this case Pakistan continues to imprison the man who gave us Osama bin Laden and continues to have a major ideological bent within the middle echelons of their government that, I think, should cause all of us pause given the size and nature of their nuclear arsenal" (Brufke 2016).

2016 Republican presidential nominee Donald Trump promised during the campaign that he could have Dr. Afridi released from prison in "two minutes" (Johnson 2016). Trump implied that he would use U.S. foreign aid as leverage to secure the release, though he did not place a percentage or dollar amount on the aid he would withhold. The promise drew a rebuke from Pakistan's minister of the interior, Chaudhry Nisar: "Contrary to Mr. Trump's misconception, Pakistan is not a colony of the United States of America" (Johnson 2016). Trump has also raised some concerns in Pakistan with statements indicating that the United States and India would be "best friends" in the event that he won the election. India and Pakistan have fought for years over the status of disputed territories that share a border with China, India, and Pakistan. Trump has offered to mediate the dispute over the Kashmir region. President Obama, while originally running for office, also offered to mediate the dispute with the consent of all parties. To this point, neither India nor Pakistan has reached out to the United States for mediation or arbitration assistance.

Further Reading

Bearak, Max, and Lazaro Gamio. "Everything You Ever Wanted to Know about the U.S. Foreign Assistance Budget." *Washington Post*. Last modified October 18, 2016. https://www.washingtonpost.com/graphics/world/which-countries-get-the-most-foreign-aid/?tid=a_classic-iphone.

Brufke, Juliegrace. "House Votes Down Amendment to Ban Aid to Pakistan." The Daily Caller. Last modified June 16, 2016. http://dailycaller.com/2016/06/16/house-votes-down-amendment-to-ban-financial-assistance-to-pakistan/.

Central Intelligence Agency. "The World Factbook: Pakistan." Last modified 2016. https://www.cia.gov/library/publications/the-world-factbook/geos/pk.html.

Chicago Council on Global Affairs. "America Divided: Political Partisanship and US Foreign Policy." Last modified 2015. https://www.thechicagocouncil.org/sites/default/files/CCGA_PublicSurvey2015.pdf.

Democratic National Committee. "2016 Democratic Party Platform." Last modified July 21, 2016. https://www.demconvention.com/wp-content/uploads/2016/07/Democratic-Party-Platform-7.21.16-no-lines.pdf.

Gaoutte, Nicole. "Obama on the Future of Terrorism after Bin Laden Raid." CNN. Last modified May 2, 2016. http://www.cnn.com/2016/05/02/politics/obama-terror-doctrine-bin-laden-raid/.

Ḥaqqaani, Ḥusain. *Magnificent Delusions: Pakistan, the United States, and an Epic History of Misunderstanding.* New York: PublicAffairs, 2013.

ICAN. "Nuclear Arsenals." International Campaign to Abolish Nuclear Weapons. Last modified 2016. http://www.icanw.org/the-facts/nuclear-arsenals/.

Johnson, Kay. "Pakistan Raps Trump over Vow to Free Doctor Who Helped Track Bin Laden." Reuters. Last modified May 2, 2016. http://www.reuters.com/article/us-pakistan-usa-trump-idUSKCN0XT1ID.

Office of the Clerk. "Final Vote Results for Roll Call 325." U.S. House of Representatives. Last modified June 16, 2016. http://clerk.house.gov/evs/2016/roll325.xml.

Pew Research Center. "Public Continues to Back U.S. Drone Attacks." Last modified May 28, 2015. http://file:///C:/Users/trubenzer.USCUPSTATE/Downloads/5-28-15-Foreign-Policy-release.pdf.

Pew Research Center. "U.S. Public, Experts Differ on China Policies." Last modified September 18, 2012. http://file:///C:/Users/trubenzer.USCUPSTATE/Downloads/US-Public-and-Elite-Report-FINAL-FOR-PRINT-September-18-2012.pdf.

Republican National Committee. "Republican Platform 2016." Last modified 2016. https://prod-static-ngop-pbl.s3.amazonaws.com/media/documents/DRAFT_12_FINAL[1]-ben_1468872234.pdf.

Riedel, Bruce. "Pakistan, Taliban and the Afghan Quagmire." Brookings Institution. Last modified August 24, 2013. https://www.brookings.edu/opinions/pakistan-taliban-and-the-afghan-quagmire/.

Rohrabacher, Juliegrace. "House Votes Down Amendment to Ban Aid to Pakistan." The Daily Caller. Last modified June 16, 2016. http://dailycaller.com/2016/06/16/house-votes-down-amendment-to-ban-financial-assistance-to-pakistan/.

Weiner, Tim. "Nuclear Anxiety: The Know-How; U.S. and China Helped Pakistan Build Its Bomb." *New York Times.* Last modified June 1, 1998. http://www.nytimes.com/1998/06/01/world/nuclear-anxiety-the-know-how-us-and-china-helped-pakistan-build-its-bomb.html?_r=0.

Wike, Richard, Bruce Stokes, and Jacob Poushter. "America's Global Image." Pew Research Center's Global Attitudes Project. Last modified June 23, 2015. http://www.pewglobal.org/2015/06/23/1-americas-global-image/.

Refugees

At a Glance

U.S. policy toward refugees, including refugee resettlement, is an issue that contains both domestic and primarily foreign elements. On the domestic side, issues related to the provision of social services and employment policy are often dealt with at the local level, with some federal assistance. Within the realm of U.S. foreign policy are issues related to refugee referral, international coordination of the response to refugee crises, and U.S. obligations under international law. Historically, refugee policy has been an area of U.S. foreign policy with a significant amount of partisan consensus. More recently, especially in the wake of the refugee crisis stemming from conflict in the Middle East, differences both between and within parties have emerged.

According to many Republicans, acceptance of refugees in America . . .

- Is unwise because on inadequate screening processes for applicants from war-torn areas;
- Should not be expanded—and should perhaps be reduced;
- Should be paused or abandoned with respect to Syrian refugees; and
- Provides for too much influence from the United Nations.

According to many Democrats, acceptance of refugees in America . . .

- Is both a moral and legal obligation;
- Should include refugees from all areas, including the Middle East;
- Is based on a rigorous screening process that protects U.S. security interests; and
- Should generally be expanded to accommodate more refugee resettlement.

Overview

The history of refugees in the United States is in some ways older than the republic itself. Millions of individuals have fled various sorts of social and political persecution around the world for the promise of a better life in the "new world"—first the colonies, and then the United States. However, the modern history of U.S. refugee policy began with the Displaced Persons Act of 1948. This post–World War II legislation established the U.S. practice of granting refugees asylum in America if they faced political persecution or had a well-founded fear of persecution. (As is the case with international law, U.S. domestic laws have never allowed for the granting of refugee status for those fleeing dire economic conditions.) Over 400,000 displaced Europeans fled and resettled in the United States under the terms of the 1948 act. At the time, Republicans were more likely to support the legislation than were Democrats in part because Democrats wanted to broaden the legislation to admit *more* refugees and in part because of disputes between Democrats about the quota system in general (Schain 2012, 172). It is also the case that early refugee law in the United States was a discriminatory extension of the National Origins Act of 1924, which placed quotas on immigration based on national origin and race.

The United States became a party to the 1967 Protocol of the 1951 Convention Relating to the Status of Refugees in 1968. The 1967 Protocol removed the temporal restriction of the original convention, making it applicable to refugees outside of Europe (UNHCR 2010). As a party to the 1967 Protocol, the United States is required to assist in refugee repatriation or, when that is not possible, temporary or permanent resettlement. The United States is not a party to the original 1951 Convention in part because of a desire to maintain the immigration quota system that has existed at various times in U.S. history. In effect, however, ratification of the 1967 Protocol binds the United States to the provisions of the original treaty, since the treaty was expanded by the protocol to include refugees from all countries.

In 1965, general immigration policy changed with the abolition of the national origins quota system. Although immigrants, who at least hypothetically enter the country voluntarily, and refugees, who enter the country as a result of political persecution, have different legal statuses, refugee quota policy often follows broader immigration quota policy. The fall of the South Vietnamese capital of Saigon to North Vietnamese troops in 1975, which finally brought the Vietnam War to an end, marked a significant change in U.S. refugee policy. Hundreds of thousands of refugees from Vietnam, as well as other areas of war-torn Southeast Asia, including Laos and Cambodia, gained permanent residence in the United States.

In 1980, Congress passed, and Democratic president Jimmy Carter signed, the Refugee Act of 1980. The act codified the 1951 Convention definition of a refugee as "a person who is unable or unwilling to return to his or her home country because of a 'well-founded fear of persecution' due to race, membership in a particular social group, political opinion, religion, or national origin" (Meissner 2010). The act passed easily with bipartisan support.

Jimmy Carter Praises the United States Refugee Act of 1980

Public Law 96-212 officially became part of the U.S. legal code on March 17, 1980, when it was signed into law by President Jimmy Carter during his last year of office. At the signing ceremony, Carter stated that "the Refugee Act reflects our long tradition as a haven for people uprooted by persecution and political turmoil. In recent years, the number of refugees has increased greatly. Their suffering touches all and challenges us to help them, often under difficult circumstances" (Carter 1980). Among the law's key provisions were measures to:

- Create a Coordinator for Refugee Affairs and Assistance;
- Establish an Office of Refugee Resettlement within the Department of Health and Human Services;
- Harmonize the U.S. definition of the term refugee with the definition used in international law;
- Exclude from the definition of refugee anyone who had engaged in political persecution in their home country; and
- Create English-language instruction and employment training programs for refugees.

Source:

Carter, Jimmy. "Jimmy Carter: Refugee Act of 1980 Statement on Signing S. 643 into Law." The American Presidency Project. Last modified March 18, 1980. http://www.presidency.ucsb.edu/ws/?pid=33154.

The 1980 Refugee Act created the Federal Refugee Resettlement Program within the Department of Health and Human Services, marking the beginning of the modern refugee resettlement era. The act authorized Congress to set an annual quota on the admission of refugees. The quota was originally set at 50,000 (though that number can be, and often has been, exceeded). It is worth noting that the process for admitting refugees under the direction of the State Department was left separate from the process for providing assistance for refugees. Thus, it is hypothetically possible for refugees to be admitted to the United States without the accompanying resettlement funds. The United States has admitted over three million refugees for resettlement since 1975 (Department of State 2015).

The refugee admission and resettlement process in the United States follows what can be a complex process. The office of the UN High Commissioner for Refugees (UNHCR) refers potential applicants to a Refugee Support Center (RSC). Close relatives of refugees in the United States may skip the UNHCR referral process. The RSCs collect biographical information and coordinate a security and medical screening process with agencies such as the Department of Homeland Security. The total screening process may last from several months to several years. In the event that a refugee obtains security and medical clearance, the person or family is paired with of nine nonprofit agencies that work with the Bureau of Refugees,

Population and Migration and the Office of Refugee Resettlement. The nonprofits assist refugees with finding housing, education, and/or employment, and becoming acclimated to the United States. The average time from referral until a refugee arrives in the United States is 18–24 months (U.S. Department of State 2013).

Overall then, refugee policy before the onset of the crisis in Syria enjoyed significant areas of bipartisan agreement. The main difference between the parties was a preference among Democrats for the admission of higher numbers of refugees. Even that difference, given the willingness of both Republican and Democrats to admit high numbers of Cuban refugees in the 1980s, was not significant enough to prevent political compromise.

In 2011, however, partisan divisions over accepting political refugees became more evident. At that time, the Arab Spring began to sweep through parts of the Middle East. The Arab Spring was a period of nonviolent and violent populist uprisings in the Middle East that began in Tunisia in December 2010. In March 2011, mass uprisings began in Syria. Under pressure from secular as well as Islamist opposition, including the Islamic State of Iraq and Syria (ISIS) terrorist group, Syria entered a state of brutal civil war. Over the next three years, the crisis led over four million Syrians to flee the country. The vast majority of these refugees are currently in Turkey, Lebanon, or Jordan (Martinez 2015). Under the direction of the Obama administration, the United States has committed to taking in 10,000 Syrian refugees in the period from September 2015 to September 2016 (Harris, Sanger, and Herszenhorn 2015). As of August 2016, approximately 10,000 Syrian refugees have resettled in the United States.

The prospect of increased Syrian refugee resettlement in the United States has opened a partisan divide between Republicans and Democrats, not only on Syrian refugee resettlement but on the resettlement of refugees from the Muslim world in general. These differences were further exposed in November 2015, when ISIS claimed responsibility for a series of attacks in Paris that killed 130 people and injured hundreds more. One of the attackers had entered Europe through Greece (a common point of entry into the EU for Syrians fleeing the conflict) as a refugee. These terrorist attacks raised fears about the prospect of similar attacks being carried out in the United States by terrorists posing as refugees. The impact of the Paris terrorist attacks has added to existing concerns about cultural differences and assimilation that have surfaced in recent years concerning broader Muslim immigration and refugee policy.

Republicans on Refugee Policy

Before the onset of the Syrian refugee crisis, it would have been difficult, at least recently, to find strong partisan divisions between Republicans and Democrats on the issue of refugee policy. In many ways, refugee policy has simply not been a high-profile issue to either political party, allowing for a certain amount of foreign policy consensus on this issue. As a result, refugees, including Muslim refugees from the Middle East and peoples fleeing war and persecution from other parts of the world, have been settling in the United States for decades, with relatively little controversy. In 2012—the year before the refugee crisis escalated in the Middle East—the Republican Party platform only mentioned the issue of refugees once, referring to the U.S. tradition of resettling refugees from "troubled lands" (Republican National Committee 2012, 46).

Public opinion on issues related to refugees has recently taken on a similar partisan dimension. Generally speaking, U.S. public opinion on issues related to refugee resettlement has, with limited exceptions, been negative (Jones 2015). In fact, with the exception of Kosovar Albanians in the 1990s, there has never been a survey finding net positive support for refugee resettlement (DeSilver 2015). It could reasonably be argued that, before the onset of the Syrian refugee crisis, the public, regardless of partisan affiliation, opposed refugee resettlement even as the United States continued to resettle millions of refugees within national borders. Generally speaking, Republican voters were even less likely to support refugee resettlement than were Democrats.

This gap between self-identified Republicans and Democrats became more pronounced once the Syrian refugee issue emerged. A 2015 Gallup poll found that 84 percent of self-identified Republicans opposed President Obama's plan to resettle 10,000 Syrian refugees in the United States while 57 percent of Democrats approved of the plan. A similar gap emerged on the issue of whether survey respondents believe that Syrian refugees will be welcome in the local communities in which they resettle (Jones 2015). It is worth noting that the Gallup survey was conducted just after the ISIS attacks in Paris. In this light, it is unclear if public opinion, or the partisan divide, will remain as stark. However, given previous negative reactions to refugee resettlement within public opinion, it would not be surprising to see public opinion remain negative toward Syrian refugee resettlement, nor would it be surprising to see members of the public identifying as Republicans opposing resettlement somewhat more than self-identified Democrats.

The position of most Republican political elites on refugee resettlement, especially Syrian refugee resettlement, seems to mirror public opinion. In November 2015, the House of Representatives passed legislation that would require increased vetting of Syrian refugees by a veto-proof majority of 289–137. Although Democrats were divided on the measure, as outlined below, only two Republicans voted against the bill. In the Senate, Democrats were able to maintain sufficient party unity to filibuster the bill, which has killed it for the time being (Barrett 2016). Republicans were unified in support of the bill. Proponents of the legislation argued that additional vetting would be necessary to ensure that terrorists from Syria are unable to use refugee status as a means to enter the United States to carry out attacks. Opponents argued that the existing vetting process is sufficient, and the new process would, in effect bar entry to almost every eligible refugee.

The Syrian refugee issue also became prominent in the 2016 Republican presidential primary. All of the Republicans in the 2016 field expressed opposition to

---

A Conservative Republican Governor Opposes Syrian Refugees in His State

On December 9, 2015, Texas governor Greg Abbott issued a brief statement concerning his decision to halt the resettlement of refugees in Texas. Abbott had previously argued that gaps in the existing vetting process acknowledged by the federal government demonstrated the need to take action. His statement reads:

> In light of alarming comments made by the House Homeland Security Committee Chairman and testimony by the Deputy Director of Homeland Security at the Texas Department of Public Safety, it is essential that a judge consider halting the Syrian refugee process—at least on a temporary basis—to ensure refugees coming to the United States will be vetted in a way that does not compromise the safety of Americans and Texans.

Source:

Abbott, Greg. "Governor Abbott Issues Statement Supporting Attorney General's Request to Halt Syrian Refugee Resettlement in Texas." Office of the Governor—Greg Abbott. Last modified December 9, 2015. http://gov.texas.gov/news/press-release/21757.

---

the idea of resettling 10,000 or more Syrian refugees in the United States. Moreover, the winner of the GOP primary, Donald Trump, argued not only in favor of banning Syrian refugees but of temporarily banning travel by *all* Muslims into the United States. Other Republican lawmakers criticized Trump's proposed ban, but it appeared to be a popular position with the Republican base. Other candidates along the continuum of Syrian refugee policy argued in favor of allowing Christian refugees from Syria to enter the United States. Both former Florida governor Jeb Bush and Texas senator Ted Cruz espoused this viewpoint. In a radio interview with talk show host Michael Medved, for example, Bush called Trump's comments "appalling. If we've screened refugees, if you're a Christian Syrian who but for the good fortune of escaping and crossing through ISIS territory, and crossing the Turkish border, stuck in a refugee camp, and go through the process to prove you're not an Islamic terrorist, you come to the United States, this noble country, to send them back to their slaughter? I find it appalling" (Kaplan and Andrews 2015). The central argument of these candidates is that Christians, as a minority community in Syria and other countries in the Middle East, are poor candidates for resettlement in the region. Muslims, by contrast, could be resettled in other Middle Eastern countries.

Syrian refugee resettlement has also created a partisan divide between Republican and Democratic governors on resettlement policy. Historically, many states and local communities have expressed opposition to refugee resettlement. These concerns generally existed across party lines. Support, especially in cases where the refugees were part of a diaspora that had already been resettling in the United

States, was also largely a nonpartisan affair. The case of Syrian refugees is divergent. Of the 30 governors who have either requested or demanded to be excluded from the resettlement of Syrian refugees as of late 2015, all but one is a Republican. Most of these governors have expressed concerns related to security in the wake of the Paris attacks. The Obama administration has argued that adequate safeguards are in place and that no Syrian refugee has ever conducted a terrorist attack in the United States. Based on the constitutional supremacy of the federal government in areas related to foreign policy, most legal experts have argued that the governors can do little to block refugees from resettling in a given state.

Democrats on Refugee Policy

Government policy regarding the acceptance and settlement of political refugees was not a particularly salient issue for Democrats before the onset of the Syrian refugee crisis. The 2012 Democratic Party platform contained one mention of refugees, and that mention only occurred in the context of climate change (Democratic National Committee 2012). To be clear, Democratic presidents such a Jimmy Carter and Bill Clinton presided over the arrival of significant numbers of refugees in the United States. However, the refugee crisis in Syria has brought us from the point where issues related to refugee policy were prominently featured in President Obama's 2016 State of the Union Address and were debated on multiple occasions in the 2016 Democratic Party primary.

As described above, there is a partisan gap between Democrats and Republicans within the general public relating to Syrian refugees. Democrats are more likely than Republicans to approve of existing plans to settle Syrian refugees in the United States. The vote in the House of Representatives on the American Security against Foreign Enemies (SAFE) Act, which would have required increased vetting of Syrian refugees, reveals that there is also a gap within the Democratic Party on this issue. The bill passed by a margin of 289–137, with a majority of Democrats voting against the measure. However, 47 Democrats crossed party lines to vote for the bill, while only two Republicans voted against it. Some Democrats, such as John Garamendi of California, argued that the bill further strengthened what is already a very stringent vetting process (Garamendi 2015). As such, the bill would complement existing procedures. Brad Ashford, representing Nebraska's second congressional district, argued that the Paris attacks required a reassessment of the refugee vetting process (Lillis 2015). He also voted for the bill. Several of the Democrats who broke ranks are part of the Blue Dog Coalition, a group best known for being a more conservative wing of the Democratic Party. The Blue Dog Coalition argued that the SAFE Act was necessary to ensure American security against terrorists who might pose as refugees in order to gain access to the United States. Ashford argued, "In the wake of the horrific attacks in Paris, we must step back and reassess our existing procedures for admitting and monitoring refugees from Iraq and Syria" (Blue Dog Coalition 2015). House minority leader Nancy Pelosi (Calif.)

made the decision not to suppress opposition to the bill within her caucus, providing Democrats with political cover to oppose the bill. Pelosi, for her part, opposed the bill and expressed support for an alternative that would have required a less stringent certification process.

Democrats who opposed the SAFE Act argued that, in effect, the bill would prevent the resettlement of any Syrian refugees in the United States. Minority Whip Steny Hoyer of Maryland argued, "The bill rests on a faulty assumption that the European refugee screening process is similar to the United States screening process. This is entirely inaccurate" (Hoyer 2015). Representative Sam Farr of California asserted that the existing refugee vetting process already takes almost two years. He also argued that acting based on the fear created by the Paris attacks would result in poor policy (Farr 2015). The central argument of most opponents of the bill is that the three sets of certifications that would have been required for each Syrian or Iraqi refugee entering the United States would have created a bureaucratic bottleneck that would have ground the process to a halt. Opponents also assert that the current vetting process, which normally takes nearly two years and involves several government agencies, is sufficient to ensure security.

Both of the major candidates for the Democratic Party presidential nomination in 2016 broadly supported President Obama's policy on Syrian refugees. Former secretary of state Hillary Clinton argued for the expansion of the existing program to allow for 65,000 Syrian refugees to be resettled in the United States (Kaplan 2015). Senator Bernie Sanders of Vermont, while not setting a numerical target for Syrian refugee resettlement, argued that those who want to halt the process in the wake of the Paris attacks were taking political advantage of a tragedy. Both candidates favor the existing vetting process, which they argue is adequate to ensure the security of Americans in communities where refugees resettle.

The partisan division between Republican governors, who have overwhelmingly called for cessation of Syrian refugee settlement, and Democratic governors, who have not, has created a further partisan divide between state and local government in some areas. Mayors of large cities within otherwise conservative states are often Democrats. Many of these mayors have indicated that their cities are willing to accept Syrian refugees, countering state demands and requests that no Syrian refugees be resettled. Former Houston mayor Annise Parker, for example, argued that Houston should accept more refugees because "not allowing refugees makes America look weak. It is the only humane thing to do" (Rhodes 2015). Andrew Gillum, Democratic mayor of Tallahassee, Florida, has also parted with the Republican governor of Florida on the issue of Syrian refugees.

The partisan division between Republican governors and Democratic mayors on this issue has multiple implications. First, neither state nor local governments can prevent refugees from resettling. Federal law leaves this decision in the hands of the national government. However, state and local governments do provide resettlement assistance, and state governments could block that assistance. At the

A Liberal Democratic Governor Supports Placing Syrian Refugees in Her State

As the Syrian refugee crisis deepened, Kate Brown, the Democratic governor of Oregon, repeatedly emphasized that her state would welcome refugees with open arms: "Clearly, Oregon will continue to accept refugees," she stated. "They seek safe haven and we will continue to open the doors of opportunity to them. The words on the Statue of Liberty apply in Oregon just as they do in every other state." She did note, however, that Oregon could not take actions regarding the refugees that would directly contravene federal laws. "As Oregonians, it is our moral obligation to help them rebuild their lives," she explained. "[But] we will continue to abide by federal laws regarding resettlement. Oregon does not have a direct role or act independently of the federal government."

Source:

Kullgren, Ian. "Kate Brown: Oregon Will Keep Accepting Syrian Refugees." OregonLive.com. November 17, 2015. http://www.oregonlive.com/politics/index.ssf/2015/11/kate_brown _oregon_will_continu.html.

same time, local governments could allocate additional money, including (hypothetically) money received from the state toward the resettlement process. Much of the funding for refugee resettlement comes from the national government and the nonprofit sector, so the potential for states to use the power of the purse to prevent refugee resettlement does have significant limits. Second, each state has a refugee coordinator who helps the federal government determine where refugees might be resettled. It is possible, given the current division, that state coordinators in states with Republican governors will say that the state lacks the capacity to resettle additional refugees, while local governments are sending a separate message. Overall, the partisan component of the refugee issue is more complicated than typical foreign policy issues because it involves many political players are levels other than the national government.

Further Reading

Barrett, Ted. "Against 2016 Backdrop, Senate to Vote on Syrian Refugees Politics.com." CNN. Last modified January 20, 2016. http://www.cnn.com/2016/01/20/politics/syrian-refugees -senate-vote-2016/.

Blue Dog Coalition. "Blue Dogs Support Ensuring FBI, Intelligence Community Coordinates Refugee Screening." Last modified November 18, 2015. http://bluedogcaucus-schrader .house.gov/media-center/press-releases/blue-dogs-support-ensuring-fbi-intelligence -community-coordinates.

Democratic National Committee. "Our Platform." Last modified 2012. https://www.demo crats.org/party-platform.

DeSilver, Drew. "US Public Often Hasn't Wanted Refugees Admitted." Pew Research Center. Last modified November 19, 2015. http://www.pewresearch.org/fact-tank/2015/11/19 /u-s-public-seldom-has-welcomed-refugees-into-country/.

Diamond, Jeremy. "Donald Trump: Ban All Muslim Travel to U.S. Politics.com." CNN. Last modified December 8, 2015. http://www.cnn.com/2015/12/07/politics/donald-trump -muslim-ban-immigration/.

Farr, Sam. "Statement on Syrian Refugee Bill." The Online Office of Congressman Sam Farr. Last modified November 19, 2015. http://farr.house.gov/index.php/newsroom/press -releases/72-newsroom/2015-press-releases/1213-statement-on-syrian-refugee-bill.

Garamendi, John. "Congressman John Garamendi's Statement on Syrian Refugee Bill." Congressman John Garamendi. Last modified November 19, 2015. https://garamendi.house .gov/press-release/congressman-john-garamendi-s-statement-syrian-refugee-bill.

Gass, Nick. "Bernie Sanders 2016: We Will Not Turn Our Backs on Syrian Refugees." Politico. Last modified November 17, 2015. http://www.politico.com/story/2015/11/bernie -sanders-syria-refugees-215967.

Harris, Gardiner, David E. Sanger, and David M. Herszenhorn. "Obama Increases Number of Syrian Refugees for U.S. Resettlement to 10,000." *New York Times*. Last modified September 10, 2015. http://www.nytimes.com/2015/09/11/world/middleeast/obama -directs-administration-to-accept-10000-syrian-refugees.html?_r=0.

Hoyer, Steny. "The Daily Whip: Thursday, November 19, 2015." The Office of Democratic Whip Steny Hoyer. Last modified November 19, 2015. http://www.democraticwhip .gov/content/daily-whip-thursday-november-19-2015.

Jones, Jeffrey M. "Americans again Opposed to Taking in Refugees." Gallup.com. Last modified November 23, 2015. http://www.gallup.com/poll/186866/americans-again-opposed -taking-refugees.aspx.

Kaplan, Rebecca. "Hillary Clinton: U.S. Should Take 65,000 Syrian Refugees." CBS News. Last modified September 20, 2015. http://www.cbsnews.com/news/hillary-clinton-u-s -should-take-65000-syrian-refugees/.

Kaplan, Thomas, and Wilson Andrews. "Presidential Candidates on Allowing Syrian Refugees in the United States." *New York Times*. November 17, 2015. http://www.nytimes .com/interactive/2015/11/17/us/politics/presidential-candidates-on-syrian-refugees .html?_r=0.

Lillis, Mike. "Blue Dog Dems to Back GOP Refugee Bill." *The Hill*. November 18, 2015. http:// thehill.com/homenews/house/260695-blue-dog-dems-to-back-gop-refugee-bill.

Martinez, Michael. "Syrian Refugees: Which Countries Welcome Them." CNN. September 10, 2015. http://www.cnn.com/2015/09/09/world/welcome-syrian-refugees-countries/.

Massie, Christopher. "Jeb Bush: Trump's Call to Send Back Syrian Refugees 'Appalling' News." BuzzFeed. Last modified November 23, 2015. http://www.buzzfeed.com /christophermassie/jeb-bush-trumps-call-to-send-back-syrian-refugees-appalling# .yd67VW3pAp.

Meissner, Doris. "Thirty Years of the Refugee Act of 1980." U.S. Department of State. Last modified September 22, 2010. http://iipdigital.usembassy.gov/st/english/publication/2 010/09/20100921144657aidan0.8100397.html#axzz4Z0rJTYOH.

Republican National Committee. "2012 Republican Platform." Last modified 2012. https:// prod-static-ngop-pbl.s3.amazonaws.com/docs/2012GOPPlatform.pdf.

Rhodes, Syan. "Gov. Abbott Says Texas Will Not Accept Refugees from Syria." KPRC. Last modified November 16, 2015. http://www.click2houston.com/news/gov-abbott-says -texas-will-not-accept-refugees-from-syria.

Schain, Martin. *The Politics of Immigration in France, Britain and the United States: A Comparative Study*. Basingstoke: Palgrave Macmillan, 2012.

Seipel, Arnie. "30 Governors Call for Halt to U.S. Resettlement of Syrian Refugees." NPR.org. November 17, 2015. http://www.npr.org/2015/11/17/456336432/more-governors-oppose-u-s-resettlement-of-syrian-refugees.

UNHCR. "Convention and Protocol Relating to the Status of Refugees." Last modified 2010. http://www.unhcr.org/3b66c2aa10.html.

U.S. Department of State. "History of U.S. Refugee Resettlement." Last modified June 19, 2015. http://www.state.gov/j/prm/releases/factsheets/2015/244058.htm.

U.S. Department of State. "U.S. Refugee Admissions Program." Last modified January 31, 2013. http://www.state.gov/j/prm/ra/admissions/index.htm.

Russia

At a Glance

Since the end of the Cold War and the collapse of the Soviet Union in 1991, the relationship between the United States and Russia has been complex. The presidency of Boris Yeltsin from 1991 to 1999 marked a period of optimism that the relationship between former belligerents would become more amicable, though tensions remained on issues such as North Atlantic Treaty Organization (NATO) expansion. Since that time, however, the nonconsecutive presidencies of Vladimir Putin, who has consolidated a personalistic dictatorship in Russia, coupled with partisan debates over the nature of U.S. foreign policy in Eastern Europe, have soured the relationship. Attempts at a "reset" in relations during the Obama administration have largely failed, and Russian political and military actions in Ukraine and Syria have heightened tensions between the two nations. During this same time, a marked partisan divide on the proper U.S. response to Russian militarism, corruption, and authoritarianism has become evident.

According to many Republicans, U.S. foreign policy toward Russia . . .

- Should be based on the willingness to use military force against Russia in the event of an attack on a NATO ally;
- Should include sending arms to Ukraine to defend against Russian aggression;
- Should not attempt to placate Russia on issues related to missile defense or NATO expansion;
- Should be based on pressuring Russia to improve its human rights record; and
- Should include targeted sanctions on Russian officials who violate human rights and/or who were involved in Crimean annexation.

According to many Democrats, U.S. foreign policy toward Russia . . .

- Should avoid sending arms to Ukraine under NATO auspices;
- Should include targeted sanctions on Russia officials who violate human rights and/or were involved with Crimean annexation;

- Should be based on cooperation in the area of nuclear arms control;
- Should be based on cooperation when interests partially or fully coincide, such as Iran; and
- Should oppose Russian efforts to support the Assad regime in Syria.

Overview

U.S. foreign policy toward Russia dates to well before the rise of the Soviet Union and the advent of the Cold War. The two countries established diplomatic relations in 1803 and formal commercial relations about 30 years later. Russia encouraged negotiation when sectional tensions escalated in the United States in the mid-19th century, but it officially supported the Union during the U.S. Civil War. Former president Ulysses S. Grant visited Russia in 1878, the last president to do so for over 100 years. The United States provided assistance to Russia and other allies before entering World War I and was the first country to recognize Russia's provisional government after the first (March) revolution of 1917, which toppled the monarchy. During World War I, the United States provided some assistance to the White Army in their efforts to defeat the Bolsheviks. Most of this assistance related to protecting U.S. interests along the Trans-Siberian Railway (Smith 2002). Vladimir Lenin, the architect of the first revolution in 1917, orchestrated a second by ultimately overthrowing the ineffective provisional government. This led to the creation of the Soviet Union, which contained Russia as a constituent Republic. The United States did not recognize the Soviet Government until 1933.

U.S. recognition of the Moscow-based Communist government that ruled the Soviet Union did little to improve the relationship between the two countries. The goal of World War I had been to make the world safe for democracy, and the Soviet Revolution did nothing to advance this goal. In addition, the general ideological differences between the two countries were an obvious source of strain. When World War II began in Europe, Soviet neutrality advanced the German cause, representing a further blow to U.S. interests. However, the German invasion of the Soviet Union in 1941 changed the strategic calculus. The United States began to provide so-called lend-lease assistance to the Soviet Union once it entered the war on the side of the Allies. Under the Lend-Lease Act, the president was allowed to transfer supplies, equipment, and arms, without compensation to any country deemed to be part of the defense interest of the United States.

After the war ended with the defeat of Germany and Japan, the United States and the Soviet Union no longer had mutual enemies to smooth over their differences. Instead, Soviet occupation of Eastern Europe and North Korea at the end of World War II helped set the stage for the Cold War. During the Cold War, the United States and the Soviet Union, with Russia as its most important republic, clashed in a variety of ways over a wide variety of issues. Contrasting economic visions, for example, led both sides to use foreign aid as leverage to encourage different economic policies. The desire of the Soviet Union to internationalize the Communist revolution—and the equally fervent wish of the United States to stop such expansion—led to proxy wars across the globe. During these conflicts, which occurred primarily in the developing world, both the Americans and Soviets poured in huge amounts of military and economic assistance. The Cold War also gave rise to nuclear and conventional arms races and higher defense spending around the world. At the diplomatic level, in spite of periods of détente, the Cold War paralyzed international organizations like the United Nations and led to increased regionalism.

Upon the dissolution of the Soviet Union in 1991, U.S. relations with Russia once again assumed center stage. The Russia Federation was not only the largest former Soviet Republic, it was also the most industrialized, possessed almost all (and eventually all) of the former Soviet nuclear stockpile, and was the successor to the Soviet Union in most treaty relationships. Boris Yeltsin, president of the Russian Federation, initially embraced neoliberal market reforms and made moves toward democratization. Republican George H. W. Bush, who was president during the period at the end of the Cold War, was suspicious of Yeltsin, who he viewed as reckless and not fully committed to reform (Goldgeier and McFaul 2003, 20–23). Relations between the two nations were also strained during the presidency of Democrat Bill Clinton, especially after the North Atlantic Treaty Organization (NATO) began to seriously consider expansion in the mid-1990s. Russia was concerned that the expansion of NATO would leave a series of potentially hostile states, with mutual assistance assurance from the United States and existing NATO allies, at its doorstep. In spite of this, Clinton and Yeltsin met on 18 different occasions, and the United States agreed to an economic assistance package to Russia. The United States also pushed for an International Monetary Fund bailout after the collapse of the Russian economy in 1998. However, political issues, including NATO expansion and U.S. involvement in the Balkan Wars of the 1990s, especially Bosnia-Herzegovina and Kosovo, were constant sources of tension.

Yeltsin's resignation, the assumption of power by Vladimir Putin, and the election of Republican George W. Bush as U.S. president in 2000 did not improve the relationship. The United States announced that it would abrogate the Anti-Ballistic Missile (ABM) Treaty in 2002, angering Russia. Continued NATO expansion, including into the Baltic Republics, was also a cause of increased tension between the two countries. One country that began consultations to join NATO was the former Soviet Republic of Georgia, which has a large ethnic Russian minority in the areas of South Ossetia and Abkhazia. Both South Ossetia and Abkhazia have attempted to break away from Georgia with the support of Russia. In 2008, Russia invaded Georgia in order to provide for the safety of its ethnic kin in the two breakaway republics. Critics in the West, including both political parties in the United States, viewed the invasion as an attempt to increase Russia's power and prestige. Georgia's flirtation with NATO, with the support of the United States, was viewed as one source of the conflict. From the U.S. perspective, bringing Georgia, which had supported the U.S. invasion of Iraq and was becoming an important ally, made sense. From the Russian perspective, expansion of NATO to include Georgia, a move that was ultimately abandoned, represented another aggressive move in Eastern Europe by the United States and NATO. Although a ceasefire between Russia and Georgia was ultimately reached, the invasion damaged the relationship between the United States and Russia. In response, the United States imposed limited economic sanctions on Russia, offered economic assistance to Georgia, and transported Georgian troops home from Iraq to participate in the defense of the country.

The relationship between the United States and Russia has remained strained during the presidency of Democratic president Barack Obama, who has clashed with Putin on a number of occasions. In 2009, Secretary of State Hillary Clinton met with her Russian counterpart in what was framed as a "reset" in relations between the two countries. The reset included the cancellation of the limited sanctions against Russia, the cancellation of planned U.S. ballistic missile defense installations in Poland and the Czech Republic, permission to use Russian airspace as part of U.S./NATO operations in Afghanistan, and the resumption of nuclear talks, which led to the New START Treaty. Although relations improved for a time, two events have served to essentially cancel the reset. First, Russia support of the Assad regime in Syria is a source of tension with the United States, who wants to see Assad removed because of his years of brutal rule and his culpability in atrocities committed against the Syrian people during the course of that country's civil war. Second, Russian military intervention in Ukraine, including annexation of the Crimean Peninsula, angered and dismayed the United States. As a result, the United States has imposed several rounds of new sanctions on 34 individuals or associations (such as banks) deemed to have assisted with the intervention.

Republicans on U.S. Relations with Russia

Overall, Republicans have been very critical of President Obama and Democrats in Congress for perceived weaknesses in their handling of the U.S. relationship with Russia. For example, the 2012 Republican Party platform asserted that the Obama administration appeased Russia by undermining U.S. missile defense capabilities (Republican National Committee 2012). The specific version of the critique made in the platform dates back to a conversation between Obama and former Russian president Dmitry Medvedev in which Obama advised Medvedev that he would have "more flexibility" on missile defense issues after the 2012 election (Nakamura and Wilgoren 2012). The conversation, which was picked up by a microphone, was not part of the public comments made by the two leaders. The platform also called for improved respect for human rights in Russia as a condition for improved trade relations.

Among the general public, people who self-identify as Republicans also tend to desire a more muscular U.S. policy toward Russia than do Democrats. Although

69 percent of Republicans would favor military intervention against Russia in the event of a Russian attack on a NATO ally, for example, a 2015 Pew Research Center poll found that only 49 percent of Democrats favor the same response (Stokes 2015). According to the same survey, 60 percent of Republicans favor sending NATO arms to Ukraine in response to the Russian annexation of the Crimea and sponsorship of the civil war in Eastern Ukraine. Thirty-nine percent of self-identified Democrats favor U.S./NATO actions to arm Ukraine in the face of Russian aggression. A majority of Republicans would also favor the U.S. military providing training for Ukrainian personnel, something opposed by most Democrats (Chicago Council on Global Affairs 2015).

It is worth noting that both Republicans and Democrats favor Ukrainian admission into NATO, a policy that would according to Article 5 of the NATO treaty, require the United States and all other NATO member states to treat an attack on Ukraine (by Russia, for instance) as an attack against them (NATO 2016). As of 2016, the only invocation of the collective security requirement of NATO occurred after the terrorist attacks of September 11, 2001 against the United States.

In addition, both Democrats and Republicans favor the use of sanctions as punishment and a coercive tool against Russia in response to its intervention in Ukraine (Pew Research Center 2014). Finally, there is bipartisan support for the idea of increasing U.S. diplomatic efforts to bring an end to the ongoing crisis (Chicago Council on Global Affairs 2015).

Republicans in Congress have also been critical of Obama administration policy toward Russia. On issues related to missile defense, for example, Republicans have argued that the United States is too willing to placate Russia by scaling back its planned missile shield. In 2015, before opening speeches at the United Nations General Assembly, President Obama met with Russian president Putin to discuss issues related to Ukraine and Syria. Republicans in Congress, including Senators Marco Rubio and John McCain, criticized the president for his willingness to meet with Putin. McCain argued that speaking with the Russian president would "play right into Putin's hands" by helping Russia break free of the isolation it faces over its actions in Syria, and, especially, Ukraine (McCain 2015). Representative Mike Rodgers of Michigan, chair of the House Intelligence Committee, stated "I think Putin is playing chess, and I think we're playing marbles" in a statement criticizing current U.S. foreign policy toward Russia related to the situation in Ukraine (Lightman 2014).

Republicans have also denounced President Obama and the Democratic Party for U.S. foreign policy toward Syria, specifically, as it relates to Russian intervention, both militarily and logistically, to prop up the Assad regime. Republicans claim that the failure of the United States to intervene more forcefully, and earlier, in the Syrian civil war enabled Assad to remain in power long enough to benefit from Russian intervention. Senator Bob Corker, chair of the Senate, posited in a statement that the lack of U.S. push back against Russia's Syria policy means that Putin can act with impunity because he has "no price to pay" (Wofford 2015).

Article 5 of the NATO Treaty

The NATO alliance was developed primarily to deter and respond to potential aggression by the Soviet Union and its Warsaw Pact allies. For a variety of reasons, including the power of the nuclear deterrent on both sides, one provision of the NATO agreement—Article 5—was never invoked during the Cold War. As NATO has expanded to include former members of the Warsaw Pact in the post–Cold War era, some analysts believe that the chances of an Article 5 invocation, which would require all NATO members to react as if they had been attacked, has risen. Article 5 reads as follows:

> The Parties agree that an armed attack against one or more of them in Europe or North America shall be considered an attack against them all and consequently they agree that, if such an armed attack occurs, each of them, in exercise of the right of individual or collective self-defense recognized by Article 51 of the Charter of the United Nations, will assist the Party or Parties so attacked by taking forthwith, individually and in concert with the other Parties, such action as it deems necessary, including the use of armed force, to restore and maintain the security of the North Atlantic area.
>
> Any such armed attack and all measures taken as a result thereof shall immediately be reported to the Security Council. Such measures shall be terminated when the Security Council has taken the measures necessary to restore and maintain international peace and security.

Article 5 has been invoked only once. After the terrorist attacks of September 11, 2001, NATO invocation of Article 5 paved the way for military action against Afghanistan. Thus, at this point in history, Article 5 has never been invoked with respect to Russian aggression, which has been confined to non-NATO countries such as Ukraine and Georgia.

Source:

"Topic: Collective Defense—Article 5." NATO. Last modified March 22, 2016. http://www .nato.int/cps/is/natohq/topics_110496.htm?

It is worth noting that congressional Republicans and Democrats have agreed on some key elements of U.S. foreign policy toward Russia. For example, in 2014, the House and Senate passed the Ukraine Freedom Support Act of 2014 without a single dissenting vote in either chamber. The act added additional targeted financial sanctions to those imposed by the president and the European Union after the initial Russian intervention in Ukraine. The act also allows, but does not require, the president to provide assistance, including arms, to Ukraine to aid in its fight against Russian-backed rebels in the east (Lakshmanan 2014). Even in this case, however, the level of bipartisanship may be less than it appears. The act passed unanimously because it is voluntary in nature. President Obama indicated on signing the bill into law that he did not intend to implement either the new sweeping sanctions against Russian gas companies authorized by the act or the armed assistance to Ukraine.

During the 2016 Republican primary, candidates for the Republican nomination for president made a wide array of claims about how they would handle Russia as president. Businessman Donald Trump, for example, argued he is not opposed to Russian involvement in Syria, as long as the main target of their military action was ISIS/ISIL. Trump has also argued that Russian intervention in Ukraine occurred because of a lack of respect for President Obama within the upper echelons of the Russian government. Trump also insisted that he would be able to develop a better working relationship with Vladimir Putin than President Obama has achieved. Overall, Trump argued that the situation in Ukraine is more of an issue for Europe than for the United States.

Senator Ted Cruz and Governor John Kasich were much more critical of Putin, a position that fits more cleanly within current Republican Party positions on the subject. Cruz, for example, asserted that more forceful action in Syria, coupled with efforts to punish Russia for its human rights abuses, is the key to countering Putin's designs in the Middle East and Eastern Europe (Cruz 2015). Cruz shared Trump's stance, however, that lack of U.S. resolve on Syria and Ukraine, has emboldened Russia. John Kasich went so far as to specifically criticize Trump's apparent affinity for Putin and his authoritarian brand of leadership, announcing a Trump–Putin ticket in jest (Levine 2015). Kasich also argued, similar to President Obama, that the Assad regime must be removed from power in order to alleviate Syrian suffering. Kasich believes that Russia is a major impediment to this goal and has suggested direct U.S. military intervention, as part of a coalition, in order to combat ISIS.

Democrats on U.S. Relations with Russia

Like Republicans, Democrats in the United States are likely to view Russian leadership and Russian foreign policy with distrust. The partisan differences exist largely in the nature of the desired response. Overall, Democrats are less likely to favor direct confrontation with Russia. Instead, Democrats are more likely to favor economic sanctions and diplomatic isolation as tools to check Russian aggression in Ukraine, Russian support for the Assad regime in Syria, and other actions deemed hostile to U.S. interests or global peace and security.

During the Obama presidency, most Democrats have emphasized cooperation with Russia on issues of mutual concern over conflict, including the New START Treaty and the imposition of sanctions on Iran. They have also emphasized that the two nations have a mutual interest in fighting terrorism. However, Democrats have also harshly condemned Russian intervention in Ukraine and the Russian decision to provide direct air and limited ground support to President Assad in Syria.

The wide partisan gap between Democrats and Republicans on the issue of arming Ukraine in the face of Russian aggression has been noted above. Overall,

Democrats within the general public are slightly less likely to favor the provision of economic aid to the Ukraine by Western countries, including the United States, and are significantly less likely to believe that the United States is not being tough enough on Russia on the Ukraine issue (Pew Research Center 2014). Democrats are also more likely to favor the intensification of diplomatic efforts to resolve the crisis; though the partisan gap with Republicans on the use of diplomacy is a comparatively small nine points (Chicago Council on Global Affairs 2015). Interestingly, Democrats and Republicans both tend to minimize the threat of Russian territorial aggression on the United States. A Chicago Council on Global Affairs survey in 2015 asked respondents to rank potential threats to the United States. Democrats ranked Russia as the 16th most significant threat to the United States, while Republicans rank Russia 13th (Chicago Council on Global Affairs 2015). This finding suggests that both Democrats and Republicans recognize that Russia's territorial ambitions have little to do with the United States.

President Obama, as well as Democratic members of Congress, have enjoyed a significant amount of unity on the issue of U.S.–Russia relations. Democrats in Congress hailed the completion of the New START Treaty as a promising step in alleviating nuclear tensions between Russia and the United States. Representative Howard Berman, who at the time was chair of the House Foreign Affairs Committee, said of Senate ratification of the New START Treaty: "This is a historic vote to safeguard U.S. national security, to further reduce the nuclear dangers facing us, and to give, indeed, a 'new start' to the cause of reducing and eliminating these most terrible of weapons" (House Committee on Foreign Affairs 2010). In the same fashion, Democrats were unified in their praise of the Obama administration and its dealings with Russia and Syria over the issue of chemical weapons. Syria agreed to give up its chemical weapons in 2013. The United States had threatened military action over Syrian use of chemical weapons and Senator Barbara Boxer of the Foreign Relations Committee credited Obama's actions with bringing Syria, under pressure from Russia, to the negotiating table to work out a solution.

This is not to say that the Obama administration has been free from criticism from Democrats for its Russia policy, especially with regard to Russian intervention in Ukraine. Before passage of the Ukraine Freedom Act in 2014, some Democrats argued that the Obama administration policy of not arming the Ukraine was a mistake. Representative Eliot Engle, a Democrat, sponsored a piece of legislation that would have called on the president to provide lethal assistance to Ukraine, which includes inherently offensive weaponry such as mortars, grenade launchers, and antiarmor missiles. The resolution, which was nonbinding, passed in the House by a vote of 348–48 with majorities of both Democrats and Republicans supporting the resolution (House Roll Call 131 2015). Although the resolution was nonbinding, it was viewed by many as a critique of Obama's refusal to arm the Ukrainian military. Representative Engle added merit to this view, arguing that the decision to arm Ukraine against Russia aggression should not be a partisan issue.

During the 2016 campaign for the Democratic Party presidential nomination, Senator Hillary Clinton generally adopted a more aggressive tone on issues related to Russia. On her campaign Web site, Clinton refers to the need to help Europe lower its dependence on Russian oil as well as the need to "contain and deter" Russian aggression in Europe (Hillary for America 2016). In addition, Clinton argued during the Democratic debates that Russia posed the greatest threat to the United States by virtue of its territorial ambitions in Europe. Senator Sanders has alternatively referred to climate change, North Korea, and ISIS as the greatest current threats to the United States. It is worth noting that both Clinton and Sanders mention the need to combat terrorism, climate change, and other foreign policy challenges much more frequently than they do the need to counter Russia.

Further Reading

Chicago Council on Global Affairs. "America Divided: Political Partisanship and US Foreign Policy." Last modified 2015. http://www.thechicagocouncil.org/sites/default/files/CCGA_PublicSurvey2015.pdf.

Cruz, Ted. "Ted Cruz: How to Push Back Putin in Syria .com." CNN. Accessed March 28, 2016. http://www.cnn.com/2015/10/09/opinions/cruz-syria-putin/.

Gibson, Ginger. "From Russia with Love: Putin, Trump Sing Each Other's Praises." Reuters. Last modified December 17, 2015. http://www.reuters.com/article/us-russia-putin-usa-trump-idUSKBN0U01NW20151217.

Goldgeier, James M., and Michael McFaul. "George H.W. Bush and Soviet Regime Change." In Power and Purpose U.S. Policy toward Russia after the Cold War. Washington, D.C.: Brookings Institution Press, 2003.

House Committee on Foreign Affairs. "Rep. Berman Lauds Historic Senate Vote for New START Treaty." House Committee on Foreign Affairs. Last modified December 22, 2010. https://democrats-foreignaffairs.house.gov/news/press-releases/rep-berman-lauds-historic-senate-vote-new-start-treaty.

Lakshmanan, Indira A. "Congress Passes Tougher Russia Sanctions but Gives Obama Leeway." Bloomberg.com/politics. Last modified December 12, 2014. http://www.bloomberg.com/politics/articles/2014-12-12/congress-passes-tougher-russia-sanctions-but-gives-obama-leeway.

Levine, Sam. "John Kasich Trolls Trump by Announcing Trump–Putin Ticket." The Huffington Post. Last modified December 19, 2015. http://www.huffingtonpost.com/entry/kasich-trump-putin-ticket_us_5675889ee4b014efe0d5b89a.

Lightman, David. "GOP Bashes Obama on Russia, Ukraine | McClatchy DC." Mcclatchydc. Last modified March 2, 2014. http://www.mcclatchydc.com/news/politics-government/congress/article24764560.html.

McCain, John. "Statement by Senator John McCain on Obama–Putin Meeting Today." Senator John McCain. September 28, 2015. http://www.mccain.senate.gov/public/index.cfm?p=press-releases&id=E950272B-5DEF-41BE-9AA4-9BD36B88B5E6.

Nakamura, David, and Debbi Wilgoren. "Caught on Open Mike, Obama Tells Medvedev He Needs 'Space' on Missile Defense." Washington Post. Last modified March 26, 2012. https://www.washingtonpost.com/politics/obama-tells-medvedev-solution-on-missile-defense-is-unlikely-before-elections/2012/03/26/gIQASoblbS_story.html.

NATO. "Topic: Collective Defense—Article 5." Last modified March 22, 2016. http://www
.nato.int/cps/is/natohq/topics_110496.htm?

Office of the Historian. "Highlights in the History of U.S. Relations with Russia, 1780–June
2006." U.S. Department of State. Last modified May 11, 2007. http://www.state.gov/p
/eur/ci/rs/200years/c30273.htm#1832treaty.

Pew Research Center. "Bipartisan Support for Increased U.S. Sanctions against Russia."
Pew Research Center for the People and the Press. Last modified April 28, 2014. http://
www.people-press.org/2014/04/28/bipartisan-support-for-increased-u-s-sanctions
-against-russia/.

Republican National Committee. "2012 Republican Platform." Last modified 2012. https://
prod-static-ngop-pbl.s3.amazonaws.com/docs/2012GOPPlatform.pdf.

Smith, Gibson B. "Guarding the Railroad, Taming the Cossacks: The U.S. Army in Russia,
1918–1920." *Prologue* 34, no. 4 (2002). http://www.archives.gov/publications/prologue
/2002/winter/us-army-in-russia-1.html.

Stokes, Bruce. "Republicans and Democrats Sharply Divided on How Tough to Be with
Russia." Pew Research Center. Last modified June 15, 2015. http://www.pewresearch
.org/fact-tank/2015/06/15/republicans-and-democrats-sharply-divided-on-how-tough
-to-be-with-russia/.

White House. "U.S.–Russia Relations: 'Reset' Fact Sheet." Whitehouse.gov. Last modified
June 24, 2010. https://www.whitehouse.gov/the-press-office/us-russia-relations-reset
-fact-sheet.

Wofford, Taylor. "Senate Republicans Blast Obama for Russian Involvement in Syria."
Newsweek, September 30, 2015. http://www.newsweek.com/john-mccain-russia-syria
-airstrikes-378407.

Sub-Saharan Africa

At a Glance

U.S. foreign policy toward the countries of sub-Saharan Africa has been a subject of significant partisan consensus in recent years. Both Democratic and Republican administrations have supported various projects in Africa related to free trade, foreign aid (including humanitarian and military aid), public health, debt relief, and biodiversity protection. To the extent that partisan divides do exist, they tend to center around the prioritization of each of these types of programs.

Sub-Saharan Africa (SSA) is a region bounded by the Sahel (the transitional area between the Sahara to the north and the savannah region to the south). Generally, North Africa is considered, though this is a bit of a simplification, to be more similar to the Middle East given the prevalence of Arab populations and followers of the Islamic faith. Although each of these distinctions can be challenged (there are many non-Arabs in North Africa, for example), it is in keeping with U.S. foreign policy conventions to consider sub-Saharan Africa as a separate region. The Bureau of African Affairs within the U.S. State Department, for example, manages U.S. relationships with only sub-Saharan African countries. The Bureau of Near Eastern Affairs, by contrast, includes the North African states of Algeria, Egypt, Libya, Morocco, and Tunisia, along with the rest of the "traditional" Middle East.

According to many Republicans, U.S. foreign policy toward sub-Saharan Africa . . .

- Should focus on free trade over foreign aid;
- Should focus on preventing the spread of communicable diseases;
- Must place a significant emphasis on defeating various terrorist groups in Africa; and
- Must take into account the need to promote individual human rights.

According to many Democrats, U.S. foreign policy toward sub-Saharan Africa . . .

- Should focus on both free trade and foreign aid;
- Should focus on preventing the spread of communicable diseases;

- Should include provisions to protect wildlife and overall biodiversity in the region; and
- Should focus on human rights, especially those of women and girls.

Overview

During the Cold War, the United States looked at SSA as a "scorecard" for its ideological competition with the Soviet Union. The large number of newly independent countries after World War II provided opportunities for Communist gains, as several sub-Saharan African states experimented with various forms of Socialism. Most countries in the region that chose Socialism as a form of economic and political organization did so in a way that defied traditional top-down Soviet-style Socialism. Other countries, most notably perhaps Ethiopia, developed Soviet-style Communist regimes and enjoyed close relations with the Soviet Union. In the case of Angola, which descended into more than a quarter-century of civil war beginning in 1975, the Soviet Union supported one rebel group (the Popular Movement for the Liberation of Angola) with aid, troops (from Cuba), and military equipment, while the United States supported another (the National Union for the Total Independence of Angola) with aid and military equipment (while relying on South Africa as a military proxy in the conflict). During the conflict, over 30 percent of the population became displaced outside of Angola as a refugee or inside Angola as an internally displaced person. In South Africa, the United States was willing to support, sometimes directly, sometimes tacitly, the white-minority government as a hedge against Communism in the region. This supported lasted until the waning years of the Cold War (the late 1980s) when the United States government was willing to apply more pressure on South Africa to democratize.

During the 1990s, U.S. foreign policy toward SSA as a broad region was defined to a significant degree by one case of humanitarian intervention that had disastrous consequences and one case of nonintervention. In 1992 and 1993, the United States intervened directly in the humanitarian crisis unfolding in Somalia, which had fallen into a state of political anarchy and lawless violence. Humanitarian aid flows were threatened by rival warlords, especially warlord Mohamed Farah Aideed. Initially, U.S. Marines acted to protect the aid flows. Later the mission expanded to the arrest of Aideed. In October 1993, 18 Army Rangers were killed in a firefight in the Somali city of Mogadishu after the downing of a two Black Hawk helicopters in a battle with Aideed's forces. Hundreds of Somalis were also killed. In the wake of the debacle, pressure came both from within the Clinton administration and from Republicans in Congress to end the mission. By March 1994, the United States had withdrawn from Somalia. The country has remained in an active state of civil war since, with the terrorist group al-Shabab at times controlling large swaths of territory.

In part because of the tragedy in Somalia in 1993, the United States made the decision in 1994 not to intervene to stop the genocide of the Tutsi ethnic group at the hands of the Hutu ethnic group in Rwanda. In spite of knowing that genocide was likely to begin as soon as five days after the assassination of Rwandan president Juvénal Habyarimana, the United States decided that there was no compelling basis, in terms of the national interest, for U.S. intervention in Rwanda. Internal discussions declassified in 1998 indicate that portions of the State Department were reticent to use the word "genocide" with respect to events in Rwanda for fear that it would require U.S. action (National Security Archive 1994). Estimates indicate that between 600,000 and 800,000 ethnic Tutsi died during the genocide (Verpoorten 2005). Clinton subsequently called the failure to stop the genocide one of his biggest regrets. The decision not to intervene more directly in Rwanda was bipartisan, however. One key Republican, Senator Bob Dole of Kansas, agreed that there was no compelling U.S. interest that would require intervention in Rwanda.

During the presidency of Republican George W. Bush, a new consensus emerged on U.S. foreign policy toward sub-Saharan Africa. One of the principles of Bush's "compassionate conservativism" was to help individuals, as directly as possible, who exhibited true need and countries willing to use the aid responsibly. During Bush's tenure, foreign aid to Africa increased by 640 percent to about $5 billion per year (Hughes 2013). In 2003, Bush launched, with the cooperation of Congress, the President's Emergency Plan for AIDS relief (PEPFAR). The program has provided billions of dollars to fight AIDS, as well as diseases such as malaria and tuberculous, worldwide. PEPFAR has been especially active in sub-Saharan Africa, which is the region most affected by HIV/AIDS. PEPFAR has subsequently been expanded to last until at least 2018 and provide increased treatment support. The George W. Bush administration, as well as Democrats and many Republicans in Congress, supported the expansion of bilateral and multilateral debt relief to states in sub-Saharan Africa. Previous debt relief, provided under a series of programs collectively known as the Highly Indebted Poor Countries Initiative (HIPC), were expanded as part of the new Multilateral Debt Relief Initiative (MDRI). Several of the poorest and most indebted countries in the world, many of which were located in sub-Saharan Africa, had up to 100 percent of their multilateral debt forgiven. In addition, the United States extended bilateral debt relief, as part of the MDRI, to all of the countries receiving multilateral relief. The result was a significant reduction in the debt burden of countries in the region.

Another program launched during the 2000s was the African Growth and Opportunity Act (AGOA). The act, signed into law by Democratic president Bill Clinton in his closing days in office, passed the House of Representatives by a vote of 235–163, with 136 of 199 Republicans and 98 of 197 Democrats supporting the legislation (House of Representatives 1999). The vote in the Senate was more bipartisan, passing 76 to 19, with 12 Democratic and six Republican votes against (U.S. Senate 1999). Incoming president Bush also supported the bill. According to the legislation's provisions, countries acting to improve the rule of law, and respect human rights and fair labor practices were granted preferential (in most cases duty free) access to U.S. markets. A majority (as many as 40) sub-Saharan African states have been declared AGOA eligible, though some, such as the Democratic Republic of Congo and Eritrea, have subsequently lost AGOA status. AGOA, which was originally scheduled to expire in 2015, has since been extended through 2025. No SSA country, before or after AGOA, is a top-20 trading partner with the United States. Collectively, the countries of SSA account for $37 billion in total trade per year with the United States (U.S. Trade Representative 2015). This means that, even if SSA were a single country, it would not qualify as one of America's top 20 trading partners.

Republicans on U.S. Foreign Policy toward Sub-Saharan Africa

The 2016 Republican Party platform mentions Africa eight times, focusing on the sub-Saharan region. Although the Republican and Democratic Party platforms share similarities, there do appear to be differences in focus. As one might expect, the Republican Party platform begins with a focus on free market reforms, as well as the promotion of individual civil and political rights. The platform goes on to mention several of the accomplishments of the Bush era, including the development of PEPFAR and AGOA. The second part of the African subsection of the Republican platform focuses on terrorism. The platform specifically mentions Boko Haram and al-Shabaab. Boko Haram is a terrorist group, acting primarily in Nigeria, which became infamous after abducting hundreds of schoolgirls from the town of Chibok in Northern Nigeria. A portion of the group, which is partially fragmented by ideological and pragmatic disagreements, has pledged its allegiance to the Islamic State of Iraq and greater Syria (ISIS). Al-Shabaab is active primarily in southern Somalia and continues to control more territory than the combined forces of the government and the African Union (AU). Al-Shabaab is currently an affiliate of the terrorist group Al Qaeda, though ISIS has made overtures toward the group that has caused a degree of fractionalization within al-Shabaab.

U.S. foreign policy toward SSA is not a high salience issue within the realm of public opinion. As a result, polling data on policies specific to SSA is not available. It is possible, however, to find public opinion data on issues that have an impact on SSA but are not specific to the region. For example, U.S. foreign aid remains important to SSA, though Chinese aid and foreign direct investment probably play a more significant role in the development of the region. With regard to foreign aid, 70 percent of self-identified Republicans favored measures to decrease aid in one 2013 poll, though the question asked was not specific to sub-Saharan Africa (Pew Research Center 2013). In addition, a 2015 poll found that only 7 percent of Republicans within the general public believe that foreign aid to developing countries is a very effective way to achieve U.S. foreign policy goals (Chicago Council on Global Affairs 2015). Given the level consistency of actual foreign aid outcomes to SSA across both Republican and Democratic administrations, however, it is not at all clear that the partisan gap in public opinion translates into policy making, at least with regard to region-specific aid.

An issue of higher salience to the public is terrorism, though not specifically terrorism in SSA. Among Republicans, terrorist attacks by Islamic extremists against America is a particularly high-priority foreign policy issue. However, general international terrorism, including terrorism in Africa, ranks higher on the Republican threat list than does the specific threat of ISIS in countries such as Iraq, Syria, and Libya (Chicago Council on Global Affairs 2015). In fact, general international terrorism makes the list of top three threats to U.S. national interests among both Democrats and Republicans (Chicago Council on Global Affairs 2015). It is also worth noting that the most notorious terrorist groups in the SSA region are ISIS and Al Qaeda affiliates primarily acting within a specific subregion. In North Africa, where activity from the core of ISIS is more common (see Libya entry), the terrorism issue is somewhat more salient to Americans in the general public.

In 2015, AGOA was extended until 2025 as part of the Trade Preferences Extension Act of 2015. Along with AGOA, Congress extended the Generalized System of Preferences (GSP) which provides preferential market access to some of the world's poorest economies. The act passed by voice vote in the GOP-controlled House of Representatives, a procedure that is generally used when there is overwhelming bipartisan consensus on a piece of legislation. Voice votes are not recorded, so it is impossible to tell which, if any, Republicans or Democrats voted against the legislation. A previous version of the legislation passed the House by a final vote of 397–32, with 212 of 243 Republicans voting in favor (GovTrack.us 2015). Another version of the legislation, which contained provisions for trade adjustment assistance, passed by a lower margin, mainly due to the inclusion of the additional provisions, which are designed to decrease the potential negative impact of free trade agreements on some sectors of the economy. The portion of the legislation providing preferences to many African countries was popular in both the House and Senate. In the Senate, the legislation passed with only one Republican vote against.

Republicans in Congress have been critical of Democrats in general and the Obama administration in particular on their stances toward terrorism in sub-Saharan Africa. One example of such criticism occurred in 2011–2012, when the U.S. State Department was determining whether to designate Boko Haram as a Foreign Terrorist Organization (FTO), a legal designation that would require the United States to take additional action to combat the organization, especially in the area of financing. Republicans in Congress wrote a letter to then secretary of state Hillary Clinton requesting that the designation be made immediately (Cohen 2014). The State Department argued that it must conduct due diligence before making the final designation. Ultimately, Boko Haram was designated an FTO in November 2013 by Secretary of State John Kerry. Republicans have argued that the delay in making the designation was evidence of weakness, both by the Obama administration and specifically by Democratic Party presidential nominee Hillary Clinton.

Issues related to the SSA region have not played a prominent role in the 2016 presidential campaign, although Republican nominee businessman Donald Trump has argued that refugees from "dangerous regions" are not being vetted before being permitted to enter the United States. At various times, he has also called for a ban on Muslims entering the United States as refugees or immigrants, though at times his stance has appeared to soften on this issue. In August 2016, for example, Trump appeared to imply at a rally in Portland, Maine, that refugees from Somalia were responsible for an increased in crimes in the Portland area. Specifically, Trump attempted to rally the crowd by saying, "So, we've just seen many many crimes getting worse all the time and as Maine knows, a major destination for Somali refugees right? Am I right?" (Bodnar 2016). Somali community leaders in Portland staged a peaceful protest in response to the comments.

Democrats on U.S. Foreign Policy toward Sub-Saharan Africa

The 2016 Democratic platform, like its Republican counterpart, has a small subsection devoted to Africa. The platform mentions Africa seven times overall. Like Republicans, Democrats primarily focus on the desirability of trade with Africa. The Democratic Party platform adds language concerning the willingness to provide foreign assistance to African countries in addition to increasing free trade. Although both the Republican and Democratic Party platforms mention the promotion of human rights in Africa, including political rights related to democracy, the Democrats also added language related to promoting the rights of women and girls around the world. Protecting the rights of women and girls, including eliminating the sex slavery trade, is a more general theme of the Democratic Party platform. Finally, Democrats, like Republicans, used their platform to emphasize their determination to combat terrorism in Africa, including Boko Haram and al-Shabaab in SSA. Where Republican specifically mentioned the need to protect persecuted Christians in the region in their platform, however, the Democratic Party omitted any discussion of interreligious persecution by terrorist groups in the region.

Perhaps the most significant difference between the two platforms, at least in an area that relates to SSA, is on the issue of refugees. Democrats argue that the United States has a responsibility to aid refugee populations fleeing conflict around the world. Although this general platform plank is not specific to SSA, the platform does mention East African refugees in the same section of the document. The world's largest and most populous refugee camp complex is located in eastern Kenya, near the Somali border. Democrats also decry the idea of banning Muslim refugees, which would include refugees from East Africa. The Republican platform mentions not admitting refugees from areas considered "breeding grounds for terrorism" (Republican National Committee 2016). Though the Republican platform does not mention Somalia or East Africa specifically, it does mention al-Shabaab, which controls a great deal of territory in Somalia.

As mentioned previously, U.S. foreign policy related to sub-Saharan Africa is not an issue that captures general public interest. Hence, public opinion polling of Democrats on matters related to SSA is largely nonexistent. Public opinion does exist on issues indirectly related to the region, however. For example, one of the largest partisan gaps on a foreign policy issue relates to the provision of American financial aid to the world's needy. Poverty remains high despite economic growth in SSA, making this a key issue for the region. One 2013 poll found that only 25 percent of self-identified Democrats would be willing to decrease aid to the world's needy, compared to 75 percent of Republicans (Pew Research Center 2013). One-third of Democrats in the general public favor increasing aid, compared to 7 percent of Republicans. It is worth noting that neither Democrats nor Republicans are convinced of the efficacy of foreign aid as a general foreign policy tool. Only 17 percent of Democrats and 7 percent of Republicans expressed a belief that aid is a "very effective" way to achieve U.S. foreign policy goals, according to one 2015 poll (Chicago Council on Global Affairs 2015). Democrats are also more likely to favor debt relief for developing countries than are Republicans. However, since the provision of debt relief often falls under the foreign aid budget, it is difficult to tease out distinct patterns in public opinion on this topic. The same is true of the refugee issue. Current opinion polling focuses on refugees from Syria, where Democrats have demonstrated more willingness to admit refugees from Syria than have Republicans.

Within Congress, Democrats, like Republicans, overwhelmingly favored the extension of AGOA until 2025. No Democrats voted against the extension in the Senate. In the House of Representatives, final passage of the act occurred by voice vote. The previous iteration of the legislation mentioned above passed the House with all but one Democrat. A second piece of bipartisan legislation, signed by the president in 2016, was the Electrify Africa Act of 2015. The act passed unanimously in both the House and Senate. The Electrify Africa Act is a policy-setting act. As such, it does not require the provision of additional aid but sets a general direction for U.S. foreign policy. In this case, the act makes it the official policy of the United States to "partner, consult and coordinate" with African states to provide access to power services to millions of SSA residents who lack access (S. 152 2016). The act avoids contentious issues that may well have drawn "nay" votes, such as pronouncements about renewable energy and climate change.

President Obama, as well as former secretary of state and Democratic presidential nominee Hillary Clinton, have largely agreed with Republicans on trade and aid issues related to Africa. Both parties have praised PEPFAR and AGOA, for example. There is a difference in focus on some issues, however. For example, Clinton has expressed support for Obama administration initiatives designed to limit trophy hunting by Americans in Africa, especially as it relates to protected species. Clinton has repeatedly denounced Trump's call for a ban on admitting refugees from majority-Muslim countries, including those in sub-Saharan Africa. Clinton has argued that the refugee admissions process already takes nearly two years, during which comprehensive vetting already takes place. Clinton has also been generally more supportive of foreign aid than has Trump, though this issue did not come up for debate with any regularity during the 2016 election cycle. With regard to most aspects of U.S. foreign policy toward SSA, with the possible exception of refugee policy, it is unlikely that a Clinton or a Trump presidency would diverge significantly in terms of actual outcomes.

Further Reading

Bodnar, Marissa. "Somali Community Responds to Trump's Comments at Rally." wgme.com. Last modified August 5, 2016. wgme.com/news/local/somali-community-responds-to -trumps-comments-at-rally.

Chicago Council on Global Affairs. "America Divided: Political Partisanship and US Foreign Policy." Last modified 2015. http://www.thechicagocouncil.org/sites/default/files /CCGA_PublicSurvey2015.pdf.

Cohen, Tom. "Clinton's Handling of Boko Haram Questioned." CNN. Last modified May 9, 2014. http://www.cnn.com/2014/05/08/politics/clinton-boko-haram/.

GovTrack.us. "H.R. 1295: Trade Preferences Extension Act of 2015." Last modified June 11, 2015. https://www.govtrack.us/congress/votes/114-2015/h345.

GovTrack.us. Text of S. 2152: Electrify Africa Act of 2015 (Passed Congress/Enrolled Bill Version). GovTrack.us, 2016. https://www.govtrack.us/congress/bills/114/s2152/text.

Hughes, Dana. "George W. Bush's Legacy on Africa Wins Praise, Even from Foes." ABC News. Last modified April 26, 2013. http://abcnews.go.com/blogs/politics/2013/04/george-w -bushs-legacy-on-africa-wins-praise-even-from-foes/.

National Security Archive. "Discussion Paper: Rwanda." Last modified May 4, 1994. http:// nsarchive.gwu.edu/NSAEBB/NSAEBB53/rw050194.pdf.

Office of the Clerk of the U.S. House of Representatives. "Final Vote Results for Roll Call 307." Last modified July 16, 1999. http://clerk.house.gov/evs/1999/roll307.xml.

Pew Research Center. "Wide Partisan Gap Exists over U.S. Aid to World's Needy." Last modified March 13, 2013. http://www.pewresearch.org/daily-number/wide-partisan -gap-exists-over-u-s-aid-to-worlds-needy/.

Republican National Committee. "Republican Platform 2016." Last modified 2016. https:// prod-static-ngop-pbl.s3.amazonaws.com/media/documents/DRAFT_12_FINAL[1] -ben_1468872234.pdf.

U.S. Senate. "U.S. Senate: Roll Call Vote 353." Last modified November 13, 1999. http:// www.senate.gov/legislative/LIS/roll_call_lists/roll_call_vote_cfm.cfm?congress=106 &session=1&vote=00353.

U.S. Trade Representative. "Africa." Last modified 2015. https://ustr.gov/countries-regions /africa.

Verpoorten, Marijke. "The Death Toll of the Rwandan Genocide: A Detailed Analysis for Gikongoro Province." *Population* (English Edition) 60, no. 4 (2005), 401–439. doi:10 .3917/popu.504.0401.

Syria

At a Glance

Significant tensions between the United States and Syria predate the Arab Spring protests that erupted in the latter country in 2011. This uprising against the authoritarian, repressive rule of President Bashar al-Assad ultimately escalated into civil war and the collapse of central authority in the country. Under the Obama administration, the official policy of the United States toward Syria is to call for the ouster of President Bashar al-Assad as part of the effort to defeat the Islamic State of Iraq and the Levant (ISIS/ISIL). The main partisan divide concerning U.S. foreign policy toward Syria relates to how best to effect regime change, as well as how to effectively bring an end to the Syria civil war on terms that are beneficial to the United States and its allies.

According to many Democrats, U.S. foreign policy toward Syria . . .

- Should be crafted with a goal of replacing President Assad;
- Should not include the involvement of U.S. ground troops with the exception of Special Operations forces;
- Should be based on supporting democratic opposition elements within the Syrian resistance;
- Must include steps, including airstrikes, to target areas held by ISIS; and
- Should include a willingness to accept Syrian refugees into the United States.

According to many Republicans, U.S. foreign policy toward Syria . . .

- Should be crafted with a goal of replacing President Assad;
- Should include the option of sending more ground troops into Syria, especially to combat ISIS;
- Should include a moratorium on accepting Syrian refugees into the United States; and
- Should include additional measures that restrict the Syrian regime's movement, including a no-fly zone.

———————

Overview

Syria and the United States established diplomatic relations in 1944, three years after Syria declared independence from France. Syria officially became an independent republic after the last French troops left the country in 1946. In 1957, Syria severed its diplomatic relationship with the United States after the United Kingdom and the United States launched a failed coup and assassination attempt on Syrian leadership. Both the United Kingdom and the United States believed that Syria was threatening oil supplies to the United States and Europe. The plan was never implemented for a variety of reasons. In 1967, Syria severed its relationship with the United States a second time. On this occasion, the Six-Day War between Israel and several Arab countries, including Syria, was the catalyst behind the decision. Although the United States did not participate in the war, it had begun to sell offensive weapons to Israel in 1965–1966 (Office of the Historian n.d.). Syria, which lost the Golan Heights in the conflict, placed part of the blame on the United States for its support of Israel. Diplomatic relations were restored between the United States and Syria in 1974.

Syria has been on the U.S. state sponsors of terrorism list since its inception in 1979, causing further tension between the two countries. Syrian support for Hezbollah, a U.S. designated terrorist group active in the Middle East, is a key reason for this designation, which carries with it mandatory sanctions (U.S. Department of State Country Reports on Terrorism 2015). For its part, Syria views Hezbollah as a liberation movement and a critical part of its efforts to counter Israeli and other Western influence in the region. Syria arms Hezbollah and, when it is unable to do so, acts as a conduit for Iranian arms transfers to Hezbollah in Lebanon, where the organization is a powerful political force.

During the 1990s and early 2000s, U.S.–Syrian relations improved for a time. Syria supported the Arab coalition that assisted in the U.S.-led response to the Iraqi invasion of Kuwait. The United States supported Syria in its attempts to end the Lebanese civil war via the so-called Taif Accord as well. Under the terms of this 1989 agreement, Syria would end its military involvement in Lebanon but remain an important presence in Lebanese politics. Syria also participated in peace talks with Israel cosponsored by the United States, further improving relations. After 9/11, Syria cooperated for a time with the United States in its attempts to combat global terrorism. This cooperation included sharing intelligence, which, according to the United States, was actionable and helped stop planned terrorist attacks.

Cooperation between the United States and Syria, however, was short-lived. Syria opposed the U.S. invasion of Iraq in 2003. Syria, as a nonpermanent member of the United Nations Security Council at the time, had supported Security Council Resolution 1441, which gave Iraq a "final opportunity" to comply with its previous resolutions (United Nations Security Council 2002). Syria, however, did not believe that the Resolution 1441 provided an automatic trigger for the invasion of Iraq in the event of noncompliance and favored allowing the weapons inspection process to play out. The United States accused Syria of becoming a major transit point for foreign fighters entering Iraq after the war began as well as developing weapons of mass destruction and supporting terrorism in Lebanon and against Israel (U.S. Department of State Bureau of Near Eastern Affairs 2014). Syria was also condemned by the administration of President George W. Bush for keeping troops in Lebanon in violation of terms of the Taif Accord. In response to these various transgressions, Congress passed and President Bush signed the Syrian Accountability and Lebanese Sovereignty Restoration Act (SALSRA) in 2003. SALSRA passed the House and Senate with only four nay votes in each chamber.

In 2007, Israel launched an airstrike against a suspected nuclear test facility in Syria. The United States initially did not comment on the strike, but later accused North Korea of providing technical assistance to Syria.

During President Obama's first term, the United States attempted limited rapprochement with Syria. Diplomatic relations were reinitiated, and the U.S. government sent an envoy to Syria. However, in 2011, as the protests associated with the Arab Spring began to escalate in Syria, the Obama administration position changed. Initially hesitant to condemn the government crackdown, which included arrests and the shooting death of four Syrians, the United States reevaluated its position as conditions worsened. Later in 2011, the United States recalled its ambassador both in protest and amid concerns that the Syrian government would not ensure the safety of diplomatic personnel. It is also at this point that the United States began to call for Assad to step down. The United States completely suspended diplomatic relations with Syria in 2014. Over time, Syria continued to descend into a civil war that has taken over 250,000 lives and has created nearly 13 million refugees and internally displaced persons.

As Syria has fallen into chaos, radical Islamist forces, most notably ISIS, have filled portions of the vacuum. Initially, the United States considered arming more moderate rebels opposing the Assad regime. The United States did provide limited humanitarian supplies and military gear in moderate rebel areas. However, the decision to arm and train rebels was postponed until 2014. The year 2014 also marked the beginning of U.S. airstrikes against ISIS positions in Syria. It is, therefore, a counterfactual question whether arming rebels earlier could have prevented the emergence of ISIS in Syria. ISIS emerged out of Al Qaeda Iraq in a complex process that included the formation of an Al Qaeda branch in Syria, called the al-Nusra front. Ultimately, ISIS broke from both al-Nusra and Al Qaeda and began referring to itself as the Islamic State of Syria and Iraq. The acronym ISIL, which is often used by the State Department and President Obama when referring to the group, stands for the Islamic State of Iraq and the Levant. The Levant is a term referring to a large crescent in the Eastern Mediterranean including parts of Israel, Jordan, Lebanon, and Syria. As of 2016, ISIS controls a large, but somewhat shrinking area of Eastern Syria and parts of Northern Iraq.

Democrats on U.S. Relations with Syria

When the last Democratic Party platform was adopted in 2012, it was not at all clear that Islamist forces would become so powerful in Syria or that the government would employ chemical weapons against civilians as part of Assad's efforts to crush the insurrection against his regime. As a result, the platform refers primarily to the need for Assad to step down and for the United States to provide assistance to help unify the various (nonterrorist) rebel groups. The type of assistance is not specified. The platform also points out that Democrats have been consistent in their criticism of Russian actions to support the Assad regime (Democratic National Committee 2012). Although the platform does mention Al Qaeda affiliates, it does not mention their operations in Syria, which at the time were not as widespread. The platform also does not mention ISIS, which was not yet separated from Al Qaeda, though it was operating independently at times.

As one might expect, a majority of Democrats defend President Obama's handling of the situation in Syria. Fifty-seven percent of self-identified Democrats believe that military operations are going well (Agiesta 2015). Only 19 percent of Republicans have a similar belief. In addition, only 36 percent of Democrats believe the ground troops should be used in Syria in the fight against ISIS. Nearly 70 percent of Republicans favor the use of ground troops. It is worth nothing that at the time the poll was taken in 2015 the issue of ISIS had risen to the forefront of public concern. At the point where U.S. ground troops might have been employed in support of moderate rebel groups, majorities within both parties opposed the deployment of U.S. troops. In fact, in 2013, as the Obama administration advanced the case for airstrikes against Syria in response to the use of chemical weapons, majorities in both parties opposed that option (Steinhauser and Helton 2013). As late as 2014, only 17 percent of the general public favored the use of ground troops in Syria (Smeltz and Daalder 2014).

President Obama has developed a variety of responses to the crisis unfolding in Syria. In 2012, the president was primarily focused on moderate resistance to the Assad regime. At this point, Obama, supported by many congressional Democrats and some Republicans, threatened the use of military force in the event that Syria used chemical weapons against the civilian population. This position became known as Obama's "red line" on Syria. In August 2013, the Syrian government used chemical weapons in an attack near the capital. The president eventually sought an Authorization for the Use of Military Force (AUMF) against Syria. However, opposition to the AUMF, which included Democrats leery or U.S. involvement in another war in the Middle East, led the president, with the support of Democratic Senate leadership, to postpone the vote (Davis 2013). Later, in 2013, Syria agreed to give up its chemical weapons after a series of negotiations with Russia. In a 2016 interview with Jeffrey Goldberg of the *Atlantic,* Obama defended what he characterized as a realistic approach to foreign policy that departs from the "Washington Playbook." Specifically, with regard to the U.S. decision not to launch airstrikes against Syria in response to Syria's use of chemical weapons against its own population, Obama argued that:

> "I'm very proud of this moment," he told me. "The overwhelming weight of conventional wisdom and the machinery of our national-security apparatus had gone fairly far. The perception was that my credibility was at stake, that America's credibility was at stake. And so for me to press the pause button at that moment, I knew, would cost me politically. And the fact that I was able to pull back from the immediate pressures and think through in my own mind what was in America's interest, not only with respect to Syria but also with respect to our democracy, was as tough a decision as I've made—and I believe ultimately it was the right decision to make." (Goldberg 2016)

The Obama administration has also attempted arming rebel groups in Syria, with varying degrees of support and little success. The train and equip program, as it is called, went into effect in 2013, but was not formally approved by Congress until 2014. One of the primary reasons for the delay between the recognition of the need to provide support for moderate rebels in Syria and the actual provision of assistance were divisions between the president and his advisers. The head of the CIA at the time, David Petraeus, as well as then secretary of state Hillary Clinton, favored arming the rebels. Obama, as well as public opinion, were against such measures (McKelvey 2015). By the time the decision was made to arm the rebels, many had already been killed, fled to other countries within Syria, or joined with ISIS or other radical Islamist groups fighting against Assad.

Divisions within the Democratic Party over the proper course of action in Syria have been significant. For example, the train and equip resolution passed the House by a vote of 273–156. Eighty-five Democrats supported the legislation, while 71 voted against it. Democratic leadership, especially Minority Leader Nancy Pelosi, favored the provision to arm Syrian rebels, claiming that the decision was "hard, but necessary" (Roll Call 2014). Several antiwar Democrats voted against the amendment that allowed continued funding of the program over concerns that arming the rebels would be a prelude to further U.S. involvement in another war in the Middle East. Representative Jackie Speier of California asserted that "we should be frank with ourselves and the American people. We are not facing a limited engagement, but a new war that will only escalate" (Marcos 2014). A similar debate occurred in the Senate, where the measure passed by a vote of 78–22. Senate leadership, as well as Democrats likely to be vulnerable in the 2014 midterm elections, tended to support the train and equip program, while antiwar Democrats warned that arming the rebels might create a slippery slope toward full U.S. military involvement.

Divisions within the Democratic Party over this issue were reflected in the differing perspectives of the two leading candidates for the Democratic presidential nomination in 2016. During the campaign, both candidates emphasized their belief that ISIS is a threat to U.S. interests. Both candidates also supported the idea

Two Prominent Democrats Clash over Arming and Training Syrian Rebels

The 2014 vote in the Senate and the House of Representatives to arm and train members of the Syrian resistance created a set of interesting and rare coalitions. One interesting dichotomy was between then Senate majority leader Harry Reid and Massachusetts senator Elizabeth Warren. Reid spoke out in favor of the authorization:

> Today, Democrats and Republicans spoke with one voice to tell the ISIS terrorists: we will find you and destroy you. The Senate has passed a strong bill to arm and train vetted Syrian opposition fighters as part of the President's strategy to destroy ISIS without repeating the mistakes of the past in the Middle East. America will lead a coalition that includes our friends and allies in European and Arab nations in a targeted, strategic mission to destroy ISIS. American air strikes will support local forces who will fight for their own countries. As the President made clear, it is up to the people of Iraq, Syria, and the region to stand up to protect their homes and families against these cruel killers.

Warren countered:

> I am deeply concerned by the rise of ISIS, and I support a strong, coordinated response, but I am not convinced that the current proposal to train and equip Syrian forces adequately advances our interests. After detailed briefings, I remain concerned that our weapons, our funding, and our support may end up in the hands of people who threaten the United States—and even if we could guarantee that our support goes to the right people, I remain unconvinced that training and equipping these forces will be effective in pushing back ISIS. I do not want America to be dragged into another ground war in the Middle East, and it is time for those nations in the region that are most immediately affected by the rise of ISIS to step up and play a leading role in this fight. Therefore, at this time, I cannot support funding for this specific action.

Sources:

Berman, Russell. "Dissecting the 5 Most Important Votes in Congress on Obama's ISIS Plan." The Wire. Last modified September 20, 2014. http://www.thewire.com/politics/2014/09/the-most-notable-votes-in-congress-on-obamas-isis-plan/380508/.

Reid, Harry. "Reid Statement on Bipartisan Senate Vote to Degrade ISIS in Syria." U.S. Senate Democratic Leader Harry Reid. Last modified September 18, 2014. http://www.reid.senate.gov/press_releases/2014-18-09-reid-statement-on-bipartisan-senate-vote-to-degrade-isis-in-syria#.Vv2pNNIrLIU.

of the United States accepting refugees from the conflict in Syria. However, the candidates diverged sharply on potential solutions to the crisis. Hillary Clinton supported the idea of arming moderate Syrian rebels at the early stages of the proposal. Clinton also supported the use of U.S. Special Forces in Syria, mainly in an effort to prevent the spread of ISIS. By contrast, Senator Sanders voted against the

Senate version of the bill providing funding to the rebels. Sanders also opposed the use of U.S. Special Forces, arguing that the United States needs instead to cultivate cooperation with key states such as Turkey in order to slow the spread of ISIS. Sanders argued that the wealthy Persian Gulf states, as well as Saudi Arabia, have not done enough to help stabilize Syria or fight ISIS.

Republicans on U.S. Relations with Syria

Much of the Republican critique of the Obama administration response to the violence and political upheaval in Syria focuses on the depth, pace, and breadth of the response. In reality, most of the proposals advanced by Republicans have been employed in Syria by the administration. However, Republicans contend that the administration's unwillingness to act quickly and decisively doomed the U.S. effort. As was the case with the Democratic Party, the 2012 platform does not dwell on Syria. The one mention of the conflict in Syria relates to Republican support for removal of President Assad. The platform criticizes President Obama's overall approach to terrorism, arguing that climate change is a greater priority to Democrats than is the global war on terror (Republican National Committee 2012).

Within the realm of public opinion, self-identified Republicans tend to display more "hawkish" tendencies with regard to the situation in Syria than do Democrats. They also are more likely, as noted above, to be critical of the president's policies in Syria and the broader Middle East. Although majorities of both parties believe that Islamic extremist groups in Iraq and Syria are a critical threat, one 2015 poll found a 12 percentage point gap between Democrats, 61 percent of whom view these groups as a critical threat, and Republicans, 73 percent of whom make the same threat level identification (Chicago Council on Global Affairs 2015). On the issue of Syrian refugees, Republicans are far less likely to support plans by President Obama to allow around 10,000 asylum-seekers from Syria resettle in the United States. Eighty-four percent of self-identified Republicans oppose the plan according to a poll by Gallup, while 57 percent of Democrats support the plan (Jones 2015). Overall, the general public falls closer to the Republican view, with 60 percent of the population opposing current Syrian refugee resettlement priorities.

Republicans in Congress have also criticized Democratic Party policies related to Syria. For example, Senator John McCain claimed that the Obama administration had not acted decisively enough to ensure the ouster of President Assad. U.S. weakness, McCain and other Republicans claim, opened a vacuum in the region that has been filled by Russia, which has used its power to bolster the regime. McCain argued that Putin "perceives the administration's inaction and caution as weakness, and he is taking full advantage" (Wofford 2015). Congressional Republicans have also charged that Obama lacks a comprehensive strategy for resolving the conflict in Syria on terms acceptable to the United States. In August 2014, President Obama remarked that it would be premature to comment on specific measures to be taken in Syria because "we don't have a strategy yet" (Boyer 2014).

Two Prominent Republican Senators Differ on Arming and Training Syrian Rebels

When the Senate voted on whether to arm and train Syrian rebels seeking to topple the Assad regime and keep ISIS from gaining power, conservative Republican senators Marco Rubio and Ted Cruz voted on opposite sides of the issue. Senator Rubio argued in favor of funding the rebels, asserting that

> first and foremost, we need to move now to degrade ISIS's capabilities. The President's decision to send 300 advisers to Iraq is a good first step, but their ability to deter ISIS will be limited unless we eventually engage in airstrikes to target their leaders as well as the supply lines that they use to transfer weapons and fighters between Syria and Iraq. We know where these supply lines are, we should not hesitate to halt the ISIS resupply to their strongholds in Anbar, Ninawa and Salah ad-Din . . . We need to begin to tackle the root causes of the problem in Syria by overtly arming the moderate Syrian rebels that are fighting ISIS in that country even as we simultaneously tackle the challenge they currently pose to Iraq.

Senator Cruz made the case against arming the rebels. He asserted that before agreeing to any intervention plan, Obama needed to explain to his satisfaction:

- Why aiding the Syrian rebels is now worth our intervention when it wasn't two years ago.
- How he has established which rebels are the appropriate recipients of this support and how this very limited support will make a material difference in Syria.
- How his team is proactively planning to keep Syria's chemical weapons out of the hands of either Hezbollah or Al Qaeda.

Sources:

Cruz, Ted. "Sen. Cruz Opposes Arming Syrian Rebels, Calls for Securing Syrian Chemical Weapons." U.S. Senator for Texas. Last modified June 20, 2013. http://www.cruz.senate .gov/?p=press_release&id=101.

Rubio, Marco. "Press Releases—U.S. Senator for Florida, Marco Rubio." Marco Rubio: U.S. Senator for Florida. Last modified July 27, 2014. http://www.rubio.senate.gov/public/index .cfm/press-releases?ID=07c08d76-2188-46ab-a315-16f0deef3c5e.

Republicans seized on the comment in an attempt to demonstrate poor handling of the situation in Syria by the administration, especially on issues related to combating ISIS. When the president did request authorization to use military force in Syria, Republicans, including House Speaker John Boehner, advanced the argument that the request was so narrow as to not provide the president with the tools necessary to implement a strategy. To date, there has been no AUMF for Syria.

Like their counterparts across the aisle, though, congressional Republicans have been wracked with a high degree of intraparty discord on the Syria issue. On the

House of Representatives vote on authorization of the train and equip program, 71 of 230 Republicans voted "nay." Some Republicans voted no out of concern that the authorization would not go far enough in weakening the Assad regime or the Islamic State. Others believed that arming remnants of the Free Syrian Army, the main bastion of moderate resistance to the Assad government, would be a mistake. Republican representative Duncan Hunter of California, for instance, expressed concerns that the Free Syrian Army had also been infiltrated by radicals, and that arming them would do little to counter the strength of ISIS. Similar divisions manifested themselves in the Senate, where 11 Republicans joined 11 Democrats to vote unsuccessfully against the measure.

During the 2016 Republican presidential primary, eventual GOP nominee Donald Trump argued in favor of a ban on all Syrian refugees, and all Muslims in general, on entering the United States, arguing that Syrian refugees are a "Trojan Horse" (Kopan 2015). Trump also did not directly oppose Russia's intervention in Syria, arguing that Russia also has an interest in destroying ISIS, which is a desirable outcome even if it means that Assad remains in power (the preferred Russian political outcome).

Further Reading

Agiesta, Jennifer. "Poll: Most Say Send Ground Troops to Fight ISIS Politics.com." CNN. Last modified December 7, 2015. http://www.cnn.com/2015/12/06/politics/isis-obama -poll/.

Boyer, Dave. "Obama Confesses: 'We Don't Have a Strategy Yet' for Dealing with Islamic State." *Washington Times*. Last modified August 28, 2014. http://www.washingtontimes.com /news/2014/aug/28/obama-admits-isil-dilemma-we-dont-have-strategy-ye/?page=all.

Chicago Council on Global Affairs. "America Divided: Political Partisanship and US Foreign Policy." Last modified 2015. http://www.thechicagocouncil.org/sites/default/files /CCGA_PublicSurvey2015.pdf.

Davis, Susan. "Senate Delays Syria Vote as Obama Loses Momentum." *USA Today*. Last modified September 10, 2013. http://www.usatoday.com/story/news/politics/2013/09/09 /obama-congress-syria-vote-in-doubt/2788597/.

Democratic National Committee. "2012 Democratic Platform." Last modified 2012. https:// www.democrats.org/party-platform.

Fenton, Ben. "Macmillan Backed Syria Assassination Plot." *The Guardian*. Last modified September 26, 2003. http://www.theguardian.com/politics/2003/sep/27/uk.syria1.

Goldberg, Jeffrey. "The Obama Doctrine: The U.S. President Talks through His Hardest Decisions about America's Role in the World." *The Atlantic*. Last modified April 2016. http://www.theatlantic.com/magazine/archive/2016/04/the-obama-doctrine/471525/.

Jones, Jeffrey M. "Americans Again Opposed to Taking in Refugees." Gallup.com. Last modified November 23, 2015. http://www.gallup.com/poll/186866/americans-again -opposed-taking-refugees.aspx.

Kopan, Tal. "Donald Trump: Syrian Refugees a 'Trojan Horse.'" CNN. Last modified November 16, 2015. http://www.cnn.com/2015/11/16/politics/donald-trump-syrian-refugees/.

Marcos, Christina. "85 Democrats Buck Obama in ISIS Vote." *The Hill*. Last modified September 17, 2014. http://thehill.com/blogs/floor-action/house/218102-85-democrats -buck-obama-on-syria.

McKelvey, Tara. "Arming Syrian Rebels: Where the US Went Wrong." BBC News. Last modified October 10, 2015. http://www.bbc.com/news/magazine-33997408.

Newsweek. "Senate Republicans Blast Obama for Russian Involvement in Syria." Last modified September 30, 2015. http://www.newsweek.com/john-mccain-russia-syria-airstrikes-378407.

Office of the Historian. "The 1967 Arab-Israeli War—1961–1968—Milestones." U.S. Department of State. Accessed March 30, 2016. .

Republican National Committee. "2012 Republican Platform." Last modified 2012. https://prod-static-ngop-pbl.s3.amazonaws.com/docs/2012GOPPlatform.pdf.

Roll Call. "House Votes to Arm Syrian Rebels; CR Passes." Last modified September 17, 2014. http://www.rollcall.com/news/house-votes-to-arm-syrian-rebels-passes-cr.

Smeltz, Dina, and Ivo Daalder. "Foreign Policy in the Age of Retrenchment." Chicago Council on Global Affairs. Last modified 2014. http://www.thechicagocouncil.org/sites/default/files/2014_CCS_Report_1.pdf.

Steinhauser, Paul, and John Helton. "CNN Poll: Public against Syria Strike Resolution." CNN. Last modified September 9, 2013. http://www.cnn.com/2013/09/09/politics/syria-poll-main/.

United Nations Security Council. *S/RES/1441 (2002)*, 2002. http://www.un.org/Depts/unmovic/documents/1441.pdf.

U.S. Department of State Bureau of Near Eastern Affairs. "U.S. Relations with Syria." Last modified March 20, 2014. http://www.state.gov/r/pa/ei/bgn/3580.htm.

U.S. Department of State. "Country Reports on Terrorism 2014." Last modified 2015. http://www.state.gov/documents/organization/239631.pdf.

Wofford, Taylor. "Senate Republicans Blast Obama for Russian Involvement in Syria." *Newsweek*. Last modified September 30, 2015. http://www.newsweek.com/john-mccain-russia-syria-airstrikes-378407.

Terrorism

At a Glance

Developing a comprehensive response to the threat of international terrorism has been a top U.S. foreign policy priority since well before the terrorist attacks of September 11, 2001. As both a global hegemon and a relatively permeable society, the United States is potentially vulnerable to terrorist attacks against its people and interests both at home and abroad. For much of U.S. foreign policy history, the perceived necessity of a unified national response to the threat of terrorism has contributed to relative comity between the Republican and Democratic parties. It is also the case that, for most of U.S. history, terrorism was not at the top of the country's foreign policy agenda. The attacks of 9/11 instantly elevated countering terrorism to priority one. The immediate reaction to the attacks was largely nonpartisan. Since then, however, the length and controversial nature of the wars in Iraq and Afghanistan, Al Qaeda's relative durability, even in its diminished form, the rise of the Islamic State, and differences over the appropriate balance between counterterrorism and protection of basic civil liberties have all combined to provide fertile ground for the development of a more significant partisan divide.

According to many Republicans . . .

- Counterterrorism policy should include the willingness to use overwhelming military force where appropriate;
- The threat of terrorism is an issue as important as domestic issues such as the economy;
- Strong domestic surveillance to combat terrorism is necessary; and
- Budget cuts to the military have decreased the ability of the United States to respond to the threat of terrorism.

According to many Democrats . . .

- Putting "boots on the ground" to combat terrorism is generally an unsound policy;
- Domestic surveillance programs designed to stop terrorism must be placed under more strict control in order to protect civil liberties;

- The U.S. military and national intelligence agencies have plenty of funding to address the threat of international terrorism; and
- Islam is no more likely than other religions to promote terrorism and political violence.

Overview

The initial reaction to the 9/11 attacks in the United States was highly aggressive, broad, and largely bipartisan. The Authorization for Use of Military Force (AUMF) requested by Republican president George W. Bush and resoundingly approved by Congress gave him the authority to use all necessary and appropriate force against those responsible for 9/11, or any entity that harbored them. The AUMF vote passed with no votes against in the Senate and a single vote, by Democratic representative Barbara Lee, against in the House of Representatives. At the time, Lee argued that the AUMF would become "a blank check for the President to wage limitless war at anytime, anywhere, for any reason, in perpetuity" (Lee 2014). Ultimately, the first AUMF became the basis for the U.S. invasion of Afghanistan, carried out in cooperation with coalition forces in October 2011.

October 2001 also marked passage of USA Patriot Act. The Patriot Act provided the national government with increased authority and a streamlined process for intercepting communications, including roving surveillance. Civil libertarians expressed concern that the Patriot Act would increase the ability of the government to monitor individual communications, including those concerning millions of innocent U.S. citizens, without effective oversight. Proponents argued that the measures were necessary to improve intelligence collection and break down barriers to information sharing between government agencies. The Patriot Act passed the Senate overwhelmingly, with the only no vote cast by Russ Feingold, a Democrat from Wisconsin. Feingold argued that the bill was a classic case of sacrificing basic constitutionally protected civil liberties in response to war.

In the House of Representatives, the Patriot Act also passed easily, but by a somewhat more partisan vote. Though a majority of Democrats and Republicans supported the bill in the House, 62 Democratic representatives voted against the Patriot Act. Mark Udall of Colorado, for example, argued that its surveillance measures were so sweeping that they would unacceptably compromise the privacy of many Americans. Ron Paul, a prominent libertarian voice within the Republican Party, was one of only three House Republicans to vote against the bill. Overall, the vast majority of no votes came from Democrats concerned with civil liberties issues. Ultimately, the Patriot Act quickly passed Congress under a procedure called suspension of the rules, which is generally designed to quickly pass ceremonial or other noncontroversial bills. Bills passed under suspension must pass by a two-thirds vote in both chambers of Congress.

The 2001 AUMF and the War in Afghanistan

Congress is often known for acting slowly, even in times of crisis. The issuance of the Authorization for the Use of Military Force (AUMF) in Afghanistan is a clear exception to this rule. Passed only seven days after 9/11, the AUMF provides sweeping authority for the invasion of Afghanistan. This sweeping authority is contained in Section 2(a) of the legislation, which reads:

IN GENERAL.—That the President is authorized to use all necessary and appropriate force against those nations, organizations, or persons he determines planned, authorized, committed, or aided the terrorist attacks that occurred on September 11, 2001, or harbored such organizations or persons, in order to prevent any future acts of international terrorism against the United States by such nations, organizations or persons. (Public Law 107-40)

It did not take long for President Bush to exercise the broad authority contained in the AUMF. By the end of September, U.S. Special Forces units had successfully entered Afghanistan. Full-scale military operations began on October 7. Few would have imagined at the time that the United States would still have combat troops in Afghanistan in 2016, long after the death of Osama bin Laden.

Source:

"PUBLIC LAW 107–40." U.S. Government Publishing Office. Last modified September 18, 2001. https://www.gpo.gov/fdsys/pkg/PLAW-107publ40/pdf/PLAW-107publ40.pdf.

The Homeland Security Act of 2002 is another example of a piece of legislation that enjoyed greater bipartisan support in the Senate than in the House of Representatives. The purpose of the act was to comprehensively reform U.S. counterterrorism policy by consolidating many counterterrorism functions within a single agency, the Department of Homeland Security (DHS). In the Senate, the Homeland Security Act passed with majorities of both Republicans and Democrats supporting the legislation. In the House of Representatives, however, a majority of Republicans supported the bill, while a majority of Democrats opposed it. One reason for Democratic Party opposition concerned labor rights. Many federal employees are part of a union, allowing them to bargain collectively for wages and benefits. The Homeland Security Act stripped DHS employees of union protections in certain cases and gave the president increased hiring and firing authority over DHS employees. Critics of Democrats who voted against the legislation argued that union activity would serve to compromise the mission of the DHS by reducing its efficiency and ability to react quickly to new information. Ultimately, 120 Democrats voted against the Homeland Security Act, while 88 Democrats supported it. Only 10 Republicans opposed that act, and it passed by a vote of 295–132 in the House (Independent Representatives account for the discrepancy in the totals).

On March 20, 2003, the United States launched Operation Iraqi Freedom, formally beginning the invasion of Iraq. The George W. Bush administration argued that Iraq was developing weapons of mass destruction, which might find their way into the hands of terrorists, including those in Al Qaeda. The Bush administration also asserted that the Iraqi government could be linked to Al Qaeda through a terrorist known as Abu Musab al-Zarqawi. The AUMF for Iraq was much more contentious than was the AUMF for Afghanistan. In the Senate, a majority of Democrats and Republicans supported the resolution. However, 21 Democrats and one Republican voted against the measure. In the House of Representatives, the results were more partisan still. A majority of Democrats voted against the AUMF, while a majority of Republicans voted for it. As was the case with the Patriot Act and the Homeland Security Act, Republicans in the House and Senate were more unified than their Democratic counterparts. With regard to the Iraqi AUMF, 81 Democrats voted with the Republicans in favor of the resolution while only six Republicans voted with the Democrats against the resolution. Although support for the war in Iraq, as well as the war in Afghanistan, fell over time, the basic partisan division has remained.

The overall trend on post-9/11 partisanship related to terrorism is clear, even if it is not universal. First, Republicans tend to be more united on issues related to terrorism than do Democrats. Second, Senators have generally been more permissive of the instruments and measures, including military measures, used to combat terrorism than have members of the House of Representatives. Third, Democrats are often more divided in the House of Representatives with respect to their position on counterterrorism policy than are Democrats in the Senate. These initial post-9/11 partisan trends have carried over into the current counterterrorism era, defined at least in part by the rise of the Islamic State of Iraq and Syria (ISIS).

Republicans on U.S. Terrorism Policy

The 2012 Republican Party platform mentioned terrorism ten times. One of the central arguments in the platform is that the Democrats, especially President Obama, are "leading from behind" on terrorism as exemplified by their support for cuts in the defense budget (Republican National Committee 2012). It is worth noting that the budget compromise between the president and congressional leaders in 2015 restored all but $5 billion (of over $600 billion) in defense spending. The Republican Party platform also referred to Cuba as a state sponsor of terror and was critical of the steps taken by the Obama administration to relax some restrictions on travel and remittances to Cuba. Republican criticism of the Obama administration's Cuba policy surged again after Obama and Cuban President Raul Castro announced in December 2014 an agreement to move toward full normalization of relations. As part of this process, Cuba was formally removed from the U.S. government's state-sponsors of terrorism list in May 2015.

The Republican Party has also been highly critical of the Obama administration's handling of the rise of ISIS, the terrorist group that has at least partially replaced Al Qaeda as the top terrorism-related security concern. As ISIS rose to prominence after separating from Al Qaeda (ISIS was originally an Al Qaeda affiliate in Iraq), Obama referred to ISIS as Al Qaeda's jayvee team in early 2014. The implication to most observers was that at least at that time, Obama felt that ISIS was not as significant a threat as Al Qaeda. In 2014, ISIS beheaded two American journalists, continued its expansion into Syria, and took the major Iraqi city of Fallujah. The Republican National Committee argued that Obama's statement, coupled with what it described as a lack of a comprehensive strategy to defeat ISIS, was a source of significant concern (Republican National Committee 2012). The RNC has also asserted that the Obama administration does not comprehend the full scope of the ISIS threat.

Within the realm of public opinion, Republicans are also very critical of U.S. efforts under the Obama administration to combat terrorism. For example, only 27 percent of Republicans believe that the government is doing well at reducing the threat of terrorism, according to one 2015 poll (Pew Research Center 2015). In that same poll, only 11 percent of Republicans approved of Obama's performance on the issue of terrorism Republican opinion of Obama's handling of the terrorist threat had previously reached a high water mark in 2011, immediately after Obama signed off on a secret Navy SEAL military operations that resulted in the death of Osama bin Laden, mastermind of the 9/11 attacks. Since then, approval of Obama's counterterrorism efforts has decreased at all points along the partisan spectrum, including among Democrats and Republicans. While it is difficult to isolate causal factors, it does appear that the decline in approval corresponds roughly to the rise of ISIS. It is also the case that Republicans are more likely than Democrats, by a nearly three-to-one margin, to view military force as the best way to combat terrorism.

One area where both Republicans and Democrats experienced intraparty discord was the vote on the USA Freedom Act. In May 2015, key provisions of the Patriot Act, including the provision that allowed for bulk data collection by the National Security Agency (NSA), expired as a result of a deadlock in the U.S. Senate. On June 2, the Senate passed the USA Freedom Act, paving the way for President Obama to sign the bill into law. The House had previously agreed to the legislation. After a period of contentious debate, which included several filibuster attempts, the bill passed the Senate by a vote of 67–32. Some opponents of the measure argued that the bill did not place stringent enough limits on bulk data collection. Other opponents, however, argued that any reduction in bulk data collection and other surveillance capability would compromise security. Proponents argued that the bill struck the proper balance between security and the protection of civil liberties (Chappell 2015). Of the 32 no votes, 30 were Republicans. Twenty-two Republican senators voted for the legislation.

Issues related to terrorism played a significant role in the 2016 Republican presidential primary. Given the propensity of self-identified Republicans within the general public to view terrorism as the top issue facing the United States, this is not a surprise. The November 2015 ISIS-sponsored attacks in Paris and the December mass shooting in San Bernardino by an individual with ties to a California Jihadist group with plans to fight for Al Qaeda in Afghanistan intensified the debate among the candidates. Donald Trump, for example, proposed a temporary ban on Muslims entering the United States in order to fight terrorism (Lee 2015). Trump has also argued in favor of profiling certain Muslims and Islamic organizations in the United States as part of U.S counterterrorism policy. During a December 2015 debate, Republican candidate Jeb Bush of Florida pushed back, arguing that the proposed ban was a demonstration of Trump's lack of seriousness. Specifically, Bush argued that the plan would be both unworkable (it is illegal to question the religious beliefs of immigrants seeking entrance into the United States) and that it would send a signal to the international community that the United States overreacts to potential security threats. All of the Republican presidential candidates favored some form of moratorium on the resettlement of Syrian and Iraqi refugees in the United States in light of the November 2015 ISIS attacks in Paris.

Republican presidential candidates have experienced areas of both unity and discord on the specific issue of how to combat the threat of ISIS. Much of the disagreement involves the question of whether U.S. "boots on the ground" are necessary in order to fight ISIS in Iraq and Syria. During his unsuccessful bid for the 2016 GOP presidential nomination, Ohio Governor John Kasich expressed support for the boots on the ground approach, arguing that the United States must be willing to commit troops to the conflict in order to avoid direct conflict in the United States (Kasich 2015). Kasich was the lone Republican candidate to specifically commit to the use of U.S. ground forces in Syria. Other candidates, such as Senator Ted Cruz, proposed increased support for other actors with boots on the ground in areas of the Middle East controlled or threatened by ISIS, specifically the Kurdish population in Syria and Iraq (Elliott 2015). All of the Republican candidates asserted that the Obama administration had not done enough to counter ISIS. There is also an emerging consensus that increased air strikes and economic coercion will be key elements in countering the terrorist group.

Democrats on U.S. Terrorism Policy

The Democratic Party platform of 2012 mentions terrorism nine times. Beyond policy, the central political argument in the Democratic Party platform is that the Obama administration kept its promise to end the war in Iraq while still hunting down terrorists abroad. The successful raid in Pakistan that resulted in the death of Osama bin Laden provided a politically useful backdrop against which to frame other counterterrorism efforts. The Democratic Party platform also draws a contrast with Republicans on the issue of civil liberties. Specifically, the platform posits that any policies used in confronting the threat of terrorism must also ensure that civil liberties and the right to privacy are protected (Democratic National Committee

The 2015 U.S. National Security Strategy

The U.S. National Security Strategy is interesting in that it is both a broad plan of action for countering threats to national security, and a partisan document, extolling the virtues of whichever party controls the White House. The 2015 National Security Strategy is no exception. With regard to strategic elements in the effort to combat terrorism, the strategy lists several priorities including:

- Degrading the capacity of ISIL both through military means and by strengthening partners;
- Cultivating stability in the Middle East in order to deny terrorist groups the opportunity to take advantage of chaotic domestic conditions; and
- Continuing the shift away from ground operations in favor of other methods of containing terrorist groups.

As a partisan political document, the National Security Strategy argues that the Obama administration has experienced several successes in the effort to combat global terrorism. These include:

- Decreasing unemployment: The National Security Strategy argues the internal economic strength is the key to domestic security;
- Ending the war in Iraq and accomplishing a major military drawdown in Afghanistan; and
- Leading over 60 coalition partners in the battle against ISIS/ISIL.

Overall, the action plan contained in the National Security Strategy with respect to terrorism is very similar to the 2012 Democratic Party platform, with the addition of significant material related to the threat of ISIS/ISIL. Given the dominant role played by the president in crafting both documents, a role that is by no means unique in the history of party platforms or national security strategies, this is not a surprise.

Source:

White House. "2015 National Security Strategy." Last modified February 2015. https://www.whitehouse.gov/sites/default/files/docs/2015_national_security_strategy.pdf.

2012). Another contrast with the Republican platform relates to the phrase "war on terror." The Democratic Party platform argues that the idea of a war on terror was internationally divisive and thus not amenable to cultivating international cooperation to confront specific individuals and groups. The Democratic Party platform shares with the Republican platform a partial focus on issues related to cybersecurity and cyberterrorism as well as a commitment to international cooperation.

Democrats within the general public also diverge from Republicans in a variety of ways. Democrats, for example, are over twice as likely to believe that the government is doing a good job of confronting the terrorist threat (Pew Research Center 2015). It is worth noting, however, that public approval ratings of U.S. government efforts to prevent terrorism have dropped over the past year among Democrats, Republicans, and independents. Net approval of current efforts, as a result, is negative for the first time during the Obama administration according to one polling organization (Pew Research Center 2015). It is also possible, though not knowable, the Democrats are more likely to approve of current efforts because they support the president, rather than because they support the policy. Democrats and Republicans also vary within the realm of public opinion on the perceived threat of Islam. A plurality of Republicans believes that Muslims should be subjected to additional scrutiny with regard to terrorism. Roughly three-fourths of Democrats disagree. Finally, Democrats diverge from Republicans on the classic "most important issue" question. A plurality of Democrats believes that the economy is the issue that will most decide their vote. Pluralities of Republicans believe that terrorism is the most important issue facing the country (Phelan 2015).

As was the case with Republicans, the Democrats experienced intraparty discord on the vote for the USA Freedom Act. However, unlike Republicans who experienced significant party-line defections in both the House and Senate, Democrats only had difficulty maintaining party unity in the House of Representatives. In the Senate, only one Democrat, Tammy Baldwin of Wisconsin, voted against passage. On May 13, 2015, the USA Freedom Act passed in the House by a vote of 338–88. Within this total, 47 Republicans broke with the majority and voted against the legislation, for many of the reasons mentioned above. Forty-one Democrats broke with the majority and also voted no. Overall, majorities of both Democrats and Republicans supported the bill in the House. Most of the Democrats who voted against the act in the House argued that it did not go enough to protect civil liberties and privacy from government intrusion. Democratic representative John Lewis of Georgia, for example, acting in concert with Representative Justin Amash, a Republican representative from Michigan, authored a letter to the Senate opposing the act on the grounds that the measure did not "adequately or appropriately reform surveillance practices or address privacy concerns" (Amash 2015).

Secretary of State Hillary Clinton and Bernie Sanders, the two principal candidates for the Democratic Party presidential nomination in 2016, both expressed support for international coalition building and the need to avoid "going it alone" as priorities in confronting the threat of terrorism. Both candidates also strongly criticized a proposal from Republican nominees to impose a ban on Muslim immigration. Although they expressed agreement on the need for a strong military in order to counter the threat of terrorism, the Clinton campaign did not dwell on military funding in the context of terrorism. The Sanders campaign, on the other hand, argued that it is necessary to take a "hard look" at the military budget, given other domestic policy priorities such as increasing funding for various social welfare programs. Finally, Clinton and Sanders expressed differing opinions on the efficacy of the USA Freedom Act. Clinton supported the act, arguing that the NSA needs to become more transparent. Sanders, by contrast, voted against the bill, arguing that indeed it did not go far enough in protecting the civil liberties and privacy of Americans.

Further Reading

Amash, Justin. "Amash, Lewis, and House Colleagues Send Letter to Senate | Congressman Justin Amash." Congressman Justin Amash | Proudly Representing the Third District of Michigan. Last modified May 20, 2015. https://amash.house.gov/press-release/amash-lewis-and-house-colleagues-send-letter-senate.

Chappell, Bill. "Senate Approves USA Freedom Act, after Amendments Fail: The Two-Way : NPR." NPR.org. Last modified June 2, 2015. http://www.npr.org/sections/thetwo-way/2015/06/02/411534447/senateis-poised-to-vote-on-house-approved-usa-freedom-act.

Democratic National Committee. "The 2012 Democratic Platform." Last modified 2012. https://www.democrats.org/party-platform.

Elliott, Phillip. "How Republican Candidates Want to Fight the Islamic State." TIME.com. Last modified November 14, 2015. http://time.com/4113042/paris-attacks-islamic-state-republican-positions/.

GOP. "The Reviews Are In: Obama's ISIS Admission Is 'Creating a Lot of Concern,' a 'Misfire,' and 'a Significant Political Blow.'" Last modified August 29, 2014. https://www.gop.com/the-reviews-are-in-obamas-isis-admission-is-creating-a-lot-of-concern-a-misfire-and-a-significant-political-blow/.

GovTrack.us. "H.J.Res. 114 (107th): Authorization for Use of Military Force against Iraq Resolution of 2002." Accessed February 7, 2016. https://www.govtrack.us/congress/votes/107-2002/s237.

GovTrack.us. "H.R. 5005 (107th): Homeland Security Act of 2002." Accessed February 7, 2016. https://www.govtrack.us/congress/votes/107-2002/h367.

Kasich, John. "John Kasich: We Need Boots on the Ground to Defeat ISIS." TIME.com. Last modified November 18, 2015. http://time.com/4119069/isis-john-kasich/.

Lee, Barbara. "Congresswoman Lee Slams Irresponsible Defense Authorization Bill, Refusal to Consider Bipartisan AUMF Repeal Amendment." Congresswoman Barbara Lee. Last modified May 22, 2014. https://lee.house.gov/news/press-releases/congresswoman-lee-slams-irresponsible-defense-authorization-bill-refusal-to.

Lee, M. J. "Republican Debate Recap: Focuses on Terror, National Security Politics.com." CNN. Accessed February 11, 2016. http://www.cnn.com/2015/12/15/politics/republican-debate-updates/.

Office of the Clerk of the U.S. House of Representatives. "Final Vote Results for Roll Call 224." Last modified May 13, 2015. http://clerk.house.gov/evs/2015/roll224.xml.

Pew Research Center. "Views of Government's Handling of Terrorism Fall to Post-9/11 Low." Pew Research Center for the People and the Press. Last modified December 15, 2015. http://www.people-press.org/2015/12/15/views-of-governments-handling-of-terrorism-fall-to-post-911-low/.

Phelan, Julie. "Terrorism Worries Are Back; Bernie Sanders Is Up, GOP Is Steady (POLL)." ABC News. Last modified November 22, 2015. http://abcnews.go.com/Politics/sanders-gop-steady-terrorism-worries-back-poll/story?id=35337895.

RealClearPolitics. "Bernie Sanders on USA Freedom Act: 'I May Well Be Voting For It,' Does Not Go Far Enough." *RealClearPolitics—Opinion, News, Analysis, Video and Polls.*

May 31, 2015. http://www.realclearpolitics.com/video/2015/05/31/bernie_sanders_on
_usa_freedom_act_i_may_well_be_voting_for_it_does_not_go_far_enough.html.

Republican National Committee. "2012 Republican Platform." Last modified 2012. https://
prod-static-ngop-pbl.s3.amazonaws.com/docs/2012GOPPlatform.pdf.

U.S. Senate. "U.S. Senate: Roll Call Vote." Last modified June 2, 2015. http://www.senate
.gov/legislative/LIS/roll_call_lists/roll_call_vote_cfm.cfm?congress=114&session=1
&vote=00201#position.

Wyden, Ron, Mark Udall, and Rand Paul. "How to End the NSA Dragnet." Latimes.com.
Last modified June 16, 2014. http://www.latimes.com/opinion/op-ed/la-oe-wyden-nsa
-surveillance-20140617-story.html.

Trade Policy

At a Glance

The most basic dichotomy in United States trade policy is between free trade and protectionism. Free trade policies suggest the absence of tariffs, export subsidies, qualitative restrictions, and any other measures that prevent the free flow of goods between countries. Protectionist policies include one or more of these elements and are designed to protect domestic industries from foreign competition, increase the amount or profit coming from exports, or both. On the one hand, free trade pacts such as the North American Free Trade Agreement (NAFTA) can lower the price of consumer goods and/or open new markets to U.S. exports. On the other hand, such agreements can also lead to the closure of U.S. businesses in the face of stiff international competition or the movement of business abroad to take advantage of less expensive labor, lower environmental standards, or some other comparative advantage. These tradeoffs have produced interesting interparty and intra-party divisions for both Republicans and Democrats. The potential benefits of free trade have also created avenues for bipartisan agreement on certain aspects of the issue such as the protection of intellectual property and the approach to competition from China.

According to many Democrats, U.S. trade policy:

- Should be generally based on free trade principles;
- Should include provisions that protect the global environment;
- Should protect U.S. sovereignty in the adjudication of trade disputes;
- Should focus on intellectual property protection; and
- Should protect workers from unfair labor practices.

According to many Republicans, U.S. trade policy:

- Should be generally based on free trade principles;
- Should include trade promotion authority (TPA) for the president;

- Should punish companies and countries that violate intellectual property protections; and
- Should only include environmental protection provisions if they are applied equally across all countries.

___

Overview

The Constitution of the United States gives Congress authority over aspects of trade such as tariffs and duties. However, the modern era of U.S. trade began in 1934 when Congress delegated this authority to the president via the Reciprocal Trade Agreements Act (Canto 1983). The act gave the president the power both to negotiate trade agreements with other countries and to set the tariff rate. Previous tariff policy centered around the Smoot-Hawley Act, which had raised tariffs to the point of having an adverse impact on the economy. The after effects of World War I, including duplicate production patterns in Europe and the United States and the resulting interest in protecting domestic industries, had further dampened trade. Congress believed that granting the president trade authority would allow the more rapid conclusion of trade agreements that would grow the economy and help the United States emerge from the Great Depression (U.S. House of Representatives, n.d.).

In the immediate post–World War II era, tariffs remained high. The United States, as one of the chief architects of the postwar order, became one of the primary forces behind the development of the General Agreement on Tariffs and Trade (GATT), which was originally signed by 23 countries in 1947. Although the GATT includes several elements, arguably the two most critical are the most-favored nation (MFN) requirement and the national treatment requirement. Under MFN, a country is required to extend trade benefits provided to one country (its most-favored-nation) to all states party to the agreement (GATT Article I). The idea is to create equal treatment between countries. The U.S. government uses the term "normal trade relations" as a substitute term for MFN. National treatment requires a country to treat an imported good identically in terms of taxes or regulations to the way it treats the same domestically manufactured good (GATT Article III). The GATT does allow parties to impose countervailing duties that raise the price of an imported good in the event that the country or company exporting the good is selling it at below-market prices (a practice referred to as dumping). Over time, the GATT was expanded to cover more goods, more countries, and more forms of protectionism.

The GATT was negotiated in several "rounds" over the course of nearly 50 years before negotiations led to the creation of the World Trade Organization (WTO) in 1995. During the GATT years, tariffs generally decreased and Congress granted the president increased authority to cut tariffs beyond GATT levels. The WTO, using GATT as its primary "rulebook," was designed to continue the negotiating process in a more permanent setting. The WTO was also empowered to address emerging trade issues such as intellectual property protection and trade in services. Trade in services involves trade in intangible products such as financial services, market research, public health consulting, and other emerging fields. Perhaps most important, the WTO has its own dispute settlement mechanism, which enables countries to bring grievances related to allegedly unfair trade practices to an international body capable of making binding rulings. For example, in 2016, the United States won a case before the WTO Dispute Settlement Mechanism (DSM) over solar panels. The United States claimed that Indian local content rules were an unfair impediment to free trade. India claimed that the rules were vital to the development of India's solar industry, which is allowed under provisions of the GATT that encourage countries to pursue sustainable development. The finding opened the Indian market to sales from U.S. solar cell companies.

The United States has also entered into a variety of regional trading agreements in the last several decades. The most famous of these is the North American Free Trade Agreement (NAFTA), which entered into force in 1994 between the United States, Canada, and Mexico. NAFTA is allowed under the WTO even though it violates the principles of MFN (Canada and Mexico receive better treatment of their goods by the United States than do other countries) because the WTO has specific provisions that allow for the development of free trade areas. NAFTA is comprehensive in that it requires the progressive elimination of all tariffs in the member countries. In order to address concerns about environmental standards and fair labor practices, supplemental agreements between the United States and Mexico were negotiated covering these areas.

Instead of requiring ratification by the Senate, many trade agreements like NAFTA are passed under congressional-executive agreements that provide for trade promotion authority (TPA, also known as fast-track). Under these types of arrangements, the president is free to negotiate the agreement in advance, with a promise by Congress to vote yea or nay on the legislation without amendment. In spite of this procedure, the passage of NAFTA was contentious. Many Democrats, including those in the Midwestern "rust" belt, as well those in the Western United States, voted against NAFTA on the grounds that it would result in a loss of American jobs to Mexico. Overall, Republicans were more supportive of the measure. NAFTA passed in the Senate by a vote of 61–38. Ten Republicans voted no while 34 voted yes. Twenty-eight Democrats voted no while 27 voted yes. The Clinton administration had lobbied congressional Democrats to raise the number of yes votes. In the House of Representatives, a majority of Democrats voted no and the enabling legislation passed by a more narrow vote of 234–200.

The most politically salient potential trade agreement during the Obama administration has been the Trans-Pacific Partnership (TPP). President Obama signed the agreement in February 2016. If approved by Congress, the TPP would create a free trade area between 12 countries, mostly in the Pacific Rim and North America. Like NAFTA, the TPP is very controversial. Opponents include both Democrats and Republicans who fear that the TPP will result in job losses in the United States, as well as decreased U.S. sovereignty over trade affairs. Democrats are especially concerned that the TPP might weaken U.S. labor and environmental protections. Republicans, meanwhile, have expressed concern about intellectual property protection under the TPP. Proponents, both Republicans and Democrats, have argued that the TPP will open new markets to U.S. goods and thus boost the American economy. Democratic proponents, including President Obama, argue that the agreement contains strong environmental and labor standards. Republicans claim that the agreement also contains significant intellectual property protections.

Democrats on U.S. Trade Policy

The Democratic Party platform has historically expressed strong support for the idea of free trade, and the 2012 version was no exception. The platform lauded new trade agreements in Latin America and Asia negotiated during the Obama administration, and supported the TPP as a means to open further markets while protecting American workers and environmental standards (Democratic National Committee 2012). On China, the platform emphasized that the United States has brought several trade cases against China, for its anti–free trade policies. China is widely accused in the United States of manipulating its currency by keeping its value artificially low to make its exports less expensive. China has also been accused of dumping products on the U.S. market at below-market prices in order to drive competitors out of business. In a more recent case, the United States sought remedy from the DSM for taxes that China levies on imported aircraft parts. The case has yet to be decided. In 2014, the United States won a case before the DSM related to Chinese accusations of U.S. dumping in the auto industry. China imposed countervailing duties, but the WTO found that China had violated its obligations under the agreement, while also finding that no dumping had occurred (U.S. Trade Representative 2014).

President Obama has also expressed his desire for increased free trade throughout his two terms in office, framing it as a key to increased economic prosperity both at home and abroad. Upon concluding trade agreements with the governments of Colombia, South Korea, and Panama, for example, the president argued that they would support tens of thousands of jobs across the country (White House 2011). The president asserted that each treaty goes further than previous treaties, such as NAFTA, to promote adequate labor standards. Some Democrats, however, have expressed concerns that free trade agreements promote decreased labor standards, which hurts workers in other countries and decreases the power and earnings of organized labor in the United States. Democrats worry that inadequate labor standards give foreign companies an unfair advantage over their U.S. counterparts. Obama has also spoken out in favor of the extension of TPA, which was granted to him in 2015 in order to conclude negotiations on the TPP. The president believes that the TPP will result in billions of dollars in new export earnings and tens of thousands of new jobs as a result.

Democratic voters appear to be more ambivalent on issues related to trade policy than does the president. For example, according to a 2015 poll by the Pew Research Center, a robust 71 percent of Democrats believe that free trade is good overall. Sixty percent believe that the TPP will result in a positive outcome (Stokes 2015). However, less than 20 percent of Democrats think that free trade creates jobs. In fact, a 2010 survey indicated that four times as many Democrats believe that free trade leads to job losses as believe that free trade generates job gains (Pew Research Center 2010). Although economic findings on this issue are inconsistent, surveys consistently indicated that a majority of Americans believe that free trade agreements lead to a net loss of jobs, especially in the manufacturing sector. Nevertheless, according to a 2015 Chicago Council on Global Affairs poll, 77 percent of Democrats believe that free trade agreements are an effective way to achieve U.S. foreign policy goals (Chicago Council on Global Affairs 2015).

Like Democrats in the general public, Democrats in Congress appear to be supportive of expansive trade policy overall—but less supportive than President Obama. For example, the vast majority of congressional Democrats supported reauthorization of the U.S. Export–Import Bank, which is designed to make U.S. products more competitive by financing foreign purchases of U.S. goods at favorable terms and by insuring U.S. companies against credit risk. On the other hand, while the president supports the extension of trade promotion authority, a majority of Democrats in both the House and Senate do not. When TPA passed the Senate by a vote of 62–37, only 14 Democrats voted yes in spite of the support of the president (Dennis 2015).

Senator Elizabeth Warren of Massachusetts joined most other Democrats in voting against TPA, arguing both that it was not reasonable to expect Congress to support TPA without seeing a current draft of the agreement, and that the TPA would give the president the ability to conclude the Trans-Pacific Partnership in a way that would sacrifice U.S. sovereignty in trade disputes. Specifically, Warren is opposed to the investor-state dispute settlement (ISDS) provisions of the TPP. Warren claims that ISDS makes it possible for investors to chip away at U.S. regulations without the involvement of U.S. courts. Proponents believe that ISDS prevents disputes between investors from becoming disputes between states. A similar phenomenon occurred in the Senate, where only 28 Democrats supported the legislation. Most Democrats who oppose TPA have also indicated that they are opposed in principle to the TPP. The TPP, which was just recently signed by the president, has yet to come before the House or Senate for approval. At present, support for trade promotion authority is a useful, though probably not perfect, surrogate for support for the TPP.

Of the 2016 Democratic Party candidates for president, Senator Bernie Sanders has been the most consistent and outspoken critic of free trade agreements. Sanders opposed NAFTA, as well as the Central American Free Trade Agreement (CAFTA), and he has opposed the TPP on the grounds that it will cost American jobs. Sanders has also criticized former senator and secretary of state Hillary

President Obama and Senator Warren Debate the Trans-Pacific Partnership

President Obama has been a consistent supporter of the Trans-Pacific Partnership, which he argues would open many markets in Asia and Latin America to U.S. goods. Obama also argues that the agreement contains the toughest worker and environmental standards in U.S. Trade History. But the progressive Democratic senator Elizabeth Warren, who agrees with Obama on most issues, has argued passionately against the agreement, which she believes would damage U.S. sovereignty, hurt American workers, and strengthen the big banks. "I understand that we want to be a nation that trades, that trade creates many benefits for us," stated Warren. "But only if done on terms that strengthen the American economy and American worker. I should say the American family, because that's what this is really about."

Source:

Sargent, Greg. "Elizabeth Warren Fires Back at Obama: Here's What They're Really Fighting About." *Washington Post.* May 11, 2015. https://www.washingtonpost.com/blogs/plum-line/wp/2015/05/11/elizabeth-warren-fires-back-at-obama-heres-what-theyre-really-fighting-about/.

Clinton for announcing her opposition to the TPP after seemingly supporting the agreement while serving in the State Department. Clinton has responded that, while she supported the negotiations and was optimistic about the results being a "gold standard" for trade agreements, the final provisions of the TPP did not meet her expectations—hence, her decision to oppose it. Her concerns relate to the ISDS process, as well as labor and environmental standards. As a senator, Clinton also voted with Senator Sanders against CAFTA. However, Clinton has supported a number of other trade agreements and is generally considered at least somewhat favorable to free trade.

Republicans on U.S. Trade Policy

The Republican Party platform is similar in many ways to its Democratic Party counterpart. The platform lays out a pro–free trade position, praising free trade agreements going back to the Reagan administration. The platform also expresses concerns about Chinese trade manipulation via currency devaluation and dumping and recognizes the need for enhanced intellectual property protections. At the same time, Republicans use the party platform, as parties normally do when they do not hold the presidency, to criticize the president on trade policy. Republicans argued in their 2012 platform, for example, that the Obama administration has not done enough to negotiate new trade agreements, claiming that those that have been completed have been negotiated too slowly (Republican National Committee

2012). The platform also claimed that President Obama had not done enough to prevent China from abusing the international trade system and stealing American intellectual property. Republicans promised that a Republican presidential administration would impose more countervailing duties and take more Chinese trade abuse cases before the World Trade Organizations Dispute Settlement Mechanism. The 2012 Republican platform did agree with Obama on the issue of TPA, asserting that it is necessary to give the president the flexibility and certainty that he needs during trade negotiations.

In public opinion polls, though, Republican voters appear to be less supportive of free trade than those who crafted that 2012 Republican Party platform. In a 2015 survey, more self-identified Republicans (42 percent) thought that free trade was good than those (39 percent) who thought it was bad on balance (YouGov 2015). However, this three-point pro-trade gap is far less than the 27-point gap in favor of free trade exhibited by Democrats. In the same survey, more Republican oppose the TPP than support it, once again conflicting with Democrats who tend to support the agreement. Interestingly, Republicans are slightly more likely to believe that free trade creates jobs than are Democrats, though minorities in both parties hold this view (Stokes 2015). Although Republican voters, in general, are skeptical of the benefits of free trade, the skepticism is even more pronounced among those Republican who identify with the Tea Party. Generally, individuals who identify with the Tea Party are more conservative on fiscal and monetary issues than other Republicans. Voters who identify themselves as Tea Party members also tend to exhibit conservative populist characteristics, such as the desire to mobilize the people against what they view as tyrannical institutions of government. In this context, it comes as little surprise that there exists a 39-point anti–free trade gap among Republican who identify with the Tea Party (Pew Research Center 2010). The gap within the sample of Republicans who do not identify with the Tea Party was 13 points smaller (but still negative).

Congressional Republicans have, generally speaking, been more likely to favor free trade agreements than congressional Democrats. This creates a somewhat counterintuitive situation where some free trade legislation supported by President Obama passes the House and the Senate with more help from Republican Party votes than Democratic Party votes. One example of this is the issue of trade promotion authority. As mentioned above, TPA passed the Senate with only fourteen Democrats supporting the measure. However, 48 of 54 Republicans supported empowering President Obama with TPA (Dennis 2015). A similar pattern occurred in the House, with President Obama relying primarily on Republican support.

On the reauthorization of the U.S. Export–Import Bank, which temporarily closed in 2015 due to congressional deadlock, Republicans were more divided. However, they still backed the position of President Obama, who favored reauthorization, thus enabling the measure to narrowly pass in both chambers in 2015. Overall, 127 Republicans favored reauthorization in the House, while 117 opposed the legislation (Office of the Clerk of the U.S. House of Representatives 2015). A similar division occurred in the Senate. Republicans who opposed reauthorization argued that the bank violates free-market principals by providing a subsidy to companies seeking to export goods. Supporters among Republicans countered that the bank is necessary to maintain U.S. trade competitiveness against other countries that use similar or more direct government intervention to enhance trade competitiveness. Senator Lindsey Graham put it simply by stating that "until you get the Chinese, the Germans and the French out of the ex-im business, I'm not going to unilaterally disarm" (Calmes 2015). Senators most closely associated with the Tea Party, or Republican senators fearing a Tea Party primary challenger in 2016, were more likely to vote against the legislation.

Within the 2016 Republican primary process, businessman Donald Trump staked out the protectionist position on trade most similar to that of the Tea Party. Trump promises a tougher stance toward China, especially on the issues of currency manipulation and intellectual property violations. Trump also promises to bring China "back to the negotiating table" to renegotiate existing agreements. Trump also opposed the TPP, arguing that it duplicated other trading agreements and would result in the loss of more American jobs. Trump asserted that the United States is already in an unannounced trade war with countries in Asia and Latin America and that it is losing that war.

Republican senator Ted Cruz, also generally admired by Tea Party Republicans, also opposed the TPP, arguing that it had not been negotiated in good faith and had the potential to encourage backdoor illegal immigration (Cruz 2015). Cruz believes that the immigration provisions in the TPP could allow workers and businesspeople to enter the United States in increased numbers using temporary visas. Overstaying those visas would be a form of illegal immigration. Cruz has taken a great deal of criticism for his apparent change in position on TPP. The fact-finding Web site Politifact found that Cruz had "flip-flopped" his position on TPA, a key tool provided to the president as part of the negotiation of the Trans-Pacific Partnership (Herring 2015). For his part, Cruz claimed that he had always opposed TPP. Governor John Kasich, whose 2016 presidential campaign was more centrist in orientation, expressed support for the TPP, as well as the fast-track authority that helped produce the agreement.

Further Reading

Calmes, Jackie. "Export-Import Bank Divides Once-Supportive Republicans." *New York Times*. Last modified June 17, 2015. http://www.nytimes.com/2015/06/18/business /international/export-import-bank-divides-once-supportive-republicans.html?_r=0.

Canto, Victor A. "U.S. Trade Policy: History and Evidence." *Cato Journal* 3, no. 3 (Winter 1983): 679–703. http://object.cato.org/sites/cato.org/files/serials/files/cato-journal/2011 /10/cj3n3-4.pdf.

Chicago Council on Global Affairs. "America Divided: Political Partisanship and US Foreign Policy." Last modified September 15, 2015. http://www.thechicagocouncil.org /publication/america-divided-political-partisanship-and-us-foreign-policy.

Cruz, Ted. "Ted Cruz: Obamatrade Enmeshed in Corrupt, Backroom Dealing." Breitbart. Last modified June 23, 2015. http://www.breitbart.com/big-government/2015/06/23/exclusive-ted-cruz-obamatrade-enmeshed-in-corrupt-backroom-dealings/.

Democratic National Committee. "2012 Democratic Platform." Last modified 2012. https://www.democrats.org/party-platform.

Dennis, Steven T. "Senate Passes Trade Promotion Authority (Updated)." Roll Call. Last modified May 22, 2015. http://www.rollcall.com/wgdb/senate-passes-trade-promotion-authority/.

Herring, Keely. "Ted Cruz Changed Position on Trade Promotion Authority, Also Called Fast-track." Politifact. Last modified July 8, 2015. http://www.politifact.com/truth-o-meter/statements/2015/jul/08/ted-cruz/ted-cruz-changed-position-trade-promotion-authorit/.

Pew Research Center. "Americans Are of Two Minds on Trade." Last modified November 9, 2010. http://www.pewresearch.org/2010/11/09/americans-are-of-two-minds-on-trade/.

Republican National Committee. "2012 Republican Platform." Last modified 2012. https://prod-static-ngop-pbl.s3.amazonaws.com/docs/2012GOPPlatform.pdf.

Stokes, Bruce. "Americans Agree on Trade: Good for the Country, but Not Great for Jobs." Pew Research Center. Last modified January 8, 2015. http://www.pewresearch.org/fact-tank/2015/01/08/americans-agree-on-trade-good-for-the-country-but-not-great-for-jobs/.

"U.S.-China Trade Reform." Make America Great Again! | Donald J. Trump for President. Last modified 2016. https://www.donaldjtrump.com/positions/us-china-trade-reform.

U.S. House of Representatives: History, Art & Archives. "The Reciprocal Trade Agreement Act of 1934." Accessed April 1, 2016. http://history.house.gov/HistoricalHighlight/Detail/36918.

U.S. Trade Representative. "United States Wins Trade Enforcement Case against China on Autos." Last modified May 2014. https://ustr.gov/about-us/policy-offices/press-office/press-releases/2014/May/US-Wins-Trade-Enforcement-Case-Against-China-On-Autos.

White House. "Statement from President Obama on the Submission of the Korea, Colombia, and Panama Trade Agreements." Whitehouse.gov. Last modified October 3, 2011. https://www.whitehouse.gov/the-press-office/2011/10/03/statement-president-obama-submission-korea-colombia-and-panama-trade-agr.

World Trade Organization. *Text of the General Agreement on Tariffs and Trade*. World Trade Organization, 1986. https://www.wto.org/english/docs_e/legal_e/gatt47_e.pdf.

YouGov. "Democrats Still More Supportive of Free Trade, TPP Than Republicans." Last modified October 12, 2015. https://today.yougov.com/news/2015/10/12/democrats-still-more-supportive-free-trade-tpp-rep/.

Trans-Pacific Partnership

At a Glance

The Trans-Pacific Partnership (commonly called the TPP), is an international trade agreement that provides for the reduction of tariffs and nontariff barriers between twelve countries in the Asia/Pacific Rim region, including the United States. It was developed after Congress granted President Obama trade promotion authority (TPA), formerly called fast track authority, to negotiate the TPP and other trade agreements. President Barack Obama strongly favors the agreement, both because of trade benefits that he argues will result from the accord and because of the Asia "pivot" designed by the administration to tie the United States closer to the Pacific Rim and counter Chinese influence in the region. Although the Barack Obama administration supports the agreement, however, it has not yet become law. Unlike normal treaties, which must pass the U.S. Senate with a two-thirds vote in order to be ratified, the TPP exists as a congressional-executive agreement. As such, it will come into force by the United States if both the House and Senate approve the measure by a simple majority vote. Under TPA terms, however, Congress must approve or decline such agreements without amendment. As of mid-2016, the Republican-controlled Congress had yet to vote on the proposed TPP.

The debate over the agreement has become one of the most salient issues of the 2016 presidential election. Although both Democratic nominee Hillary Clinton and Republican nominee Donald Trump oppose the agreement as written, the stark differences between the candidates on whether the agreement can be salvaged, as well as interparty and intraparty disputes over the agreement, promise to make the TPP a key issue well beyond the election.

According to many Democrats, the Trans-Pacific Partnership . . .

- Must do more to protect American workers from unfair trade practices that might result in lost manufacturing or service jobs;
- Should not be voted on in the "lame-duck" Senate session after the 2016 election;
- Should protect U.S. sovereignty in the adjudication of trade disputes; and
- Should do more to protect the environment from lower environmental standards in other nations that are parties to the agreement.

According to many Republicans, the Trans-Pacific Partnership . . .

- Must do more to address U.S. intellectual property protection concerns;
- Should include TPA for the president;
- Should not be voted on in the "lame-duck" Senate session after the 2016 election; and
- Should only include environmental protection provisions if they are applied equally across all countries.

Overview

The TPP began as a more geographically limited agreement negotiated in the early 2000s and finalized in 2006 between Brunei, Chile, New Zealand, and Singapore. In spite of this agreement's relatively small size, both in terms of the countries involved and the amount of trade between them, the goal of the original negotiators has always been to expand the number of countries that are part of the agreement. The United States announced its conceptual support for the TPP in 2008, and formally joined the negotiations in 2009. There is continuity in this respect between the George W. Bush administration and the Obama administration in that both strongly supported, at least in principle, the development of a broad-based trade agreement that would encompass nations on both sides of the Pacific. After several years of negotiations, final international agreement on the TPP was reached in October 2015 by Australia, Brunei, Canada, Chile, Japan, Malaysia, Mexico, New Zealand, Peru, Singapore, the United States, and Vietnam. The treaty will enter into force when either all of the signatories have ratified the instrument, or, after two years, if signatories representing 85 percent of total gross domestic product (GDP) within the TPP ratify the agreement. As such, the agreement cannot enter into force without the United States' ratification because that 85 percent threshold is impossible to reach without the inclusion of the massive American economy. The countries that have signed the TPP currently make up approximately 40 percent of the world's GDP.

In total, the TPP contains over 2,000 pages, 30 chapters, four annexes relating to a variety of issues not covered directly in the body of the treaty, and several "related instruments" which cover bilateral understandings that needed to occur in order for the multilateral agreement to work. However, some of the main provisions of the TPP can be summarized as follows:

- *Market access/tariff reductions:* Over the course of time (ranging from immediately to 30 years) the TPP will eliminate tariffs on 88 percent of products exported by the United States to member countries and 90 percent of U.S. imports from member countries (Fergusson, McMinimy, and Williams 2016).

- *Labor and environmental issues:* From the perspective of the United States, especially Democrats in the United States, developing countries have used unfair labor practices and lax environmental standards to lower the cost of production in ways that give them an inequitable competitive advantage. The TPP makes it more difficult for members to use compulsory labor or poor work conditions to lower prices. On issues related to the environment, the TPP requires members to follow environmental agreements to which they are already members and prohibits some unsustainable fishing subsidies.
- *E-commerce:* Members of the TPP are prohibited from blocking data flows across national borders with other members. Democrats and Republicans in the United States believe that many countries have used data restrictions to hamper online businesses in the United States.
- *National treatment for trade in services:* A number of countries, including the United States, generate a significant portion of their GNP through trade in services like financial services and telecommunications services. National treatment requires member countries to treat and regulate the service provided from another member country as if that service were provided by the home country.
- *State-owned enterprises (SOEs):* Most states, including the United States, have state-owned enterprises that at times engage in international trade. The U.S. Postal Service, for example, competes with domestic and foreign enterprises of the same type (public and private). The TPP includes some limits on subsidies to SOEs and exemptions for SOEs (like the U.S. Postal Service) that generate most of their revenue from delivering services in the home country.
- *Investment:* Generally, countries are allowed to regulate investments made by actors in other states as part of the national interest. States retain these rights under the TPP. One aspect of investment that has been controversial in the United States is Investor-State Dispute Settlement (ISDS). Many Democrats believe that ISDS will enable foreign actors to circumvent U.S. law by having contentious cases heard outside of the U.S. court system (which is allowed in some case under ISDS). Republicans tend to argue that ISDS is a vital part of most modern trade agreements that opens countries up to increased investment and improves the flow of capital.

As of mid-2016, the TPP has yet to come up for a vote in the House of Representatives or the Senate. Many members of Congress consider the TPP controversial enough to avoid taking a definitive position, or a vote requiring the expression of a final position, on the agreement before the 2016 election. The fact that President Obama, a Democrat, and Speaker of the House Paul Ryan, a Republican, and Senate majority leader Mitch McConnell, another Republican, all favor the deal has led some observers to speculate that there may be a vote on the measure during the lame-duck session of Congress that occurs between the 2016 election and new members of Congress take office on January 3, 2017. However, the fact that both the Democratic and Republican Party nominees for president oppose a lame-duck vote, and the fact that the Republican Party platform officially opposes a lame-duck vote, make this option politically risky as well.

Democrats on the TPP

Since the 1990s a moderate, generally business-friendly wing of the Democratic Party has dominated policy making, at least at the national level. In this environment, trade deals such as the North American Free Trade Agreement (NAFTA) have enjoyed at least a degree of bipartisan support. In 2016, a very strong challenge from the more liberal wing of the Democratic Party, led by high-profile elected officials such as Vermont senator Bernie Sanders and Massachusetts senator Elizabeth Warren, has pushed the party further toward a more traditional protectionist (anti–free trade) position. In this context, it is perhaps not surprising that the 2016 Democratic Party platform only mentions the TPP by name once. The platform contains language suggesting that any trade agreements must support American jobs, national security, and the environment—and applies this language directly to the TPP. An earlier draft of the platform contained language acknowledging the diversity of views within the party surrounding the TPP. Ultimately, this language was removed before passage of the final draft.

Democrats within the general public appear to support the TPP by narrow margins. In 2015, Pew Research found that 51 percent of Democrats believed that the TPP would be a "good thing" for the United States (Poushter 2015). In more indirect polling, Gallup found that 40 percent of Democrats thought that removing the United States from the TPP would be either a very effective or somewhat effective measure to improve the U.S. economy (Newport 2015). In the case of the Gallup measure, the impact is less clear because the question asks about the potential impact on the economy of an agreement that currently does not exist. A 2016 Morning Consult poll found more support than opposition for the TPP among Democrats (32 percent support to 23 percent opposition). However, the same poll found that a plurality of Democrats either had no opinion of the TPP or did not know about the agreement (Rainey 2016).

In spite of the lack of general public knowledge of the TPP, the issue has proved to be salient among the political elite, including elected officials from both parties. In order to finalize negotiations on the TPP, the president requested an extension of TPA from Congress, only to have Senator Warren and some other Democratic senators voice their opposition. Warren argued that the ISDS provisions of the agreement, coupled with the fact that senators were asked to extend TPA without seeing a current draft of the agreement, made the measure unpassable. She argued that ISDS was a violation of U.S. sovereignty that would allow large foreign and

U.S. corporations to bypass the U.S. legal system by settling disputes by arbitration in an international forum. Supporters counter that, under the TPP, ISDS rulings are subject to review by domestic courts. In addition, the U.S. Trade Representatives Offices argues that ISDS benefits the United States because U.S. laws are already compatible with the type of requirements that exist under the TPP (U.S. Trade Representative 2015).

In the end, the Senate was able to pass TPA, with primarily Republican Support. Of the 44 Democrats who voted, only 13 voted in favor of extension (*New York Times* 2015). A similar phenomenon occurred in the House, where 158 of 186 Democrats opposed the extension of TPA. Only the strong support of Republicans made passage possible. Passage of TPA under these conditions was seen as a strong rebuke of President Obama, who had personally lobbied his fellow Democrats for the extension of TPA. Once TPA passed, Democrats became somewhat more supportive of the passage of and extension of Trade Adjustment Assistance (TAA) which is designed to help workers adversely affected by free trade agreements. Still, TAA only passed as a last-minute addition to the African Growth and Opportunity Act, which was more heavily favored by Democrats.

TPP dynamics have caused other divisions among Democrats. President Obama favors the TPP as a mechanism to reduce trade barriers in other countries, opening their markets to more U.S. products. In Obama's view, the TPP is also a critical component of the so-called "pivot" to Asia, a series of foreign policy initiatives announced in 2011 to develop closer ties between the United States and Asian countries. The pivot, at least in part, is designed to address growing Chinese influence in the region. The Obama administration believes that the economic interdependence fostered by free trade agreements will lead to closer political ties while preventing China from reaching full hegemonic status. Although the TPP is not the only element of the pivot, it is a critical component. From President Obama's perspective, the TPP would supplement existing bilateral trade agreements, as well as security cooperation such as the joint naval exercises that the United States began with Vietnam in 2014.

Democratic presidential nominee Hillary Clinton originally favored the TPP, in part because she served as secretary of state during a portion of the negotiating process. In 2012, Clinton referred to the TPP as the "gold standard in trade agreements" (Carroll 2015). However, during the 2015–2016 campaign season, Clinton reversed course, arguing that the TPP does not do enough to prevent currency manipulation among member states. Countries, especially authoritarian countries or those with hegemonic central banks, can artificially lower the value of their home currency beyond its value in a hypothetical free market. Although this tactic raises prices in the home country, it lowers the costs of exports, which can lead to significant economic growth. Clinton has also argued that the some of the intellectual property provisions in the TPP will make it more difficult to bring generic prescription drugs to market, especially in developing countries, thereby hurting the poor.

Conventional political wisdom has it that Clinton changed her position on TPP as a result of political pressure from her left. Senator Bernie Sanders, an independent from Vermont who made the Democratic Party nomination process closer than anyone expected at the outset, used his opposition to the TPP to draw a contrast with Secretary Clinton on trade. Sanders argued that both manufacturing and service sector jobs would be lost. With regard to manufacturing jobs, Sanders stated:

> As a result of NAFTA, the U.S. lost nearly 700,000 jobs. As a result of Permanent Normal Trade Relations with China, the U.S. lost over 2.7 million jobs. As a result of the Korea Free Trade Agreement, the U.S. has lost 70,000 jobs. The TPP would make matters worse by providing special benefits to firms that offshore jobs and by reducing the risks associated with operating in low-wage countries. (Sanders 2016)

Clinton has also been associated with North American Free Trade Agreement (NAFTA) as a result of her status as First Lady during the time that international treaty between the United States, Canada, and Mexico was finalized. Sanders's argument that the TPP is bad both for the environment and the American worker resonated through the primary season and into the Democratic National Convention in July 2016.

Republicans on the TPP

Given the significant role played by Republicans in Congress in providing the president with the authority to negotiate the TPP, one might expect a more pro-TPP stance in the 2016 Republican platform. The politics of the 2016 presidential election has negated that possibility, however. In fact, the Republican platform does not explicitly mention the TPP at all. However, there are two strong indirect mentions of the TPP in the platform. One refers to the need to be willing to walk away from a negotiation if it does not advance U.S. interests, a clear nod to the Donald Trump wing of the Republican Party, which believes that the TPP is fatally flawed. The other refers to the desire to avoid a congressional vote on "trade agreements" during the lame-duck session of Congress after the 2016 election. This statement is telling in that a lame-duck vote might be the best chance to pass the TPP in its current form given President Obama's support of the deal and the support of most congressional Republicans.

Within the general public, polls indicate that Republicans are more likely than Democrats to oppose the TPP. One 2015 poll, for example, found only 43 percent of Republicans in support of the treaty, 8 percent less than Democrats (Poushter 2015). A 2016 Morning Consult poll, in which a plurality of respondents either had no position or had not heard about the TPP, contained an identical gap in support (Rainey 2016). As was the case with Democrats, it will be impossible to know until after the new president takes office whether this opposition is a partisan response to the Obama administration or a more deep-seated mistrust of free trade of the type that has propelled the protectionist wing of the Republican Party to prominence under Donald Trump.

Overall, Republicans in Congress have been more supportive of the TPP than have Democrats. When the Senate passed TPA, for example, 47 of 52 Republicans voted in favor of the resolution which strengthened the president's hand to negotiate the TPP (*New York Times* 2015). In the House, 190 of 240 Republican representatives voted in favor of TPA. The higher percentage of Republican no votes in the House can be attributed to two main factors. First, Republicans in states that have lost large numbers of manufacturing jobs, such as Michigan and New York, were more likely to vote against TPA in an effort to prevent final negotiation of the TPP, as well as to satisfy their antitrade constituents. Second, Tea Party Republicans, while not unified on the TPP, were more likely to vote against the measure. Overall, Tea Party Republicans are more likely to believe that free trade hurts American workers. In general, however, Republicans were as unified in their support of TPA as Democrats were in opposition.

Experts agree if the TPP does not pass in 2016, despite the support of Obama, House Speaker Paul Ryan, and Senate majority leader Mitch McConnell, its prospects look dim. Regardless of the outcome of the 2016 U.S. presidential election, both major party candidates are on record as opposing the agreement, with Republican nominee Donald Trump expressing even more vehement opposition to the TPP than Clinton. At a 2016 rally in Ohio, which has lost a large number of manufacturing jobs since the 1990s, Trump stated that "the Trans-Pacific Partnership is another disaster done and pushed by special interests who want to rape our country, just a continuing rape of our country" (Lima 2016).

Trump objects to the TPP on several grounds. First, he asserts that the TPP would hurt the United States by making U.S. markets more permeable to foreign goods, which would further decrease the number of domestic manufacturing jobs. In a related vein, Trump believes that the lack of a mechanism to deter currency manipulation would further lower the price of foreign imports, also hurting manufacturing. Second, Trump has argued that China, which is not part of the TPP process, would ultimately be able to take advantage of TPP market access in order to increase exports to the United States. Given China's exclusion from the TPP, it is unclear how that might occur. However, Trump has consistently argued that both India and China use unfair trade practices at the expense of U.S. domestic and international interests.

Given the opposition of both current presidential candidates to the agreement, it will be difficult for the United States to become a party to the TPP unless there is a vote in the 2016 lame-duck session. However, it is likely that negotiations will continue to create either a new agreement or to amend the existing agreement to make it more palatable to the United States. It is also possible that the other member states will craft a similar agreement without U.S. inclusion. In any case, the controversy over the TPP has created partisan tensions that are likely to drive foreign policy debates related to trade for years to come.

Further Reading

Carroll, Lauren. "What Hillary Clinton Really Said about TPP and the 'Gold Standard.'" Politifact. Last modified October 13, 2015. http://www.politifact.com/truth-o-meter /statements/2015/oct/13/hillary-clinton/what-hillary-clinton-really-said-about-tpp -and-gol/.

Democratic National Committee. "2016 Democratic Party Platform." Last modified July 21, 2016. https://www.demconvention.com/wp-content/uploads/2016/07/Democratic -Party-Platform-7.21.16-no-lines.pdf.

Dennis, Steven T. "Senate Passes Trade Promotion Authority (Updated)." Roll Call. Last modified May 22, 2015. http://www.rollcall.com/wgdb/senate-passes-trade-promotion -authority/.

Fergusson, Ian F., Mark A. McMinimy, and Brock R. Williams. "The Trans-Pacific Partnership (TPP): In Brief." Congressional Research Service. Last modified February 9, 2016. https://www.fas.org/sgp/crs/row/R44278.pdf.

Herring, Keely. "Ted Cruz Changed Position on Trade Promotion Authority, Also Called Fast-track." Politifact. Last modified July 8, 2015. http://www.politifact.com/truth-o -meter/statements/2015/jul/08/ted-cruz/ted-cruz-changed-position-trade-promotion -authorit/.

Lima, Cristiano. "Trump Calls Trade Deal 'a Rape of Our Country.'" Politico. Last modified June 28, 2016. http://www.politico.com/story/2016/06/donald-trump-trans-pacific -partnership-224916.

New York Times. "Congressional Bills and Votes." Last modified June 24, 2015. http://politics .nytimes.com/congress/votes/114/senate/1/219.

Office of the Clerk of the U.S. House of Representatives. "Final Vote Results for Roll Call 576." Last modified October 27, 2015. http://clerk.house.gov/evs/2015/roll576.xml.

Newport, Frank. "Americans and the Economic Impact of the Trans-Pacific Partnership." Gallup.com. Last modified October 12, 2015. http://www.gallup.com/opinion/polling -matters/186083/americans-economic-impact-trans-pacific-partnership.aspx.

Poushter, Jacob. "Americans Favor TPP, but Less Than Those in Other Countries Do." Pew Research Center. Last modified June 23, 2015. http://www.pewresearch.org/fact -tank/2015/06/23/americans-favor-tpp-but-less-than-other-countries-do/.

Rainey, Ryan. "As Trade Plays in Campaigns, Most Americans Don't Know What TPP Is." Morning Consult. Last modified April 21, 2016. https://morningconsult.com/2016/04 /21/trade-talk-may-play-trail-americans-dont-know-tpp/.

Republican National Committee. "Republican Platform 2016." Last modified 2016. https:// prod-static-ngop-pbl.s3.amazonaws.com/media/documents/DRAFT_12_FINAL[1] -ben_1468872234.pdf.

Sanders, Bernie. "Senator Bernie Sanders: The Trans-Pacific Trade (Tpp) Agreement Must Be Defeated." Senator Bernie Sanders of Vermont. Last modified 2016. https://www.sanders .senate.gov/download/the-trans-pacific-trade-tpp-agreement-must-be-defeated?inline =file.

Stokes, Bruce. "Americans Agree on Trade: Good for the Country, but Not Great for Jobs." Pew Research Center. Last modified January 8, 2015. http://www.pewresearch.org/fact -tank/2015/01/08/americans-agree-on-trade-good-for-the-country-but-not-great-for -jobs/.

U.S. Trade Representative. "Frequently Asked Questions on the Trans-Pacific Partnership." Last modified 2015. https://medium.com/the-trans-pacific-partnership/frequently-asked -questions-on-the-trans-pacific-partnership-eddc8d87ac73#.hc4ebxn37.

U.S. Trade Representative. "Overview of TPP." Last modified 2016. https://ustr.gov/tpp
/overview-of-the-TPP.

YouGov. "Democrats Still More Supportive of Free Trade, TPP Than Republicans." Last
modified October 12, 2015. https://today.yougov.com/news/2015/10/12/democrats-still
-more-supportive-free-trade-tpp-rep/.

Ukraine

At a Glance

Given Russian intervention in the Ukraine and the resulting annexation of Crimea (the Crimean Peninsula), it is difficult to examine U.S./Ukrainian relations without also considering America's strained relations with Moscow. For example, America's stated desire to move Ukraine closer to the European Union through economic liberalization and integration is clearly aimed at checking Russian ambitions in Eastern Europe. In the mid-2010s, the main partisan divide over U.S. foreign policy toward Ukraine relates to the degree to which the United States ought to assist Ukraine, through military or other means, in its effort to ensure the territorial integrity of the country. Calibrating the correct level of assistance is not easy, given Ukrainian proximity to Russia and the large number of ethnic Russians who live in eastern Ukraine (the latter of which is due in part to arbitrary boundary changes during the Soviet era).

According to many Republicans . . .

- The United States should be willing to provide military assistance to Ukraine in its attempt to maintain its territorial integrity;
- Ukraine should be invited to join NATO;
- The United States must be willing to intensify sanctions against Russia to deter its intervention in Ukraine; and
- The Obama administration is appeasing Russia in other areas of Ukraine and Eastern Europe by failing to provide sufficient support to the government in Kiev.

According to many Democrats . . .

- The United States should avoid sending arms to Ukraine;
- Ukraine should be invited to join NATO or, at the very least, maintain a close relationship with the organization;

- The United States should continue to use sanctions, diplomatic isolation, and other measures to pressure Russia to end its interventionist actions in Ukraine; and
- The Obama administration is correct in its unwillingness to get more involved in Ukraine, as such intervention could bring the United States into a direct confrontation with Russia on Russian terms.

Overview

The history of Ukraine dates back to the late 800s CE, with the establishment of Kievan Rus, an early eastern Slavic state. However, much of Ukrainian history involves brief periods of sovereignty followed by longer periods of foreign rule. In 1917, after the collapse of the Russian empire, Ukraine enjoyed one such period of independence. By 1921, however, the Ukrainian Soviet Socialist Republic (SSR) was formed as Ukraine was absorbed into the Union of Soviet Socialist Republics (USSR). In 1954 the Soviet government transferred Crimea, which had been part of Russia since 1783, to the Ukrainian SSR. The transfer occurred with little fanfare and did not have a significant impact on the USSR at the time given its structure of party-controlled governance rather than true federalism, as enumerated in the Soviet Constitution.

After the collapse of the Soviet Union in 1991, more information about the transfer became available. Documents indicated that the main rationales for transferring Crimea into Ukraine were territorial proximity, common economic structure, and a celebration of the 300th anniversary of Ukrainian reunification with Russia (Kramer 2014). Much of Crimea is ethnically Russian, and the peninsula occupies a geostrategically important location on the Black Sea. These facts made the peninsula's political status much more salient in the post-Soviet era.

In 1991, Ukraine declared its independence as part of the formal breakup of the Soviet Union. Though the United States recognized Ukrainian independence without reservation, Republican president George H. W. Bush gave a widely publicized speech in which he advised against the dangers of "suicidal nationalism." The U.S. government was worried that nationalism in the former Soviet Republic might become a source of conflict between the former SSRs and Russia (*New York Times* 1991). The "Chicken Kiev" speech, as it became known, was criticized by both Republicans (especially more conservative Republicans) and many Democrats in the United States, as aligning too closely with Russia's desires and not adequately defending rights of national self-determination. In 1994, Ukraine gave up its nuclear arsenal in exchange for economic and security assurances from Russia and the United States. During the 1990s and 2000s, the United States attempted to steer Ukrainian politics in a more pro-Western direction, with varying levels of success. In 2004, for example, the United States joined with the European Union to support opposition candidate Viktor Yushchenko for election. Yushchenko ultimately emerged as president, but only after a protracted constitutional crisis.

However, in 2010, Party of Regions candidate Viktor Yanukovych, a former prime minister who had originally been declared the victor in the 2004 elections, became president. Yanukovych, who was backed by Russia, brought Ukraine into a closer relationship with Moscow. Yanukovych pulled back from closer Western European ties, including the EU-Ukraine Association Agreement, which would have brought closer economic and political integration between the two governments.

Yanukovych's refusal to sign the agreement, coupled with discontent with the government, led to a series of protests that brought down the government and forced Yanukovych to flee to Russia. Russia considered the protests and removal of Yanukovych to be a coup backed by the West, including the United States. The new government in Ukraine signed the EU-Ukraine Association Agreement.

Russia's belief that Ukraine's government had been unfairly captured by the United States and Europe led them to expand their military and political maneuverings in Eastern Ukraine, including Crimea. Russian troops helped ethnic Russians in Crimea gain an upper hand in the conflict in the hope that Crimea would secede from Ukraine and join Russia. Russia then annexed Crimea after a referendum indicated that a majority of people in Crimea wished to separate from Ukraine and integrate into the Russia Federation. However, the government in Kiev, as well as officials in the EU and the United States charged that the referendum was rife with voting fraud and other irregularities.

Since then, the Ukrainian government has repeatedly claimed that the Russian intervention in Crimea in 2014 constituted a clear violation of the 1994 agreement guaranteeing Ukrainian sovereignty. Ukraine has urged the United States to live up to its obligations as a guarantor of Ukrainian territorial integrity and provide increased military, economic, and political help to get their territory back. After the 2014 Russian military intervention and subsequent referendum, though, the Russian government of President Vladimir Putin has issued many statements emphasizing their belief that Crimea had been "fully integrated" into Russia. Meanwhile, other parts of Eastern Ukraine are also engaged in active rebellion against the central government and are currently fighting either for independence or integration with the Russian Federation. The Ukrainian government and the United States has also attributed this unrest to Russian interference in Ukrainian affairs.

In 2014, the U.S. Congress passed and Democratic president Barack Obama signed the Ukraine Freedom Support Act, which imposed sanctions on Russia, as well as secessionists in Eastern Ukraine. The act also allowed, but does not require, the president to provide arms to Ukraine as part of the effort to maintain its territorial integrity. The debate over the proper scope of U.S. assistance in this regard remains a subject of partisan debate.

Republicans on U.S. Relations with Ukraine

Until very recently, the Republican Party seemed unified in its stance that the United States should provide armed assistance to the Ukraine in its conflict with separatists and Russian military and paramilitary forces in the East. An original draft amendment to the Republican platform contained a call for the provision of lethal assistance (weapons) to the Ukrainian government (Rogin 2016). Republicans had hoped to use their willingness to provide lethal assistance to Ukraine to paint Democrats as weak on defending U.S. interests abroad. However, the final platform reads that "we [Republicans] also support providing appropriate assistance to the armed forces of Ukraine and greater coordination with NATO defense planning" (Republican National Committee 2016). The removal of the phrase "lethal assistance" from the platform in favor of "appropriate assistance" was seen as a disappointment to many more hawkish Republicans. The campaign of 2016 Republican presidential nominee Donald Trump stated publicly that it did not intervene to alter the platform language. Later, however, Trump stated that the campaign was involved in tweaking the platform language, but that he (Trump) was not personally involved (Graves 2016). Trump has argued that, given the fact that a majority of Crimean residents are Russian, one should not be surprised that the region desires to be part of Russia. Overall, the Republican platform expresses the goal of maintaining the territorial integrity of Ukraine. The change in platform language does raise questions, however, about what Republicans feel is the best way to attain this goal.

For most Republicans, as well as most Democrats, general issues related to U.S.–Ukraine relations are not of the highest priority. However, the U.S. relationship with Russia is a more prominent issue, and those aspects of the situation in Ukraine that relate more directly to Russia are, by extension, more likely to elicit opinions from members of the general public. According to a 2015 poll by the Chicago Council on Global Affairs, 59 percent of self-identified Republicans in the general public favor providing training to Ukrainian military troops (Chicago Council on Global Affairs 2015). Sixty-five percent of Republicans favored increasing sanctions against the Russian Federation in response to the situation in Ukraine. Forty-seven percent of Republicans favored directly arming Ukraine against the threat. A Pew Research Center survey, also set in 2015, found a larger percentage of Republicans (60 percent) in favor of providing arms to Ukraine (Simmons, Stokes, and Poushter 2015). According to the same Pew Research Center Survey, 71 percent of Republicans believe that Ukraine should be a member of NATO. This would require mutual assistance by NATO members in the case of aggression by a foreign power. Finally, a near-majority of Republicans (50 percent) blamed Russia directly for the violence in Eastern Ukraine (as opposed to Ukrainian separatists, the Ukrainian government, or the Western powers including the United States).

Republican members of Congress have also weighed in on the situation in Ukraine. In 2014, for example, all Republicans in the House and Senate supported the Ukraine Freedom Support Act. The act required the president to impose targeted sanctions against any Russian entity supporting secession in Ukraine and authorizes but did not require the president to impose sanctions against anyone investing in Russian crude oil (Congress.gov 2014). Several Republicans, including then House Speaker John Boehner, indicated a desire to require the president to provide "lethal assistance" to the government of Ukraine. However, the provision became voluntary in the final bill under a veto threat by President Obama, who was willing to sign the voluntary language into law. In 2015 a group of eight high-ranking House Republicans and three House Democrats sent a letter to President Obama which stated, in part:

> The Congress has already, with overwhelming bipartisan support, provided you with the authorities, resources, and political support to provide assistance, including lethal, to the government and people of Ukraine. We urge you in the strongest possible terms to use those authorities and resources to meet the specific and direct requests the government of Ukraine has made of your administration. (speaker.gov 2015)

Other Republican political elites have been more directly critical of the president. Former vice president Dick Cheney, for example, said that President Obama has projected an "image of weakness" that encourages aggression on the part of states like Russia (Curry 2014). Senator Ted Cruz argued that ineffectual policies enacted by the Obama administration toward Syria and Libya (specifically with regard to the consulate attack in Benghazi) sent a message to Putin that Russia could annex Crimea without repercussions. Trump argued that Russia acted in Eastern Ukraine because Putin "does not respect our president whatsoever" (Birnbaum and DelReal 2015). Trump also argued that the key to preventing Russia aggression would be united European action against Russia. Once again, this is consistent with Trump's position that U.S. military aid to Ukraine is not the correct policy. It is also consistent with Trump's position on NATO, which reflects his belief that many NATO countries do not do their fair share as part of the alliance. Though Ukraine is not part of NATO, Trump views the situation in Ukraine as primarily a European issue that is best resolved by a more muscular foreign policy on the part of European states.

Democrats on U.S. Relations with Ukraine

The 2016 Democratic Party platform mentions Ukraine twice. In one mention, Democrats commit to "continue to support a close relationship with states that seek to strengthen their ties to NATO and Europe, such as Georgia and Ukraine" (Democratic National Committee 2016). The second mention refers directly to Russian intervention in Ukraine as a violation of Ukrainian sovereignty. While the Republican platform, and the debates around it, reflect an argument about the nature of lethal versus nonlethal assistance to Ukraine, the Democratic Party platform does not specifically mention assistance of any type. Such a debate does exist among Democrats; however, party elites have maintained enough unity to keep the debate out of platform committee discussions and to keep congressional directives with regard to lethal assistance strictly voluntary. Generally speaking, most Democrats favor the provision of economic and humanitarian assistance to Ukraine in the face of Russian aggression. Democrats also favor the continued diplomatic and economic isolation of Russia in response to the crisis.

Within the realm of public opinion, Democrats are much less likely to support the provision of military assistance to Ukraine than are Republicans. For example, in 2015, 39 percent of Democrats in a Pew Research Center survey supported NATO sending lethal assistance to Ukraine (Simmons, Stokes, and Poushter 2015). By contrast, 60 percent of Republicans favored lethal assistance. Strong majorities of both parties (60 percent of Democrats and 69 percent of Republicans) favored providing Ukraine with economic assistance. Ukrainian economic output has fallen significantly since 2014 for a variety of reasons. In addition, Ukraine has been forced to diversify its sources of natural gas, a major source of fuel, in response to the conflict with Russia (a major supplier to Ukraine and all of Europe). Economic assistance is thus considered by many strategists to be vital resistance in this regard.

Finally, while a majority of Democrats (59 percent) favor Russian admission into NATO, overwhelming support (71 percent) among Republicans also creates a partisan gap in this area of U.S.–Ukraine policy.

Like their Republican counterparts, Democrats in Congress voted unanimously for the Ukraine Freedom Support Act, which passed Congress and was signed by President Obama in late 2014. Democrats opposed to arming Ukraine with U.S. weapons were able to vote for the bill for two reasons. First, the language of the bill authorizing lethal assistance to Ukraine made it clear that Obama was not obligated to provide such assistance. Instead, it was made voluntary, at the discretion of the president. Second, President Obama indicated, both before and after passage of the legislation, that he did not intend to use the authorization provided in the bill in order to provide arms to Ukraine. The United States had already provided about $200 million in nonlethal security assistance to Ukraine, including defense civilian and military experts, and facility security assistance, and items such as night-vision goggles, surveillance drones, and armored Humvees (White House 2015). Lethal defensive assistance, were it ever provided, would likely include antitank (armor) weapons, as well as mortars, grenade launchers, and other small-arms (Medynskyi 2016).

Although the push to provide Ukraine with lethal defensive armaments is stronger among Republicans, there are Democrats who believe that Ukraine will need access to more advanced U.S. weaponry in order to resist both Russia and pro-Russian separatists (who have access to advanced Russian weapons). For example, Senator Robert Menendez (D-N.J.) argued that "providing nonlethal equipment like night vision goggles is all well and good, but giving the Ukrainians the ability to see Russians coming but not the weapons to stop them is not the answer" (Herb 2015). As mentioned earlier, three high-ranking House Democrats joined Republicans in March 2015 to urge the president to send lethal defensive assistance to Ukraine. However, as of mid-2016 none of the Democrats in question had indicated a willingness to vote to make the provision of lethal defensive assistance mandatory. This is important because it would require Democrats working with Republicans to pass a mandatory measure over a likely presidential veto.

Both Obama and 2016 Democratic Party presidential nominee Hillary Clinton have refused to rule out sending weapons to Ukraine at some point in the future, however. There are multiple factors at play here. First, presidents from both parties are generally loath to cede what they view as powers granted under Article II of the Constitution (which covers the executive branch) to Congress. A congressional act requiring the provision of weapons blurs the line between the Article I power of the purse (power over spending) and Article II Section 2 (Commander in Chief of the Armed Forces) powers. Second, it is very common for a president to "leave all options on the table" for the sake of strategic ambiguity (not wanting an opponent to know how the United States will react in a given situation). Third, it is possible that the president would use congressional authorization to send lethal assistance to Ukraine without making this assistance public. Finally, Russia has already indicated that it would view lethal assistance as a provocative act, subject to escalation of its own military activities in Ukraine. Aside from the fact that the Pentagon has indicated at least partial support for lethal assistance, the opinions of Obama's closest advisers on the issue are hazy. It is possible that they believe that the benefits of arming Ukraine would be outweighed by further Russian intervention, forcing the U.S. to choose between escalation and acquiescence to Russian dominance of Ukraine.

For her part, former secretary of state Clinton has called for a tougher approach to Russia in response to its intervention in Ukraine. However, Clinton has not indicated whether she would provide defensive weapons to Ukraine as part of this tougher approach. Generally speaking, Clinton is viewed as more "hawkish" on foreign policy issues than most Democrats. This poses an interesting contrast with Donald Trump, who appears to be running slightly to the left of Clinton on the issue of Ukraine, and the response to Russia in general. In part, Clinton's stance finds its genesis in the failed "reset" with Russia, in which Clinton hoped to forge close ties with its foe after years of cold relations during the first Putin presidency. Clinton is widely regarded as having failed in her assessment of the power structure in Russia during the reset, which has, in part, caused her to take a more aggressive stance toward Russia in general during her election run.

Further Reading

Birnbaum, Michael, and Jose A. DelReal. "Trump Tells Ukraine Conference Their Nation Was Invaded Because 'There Is No Respect for the United States.'" *Washington Post*. Last modified September 11, 2015. https://www.washingtonpost.com/news/post-politics/wp/2015/09/11/trump-tells-ukraine-conference-their-nation-was-invaded-because-there-is-no-respect-for-the-united-states/.

Chicago Council on Global Affairs. "America Divided: Political Partisanship and US Foreign Policy." Last modified 2015. https://www.thechicagocouncil.org/sites/default/files/CCGA_PublicSurvey2015.pdf.

Congress.gov. "H.R.5859—113th Congress (2013–2014): Ukraine Freedom Support Act of 2014." Last modified December 18, 2014. https://www.congress.gov/bill/113th -congress/house-bill/5859/.

Curry, Tom. "Republicans Heighten Criticism of Obama's Ukraine Response." NBC News. Last modified March 9, 2014. http://www.nbcnews.com/storyline/ukraine-crisis/repub licans-heighten-criticism-obamas-ukraine-response-n48386.

Democratic National Committee. "2016 Democratic Party Platform." Last modified July 21, 2016. https://www.demconvention.com/wp-content/uploads/2016/07/Democratic -Party-Platform-7.21.16-no-lines.pdf.

Graves, Allison. "Did Trump Campaign Soften Platform Language to Benefit Russia?" Politi-Fact. Last modified August 4, 2016. http://www.politifact.com/truth-o-meter/article /2016/aug/04/did-trump-campaign-soften-platform-language-benefi/.

Herb, Jeremy. "Obama Pressed on Many Fronts to Arm Ukraine." Politico. Last modified March 11, 2015. http://www.politico.com/story/2015/03/obama-pressed-on-many-fronts -to-arm-ukraine-115999.

Kramer, Mark. "Why Did Russia Give Away Crimea Sixty Years Ago?" Wilson Center: Cold War International History Project. Last modified March 19, 2014. https://www.wilson center.org/publication/why-did-russia-give-away-crimea-sixty-years-ago.

Medynskyi, Ivan. "U.S. Military Assistance to Ukraine under Obama and Beyond." *Institute of World Policy*, 2016. Accessed August 14, 2016. http://kennankyiv.org/wp-content /uploads/2016/04/Medynskyi_Agora_V16_final-2.pdf.

New York Times. "After the Summit—Excerpts from Bush's Ukraine Speech—Working 'for the Good of Both of Us.'" Last modified August 2, 1991. http://www.nytimes.com /1991/08/02/world/after-summit-excerpts-bush-s-ukraine-speech-working-for-good -both-us.html?pagewanted=all.

Republican National Committee. "Republican Platform 2016." Last modified 2016. https:// prod-static-ngop-pbl.s3.amazonaws.com/media/documents/DRAFT_12_FINAL[1] -ben_1468872234.pdf.

Rogin, Josh. "Trump Campaign Guts GOP's Anti-Russia Stance on Ukraine." *Washington Post*. Last modified July 18, 2016. https://www.washingtonpost.com/opinions/global -opinions/trump-campaign-guts-gops-anti-russia-stance-on-ukraine/2016/07/18 /98adb3b0-4cf3-11e6-a7d8-13d06b37f256_story.html?utm_term=.9e3881df8dcc.

Simmons, Katie, Bruce Stokes, and Jacob Poushter. "NATO Publics Blame Russia for Ukrainian Crisis, but Reluctant to Provide Military Aid." Pew Research Center. Last modified June 10, 2015. http://file:///C:/Users/Administrator.USL050228/Downloads/Pew-Research -Center-Russia-Ukraine-Report-FINAL-June-10-2015.pdf.

Speaker.gov. "Bipartisan Group of Lawmakers Urges President Obama to Arm Ukraine." Last modified March 5, 2015. http://www.speaker.gov/press-release/bipartisan-group -lawmakers-urges-president-obama-arm-ukraine.

White House. "Fact Sheet: U.S. Assistance to Ukraine." Whitehouse.gov. Last modified December 7, 2015. https://www.whitehouse.gov/the-press-office/2015/12/07/fact-sheet -us-assistance-ukraine.

United Nations

At a Glance

As one of the chief architects of the post–World War II international order, the United States has always played a critical role at the United Nations (UN). The importance of the UN in the eyes of the U.S. government, however, has varied significantly over time. At present, the United States continues to turn to the organization as an instrument of international cooperation on a variety of issues including international peace and security, enforcement of universal human rights norms, and social and humanitarian assistance. At the same time, a significant partisan gap exists between Republicans and Democrats with respect to both the utility of the UN and what efforts it must undertake to be more relevant to U.S. foreign policy in the new millennium.

According to many Republicans, the United Nations . . .

- Is generally less important than international linkages of other sorts, such as alliances and trade agreements;
- Is in desperate need of financial and bureaucratic reform, including the elimination of duplicative agencies and efforts;
- Contains agencies like the UN Population fund that should be prevented from financing abortions in other countries; and
- Interferes too much in the sovereign affairs of member states.

According to many Democrats, the United Nations . . .

- Should promote universal human rights norms;
- Is a cooperative body, and international cooperative agreements benefit the United States and the world;
- Has a legitimate role to play in providing family planning services, including access to safe abortion, in the developing world; and
- Should be fully funded, with the United States maintaining its historic commitment levels.

Overview

U.S. involvement in the United Nations is older than the organization itself. In early 1941, before the United States had entered World War II, President Franklin D. Roosevelt and British prime minister Winston Churchill met to discuss the postwar order. The agreement they produced became known as the Atlantic Charter and was agreed on by all of the allied countries that fought the Axis Powers in the war. Among the principals agreed on by the Allies were the ideas that countries would not seek territorial gains from the war, that states should promote economic cooperation and free trade, and that the ultimate goal should be to eliminate the use of force from international relations.

It was also Roosevelt who first used the term "United Nations" to refer to the Allies collectively. In 1942, the Declaration by United Nations, which later became known as the Declaration of the United Nations, was signed by 26 states. It committed the signatories to strive for human rights, religious freedom, and to fight together against the Axis powers without making separate peace agreements.

The founding members of the United Nations, including the United States, negotiated the final details of the organization's charter at the United Nations Conference on International Organization in San Francisco. The basic elements of the organization had been negotiated at the Dumbarton Oaks Conference in Washington, D.C. over a three-week period in 1944. On July 28, the United States became the first state to ratify the treaty creating the UN by a 98–2 vote in the Senate. The bipartisan vote occurred only after Senate Republicans received assurances that the UN would not supersede in any case the Constitution of the United States. Congress was also insistent that it would not ratify the agreement if the United States did not have a veto in the United Nations Security Council. In addition, the United States was the first country to deposit its instrument of ratification, becoming the first member of the organization. The United Nations was officially founded on October 24, 1945.

The UN Charter contains several key provisions of particular relevance to the United States and its conduct of foreign affairs. Chapter V, VI, and VII, however, contain the most significant powers of the organization in the form of the United Nations Security Council (UNSC). Chapter V describes the functions and membership of the UNSC. The primary victors of World War II, China (at the time the Republic of China), France, Great Britain, the United States, and the Soviet Union (USSR) were all granted permanent membership and a veto of any organization activity with which they disagreed. When the Cold War began, the existence of the veto caused immediate paralysis within the UN Security Council. Chapter VI of the charter relates to the pacific (peaceful) settlement of disputes. It enjoins states from breaches of the peace and acts of aggression and allows the UNSC to suggest measures, such as mediation or arbitration, to resolve disputes. Chapter VII of the UN Charter allows the Security Council to levy economic or other sanctions against countries that threaten international peace and security or to use force.

The Atlantic Charter of 1941

The Atlantic Charter was a joint declaration made by President Franklin D. Roosevelt and Winston Churchill in 1941, before the United States had even entered the war. Although the charter is not an international law, its ideals are reflected in many international laws that exist today, including the charter of the United Nations and the Law of the Sea. The charter is short, but it described several key principles of foreign relations that Roosevelt and Churchill declared to be held in common by the two nations:

First, their countries seek no aggrandizement, territorial or other;

Second, they desire to see no territorial changes that do not accord with the freely expressed wishes of the peoples concerned;

Third, they respect the right of all peoples to choose the form of government under which they will live . . .

Fourth, they will endeavor, with due respect for their existing obligations, to further the enjoyment by all States, great or small, victor or vanquished, of access, on equal terms, to the trade and to the raw materials of the world which are needed for their economic prosperity;

Fifth, they desire to bring about the fullest collaboration between all nations in the economic field with the object of securing, for all, improved labor standards, economic advancement and social security;

Sixth, after the final destruction of the Nazi tyranny, they hope to see established a peace which will . . . afford assurance that all the men in all lands may live out their lives in freedom from fear and want;

Seventh, such a peace should enable all men to traverse the high seas and oceans without hindrance;

Eighth, they believe that all of the nations of the world, for realistic as well as spiritual reasons must come to the abandonment of the use of force . . . They will likewise aid and encourage all other practicable measure which will lighten for peace-loving peoples the crushing burden of armaments.

Source:

NATO. "Atlantic Charter." August 14, 1941. Last updated October 1, 2009. North Atlantic Treaty Organization. http://www.nato.int/cps/en/natohq/official_texts_16912.htm.

In practice, the use of force by the UN, which was to be organized under a Military Staff Committee, has never occurred in the manner envisioned in the charter, which would have required member states to commit standby forces to the UN. For a variety of reasons, including Cold War gridlock and the desire of states to maintain sovereign use of their armed forces, the UN never developed its own response capability. During the Cold War, so-called peacekeeping missions, where lightly armed UN troops and observers would interpose themselves between warring states (with the permission of those states), became the norm. Only at the onset of the Korean War did the UN authorize the use of direct military force by member states against an aggressor (North Korea in that instance). The Security Council was only able to act in that instance because of the absence of the Soviet Union, which was protesting the fact that the Western powers were unwilling to allow the People's Republic of China to take the seat designated for China on the UNSC. Instead, the Republic of China (ROC) maintained its membership even though its leadership had fled to Taiwan after losing control of the government to communist rebels.

Over the course of its history, the United States and the UN have had a strained relationship. At the founding of the organization, the United States had an advantage in its voting coalition within the United Nations General Assembly, where every country has one vote. As the number of developing countries joining the UN grew, however, the United States often found itself on the losing side of General Assembly votes. Although General Assembly Resolutions are not binding on the membership, they do express the collective will of the international community. Over time, the United States has one of the lowest rates of overall voting coincidence with other UN members. Voting coincidence measures the percentage of times that the United States votes the same way as another member of the General Assembly or UNSC, aggregates across all countries. Essentially, voting coincidence is a measure of isolation, and the United States has found itself more isolated at the UN over time.

Partially as a result of this isolation, calls from some American lawmakers and foreign policy observers for UN reform—or for the United States to leave the United Nations altogether—have grown louder over time. Advocates of reform charge the size of the UN bureaucracy has become bloated, that UN officials are too well-compensated, and that corruption within the United Nations System is widespread. On the whole, the Republican Party, as well as many moderate Democrats, tends to support the reform movement. Calls for reform of the UN were an area of continuity between the presidencies of Bill Clinton and George W. Bush.

Advocates of withdrawal from the United Nations, who to this point have gained little momentum, also point out that it is not uncommon for countries with poor human rights records to be elected to the UN Human Rights Council. They say that this sometimes leaves the United States without the means to promote respect for individual human rights through the UN. Other American advocates for withdrawal also claim that the UN is biased against Israel to the point where the organization fails to consider the role of the Palestinian Authority, now called the State of Palestine in the UN General Assembly, or belligerent Arab states as sources of instability in the region.

Republicans on U.S. Policy toward the United Nations

The 2012 Republican Party platform mentioned the United Nations four times. The overall theme is that, while the United Nations has its place in global affairs,

Bill Clinton Makes the Case for UN Reform

During his first two years in office, President Bill Clinton enjoyed Democratic majorities in both the House and Senate. Pressure from Republicans in Congress to reform the United Nations bureaucracy was strong during this period, but Republicans did not have the clout to dictate UN policy. However, Clinton showed some support for this perspective in a 1993 address to the United Nations General Assembly:

Changes in the U.N.'s peacekeeping operations must be part of an even broader program of United Nations reform. I say that again not to criticize the United Nations but to help to improve it. As our Ambassador Madeleine Albright has suggested, the United States has always played a twin role to the U.N., first friend and first critic.

I applaud the initial steps the Secretary-General has taken to reduce and to reform the United Nations bureaucracy. Now, we must all do even more to root out waste. Before this General Assembly is over, let us establish a strong mandate for an Office of Inspector General so that it can attain a reputation for toughness, for integrity, for effectiveness. Let us build new confidence among our people that the United Nations is changing with the needs of our times.

Ultimately, the key for reforming the United Nations, as in reforming our own Government, is to remember why we are here and whom we serve. It is wise to recall that the first words of the U.N. Charter are not "We, the government," but, "We, the people of the United Nations." That means in every country the teachers, the workers, the farmers, the professionals, the fathers, the mothers, the children, from the most remote village in the world to the largest metropolis, they are why we gather in this great hall. It is their futures that are at risk when we act or fail to act, and it is they who ultimately pay our bills.

Source:

U.S. Department of State. "Address by President Bill Clinton to the UN General Assembly." Last modified September 27, 1993. http://www.state.gov/p/io/potusunga/207375.htm.

the United States must be prepared to "go its own way" when necessary (Republican National Committee 2012). The platform enumerates a litany of problems with the United Nations, including a scandal-ridden bureaucracy, isolation of Israel, human rights abusers gaining positions of power on the Human Rights Council, overpayment issues in the Secretariat, promotion of abortion, and a general lack of transparency. The platform also warns of excessive UN power over domestic environmental policy and the potential for it to exert supranational control over the Internet. Missing from the 2012 platform was a call for a reduction in United States dues to the UN (dues owed by each member nation are calculated based on a formula that incorporates factors like national income and population size). The United States has always paid the top rate due to the size of the economy and higher per capita income. The 2016 Republican platform echoes the concern that that United Nations is pushing a political, rather than a science-driven, agenda on climate change. The 2016 platform also argues that Obama's administration should cut all U.S. funding to the UN Framework Convention on Climate Change as a result of Palestine being allowed to join the organization. The United States does not recognize Palestine, a set of territories currently occupied by Israel.

Public opinion among self-identified Republicans largely mirrors the arguments made in the 2012 platform. At the most general level, only 41 percent of Republicans had a positive view of the United Nations according to a Pew poll taken around the same time period (Pew Research Center's Global Attitudes Project 2013). In addition, only 25 percent of Republicans believed that one of the major policy goals of the United States should be to strengthen the United Nations (Drake 2013). In a separate survey conducted three years later, 13 percent of Republicans thought that strengthening the United Nations would be a very effective way to help the United States effectively meet its foreign policy goals (Chicago Council on Global Affairs 2015). Overall, Republicans are less likely than Democrats to favor multilateral solutions, such as those crafted by international organizations such as the UN, to the challenges facing the United States. The general trend in public opinion concerning the United Nations also applies to specific cases. For example, on the eve of the U.S. invasion of Iraq in 2003, a plurality of Americans favored making the invasion contingent on the approval of the UN Security Council. By contrast, a plurality of Republicans favored the invasion even if the United Nations did not issue its approval (Moore 2002).

Republicans in government have also tended to be quite critical of the United Nations. In 1983, President Reagan famously withdrew the United States from the United Nations Educational Scientific and Cultural Organization (UNESCO) over its alleged promotion of collective rights over individual human rights. The United States did not withdraw from the UN itself or any of its other specialized agencies, however, and the United States quietly rejoined UNESCO in 2002. Nearly every year, meanwhile, a small group of Republicans in the House or Senate sponsor a resolution to disassociate the United States from the United Nations. These resolutions normally take on one of two forms. In the first form, such as the Resolution sponsored by Republican senator Rand Paul in 2013, Congress strips all U.S. funding from the organization. At current assessment rates, that is just over $7 billion. Paul's 2013 bill never made it beyond the committee state, where no action was taken on the legislation. In the second form, typified by a bill introduced by Republican Mike Rogers in 2013, the United States formally withdraws from the United Nations, including its specialized agencies. In the bill sponsored by Rogers, the United States would also have withdrawn from all UN-based treaties and covenants, such as the International Covenant on Civil and Political Rights. Rogers's bill also never made it past the committee phase. Generally, there is enough support for the United Nations, even among Republicans, that these bills die in committee out of recognition that they would never survive a vote on the floor of the House or Senate, much less a veto-override vote.

Other Republican elected officials have taken aim at specific United Nations bodies or policies with which they disagree. For example, in 2010, Representative

Ileana Ros-Lehtinen of Florida introduced legislation that would have cut U.S. funding for the United Nations by an amount equal to U.S. budgetary support of the UN Human Rights Council (Rubin 2010). The bill would also have withdrawn the United States from the Council. Republicans object to the fact that countries known for individual human rights abuses, such as Iran and Vietnam, are able to gain seats on the Human Rights Council. Republicans also believe that the Council does not go far enough to call out human rights abuses in countries such as China. During the George W. Bush administration, the United States withheld funding from the United Nations Population Fund (UNFPA) because, in its view, the organization promoted abortion as a family planning option in China. The UNFPA has responded that it does not promote abortion in countries where abortion is not legal, though it does promote access to postabortion care and safe abortion facilities in countries where abortion is already legal.

Republicans have, however, sometimes sought approval from the United Nations to help them advance desired foreign policy outcomes. For example, the United States turned to the United Nations for authorization to liberate Kuwait from Iraq in 1990–1991. The Bush administration also sought UN authorization for the Invasion of Iraq in 2003 in response to concerns about Saddam Hussein's links to Al Qaeda and the development of weapons of mass destruction. Though the United Nations never formally authorized the invasion, the United States cited a violation of a previous UN Security Council Resolution (1441 of 2002) as justification for the invasion of Iraq in 2003.

Generally speaking, the major Republican candidates for their party's 2016 presidential nomination expressed skepticism about the United Nations' ability to help the United States meet its foreign policy goals. Senator Ted Cruz, for example, argued that the Obama administration has used the UN to "bind the United States and take away our sovereignty" (Real Clear Politics 2015). Cruz also criticized the oft-maligned Human Rights Council for its condemnation of what the council called Israeli human rights violations in the occupied Gaza Strip. Ohio governor John Kasich, meanwhile, emphasized his belief that the United Nations should spend more time focused on ISIS rather than climate change (Doris 2016). Kasich also criticized the UN for its endorsement of the Joint Comprehensive Framework—the Iran nuclear deal negotiated by the Obama administration. Businessman (and eventual nominee) Donald Trump, meanwhile, argued that the United States spends too much money on intergovernmental organizations such as the North Atlantic Treaty Organization (NATO) and the United Nations, and he implied that the United Nations was incapable of dispute resolution, one of the organizations' primary functions (Parker 2016).

Democrats on U.S. Policy toward the United Nations

Unlike the Republican platform of the same year, the Democratic Party's 2012 platform emphasized the utility of the UN in areas such as international peace and security. The platform specifically mentioned Iran and North Korea, both of which were placed under sanctions under Chapter VII of the UN Security Council in response to their efforts to develop nuclear weapons programs, as examples of productive UN actions (Democratic National Committee 2012). The platform also stated that the party was dedicated to restoring American leadership at the UN, an attempt to draw a contrast with Republicans on the issue of multilateralism and international cooperation in general. For the most part, Democrats are more likely to favor a stronger role for the United Nations and are less likely to caution the public about attempts by the organization to influence domestic politics. The platform only refers to reform in the context of modernizing the UN infrastructure. Still, the United Nations has not been exempt from Democratic Party criticism.

For many years Democrats in the general public have generally held a more favorable view of the United Nations than Republicans. In a 2013 survey, for example, 71 percent of Democrats expressed favorable opinions concerning the United Nations compared to 41 percent of Republicans (Pew Research Center's Global Attitudes Project 2013). According to the same poll, 50 percent of Democrats also believe that strengthening the United Nations should be a top U.S. foreign policy priority, compared with 25 percent of Republicans who hold this viewpoint (Drake 2013). In one of the widest partisan gaps, the percentage of Democrats who believe that the UN should play a major role in world affairs exceeds the percentage of Republicans who make the same argument by over 50 percent. These views are consistent with a trend that has existed since the U.S. Senate debated whether or not the country would join the United Nations, namely that Democrats are more comfortable with an assertive role for the UN in global affairs than are Republicans.

The relationship between Democratic Party presidents and the United Nations has been uneven. President Clinton, for example, blocked United Nations secretary general Boutros Boutros-Ghali from serving a second term. Boutros-Ghali became the first secretary general to be denied this possibility. In part due to his own views on the issue and in part due to pressure from congressional Republicans, Clinton argued that the UN bureaucracy had become too bloated and too costly and that new leadership could better institute necessary bureaucratic reforms. The Clinton administration was also highly critical of the UN's unwillingness to act more forcefully to stop the genocide in Bosnia. The United Nations Protection Force (UNPROFOR) was, for a significant period of time, not allowed to conduct the robust and effective strikes against Bosnian-Serb positions that the Clinton administration thought necessary to protect Bosnian Muslims from violence. In spite of this tension, however, Clinton did advocate payment of U.S. arrears (back dues) to the United Nations. Congressional Republicans had blocked payment of arrears due to their own concerns about the inefficiency and corruption of the United Nations.

By contrast, President Obama is generally viewed as having a more positive relationship with the United Nations. In his first address to the General Assembly of the United Nations, Obama pledged to abandon what Democrats viewed as the unilateral approach of his predecessor, Republican president George W. Bush.

In multiple cases, the Obama administration has shown a willingness to go to the UN even when this angers key allies like Israel. On the issue of the Iranian nuclear program, for example, Israel, as well as Republicans in Congress, urged the president to consider air strikes against Iranian nuclear facilities. Instead, President Obama sought the imposition of new and stronger economic sanctions in the UNSC, which obliged. Iran eventually came to the negotiating table and traded concessions on its nuclear program for partial sanctions relief. The resulting Joint Comprehensive Plan of Action has been assailed by Republicans as leaving Iran with too many paths to a nuclear weapon. Obama has insisted that the multilateral negotiations produced a more durable result than would airstrikes, new unilateral sanctions (the United States already uses sanctions against Iran for other reasons), or a combination of both. Hillary Clinton, who won the Democratic presidential nomination in 2016, has promised to continue the commitment to multilateralism and the UN displayed by Obama.

Within Congress, Democrats also tend to favor the UN more than Republicans. Democrats, for example, have not sponsored bills to withdraw the United States from the United Nations or to cut UN funding entirely. Also, Democrats in Congress are less likely than their Republican counterparts to vote in favor of withholding U.S. funding from specific United Nations programs, such as the UNFPA or UNESCO or opposing tying payment of U.S. arrears to UN reform benchmarks, as dictated in the Helms-Biden Agreement of 1997 (Bongang 2007, 178). This does not mean, however, the Democrats are unwilling to criticize the UN or use U.S. financial leverage against the organization. In 2015, for example, Democrats in Congress were heavily critical of the Obama administration for bringing the Joint Comprehensive Plan of Action (JCPOA) with Iran before the UN Security Council before bringing it before Congress. Democratic senator Ben Cardin argued that Congress should have been allowed to voice its opinion on the bill first. Both Democrats and Republicans expressed concern that the move to consult the UN first amounted to bypassing Congress in favor of a supranational organization, something with which even multilateralist Democrats are uncomfortable. Democrats were not, however, willing to allow displeasure with President Obama for going to the United Nations first to allow the JCPOA from taking effect. Democrats were able to mount a successful filibuster on a Republican-led effort to vote down JCPOA in the Senate (see Iran entry).

Further Reading

Bite, Vita. "United Nations System Funding: Congressional Issues." Congressional Research Service. Last modified September 21, 2005. http://fpc.state.gov/documents/organiza tion/55841.pdf.

Bongang, Benn L. *The United States and the United Nations Congressional Funding and U.N. Reform*. New York: LFB Scholarly Pub, 2007. http://public.eblib.com/choice/public fullrecord.aspx?p=3016839.

Chicago Council on Global Affairs. "America Divided: Political Partisanship and US Foreign Policy." Last modified 2015. https://www.thechicagocouncil.org/sites/default/files /CCGA_PublicSurvey2015.pdf.

Clinton, Bill. "Address by President Bill Clinton to the UN General Assembly." U.S. Department of State. Last modified September 27, 1993. http://www.state.gov/p/io/potusunga /207375.htm.

Democratic National Committee. "2012 Democratic Platform." Last modified 2012. https:// www.democrats.org/party-platform.

Doris, Margaret. "John Kasich: 'I Know That Human Beings Affect the Climate.'" *Esquire.* February 29, 2016. http://www.esquire.com/news-politics/politics/news/a42549/john -kasich-climate-change/.

Drake, Bruce. "Republicans Gloomier about U.S. Role in the World." Pew Research Center. Last modified December 5, 2013. http://www.pewresearch.org/fact-tank/2013/12/05 /republicans-gloomier-about-u-s-role-in-the-world/.

Fox News. "Exclusive: John Kasich on Why He Should Be the Next President." July 21, 2015. http://www.foxnews.com/transcript/2015/07/21/exclusive-john-kasich-on-why -should-be-next-president/.

Lillian Goldman Law Library. "Atlantic Charter." Last modified 2008. avalon.law.yale.edu /wwii/atlantic.asp.

Moore, David W. "Support for Invasion of Iraq Remains Contingent on U.N. Approval." Gallup. Last modified November 12, 2002. http://www.gallup.com/poll/7195/support -invasion-iraq-remains-contingent-un-approval.aspx.

Parker, Ashley. "Donald Trump Says NATO Is 'Obsolete,' UN Is 'Political Game.'" *New York Times.* Last modified April 2, 2016. http://www.nytimes.com/politics/first-draft /2016/04/02/donald-trump-tells-crowd-hed-be-fine-if-nato-broke-up/.

Pew Research Center's Global Attitudes Project. "UN Retains Strong Global Image." Last modified September 17, 2013. http://www.pewglobal.org/2013/09/17/united-nations -retains-strong-global-image/.

RealClear Politics. "Cruz: Obama 'Wants to Use the United Nations to Bind the United States and Take Away Sovereignty.'" September 16, 2015. http://www.realclearpolitics .com/video/2015/09/16/cruz_obama_wants_to_use_the_united_nations_to_bind_the _united_states_and_take_away_sovereignty.html.

Republican National Committee. "Republican Party Platform 2012." Republican National Committee. Accessed January 7, 2016. https://prod-static-ngop-pbl.s3.amazonaws.com /docs/2012GOPPlatform.pdf.

Rubin, Jennifer. "Right Turn: A Change in Foreign Affairs?" *Washington Post.* Last modified December 12, 2010. http://www.washingtonpost.com/wp-dyn/content/article/2010/12 /10/AR2010121007440.html.

Glossary

African Growth and Opportunity Act (AGOA): A nonreciprocal (the African countries in the program do not have to provide the same benefits to the United States that are provided to them) trade preference program that provides duty-free treatment to U.S. imports of certain products from eligible sub-Saharan African (SSA) countries. As of 2016 there are 49 candidate SSA countries, with 39 eligible for the preference benefits.

African Union (AU): A continent-wide, political, economic, and social organization with 54 member states. Its main goals are the promotion of democracy, human rights, economic development, and peace and security. The AU is headquartered in Addis Ababa, Ethiopia.

All-of-the-Above Energy Strategy: A strategy designed to increase American energy independence by cultivating domestic sources of energy. These sources include both increasing renewable energy options such as solar, wind, and hydroelectric power and increasing access to fossil fuels through increased exploration and exploitation of domestic sources of coal, oil, and natural gas.

Al Qaeda: A terrorist group founded by Osama bin Laden in the late 1980s. The group is most infamous for its attacks on the World Trade Center buildings and the Pentagon on September 11, 2001. Al Qaeda has several affiliate organizations that operate in Africa, the Middle East, and Asia.

American Israel Public Affairs Committee (AIPAC): AIPAC is the largest and most influential pro-Israel lobbying group in the United States. Its goal is to influence public opinion and public policy on issues related to U.S. foreign policy toward Israel. AIPAC is generally considered to be the most powerful of the ethnic/religious lobbying groups in the United States.

American Recovery and Reinvestment Act: Passed in 2009, the American Recovery and Reinvestment Act was a far-reaching bill crafted by Democrats and the Obama administration to stimulate the economy after the Great Recession that began in 2007. Although focused on the domestic economy, the stimulus did provide additional resources to a variety of State Department foreign policy projects. The act also focused on the development of clean energy policy as part of the all-of-the-above energy strategy.

Anti-Ballistic Missile (ABM) Treaty: A treaty between the United States and the Soviet Union (later Russia) that was signed in 1972. The treaty limited the ability of both countries to use missile defense platforms to defend against attacks from the other state. The idea was to make nuclear war unthinkable by limiting the ability of each side to defend against it (see mutually assured destruction). The United States withdrew from the treaty in 2002, announcing that it would develop missile defense designed to stop attacks from "rogue states" like Iran and North Korea.

Arab Spring: The Arab Spring refers to a series of political uprisings that began in Tunisia in 2011 and spread to many areas of the Arab world. Although observers hoped that the

Arab Spring would bring democratic reform, it has led to significant instability and conflict in Arab countries such as Egypt and Syria.

Authorization for the Use of Military Force (AUMF): AUMFs allow the president to deploy troops into harm's way without a formal declaration of war. For example, AUMFs authorized the invasion of Afghanistan and Iraq as part of the Global War on Terror.

Benghazi Attack: An attack on the U.S. consulate in Benghazi, Libya, on September 11, 2012. Four Americans, including Ambassador Christopher Stevens, died in the attack. The tragedy became a political lightning rod in both the 2012 and the 2016 presidential elections, with Republicans accusing Democrats of not doing enough to protect the consulate and Democrats accusing Republicans of politicizing the issue.

Biological Weapons Convention (BWC): Bans the development, stockpiling, and use of biological weapons. The BWC entered into force in 1975. The treaty is known for its weak enforcement provisions.

Bipartisan Budget Act of 2015: A budget compromise designed to prevent the government from shutting down or defaulting on any debt payments during 2016 and 2017. The legislation ends the sequester era cuts on discretionary spending, including military spending.

Blue Dog Democrat: Blue dog Democrats are conservative Democrats, especially on matters related to fiscal policy. Blue dog Democrats are often, though not always, from Southern states.

Boosted Fission Nuclear Weapon: A fission (atom-splitting) nuclear device that uses a small amount of fusion (atom combination) material. This type of bomb has a higher yield than a traditional fission device, but a much lower yield than fusion devices; however, they are much easier to produce than fusion weapons.

Brexit: A combination of the terms "Britain" and "exit" designed to cleverly portray the process by which the United Kingdom, most of which is Great Britain, voted to leave the European Union. The U.K. vote on Brexit occurred in June 2016.

Caliphate: A caliphate is an Islamic state governed by Islamic law and ruled by and Islamic Caliph. The terrorist group the Islamic State of Iraq and Syria (ISIS) has declared a caliphate in parts of Iraq and Syria. The ISIS caliphate is not, however, recognized by most Muslims.

Camp David Accords: Concluded in 1978, the Camp David Accords were a peace and mutual recognition agreement between Egypt and Israel, facilitated by President Carter.

Central American Free Trade Agreement (CAFTA): A regional free trade agreement between the United States and Costa Rica, El Salvador, Guatemala, Honduras, Nicaragua, and the Dominican Republic (which joined the agreement after it entered into force). CAFTAs main provisions call for the elimination of tariffs between parties, which lowers barriers to trade.

Chemical Weapons Convention: An international treaty that bans the stockpiling, development, and use of chemical weapons. The treaty, which entered into force in 1997, is known for its strong verification provisions, which require states to submit to random inspections of previous chemical weapons sites and monitor dual-use technologies.

Chinese Exclusion Act: Signed into law in 1882, the Chinese Exclusion Act imposed a 10-year moratorium on Chinese labor immigration into the United States. Naturalization of existing Chinese aliens was also severely restricted. The act was extended, and parts of the exclusion lasted until the 1940s, when a quota-based immigration policy became the law of the land.

Civil Liberties: Basic rights and freedoms that the government cannot take away. In the United States, many of these liberties are enumerated in the Bill of Rights, which consists of the first 10 amendments to the U.S. Constitution.

Civil Society: A voluntary network of groups and organizations working in the interest of citizens to enhance their vision of the public good.

Clean Power Plan: Announced by President Obama in August 2015, the Clean Power Plan is a series of regulations designed to cut carbon pollution, increase fuel efficiency, and improve greenhouse gas monitoring. Emplaced by executive order, the plan has been enjoined from taking effect until the U.S. Supreme Court hears a case as to its constitutionality.

Climate Change: Altered regional and global climate patterns largely attributed to increased emissions of carbon dioxide and other greenhouse gases during the 20th and 21st centuries. "Anthropogenic climate change" is a term for climate change directly attributable to human activity.

Coalition of the Willing: The group of countries, led by the United States, that allied to invade Iraq in 2003. After the United Nations failed to formally authorize the war, the United States went about assembling a group of countries willing to lend some assistance, as well as international legitimacy, to the invasion.

Coalition Support Funds: Money made available by the United States to reimburse countries for their contributions to antiterrorism and counterterrorism efforts, especially those countries that incur significant expenses combating terrorism in their own countries or that provide facilities and support to U.S. troops engaged in such efforts.

Cold War: An ideological struggle, manifesting itself in political and military tension, between the United States and its allies and the Soviet Union and its allies. The Cold War began shortly after World War II and ended in 1991 with the collapse of the Soviet Union.

Communism: Communism is a theory and a political system based on the idea of common ownership of the means of production, including land and capital, by the people. In practice, Communism has been associated with state monopolization of the means of production, as well as all political institutions within the Communist state.

Comprehensive Test-Ban Treaty (CTBT): A multilateral agreement that would ban the testing of nuclear explosive devices, including nuclear weapons. The CTBT was opened for signature in 1996 but has not entered into force. The United States has refused to ratify the treaty, though it does not currently test nuclear weapons, because it wishes to reserve the right to do so in order to ensure the continued viability of U.S. stockpiles.

Convention on the Rights of the Child: A multilateral agreement designed to enumerate the rights of children, including the right to basic protection, freedom from hazardous child labor, and freedom not to fight in war (through optional protocol). Though the United States protects many of these rights, it is the only country in the world not to have ratified the convention.

Council on Foreign Relations: A nonpartisan think tank that attempts to educate policy makers, educators, and all citizens on issues related to foreign policy. The council publishes the widely read journal, *Foreign Affairs*.

Coup d'état: An extraconstitutional and illegal seizure of political control in a country, often undertaken by the military, or with the direct support of the military.

Crimea: A piece of territory in Eastern Ukraine, also called the Crimean Peninsula. Crimea has a large number of ethnic Russians. With the assistance of direct military intervention on the part of Russia, Crimea seceded from Ukraine and voted to join the Russian Federation in 2014. The move has not been recognized by the international community.

Cuban American National Foundation (CANF): An interest group dedicated to bringing human rights and democracy to Cuba. The CANF was started by Cuban Americans living as exiles in the United States. The organization has lobbied for the imposition and maintenance of comprehensive sanctions against Cuba.

Cuban Missile Crisis: A foreign policy and military crisis between the United States and the Soviet Union that occurred in 1962 after the discovery of Soviet nuclear missiles in Cuba. The United States under President Kennedy placed a blockade around Cuba to prevent further nuclear supplies from arriving and threatened to take action to neutralize the existing threat. The Soviet Union ultimately relented, removing the missiles in exchange for guarantees from the United States not to invade Cuba and to remove U.S. nuclear weapons from Turkey.

Currency Manipulation: A practice normally designed to control the value of one's currency, rather than allowing value to float on the open market. Often, countries will attempt to lower the value of their own currency by selling it and purchasing foreign reserves. Cheaper currency allows a country's exports to sell for less on international markets, improving competitiveness. The United States frequently accuses China of currency manipulation.

Cybersecurity: Preventing the authorized use of electronic data and computer networks, as well as preventing unauthorized access to data networks.

Cybersecurity Act of 2015: Provides mechanisms for cybersecurity information sharing between the public and private sector. To protect civil liberties, private entities must remove personal data before sharing with the government. The information sharing provisions of the act are voluntary and do not create a duty to act under the law.

Cyberterrorism: Using information technology to spread fear for political or other ideological purposes, or attacking information technology systems for political or other ideological purposes.

Deferred Action for Childhood Arrivals (DACA): Deferred action refers to the ability of the Department of Homeland Security to delay deportation of undocumented immigrants at its discretion. DACA, which was announced in 2014 by President Obama, would have extended this deferred action to include undocumented immigrants who arrived in the United States as children. DACA was blocked at the appellate court level, and the Supreme Court deadlocked 4-4, leaving the ban on DACA (and DAPA) in place.

Deferred Action for Parents of Americans (DAPA): Deferred action refers to the ability of the Department of Homeland Security to delay deportation of undocumented immigrants at its discretion. DAPA, which was announced in 2014 by President Obama, would have extended this deferred action to parents of children born in the United States, as long as the undocumented immigrant has lived in the United States since 2010. DAPA was blocked at the appellate court level, and the Supreme Court deadlocked 4–4, leaving the ban on DAPA (and DACA) in place.

Demilitarized Zone (DMZ): Refers to a 150-mile long zone following the 38th parallel that marks the ceasefire line between North and South Korea at the end of the Korean War in 1953.

Development, Relief, and Education for Alien Minors (DREAM) Act: A law proposed in multiple sessions of Congress, but never passed, that would provide a path to citizenship for undocumented immigrants who arrived in the United States as children and seek higher education or to serve in the military. The DREAM Act has never passed Congress.

Disarmament: Refers to reductions or the elimination of weapons and military forces. Disarmament often takes place in the context of bilateral or multilateral treaties.

Drug Cartel: A criminal organization that engages in drug production and trafficking.

Drug War: The War on Drugs was declared in 1971 by President Nixon. Domestically, the war on drugs includes prohibition and punishment for use, distribution, and production. In foreign policy, the drug war includes U.S. financial, technical, and logistical support to countries attempting to eliminate drug production and trafficking.

Dual-Use Technology: Refers to technology that has both military and civilian uses. In the context of weapons of mass destruction, dual-use technology is anything that can be used both in peaceful civilian applications and in the production of biological, chemical, and nuclear weapons. Dual-use technologies are often grouped or "scheduled" according to the threat of diversion to nonpeaceful purposes or their level of use in peaceful applications.

Environmental Protection Agency (EPA): The EPA is the main environmental regulation agency in the United States. The agency also monitors environmental degradation and conducts research on environmental issues.

European Monetary Union: A subset of EU countries that have also agreed to use a common currency (the Euro) and set all monetary policy together, rather than as individual states.

European Union (EU): The EU is an intergovernmental organization created by an agreement between 28 countries. Those countries give up a portion of their sovereignty and agree to allow free movement of goods, services, and people between the members. They also agree to make some decisions at the European level, rather than their home states.

Filibuster: A parliamentary procedure technique that allows a minority of U.S. senators (as few as 41) to block a vote on a piece of pending legislation. Under Senate rules, a speaker may speak to a resolution as long as desired. The only way to stop a senator speaking endlessly is to invoke cloture (a motion to cut off debate), which requires 60 votes to pass. If cloture cannot be invoked, the senator may continue to speak, blocking a vote on the resolution until the Senate agrees to move to another matter. Currently, the filibuster does not require a continuous floor speech to operate. A senator need only state their intention to launch a filibuster to require the invocation of cloture.

Fissile Material: Material (usually specific isotopes of uranium or plutonium) that is capable of sustaining a nuclear reaction via fission (the splitting of atoms). Fissile material may be used in the generation of nuclear power or the construction of nuclear weapons, provided it is purified to the correct level (normally greater than 90 percent pure for the creation of nuclear explosive devices).

Foreign Assistance Act: Originally passed in 1961, and modified several times, the act governs how the United States distributes foreign aid. The act created the U.S. Agency for International Development (USAID) to govern the distribution of aid within broad federal guidelines.

Foreign Direct Investment (FDI): An investment made by individual(s), a company, or a country in the business sector of another country.

Foreign Terrorist Organization Designation: The Immigration and Nationality Act requires the secretary of state to create a list of organizations engaged in terrorist activity.

This designation requires the United States to monitor the group to ensure that no U.S. nationals or the U.S. government provide it material support.

Free Rider: An individual (or a country within an intergovernmental organization) that gains the benefits of membership or the fruits of the efforts of an organization or collective activity without engaging in any of the work. For example, a country the benefits from the global reduction in greenhouse gases, but does not itself reduce emissions of greenhouse gases, could be considered a free rider.

General Agreement on Tariffs and Trade (GATT): Established in 1948 and lasting until the creation of the World Trade Organization in the mid-1990s. GATT was a series of agreements to reduce import quotas and reduce tariffs on a variety of individually negotiated goods.

Generalized System of Preferences (GSP): Provides preferential access (normally duty free) for 5,000 different types of products imported into the United States from eligible developing countries. There are currently 122 eligible beneficiary countries.

Geneva Protocol of 1925: Official known as the Protocol for the Prohibition of the Use in War of Asphyxiating, Poisonous or other Gases, and of Bacteriological Methods of Warfare, the treaty prohibits the use of chemical and biological weapons in international warfare but does not prohibit their development, stockpiling, or use in domestic conflicts.

Grand Strategy: Refers formally to the collection of plans and policies that comprise the state's deliberate effort to harness political, military, diplomatic, and economic tools together to advance that state's national interest. The term is mostly used by academics who study U.S. foreign policy.

Greenhouse Gas: Any gas that traps heat in the Earth's atmosphere. Carbon dioxide and methane are examples of greenhouse gases.

Guantanamo Bay: Location of a naval base and terrorist detention center. Guantanamo is in Cuba, but the United States directly controls the area and pays Cuba rent to maintain a base there. Cuba does not currently recognize what it considers to be an occupation and does not accept transfer payments for the U.S. base. The United States has controlled Guantanamo Bay since 1903.

Heavily Indebted Poor Countries Initiative (HIPC): A multilateral debt relief initiative, later joined by bilateral lenders, designed to reduce the debt of the world's poorest countries to more manageable levels.

Helms-Burton Act: Passed in 1996 as the Cuban Liberty and Democratic Solidarity Act, Helms-Burton strengthened U.S. sanctions against Cuba and placed control for larger portions of the Cuban embargo in the hands of Congress.

Hezbollah: Translated as "Party of God," Hezbollah is a Shiite Islamic political movement and a terrorist group. It is especially powerful in Lebanon and has tried to remove all Israeli influence from the country. Hezbollah is backed heavily by Iran.

Humanitarian Intervention: The use of military force by one state or intergovernmental organization in the territory of another with the purpose of protecting human rights or delivering humanitarian aid.

Hydraulic Fracking: A process designed to release natural gas and oil from shale deposits by pumping a mixture of water, sand, and chemicals into cracks in the deposits. This releases the trapped fossil fuels.

Hydrogen Bomb: A hydrogen bomb produces its energy through fusion (combining isotopes) rather than fission (splitting atoms). Fusion releases much more energy than fission, resulting in higher explosive yields.

Immigration Act of 1924: The first piece of comprehensive immigration legislation to set a quota on immigration from other countries. The original quota was 2 percent per year of the number of people from that country already living in the United States (based on census data).

Intercontinental Ballistic Missile (ICBM): A guided missile designed to deliver a payload to a target anywhere in the world. Generally, ICBMs carry a nuclear warhead or multiple warheads.

Intergovernmental Panel on Climate Change (IPCC): A scientific body set up by the international community in 1988 to provide the world with clear, scientific data on the current state of climate change and its impact.

Intermestic: A term coined by foreign policy scholar Bayless Manning to refer to an issue that has both foreign policy and domestic dimensions. Trade policy, for example, is intermestic in that tariffs have clear domestic and foreign policy dimensions.

Internally Displaced Person: Like a refugee, an internally displaced person flees their home because of a well-founded fear of political persecution for reasons of race, nationality, religion, or political opinion. However, an internally displaced person fleas to a location within their home state. Unlike refugees, internally displaced persons are not covered under international law. However, internal migration can lead to increased instability, which can become a basis for humanitarian intervention.

International Atomic Energy Agency (IAEA): An intergovernmental organization designed to promote cooperation in the peaceful use of nuclear technology. Also, serves as the principal verification mechanism for the Nuclear Nonproliferation Treaty.

International Covenant on Civil and Political Rights: A multilateral treaty that entered into force in 1976. The treaty covers rights such as freedom of speech, religion, and assembly, as well as the right to vote. The treaty also protects due process rights.

International Development Association (IDA): The IDA is the part of the World Bank that provides loans and grants to the world's poorest countries in order to enable these countries to undertake development programs.

International Monetary Fund (IMF): An organization dedicated to promoting financial stability and monetary policy cooperation between states. The IMF makes loans to countries facing balance of payment difficulties.

International Security Assistance Force (ISAF): A NATO force designed to provide internal security and training in Afghanistan in the wake of the 2001 U.S. invasion. In 2011, the ISAF began to transition international security responsibilities directly to the Afghan government.

Intifada: A term meaning "tremor" or a "shaking off" in Arabic that denotes periods of Palestinian uprisings in the occupied territories of the West Bank and Gaza Strip. The two commonly cited intifadas occurred from roughly 1987–1991 and 2000–2005.

Investor-State Dispute Settlement (ISDS): An international arbitration procedure that allows investors to sue a state for alleged discriminatory behavior under the terms of an international treaty. The Trans-Pacific Partnership (TPP) contains ISDS provisions that have made it controversial among critics who argue that ISDS decreases state sovereignty.

Islamism: A political movement within Islam that generally desires to replace secular laws with Islamic laws.

Islamic State of Iraq and Greater Syria (ISIS): An Islamist terrorist group that wishes to establish an Islamic Caliphate in large portions of the Middle East. Often referred to as the Islamic State or Iraq and the Levant (an area of the eastern Mediterranean containing parts of Israel, Jordan, Iraq, Syria, Lebanon, Turkey, and Egypt.

Joint Comprehensive Plan of Action (JCPOA): An agreement between Iran, the United States, China, France, Russia, the U.K., and Germany, designed to curtail Iran's nuclear weapons program in exchange for sanctions relief. Iran will decrease its stock of enriched uranium and reduce its enrichment capability by two-thirds.

Least Developed Country (LDC): A classification by the United Nations that denotes countries with very low per capita income, low levels of overall health, and high economic vulnerability.

Lockerbie Bombing: Refers to the bombing of Pan-American Airways Flight 103, killing over 250 passengers and crewmembers. The attack was carried out under the sponsorship of Libyan leader Muammar Qaddafi.

Major non-NATO Ally Designation: A non-NATO member state designated by the president as a strategic partner of the United States. The status does not imply automatic U.S. assistance in case of an attack, but normally includes increased military aid and cooperative defense research.

Marshall Plan: Officially known as the European Recovery Program (ERP), the Marshall Plan was designed to help western European economies to rebuild after World War II. The United States provided $12 billion in Marshall Plan aid, which would be valued at over $120 billion today.

Mérida Initiative: A security agreement between Mexico and the United States designed to fight organized crime and associated drug production and trafficking. The United States has provided nearly $2.5 billion in security aid to Mexico under the terms of the plan.

Millennium Challenge Corporation: An independent U.S. foreign assistance agency established by Congress in 2004. Countries compete for aid from the corporation by meeting certain good governance benchmarks and submitting specific proposals for how all aid will be spent.

Millennium Development Goals: A series of eight goals developed within the United Nations system to establish a peaceful and healthy global economy by the year 2015.

Missile Defense Agency: Agency responsible for research, development, and acquisitions necessary to defend the United States against an incoming ballistic missile attack.

Monroe Doctrine: Announced in 1823, the Monroe Doctrine sets U.S. foreign policy toward European intervention in the Western Hemisphere by saying that it will be viewed as unfriendly toward the United States. As the U.S. grew in power, it became the basis for intervention in the Western Hemisphere.

Most-Favored Nation (MFN): A principle of international trade where one country agrees to give another country (or all countries) the same trading terms that it grants to its most-favored trading partner. MFN as a more specific term refers to a status granted by the United States to another country providing the best trading terms for that country. The United States refers to MFN as Permanent Normal Trade Relations (PNTR).

Mujahideen: Can refer to Islamic fighters combating non-Muslims in majority Muslim countries (Mujahideen comes from the same Arabic root as jihad, which means "struggle" or "holy war.") Specifically, refers to Islamic rebels from a variety of countries who fought to resist the Soviet occupation of Afghanistan in the 1980s.

Multilateral Debt Relief Initiative (MDRI): An extension of the HIPC program that provided 100 percent of debt owed to the IMF, the World Bank, and the African Development Bank to HIPC eligible countries. The Paris Club of bilateral creditors also participated in the MDRI.

Mutually Assured Destruction (MAD): The idea that any nuclear war would result in losses so significant that it would be impossible to say that anyone "won" the war due to the scope of the destruction. Hence, no state could ever rationally turn to a nuclear strike as a viable option as long as the other side had a sufficient retaliatory nuclear deterrent.

Nation-Building: The act of constructing new political, economic, and social, and (sometimes) physical, structures in a state. Nation-building often occurs in the aftermath of an invasion of one state by another.

North American Free Trade Agreement (NAFTA): An agreement that entered into force in 1994 creating a free trade zone between Canada, the United States, and Mexico. Most tariff and nontariff barriers (such as import quotas) have been eliminated under NAFTA.

North Atlantic Treaty Organization (NATO): A defense alliance between 28 member nations, including the United States, Turkey, and most of the European Union. Under the terms of the treaty, an attack against one member is considered an attack on all members. Formed primarily to deter Soviet aggression during the Cold War, NATO has engaged in peacekeeping and peace enforcement operations in the post–Cold War era.

North Korean Sanctions and Policy Enhancement Act: Passed in 2016, the act increases sanctions against North Korea in response to its nuclear and ballistic missile programs, as well as human rights abuses and history of cyberattacks against U.S. interests.

Nuclear Fuel Cycle: The process of making nuclear material ready for use, using it, and then storing any resulting waste. Fissile material diverted during the nuclear fuel cycle could be used in the construction of a nuclear explosive device, making it necessary to safeguard such material against diversion.

Office of National Drug Control Policy: Part of the Executive Office of the President, the Office of National Drug Control Policy runs the nation's antidrug programs. The office is headed by a "Drug Czar" The czar attempts to reduce use, production, and trafficking of illicit drugs.

Organization for Economic Cooperation and Development (OECD): A group of 34 developed market economies that attempt to promote free markets, economic growth, and sustainable development in their own economies as well as in the developing world.

Organization for the Prohibition of Chemical Weapons (OPCW): The organization responsible for verifying compliance with the Chemical Weapons Convention. Known for intrusive verification methods, including challenge inspections.

Overseas Contingency Operations Funds: Special appropriations, made apart from the regular defense funding, designed to fight the Global War on Terror. Originally referred to as Global War on Terror (GWoT) funding.

Palestinian Authority (PA): Name for the interim government designed to rule over the Gaza Strip and the West Bank as autonomous regions. Established as part of a 1994 peace agreement between Israel and the Palestine Liberation Organization (the Oslo Accords).

Paris Climate Agreement: Adopted within the UN Framework Convention on Climate Change, the Paris Climate Agreement attempts to limit greenhouse gas emissions in a way that will limit global temperature increases to 1.5 degrees Celsius above preindustrial levels. The agreement is voluntary in that each party is allowed to establish a National Determined Contribution (NDC) to the agreement.

Paris Club: A group of major creditor countries that coordinate policy in providing debt relief to developing countries.

Party Platform: A set of principles, policy proposals, and goals formally adopted by a political party. The Democratic and Republican Parties in the United States update their platforms every four years.

Permanent Normal Trade Relations (PNTR): A designation by the United States that replaces the term most-favored nation (MFN). Under PNTR, the United States agrees to provide the most preferential trade terms available to the designated state.

Power of the Purse: Refers to the power of Congress to pass, or refuse to pass, funding resolutions. The power of the purse is designed to be a mechanism to limit the executive branch's ability to act in ways contrary to the wishes of Congress.

Preemptive Military Intervention: Military intervention designed to prevent an imminent attack on the territory of the attacking state.

President's Emergency Plan for AIDS Relief (PEPFAR): A government initiative designed to prevent the spread of AIDS and manage its impact. Most PEPFAR programs are in sub-Saharan Africa.

Preventive Military Intervention: Military intervention designed to stop a potential future threat to the intervening country.

Rally 'Round the Flag Effect: A short-term surge in public opinion of the president, and the government in general, during times of war or other international crises.

RAND Corporation: A nonprofit policy think tank funded in part by the U.S. government and in part by private endowment. Provides advice and analysis to the U.S. armed forces.

Realism: An approach to politics, especially foreign policy, that focuses on the pursuit of discrete national interests through the application of power.

Reciprocal Trade Agreement Act: Passed in 1934; allows the president, instead of Congress, to negotiate reciprocal trade agreements with other countries.

Refugee: Under international law, a refugee is someone who has been forced to flee his or her country because of persecution, war, or violence. A refugee has a well-founded fear of persecution for reasons of race, religion, nationality, political opinion or membership in a particular social group.

Sectarianism: Conflict that results attaching inferior or superior attributes to a group (a sect) based on identifiable characteristics such as ethnicity, race, language, or religion.

Secularism: The formal separation of church and state as a matter of public law.

Sequestration: Automatic, across the board cuts in discretionary spending, triggered in 2013 as a result of the Budget Control Act of 2011. Sequestration cuts were mostly reversed by the Bipartisan Budget Act of 2015.

Shia Islam: Minority sect within Islam that believes that Allah (God) chose Ali to be the Prophet Muhammed's successor. The division between Shia and Sunni Islam is one basis of conflict within the Muslim world.

Sovereignty: Absolute authority or a monopoly on the legitimate use of force within the boundaries of a state. Note: in international terms, the words "state" and "country" are mostly synonymous.

Strategic Arms Limitation Talks (SALT): Refers to two sets of nuclear disarmament talks between the United States and the Soviet Union. SALT I resulted in the ABM Treaty and also limited the number of strategic nuclear weapons. SALT II resulted in limiting the number of ICBM systems to 2,400 on each side.

Strategic Arms Reduction Treaty (START): Signed in 1991, the original START limited the number of ICBMs to 1,600 and the number of warheads to 6,000 in both the United States and the Soviet Union (later Russia). The new START was signed in 2011 and reduced the number of allowed warheads to 1,550. The number of deployed missiles was limited to 700 per side.

Strategic Defense Initiative (SDI): Nicknamed "star wars," SDI was a proposed system to defend against a Soviet nuclear attack. Though never realized as envisioned, SDI formed part of the basis for modern missile defense systems.

Stuxnet Virus: A computer worm that can be deployed against industrial control systems such as those used to operate hydroelectric dams and nuclear facilities. The United States deployed Stuxnet against Iranian nuclear facilities, resulting in failure of a number of Iranian uranium enrichment centrifuges.

Sunni Islam: Sunni Muslims make up a majority of the world's Muslim population. Sunnis believe that the Muslim community should select successors to the Prophet Muhammed. Shia Muslims, by contrast, believe that a decedent of the Prophet should rule the faithful. The original schism occurred in the year 632, after the death of Muhammed.

Tariff: A tax or a duty applied to certain imports into a country.

Tea Party Movement: A social movement known for its conservative positions and general distrust of the national government. Emphasizes populism and small government, especially in the economic realm. The Tea Party became prominent in 2010 when its members won several primary elections over more mainline Republicans (most Tea Party members also identify as Republicans). Critics argue that the Tea Party represents racist and xenophobic positions, such as the belief that President Obama is secretly a Muslim.

Terrorism: The use of violence and fear, primarily against civilians or government institutions, in order to advance a political or ideological purpose.

Think Tank: An organization composed of policy experts designed to provide advice to governments and influence the policy-making process.

Trade Promotion Authority (TPA): Previously known as "fast track," TPA allows the executive branch to negotiate trade agreements knowing that Congress will only be allowed an up or down vote on the resulting measure. Congress can block implementation of an agreement but agrees in advance not to amend the agreement.

Train and Equip Program: A program that identifies, trains, and provides military aid to moderate opposition forces in and around Syria. The program aims to enlist opposition fighters to aid in the defeat of ISIS within Syria.

Trans-Pacific Partnership (TPP): A potential trade agreement, involving 12 countries (including the United States) that would eliminate tariffs on over 18,000 goods and services traded between the member states. President-elect Donald Trump opposes the TPP, much of which was negotiated during the Obama administration. As a result, the United States is unlikely to become party to the agreement, if it enters into force at all.

Treaty on the Nonproliferation of Nuclear Weapons (NPT): Upon its entry into force in 1970, the NPT limited the number of parties allowed to have nuclear weapons to five (United States, United Kingdom, Soviet Union/Russia, China, and France). In exchange for signing the treaty as nonnuclear weapons states, other parties were to receive benefits from the transfer of peaceful nuclear technology. States that have not become party to the treaty are not bound by its provisions. Several nuclear weapons states, including India, Pakistan, and Israel, never signed the treaty. North Korea withdrew from the treaty in order to allow itself to develop nuclear weapons.

Two-State Solution: The idea that negotiations between Israel and the Palestinian Authority should be guided by the goal of having an independent and secure Palestine and an independent and secure Israel living peacefully adjacent to each other.

United Kingdom Independence Party (UKIP): A populist, right-wing political party. UKIP was one of the main proponents of Brexit.

United National Framework Convention on Climate Change (UNFCCC): A treaty negotiated during the Rio Earth Summit and entered into force in 1994. The goal of the treaty is to stabilize the climate by limiting greenhouse gas emissions. The Paris Climate Agreement is considered part of the UNFCCC framework.

United Nations (UN): An intergovernmental organization, headquartered in New York and designed to promote international peace and security, respect for human rights, and international development. The United Nations has 193 members as of 2016.

United States Agency for International Development (USAID): Operating under the State Department, USAID works to eradicate poverty and promote good governance by providing foreign aid to developing countries, either directly or through nongovernmental organizations (NGOs) that carry out activities promoted by USAID.

Universal Declaration of Human Rights (UDHR): Adopted by the United Nations General Assembly in 1948, the UDHR states basic rights and freedoms to which all individuals are entitled.

U.S.–China Joint Statement on Climate Change: An agreement, announced in 2014, between the United States and China as part of the Paris Climate talks. Both parties agreed to ratify the Paris agreement. The United States undertook to reduce greenhouse gas emissions to 26–28 percent below 2005 levels by 2030. China undertook to stop increasing its emissions levels by 2030.

U.S. CYBERCOM: U.S. Cyber Command coordinates the defense of U.S. military cyber resources and activities.

USA Freedom Act: A revision of the Patriot Act, enacted in 2015, that reauthorizes the USA Patriot Act with limits on bulk data collection.

USA Patriot Act: Passed in October 2011, the Patriot Act was designed to make it easier for domestic and foreign intelligence gathering agencies to find terrorists and prevent terrorism. The act was controversial in that it allowed bulk data collection of phone records, wiretapping with an expedited warrant process, and other provisions of concern to civil liberties advocates. The USA Freedom Act restricts bulk data collection but maintains some provisions related to expedited wiretapping and the tracking of "lone wolf terrorists" (terrorists operating outside of a traditional terrorist network).

War on Terror (Global War on Terror): A term coined by the Bush administration after the terrorist attacks of September 11, 2001, referring to efforts to combat terrorism through the use of U.S. military resources (as opposed to as a crime to be prevented and punished using more traditional police and domestic intelligence gathering resources).

War Powers Resolution: An act passed by Congress over the veto of President Nixon in 1973 designed to limit the ability of the president to deploy troops into combat situations without the authorization of Congress. Forces deployed into combat must be withdrawn within 60 days unless authorized by Congress.

Weapons of Mass Destruction (WMD): An inherently offensive class of weapons known for their inability to distinguish between civilian and military targets. The four generally recognized classes of WMD are nuclear (fission and fusion), chemical, biological, and radiological (radioactive material triggered with a conventional explosive).

World Bank: Officially known as the International Bank for Reconstruction and Development, the World Bank provides financial and technical assistance to the developing world, often in the form of concessional loans (loans at below market interest rates with extended repayment terms). These loans are designed to be used for projects that enhance the economic development prospects of the borrower.

World Trade Organization (WTO): The only global organization dealing with the rules of trade between states. The WTO resolves trading disputes between members and promotes free and rules-based trade. WTO agreements are designed to be permanent and replace those ad hoc agreements made under the GATT.

Bibliography

African Development Bank. *Debt Relief Initiatives, Development Assistance and Service Delivery in Africa.* Oxford: Oxford University Press, 2009.

Al-Ali, Zaid. "How Maliki Ruined Iraq." *Foreign Policy.* Last modified June 19, 2014. http://foreignpolicy.com/2014/06/19/how-maliki-ruined-iraq/?wp_login_redirect=0.

Arms Control Association. "Chronology of U.S.–North Korean Nuclear and Missile Diplomacy." February 2016. https://www.armscontrol.org/factsheets/dprkchron.

Arnone, Marco, and Andrea F. Presbitero. *Debt Relief Initiatives: Policy Design and Outcomes.* Farnham, Surrey, England: Ashgate, 2010.

Asmus, Ronald D. *Opening NATO's Door: How the Alliance Remade Itself for a New Era.* New York: Columbia University Press, 2004.

Bailey, Beth L., and Richard H. Immerman. *Understanding the U.S. Wars in Iraq and Afghanistan.* New York: NYU Press, 2015.

Barbour, Emily C. "International Agreements on Climate Change: Selected Legal Questions." Congressional Research Service. Last modified April 12, 2010. http://fpc.state.gov/documents/organization/142749.pdf.

Barnes, Julian E., and Gordon Lubold. "U.S., Allied Military Review New Options for Afghan Pullback." *Wall Street Journal.* Last modified September 24, 2015. http://www.wsj.com/articles/u-s-allied-military-review-new-options-for-afghan-pullback-1443139109.

Bearak, Max, and Lazaro Gamio. "Everything You Ever Wanted to Know about the U.S. Foreign Assistance Budget." *Washington Post.* Last modified October 18, 2016. https://www.washingtonpost.com/graphics/world/which-countries-get-the-most-foreign-aid/?tid=a_classic-iphone.

Bite, Vita. "United Nations System Funding: Congressional Issues." Congressional Research Service. Last modified September 21, 2005. http://fpc.state.gov/documents/organization/55841.pdf.

Bongang, Benn L. *The United States and the United Nations Congressional Funding and U.N. Reform.* New York: LFB Scholarly Pub., 2007. http://public.eblib.com/choice/publicfullrecord.aspx?p=3016839.

Bonner, Robert C., and Andres Rozental. "Managing the United States–Mexico Border: Cooperative Solutions to Common Challenges." Wilson Center. Last modified July 7, 2011. https://www.wilsoncenter.org/sites/default/files/PCIP%20Comexi%20Full%20Report-%20english%20version.pdf.

Carson, Jayne A., and James Helis. "Nation-Building, the American Way." Federation of American Scientists. Last modified April 7, 2003. https://fas.org/man/eprint/carson.pdf.

Chicago Council on Global Affairs. "America Divided: Political Partisanship and US Foreign Policy." Last modified 2015. http://www.thechicagocouncil.org/sites/default/files/CCGA_PublicSurvey2015.pdf.

Churchill Centre. "The Sinews of Peace 'Iron Curtain Speech'" Last modified 2016. http://www.winstonchurchill.org/resources/speeches/1946-1963-elder-statesman/120-the-sinews-of-peace.

Cooper, Helene, and Robert F. Worth. "Arab Spring Proves a Harsh Test for Obama's Diplomatic Skill." *New York Times*. Last modified September 24, 2012.

Corner, Mark. *The European Union: An Introduction*. London, United Kingdom: Tauris, 2014.

Cuban American National Foundation. "CANF Responds to Today's Announcement Regarding U.S.–Cuba Policy." Accessed January 7, 2016. http://canf.org/news-item /canf-responds-to-todays-announcement-regarding-u-s-cuba-policy/

Dao, James, and Steven L. Myers. "Attack on Iraq: The Overview." *New York Times*. Last modified February 17, 2001. http://www.nytimes.com/2001/02/17/world/attack-iraq -overview-us-british-jets-strike-air-defense-centers-iraq.html?pagewanted=all.

Davis, John. *Presidential Policies and the Road to the Second Iraq War: From Forty One to Forty Three*. Aldershot, England: Ashgate Pub., 2006.

Democratic National Committee. "The 2012 Democratic Platform." Last modified 2012. https://www.democrats.org/party-platform.

Democratic National Committee. "2016 Democratic Party Platform." Last modified 2016. https://www.demconvention.com/wp-content/uploads/2016/07/Democratic-Party -Platform-7.21.16-no-lines.pdf.

Deutch, John M. *The Crisis in Energy Policy*. Cambridge, MA: Harvard University Press, 2011.

Duarte, Sergio. "Disarmament and Non-Proliferation: A Historical Review." United Nations. Last modified March 28, 2011. http://www.un.org/disarmament/HomePage/HR/docs /2011/2011-03-28_OAS_statement.pdf.

Epstein, Susan E., and Lynn M. Williams. "Overseas Contingency Operations Funding: Background and Status." Congressional Research Service. Last modified June 13, 2016. https://www.fas.org/sgp/crs/natsec/R44519.pdf.

Ford, Matt. "The Fifth Circuit Court of Appeals Rules against Obama's Executive Actions on Immigration." *The Atlantic*. Last modified November 10, 2015. http://www.theatlantic .com/politics/archive/2015/11/fifth-circuit-obama-immigration/415077/.

Fuller, Christine. *The Rise of ISIS: Background and Perspective from the UK and US*. Nova Science Publishers, 2015.

Goldberg, Jeffrey. "President Obama's Interview with Jeffrey Goldberg on Syria and Foreign Policy." *The Atlantic*. Last modified April 2016. http://www.theatlantic.com/magazine /archive/2016/04/the-obama-doctrine/471525/.

Goldgeier, James M., and Michael McFaul. "George H.W. Bush and Soviet Regime Change." In *Power and Purpose: U.S. Policy toward Russia after the Cold War*. Washington, D.C.: Brookings Institution Press, 2003.

Gonzalez-Barrera, Ana, and Jens M. Krogstad. "What We Know about Illegal Immigration from Mexico." Pew Research Center. Last modified November 20, 2015. http://www .pewresearch.org/fact-tank/2015/11/20/what-we-know-about-illegal-immigration -from-mexico/.

Haney, Patrick J., and Walt Vanderbush. 1999. "The Role of Ethnic Interest Groups in U.S. Foreign Policy: The Case of the Cuban American National Foundation". *International Studies Quarterly* 43 (2) [International Studies Association, Wiley]: 341–361. http:// www.jstor.org/stable/2600759.

Ḥaqqānī, Ḥusain. *Magnificent Delusions: Pakistan, the United States, and an Epic History of Misunderstanding*. New York: PublicAffairs, 2013.

History of Congress: President's Annual Message. American Memory: Library of Congress, 1823. Accessed October 2, 2016. https://memory.loc.gov/cgi-bin/ampage?collId=llac &fileName=041/llac041.db&recNum=4.

Kafura, Craig, and Sara McElmurry. "Growing Partisan Divides on Immigration." Chicago Council on Global Affairs. Last modified September 8, 2015. http://www.thechicago council.org/publication/growing-partisan-divides-immigration?utm_source=Informz &utm_medium=Email&utm_campaign=Council.

Kahn, Greg. (n.d.). "The Fate of the Kyoto Protocol under the Bush Administration." *Berkeley Journal of International Law* 21 (3): 548–571. http://scholarship.law.berkeley.edu /cgi/viewcontent.cgi?article=1248&context=bjil.

Kaplan, Eben. "How Libya Got Off the List." Council on Foreign Relations. Last modified October 16, 2007. http://www.cfr.org/libya/libya-got-off-list/p10855.

Kerr, Orin. "How Does the Cybersecurity Act of 2015 Change the Internet Surveillance Laws?" *Washington Post.* Last modified December 24, 2015. https://www.washingtonpost .com/news/volokh-conspiracy/wp/2015/12/24/how-does-the-cybersecurity-act-of -2015-change-the-internet-surveillance-laws/.

Kramer, Mark. "Why Did Russia Give Away Crimea Sixty Years Ago?" Wilson Center: Cold War International History Project. Last modified March 19, 2014. https://www.wilson center.org/publication/why-did-russia-give-away-crimea-sixty-years-ago.

Krogstad, Jens M., Jeffrey S. Passel, and D'Vera Cohn. "5 Facts about Illegal Immigration in the U.S." Pew Research Center. Last modified September 20, 2016. http://www .pewresearch.org/fact-tank/2016/09/20/5-facts-about-illegal-immigration-in-the-u-s/.

Lasensky, Scott. "Underwriting Peace in the Middle East: U.S. Foreign Policy and the Limits of Economic Inducements." *Middle East Review of International Affairs.* Last modified March 2002. www.rubincenter.org/2002/03/lasensky-2002-03-07/.

Lee, Brianna. "Mexico's Drug War." Council on Foreign Relations. Last modified March 5, 2014. http://www.cfr.org/mexico/mexicos-drug-war/p13689.

Matray, James I. (n.d.). "The Failure of the Bush Administration's North Korea Policy: A Critical Analysis." *International Journal of Korea Studies* 17 (1): 140–177.

Mearsheimer, John J. *The Tragedy of Great Power Politics.* New York: Norton, 2001.

Mearsheimer, John J., and Stephen M. Walt. *The Israel Lobby and U.S. Foreign Policy.* New York: Farrar, Straus, and Giroux, 2007.

NATO. "Official Text: The North Atlantic Treaty, 04-Apr.-1949." Last modified 2016. http:// www.nato.int/cps/en/natolive/official_texts_17120.htm.

Office of the Historian. "The United States, Cuba, and the Platt Amendment, 1901—1899– 1913—Milestones." Accessed January 6, 2016. https://history.state.gov/milestones /1899-1913/platt.

Pei, Minxin, and Sara Kasper. "Lessons from the Past: The American Record on Nation Building." Carnegie Endowment for International Peace. Last modified May 2003. http://carnegieendowment.org/files/Policybrief24.pdf.

Remnick, David. "Going the Distance: On and Off the Road with Barack Obama." *New Yorker.* Last modified January 27, 2014. http://www.newyorker.com/magazine/2014/01/27 /going-the-distance-david-remnick.

Republican National Committee. "2012 Republican Platform." Last modified 2012. https:// prod-static-ngop-pbl.s3.amazonaws.com/docs/2012GOPPlatform.pdf.

Republican National Committee. "Republican Party Platform 2016." Last modified 2016. https://prod-static-ngop-pbl.s3.amazonaws.com/media/documents/DRAFT_12 _FINAL[1]-ben_1468872234.pdf.

Riedel, Bruce. "Pakistan, Taliban and the Afghan Quagmire." Brookings Institution. Last modified August 24, 2013. https://www.brookings.edu/opinions/pakistan-taliban-and -the-afghan-quagmire/.

Schain, Martin. *The Politics of Immigration in France, Britain and the United States: A Comparative Study*. Basingstoke: Palgrave Macmillan, 2012.

Schoenbaum, David. *The United States and the State of Israel*. New York: Oxford University Press, 1993.

Shapiro, Andrew J. "Ensuring Israel's Qualitative Military Edge." U.S. Department of State. Last modified November 4, 2011. http://www.state.gov/t/pm/rls/rm/176684.htm.

Sharp, Jeremy. "Egypt–United States Relations." Congressional Research Service. Last modified June 15, 2005. http://www.au.af.mil/au/awc/awcgate/crs/ib93087.pdf.

Sharp, Jeremy M. "U.S. Foreign Aid to Israel." Congressional Research Service. Last modified June 10, 2015. https://www.fas.org/sgp/crs/mideast/RL33222.pdf.

Sloan, Stephen. *Terrorism: The Present Threat in Context*. Oxford, U.K.: Berg, 2006.

Smeltz, Dina, and Ivo Daalder. "Foreign Policy in the Age of Retrenchment." Chicago Council on Global Affairs. Last modified 2014. http://www.thechicagocouncil.org/sites/default/files/2014_CCS_Report_1.pdf.

Snyder, Scott A. "U.S. Policy toward North Korea." Council on Foreign Relations. January 2013. http://www.cfr.org/north-korea/us-policy-toward-north-korea/p29962.

Somander, Tonya. "President Obama on the U.S.–Mexico Relationship." Whitehouse.gov. Last modified July 25, 2016. https://www.whitehouse.gov/blog/2016/07/25/president-obama-us-mexico-relationship.

Staten, Clifford L. *The History of Cuba*. Westport, CT: Greenwood Press, 2003.

Stokes, Bruce. "Americans Agree on Trade: Good for the Country, but Not Great for Jobs." Pew Research Center. Last modified January 8, 2015. http://www.pewresearch.org/fact-tank/2015/01/08/americans-agree-on-trade-good-for-the-country-but-not-great-for-jobs/.

Tarnoff, Curt, and Marian L. Lawson. "Foreign Aid: An Introduction to U.S. Programs and Policy." Federation of American Scientists. Last modified February 10, 2011. https://www.fas.org/sgp/crs/row/R40213.pdf.

Text of the General Agreement on Tariffs and Trade. World Trade Organization, 1986. https://www.wto.org/english/docs_e/legal_e/gatt47_e.pdf.

Theodore Roosevelt's Corollary to the Monroe Doctrine (1905). ourdocments.gov, 1904. https://www.ourdocuments.gov/doc.php?doc=56.

Theohary, Catherine A., and John Rollins. "Terrorist Use of the Internet: Information Operations in Cyberspace." Congressional Research Service. Last modified March 8, 2011. https://www.fas.org/sgp/crs/terror/R41674.pdf.

Udall, Morris K. "Special Report: The Foreign Assistance Act of 1961." University of Arizona Libraries. Last modified 1961. http://www.library.arizona.edu/exhibits/udall/special/foreign.html.

UNHCR. "Convention and Protocol Relating to the Status of Refugees." Last modified 2010. http://www.unhcr.org/3b66c2aa10.html.

United Nations. "The Universal Declaration of Human Rights." Last modified 2016. http://www.un.org/en/universal-declaration-human-rights/.

United Nations Office on Drugs and Crime, 2015. *World Drug Report 2015*. Accessed September 18, 2016. https://www.unodc.org/documents/wdr2015/World_Drug_Report_2015.pdf.

United Nations Treaty Collection. "Charter of the United Nations." Accessed March 20, 2016. https://treaties.un.org/doc/publication/ctc/uncharter.pdf.

U.S. Department of State. "U.S. Refugee Admissions Program." Last modified January 31, 2013. http://www.state.gov/j/prm/ra/admissions/index.htm.

U.S. Department of State Bureau of Near Eastern Affairs. "U.S. Relations with Syria." Last modified March 20, 2014. http://www.state.gov/r/pa/ei/bgn/3580.htm.

U.S. Department of State Office of the Historian. "Highlights in the History of U.S. Relations with Russia, 1780–June 2006." Last modified May 11, 2007. http://www.state.gov/p/eur/ci/rs/200years/c30273.htm#1832treaty.

U.S. Environmental Protection Agency. "Fact Sheet: Clean Power Plan by the Numbers | Clean Power Plan." Last modified 2015. http://www.epa.gov/cleanpowerplan/fact-sheet-clean-power-plan-numbers.

Vanderbush, Walt, and Patrick Jude Haney. *The Cuban Embargo*. University of Pittsburgh Press, 2005.

Waltz, Kenneth N. *Man, the State, and War: A Theoretical Analysis*. New York: Columbia University Press, 1959.

Wertz, Daniel, and Chelsea Gannon. "A History of U.S.–DPRK Relations." The National Committee on North Korea. November 2015. http://www.ncnk.org/resources/publications/US_DPRK_Relations.

Wheeler, Brian, and Alex Hunt. "Brexit: All You Need to Know about the UK Leaving the EU." BBC News. Accessed July 21, 2016. http://www.bbc.com/news/uk-politics-32810887.

White House. "Fact Sheet: U.S. Assistance to Ukraine." Whitehouse.gov. Last modified December 7, 2015. https://www.whitehouse.gov/the-press-office/2015/12/07/fact-sheet-us-assistance-ukraine.

White House. "Foreign Policy Cyber Security Executive Order 13636." Last modified February 12, 2013. https://www.whitehouse.gov/issues/foreign-policy/cybersecurity/eo-13636.

White House. "Presidential Determination—Major Drug Transit or Major Illicit Drug Producing Countries for Fiscal Year 2016." Whitehouse.gov. Last modified September 4, 2015. https://www.whitehouse.gov/the-press-office/2015/09/14/presidential-determination-major-drug-transit-or-major-illicit-drug.

White House. "Remarks by the President in Address to the Nation on the Way Forward in Afghanistan and Pakistan." Whitehouse.gov. Last modified December 1, 2009. https://www.whitehouse.gov/the-press-office/remarks-president-address-nation-way-forward-afghanistan-and-pakistan.

White House. "U.S.–China Joint Announcement on Climate Change." Whitehouse.gov. Last modified November 12, 2014. https://www.whitehouse.gov/the-press-office/2014/11/11/us-china-joint-announcement-climate-change.

Zartman, I. William. *Arab Spring: Negotiating in the Shadow of the Intifadat*. Athens: University of Georgia Press, 2015.

Zhu, Zhiqun. *US–China Relations in the 21st Century: Power Transition and Peace*. London: Routledge, 2006.

Index

About the Author

Trevor Rubenzer, PhD, is an associate professor of political science at the University of South Carolina, Upstate. Dr. Rubenzer's research specializes in the impact of ethnic identity groups on U.S. foreign policy. His work has appeared in several journals, including the *American Journal of Political Science, International Studies Quarterly,* and *Foreign Policy Analysis.*